Home Recording

WITHDRAWN

D1292148

Home Recording

6th Edition

by Jeff Strong

COVINGTON BRANCH LIBRARY
NEWTON COUNTY LIBRARY SYSTEM
7116 FLOYD STREET
COVINGTON GA 30014

Home Recording For Dummies®, 6th Edition

Published by: **John Wiley & Sons, Inc.**, 111 River Street, Hoboken, NJ 07030-5774, www.wiley.com

Copyright © 2021 by John Wiley & Sons, Inc., Hoboken, New Jersey

Published simultaneously in Canada

No part of this publication may be reproduced, stored in a retrieval system or transmitted in any form or by any means, electronic, mechanical, photocopying, recording, scanning or otherwise, except as permitted under Sections 107 or 108 of the 1976 United States Copyright Act, without the prior written permission of the Publisher. Requests to the Publisher for permission should be addressed to the Permissions Department, John Wiley & Sons, Inc., 111 River Street, Hoboken, NJ 07030, (201) 748-6011, fax (201) 748-6008, or online at http://www.wiley.com/go/permissions.

Trademarks: Wiley, For Dummies, the Dummies Man logo, Dummies.com, Making Everything Easier, and related trade dress are trademarks or registered trademarks of John Wiley & Sons, Inc. and may not be used without written permission. All other trademarks are the property of their respective owners. John Wiley & Sons, Inc. is not associated with any product or vendor mentioned in this book.

LIMIT OF LIABILITY/DISCLAIMER OF WARRANTY: THE PUBLISHER AND THE AUTHOR MAKE NO REPRESENTATIONS OR WARRANTIES WITH RESPECT TO THE ACCURACY OR COMPLETENESS OF THE CONTENTS OF THIS WORK AND SPECIFICALLY DISCLAIM ALL WARRANTIES, INCLUDING WITHOUT LIMITATION WARRANTIES OF FITNESS FOR A PARTICULAR PURPOSE. NO WARRANTY MAY BE CREATED OR EXTENDED BY SALES OR PROMOTIONAL MATERIALS. THE ADVICE AND STRATEGIES CONTAINED HEREIN MAY NOT BE SUITABLE FOR EVERY SITUATION. THIS WORK IS SOLD WITH THE UNDERSTANDING THAT THE PUBLISHER IS NOT ENGAGED IN RENDERING LEGAL, ACCOUNTING, OR OTHER PROFESSIONAL SERVICES. IF PROFESSIONAL ASSISTANCE IS REQUIRED, THE SERVICES OF A COMPETENT PROFESSIONAL PERSON SHOULD BE SOUGHT. NEITHER THE PUBLISHER NOR THE AUTHOR SHALL BE LIABLE FOR DAMAGES ARISING HEREFROM. THE FACT THAT AN ORGANIZATION OR WEBSITE IS REFERRED TO IN THIS WORK AS A CITATION AND/OR A POTENTIAL SOURCE OF FURTHER INFORMATION DOES NOT MEAN THAT THE AUTHOR OR THE PUBLISHER ENDORSES THE INFORMATION THE ORGANIZATION OR WEBSITE MAY PROVIDE OR RECOMMENDATIONS IT MAY MAKE. FURTHER, READERS SHOULD BE AWARE THAT INTERNET WEBSITES LISTED IN THIS WORK MAY HAVE CHANGED OR DISAPPEARED BETWEEN WHEN THIS WORK WAS WRITTEN AND WHEN IT IS READ.

For general information on our other products and services, please contact our Customer Care Department within the U.S. at 877-762-2974, outside the U.S. at 317-572-3993, or fax 317-572-4002. For technical support, please visit https://hub.wiley.com/community/support/dummies.

Wiley publishes in a variety of print and electronic formats and by print-on-demand. Some material included with standard print versions of this book may not be included in e-books or in print-on-demand. If this book refers to media such as a CD or DVD that is not included in the version you purchased, you may download this material at http://booksupport.wiley.com. For more information about Wiley products, visit www.wiley.com.

Library of Congress Control Number: 2020945324

ISBN 978-1-119-71110-0 (pbk); ISBN 978-1-119-71163-6 (ebk); ISBN 978-1-119-71164-3 (ebk)

Manufactured in the United States of America

SKY10021530_093020

Contents at a Glance

Table of Contents

Introduction

If you're like most musicians, you've been noodling around on your instrument for a while and you've finally decided to take the plunge and get serious about recording your ideas. You may just want to throw a few ideas down onto tape (or hard drive) or capture those magical moments you have with your band. Or you may want to compose, record, produce, and release the next great platinum album. Either way, you'll find that having a home studio can give you hours of satisfaction.

Well, you've chosen a great time to get involved in audio recording. Not long ago, you needed to go to a commercial recording studio and spend thousands of dollars if you wanted to make a decent-sounding recording. Now you can set up a first-class recording studio in your garage or spare bedroom and create music that can sound as good as that coming out of top-notch studios (that is, if you know how to use the gear).

Home Recording For Dummies, 6th Edition, is a great place to start exploring the gear and techniques you need to create great recordings (if I do say so myself). This book introduces you to home recording and helps you to get your creative ideas out into the world.

About This Book

Home Recording For Dummies not only introduces you to the technology of home recording but also presents basic multitrack recording techniques. In the pages that follow, you find out about the many types of digital recording systems available, including computer-based systems, all-in-one recorder/mixer systems (called *studio-in-a-box systems*), and phone and tablet recording.

You get acquainted with the basic skills you need to make high-quality recordings. These skills can save you countless hours of experimenting and searching through owner's manuals. In this book, you discover

- The ins and outs of using the various pieces of equipment in your studio
- Tried-and-true engineering techniques, such as microphone choice and placement

» The concepts of multitracking, mixing, and mastering

» How to turn all your music into complete songs

» How to assemble and release an album

Home Recording For Dummies puts you on the fast track toward creating great-sounding recordings because it concentrates on showing you skills that you can use right away and doesn't bother you with tons of technical jargon or useless facts.

Throughout the book, you see *sidebars* (text in gray boxes) and text marked with the Technical Stuff icon. Both of these are skippable — they provide interesting information, but it's not essential to your understanding of the subject at hand.

Finally, within this book, you may note that some web addresses break across two lines of text. If you're reading this book in print and want to visit one of these web pages, simply key in the web address exactly as it's noted in the text, pretending as though the line break doesn't exist. If you're reading this as an e-book, you've got it easy — just click the web address to be taken directly to the web page.

Foolish Assumptions

I have to admit that when I wrote this book, I made a couple of assumptions about you, the reader. First, I assume you're interested in recording your music (or someone else's) in your home and not interested in reading about underwater basket-weaving (a fascinating subject, I'm sure, but not appropriate for a book entitled *Home Recording For Dummies*).

I assume you'll most likely record your music using a digital hard drive recording system because these are the most common types of systems available. I also assume you're relatively new to the recording game and not a seasoned professional. (Although if you were, you'd find that this book is a great reference for many audio engineering fundamentals.) Oh, and I assume you play a musical instrument or are at least familiar with how instruments function and how sound is produced.

Other than these things, I don't assume you play a certain type of music or that you ever intend to try to "make it" in the music business (or even that you want to treat it as a business at all). If course, if you aspire to make music your career, you'll find the information in this book invaluable in helping you make the best sounding music possible.

Icons Used in This Book

Throughout this book, I use a few icons to help you along your way. These icons are as follows:

TIP

The Tip icon highlights expert advice and ideas that can help you to produce better recordings.

REMEMBER

Certain techniques are important and bear repeating. The Remember icon gives you those gentle nudges to keep you on track.

TECHNICAL STUFF

Throughout the book, I include some technical background on a subject. The Technical Stuff icon shows up in those instances so that you know to brace yourself for some dense information.

WARNING

The Warning icon lets you know about those instances when you could damage your equipment, your ears, or your song.

Beyond the Book

In addition to what you're reading now, this book also comes with a free access-anywhere Cheat Sheet that gives you even more pointers on how to successfully record music in your home. To get this Cheat Sheet, simply go to `www.dummies.com` and search for "*Home Recording For Dummies* Cheat Sheet" in the Search box.

Where to Go from Here

This book is set up so that you can read it from cover to cover and progressively build on your knowledge, or you can jump around and read only those parts that interest you at the time. For instance, if you're getting ready to record your band and you need some ideas on how to get the best sound out of your microphones, go straight to Part 2. If you're new to this whole home recording thing and want to know what kind of gear to buy, check out Chapters 1 and 2.

For the most part, starting at Chapter 1 gets you up to speed on my way of thinking and can help you understand some of what I discuss in later chapters.

1 Getting Started with Home Recording

IN THIS PART . . .

Discover the gear you need to build your studio.

Understand how the home recording process works.

Choose the best recording system for your needs and goals.

Set up your studio so that it both sounds good and is easy to work in.

Get to know the way the signal flows through different systems.

Understand the purpose of all the knobs, buttons, and connectors in recording systems.

IN THIS CHAPTER

» Exploring the components of a home studio

» Peering into the process of recording

» Making sense of mixing and mastering

» Finishing up your project

Chapter 1

Understanding Home Recording

Audio recording is a fun and exciting activity. Being able to put down your musical ideas and craft them into an album is nearly every musician's dream. The only problem is the learning curve that comes with being able to record your music at home; most musicians would rather spend their time and energy making music.

In this chapter, I help you get a handle on the basics of home recording and show you what's involved in the process. You discover the basic components of a recording studio and find out what gear you need to buy first. In addition, you explore the multitracking process and find out what's involved in mixing your tracks. You move on to exploring mastering and finding ways to share your music with your listeners.

Examining the Anatomy of a Home Studio

Whether it's a free phone app or a million-dollar commercial facility, all audio recording studios contain the same basic components. Understanding these basic components is an area where many people get lost and one about which I receive the most email. As you glimpse the recording world, you'll inevitably think that recording your own music will cost way too much and be way too complicated. Well, it can be. But it can also be pretty simple and cost-efficient. In the following sections, I present a list of audio-recording essentials and offer insight into cost-saving and efficient systems that you can find on the market.

Exploring the recording essentials

To take the mystery out of recording gear, here are the essentials that you need to know:

- **Sound source:** The sound source is your voice, your guitar, your ukulele, or any other of the many sound makers in existence. As a musician, you probably have at least one of these at your disposal right now.
- **Input device:** Input devices are what you use to convert your sound into an electrical impulse that can then be recorded. Here are the four basic types of input devices:
  - **Instruments:** Your electric guitar, bass, synthesizer, and drum machines are typical instruments you plug into the mixer. These instruments constitute most of the input devices that you use in your studio. The synthesizer and drum machine can plug directly into your mixer or recorder, whereas your electric guitar and bass need a direct box (or its equivalent, such as an instrument or Hi-Z input in your audio interface) to plug into first. A *direct box* is an intermediary device that allows you to plug your guitar directly into the mixer. Chapter 9 explores instruments and their connections to your system.
  - **Microphones:** A microphone (or mic) enables you to record the sound of a voice or an acoustic instrument that you can't plug directly into the recorder. A microphone converts sound waves into electrical energy that can be understood by the recorder. I detail several types of microphones in Chapter 6.
  - **Sound modules:** Sound modules are special kinds of synthesizers and/or drum machines. What makes a sound module different from a regular synthesizer or drum machine is that a sound module contains no triggers or keys that you can play. Instead, sound modules are controlled externally by another synthesizer's keyboard or by a Musical Instrument Digital Interface (MIDI) controller (a specialized box designed to control MIDI instruments). Sound modules have MIDI ports (MIDI jacks) that enable you to connect them to other equipment. Chapter 11 digs into the details about sound modules.
  - **Software synthesizers:** Software synthesizers (also known as *softsynths*) are software programs that don't need hardware MIDI connections because the sound modules are stored on your computer's hard drive.

REMEMBER

Depending on what your sound source is, it may also be an input device. For example, an electric guitar has pickups that allow you to plug it directly into a mixer input without having to use a microphone. On the other hand, your voice can't accept a cord, so you need to use a mic to turn your singing into an electrical impulse that can be picked up by your mixer or equivalent device. You can find out more about input devices in Chapter 9.

» **Mixer:** You use a mixer to send the electrical signal of your input device into your recorder and to route signals in a variety of ways. Traditionally, a mixer serves the following purposes:

- **Routing your signals into your recorder:** This allows you to set the proper level for each input device so that it's recorded with the best possible sound. Chapter 4 explores the different mixer-type devices for this purpose.
- **Blending (mixing) your individual tracks into a *stereo pair* (the left and right tracks of your stereo mix) or surround sound channels:** This role of the mixer is where your vision as a music producer takes center stage and where you can turn raw tracks into a polished piece of music. Chapter 16 explores this use of a mixer.

» **Recorder:** The recorder stores your audio data. For most home recordists, the recorder is digital. You can find out more about the different types of recorders in the next section of this chapter.

» **Signal processors:** Most of the time, you have to tweak your recorded tracks. Signal processors give you the power to do this. Signal processors can be divided into the following basic categories:

- **Equalizers:** Equalizers let you adjust the frequency balance of your tracks. This is important for making your instruments sound as clear as possible and for getting all your tracks to blend well.
- **Dynamics processors:** Dynamics processors are used to control the balance between the softest and loudest parts of your tracks. They have many uses in the studio to help you make your tracks sit well together and to keep from overloading your system. Chapters 9, 19, and 22 explore ways to use dynamics processors in your music.
- **Effects processors:** Effects processors allow you to change your tracks in a variety of ways, such as to create a more realistic sound or unusual effects. Typical effects processors include reverb, delay, chorus, and pitch shifting. You can find out more about these processors in Chapter 19.

- **Monitors:** Monitors, such as quality headphones or speakers, enable you to hear the quality of your recording and mixing. Monitors come in three basic designs:
  - **Headphones:** Headphones come in an astonishing variety. Some are good for listening to music, while others are good for recording and mixing music. Most home recordists start with headphones because they typically cost a lot less than speakers and serve the double duty of allowing you to hear yourself while you record and allowing you to hear the mix when all your tracks are done.
  - **Passive:** Passive monitors are like your stereo speakers in that you also need some sort of amplifier to run them. A ton of options are available with prices from around $100. Just remember that if you go this route, you need to budget money for an amp, which can run a few hundred dollars or more.
  - **Active:** Active monitors have an integrated amplifier in each speaker cabinet. Having a built-in amp has its advantages, including just the right amount of power for the speakers and short runs of wire from the amp itself to the speakers (this is kind of a tweaky area that some people claim produces a better sound). You can find quite a few active monitors on the market starting at just a couple hundred dollars.

Checking out recording system types

With the long list of equipment that I present in the previous section, you may think that you need to spend a ton of money to get everything you need. Fortunately, home-recording systems are available that contain many of the components you need, so you don't have to buy everything separately. I go into detail about these systems in Chapter 2, but here's a basic overview:

- **Studio-in-a-box (SIAB) systems:** These are all-in-one units that have everything in them except for the sound source, input device, and monitors. For very little money (starting well under $500), you get almost everything you need to start recording. These types of systems are also easy for a beginner to use and are great for musicians who don't want to spend a ton of energy tweaking their setups.
- **Computer-based systems:** These systems, often referred to as Digital Audio Workstations (DAWs) use the processing power of your computer to record, mix, and process your music. Computer-based systems, similar to the SIAB systems, perform many of the typical recording functions at once. When you have one of these systems, you only need your sound source, your input devices, and your monitors.

» **Ultra-portable systems:** Even though the rest of the systems I describe here can be portable, ultra-portable systems are designed so that you can record nearly anywhere with little fuss. These types of systems include smartphones, linear recorders, and tablet computers, which I introduce in Chapter 2. Like SIAB and computer-based systems, most of what you need is included, so all you have to worry about are your sound sources, input devices (or not — some come with mics already), and monitors (most often just a set of headphones).

Getting a Glimpse into the Recording Process

It's easy to focus on all the gear that's used in audio recording and think that the process must be pretty complicated. Well, it can be if you want it to, but it doesn't have to be. The heart of recording over the last 60 years or so has been an approach called *multitracking.* At its core, multitracking involves recording all the instruments on separate tracks so that you can mix them later almost any way you want. You can multitrack by recording everything — or at least most of the instruments — at one time, just like a live performance, or you can go to the other extreme and record each instrument separately. Either way, you need a bunch of tracks to be able to record to, and you need to understand how to blend all these separate pieces into something musical.

Setting up a song

The first step in recording your music is to set up your system to record. Because you're probably using a digital system, you need to configure your song. This usually involves setting the file type, bit depth, and sample rate. This process is one that you'll become very good at in no time. For the lowdown on setting up songs in various systems, check out Chapter 5.

Getting a great sound

Getting your sound source to sound great in your system is the most important aspect of recording quality music (well, aside from the song and the performances). This is also an area where you'll constantly be growing and learning. I've been recording professionally since 1985, but I still discover something new every time I set up a mic or plug in an electronic instrument. Any time you spend tweaking your mic placement or recording chain setup (configuration and levels) is time well spent, and the reward is often added clarity or at least a more interesting sound. For an introduction to the intricacies of recording high-quality source sounds, check out Parts 2 and 3 of this book.

Recording

After you have everything set up, the actual process of recording your music properly is pretty straightforward: You enable your track and press the Record button. This is easier said than done when the clock is ticking and you know that every mistake you make is being documented. Luckily, digital recording makes it easy to redo a track without costing you anything in audio fidelity. (It will cost you time, but because you record at home, you may have more time to get your recording right.) Check out Chapter 10 for the specifics on recording using a variety of digital systems.

Overdubbing

With one track recorded, you're ready to dig into one of the most invigorating parts of the multitracking process: overdubbing. *Overdubbing* is the process of adding new tracks to your existing ones. This feature allows you to be the one-man band or to bring in other musicians to spice up your music. Overdubbing is easily done with digital multitrack recorders. To get you going quickly, I cover the details in Chapter 10.

Making Sense of Mixing

For most recordists, the process of mixing is what turns their mishmash of musical tracks into a song. Mixing involves the following steps:

- Cleaning up your tracks by removing unwanted noise and performance glitches
- Equalizing each track so that it blends well with all the others
- Adding signal processing to enhance each track
- Blending your tracks to tell the story you want to tell with your song
- Embellishing your tracks with special effects or unique sounds

The following sections offer an overview of these steps.

Cleaning up tracks using editing

When you record, you want the best possible sound and performance for each instrument that you can get, but try as you might, sometimes you run into problems. These can include picking up unwanted sounds, such as chair squeaks, coughs, or other instruments, and can include (and often does) mistakes a musician makes that need to be cut out. In the olden days of tape recording, this editing process, which involved physically cutting out the bad parts of the tape with a razor blade, took time and skill. Today, you can do the necessary editing by using the editing functions in digital systems. This is nice, but it can also tempt you into editing your tracks more than is necessary and, as a result, can suck the life out of them. To help you understand what you can do with digital recording systems and to help keep you on track with your editing, check out Chapter 15.

Equalizing your tracks

When you start mixing a bunch of instruments, you often need to adjust the frequencies present in each instrument so that they all blend without creating mush (a highly technical term). By adjusting the frequencies of each instrument in the mix, you can make sure that each can be heard. This process is simple, but it can be time consuming. To make it easier for you, I cover equalization (EQ) in detail in Chapter 17.

Processing your signal

In the world of multitracking in small, acoustically untreated recording rooms (most home recordists use a spare bedroom or basement to record in and don't have a ton of money to make the room sound great), it's almost essential to process the sound with effects or dynamics processors. Doing so is usually intended to add the feel of a live concert to the recording, although many people also use signal processing to create interesting effects. Because the possibilities for processing your track using a digital system are almost limitless, this is an area where most beginners overdo it. The ability to alter your tracks can be used and abused — I cover the basics of processing in Chapter 19 to help you keep the abuse to a minimum.

Blending your tracks

This is also a process in which most new recordists run into problems. Properly mixing your tracks means keeping levels from getting out of hand, placing things where you want them in the sound field (left to right and front to back), adjusting EQ to blend all your instruments in a pleasing way, and using signal processors, such as compression and reverb, to make the most of each track. This process is a circular one and takes skill and patience to get right. Cutting corners always results in an end product that falls short of its potential. To help you make this process easier, I cover mixing in detail in Chapters 20 and 21.

Adding the Final Touches

After your songs are recorded and mixed, all that's left to do is add the finishing touches. These include mastering your songs, putting them all on CD, and getting them out into the world through promotion.

Mastering your mixes

Mastering is an often-misunderstood (and even unknown to many) part of the music production process that can make or break a CD (well, not literally). Mastering consists of several important steps that are intended to polish your songs so that they make up a complete collection on a CD, commonly referred to as an album. Here are the steps for mastering your songs:

1. **Optimize the dynamics.**

   The goal here is to get the dynamic levels within and between each song to their best. It also means making your music *smooth* (no sharp edge to the music) or *punchy* (a pronounced attack) — or something in between. Unfortunately, most people are concerned only with getting their CDs as loud as possible when performing this part of mastering. This isn't a good idea, as you find out in Chapter 22.

2. **Adjust the overall tonal balance.**

   The point of this part of the mastering process is to create tonal continuity among all the songs on your CD. Because you probably recorded and mixed all your tunes over a period of months, each song may have slightly different tonal characteristics. This part of mastering is where you make all your songs consistent so that they sound like part of an album and not a bunch of disjointed tunes thrown together haphazardly.

3. **Match the song-to-song volume.**

   When your listeners play your CD, you don't want them to have to adjust the volume of each song as it plays (unless they absolutely love a particular tune and want to turn it up, of course). The goal with this part of mastering is to get the volume of all the songs on a CD at pretty much the same level. This keeps one song from barely being heard while another threatens to blow the speakers.

4. **Set the song sequence.**

   How your songs are arranged on your CD helps tell your story. Think about how the order of each song on your album can make the most compelling musical statement. This part of the mastering process involves not only deciding what order everything should be in but also the steps you take to make it happen.

Putting your music out into the world

Formatting your finished and mastered songs for distribution and sales is one of the most exciting parts of the recording process. At last, you have a product, a complete musical statement that you can share with (or sell to) others. Like a lot of audio recording and production, the act of making distributable and saleable music is more involved than simply clicking the Burn button in your CD-recording program (at least if you want to make more than one copy) or uploading your music to a website.

In today's largely digital world you have two basic distribution methods: streaming/downloadable music and physical CDs. As a throwback, more and more people are releasing music on vinyl records today.

Dealing with digital distribution

All music is now delivered, first and foremost, as a digital file. MP3 and AAC are the most popular formats. Depending on where your music goes, such as Spotify, Apple Music, or any of a myriad of other Internet music sites, you need to encode your music to meet the site's requirements. It's a pretty simple process, but one that's closely tied to an area most musicians would rather not have to deal with: promotion. I cover this topic in Chapter 25.

Creating CD copies

For CD copying, you can either duplicate or replicate your CDs to make copies to give or sell to your fans. Here's a quick rundown on the differences between these two approaches (Chapter 23 explains them in detail):

- **Duplication:** Duplication consists of burning multiple CD-Rs from an audio file. Duplication requires very little setup, so it doesn't cost much to make smaller quantities, such as 50 to 500 CDs.
- **Replication:** The replication process starts with producing a glass master from your finished CD-R. This master CD is then used to create CDs using special CD presses, just like the major-label releases. Replication costs a bit more for setup, but the cost to create larger quantities of CDs is lower than that for duplication. This is a good choice for quantities of 500 or more.

Embracing vinyl

Many indie musicians are also embracing vinyl as a medium for their music. There are several reasons, many of which relate to creating a more compelling product. It's also worth mentioning that vinyl is much harder to pirate than a downloadable digital file. This is adding to appeal of vinyl records as a cost worth considering. I cover the details of making vinyl records in Chapter 23.

Promoting your music

The final and most grueling step of recording and putting out a CD is the promotion process. This is where you either make it or break it as an independent artist. To help you along, I offer ideas and insights in Chapter 25.

IN THIS CHAPTER

» Understanding your home recording needs

» Taking a look at digital recorders

» Understanding analog studio equipment

» Exploring a few different recording systems

Chapter 2 Getting the Right Gear

For many people, building a home studio is a gradual thing. You may start out with a synthesizer and a two-track recorder and add a microphone. Then you may decide to buy a multitrack recorder. Then you trade in your stereo speakers for real studio monitors. And before you know it, you've invested thousands of dollars in a first-rate home studio.

When setting up your home studio, you can go a couple of routes. You can walk into your local musical instrument store or pro audio shop without any forethought, buy the pieces of gear that catch your eye, and then figure out where you may use them in your studio. (Hey, don't laugh — I've done this.) Or, you can determine your goals ahead of time and research each piece of equipment before you buy it to make sure it's the best possible solution for you at the best price point. I recommend the latter approach because you end up with only the equipment you need and not a bunch of useless gear that may only ever look good sitting in your studio.

The process of choosing the right equipment doesn't have to be difficult. All it takes is a little self-assessment and some basic knowledge about the different equipment options. This chapter helps you discover these things. Here you explore a few different system configurations and begin to understand what can work for your situation. You also become familiar with some of the many analog extras that so many people who favor digital recording want today.

REMEMBER

Digital recording technology is evolving at an incredible rate. As soon as the ink dries on this paper, the next best thing in recording gear may surpass much of the technology that I write about in this chapter. It's tempting to always look to the next great innovation before you decide on a recording system, but I caution you against this wait-and-see attitude. Digital recording technology is now at the point that what you can record in your meager home studio can sound as fat, as clean, or as (insert your favorite recording adjective here) as the best recordings that have been released in the last 40 years.

Don't be afraid to just jump in and start recording. The way to great-sounding recordings is through hours of recording experience (not to mention having great songs with which to work).

TIP

Some of the equipment I describe in this chapter isn't on the top of the list for most home recordists. I discuss this equipment, though, because you'll likely be taken over by a disease that runs rampant in the audio recording world. Yes, I'm sorry to inform you that you're almost assuredly going to get a chronic case of GAS *(gear acquisition syndrome).* Don't worry; it's not terminal (unless, of course, you don't run your future purchases by your family first), but it can be uncomfortable. Nothing much is worse than having your eye on a piece of gear you just can't afford. "Let's see, food for a month or that new compressor I've just gotta have? . . . Oh well, I needed to go on a diet anyway."

The good news is that you'll never run out of new equipment to drool over and you'll never be alone in your suffering — everyone who owns a recording studio (private or commercial) suffers from GAS to some extent. The best way to keep GAS at bay is to decide on a system and buy it. Then stop looking at gear and get to work making music. After all, that's why you bought the stuff in the first place.

Determining Your Home Studio Needs

Home studios can vary tremendously. A home studio can be simple, like a handheld digital recorder with a built-in microphone set up in the corner of your bedroom. Or you can opt for something elaborate, like a multitrack digital recorder with thousands of dollars in outboard gear and expensive instruments residing in an acoustically treated addition to your house (whew!).

Whatever your budget, your first step before purchasing a home recording system is to determine your recording goals. Use the following questions to help you uncover what you truly need (and want) in your home studio. As you answer these questions, remember that most recording studios aren't built all at once — pieces of equipment are added slowly over time (a mic here, a preamp there). When getting your first home studio system, start with only those pieces of gear that you *really* need and then add on slowly as you get to know your equipment.

TIP

For most home recordists, the weakest link in their recording system is their engineering know-how. A $4,000 mic is useless until you gain an understanding of the subtleties of mic placement, for instance. (Check out Chapters 7 and 8 for more on such subtleties.) I recommend you wait to buy that next piece of gear until you completely outgrow your present piece of equipment.

To get an understanding of what kind of home studio is best for you, ask yourself the following questions:

- **How much money can I spend on equipment?** For most people, money is the ultimate determining factor in choosing their studio components. Set a budget and try to stay within it. The sky's the limit on what you can spend on recording equipment for your home studio, but you don't need to spend a ton of money. If you know your goals and do your research, you can create top-quality recordings without having the best of everything.

  In fact, your skill as a recording engineer has a much greater effect on the overall quality of your sound than whether you have a $3,000 preamp. With the techniques that you discover in this book and tricks that you uncover as you get to know your equipment, you can make recordings good enough to compete in the marketplace.

  REMEMBER

  Digital recording technology has improved tremendously over the last few years and will continue to improve in the years to come. Don't get sucked into the belief that you have to have the latest, greatest thing to make great music: otherwise you'll always be buying something. After all, great albums and number-one hits throughout history were recorded on lesser equipment than you can find in most home studios today. Focus on the song and the arrangement — practicing solid recording techniques — and you can get by with any of the pro or semipro recording systems available.

- **Is this studio just for me, or do I intend to hire it out to record others?** Your answer to this question may help you decide how elaborate a system you need. For example, if you eventually want to hire yourself and your studio out to record other people, you need to think about the compatibility of your system with other commercial studios. Your clients need to be able to take the music that they record at your studio and mix or master it somewhere else. You may also have to buy specific gear that clients want to use, which often means spending more money for equipment from sought-after manufacturers that may sound the same as lesser-name stuff. If you're interested in going the commercial studio route, check out other commercial studios in your area and find out what they use and what type of equipment their clients ask for.

If this studio is just for your use, you can focus on getting the best bang for the buck on gear without worrying about compatibility or marketability issues.

- **Will I be recording everything directly into the mixing board, or will I be miking most of the instruments?** Your answer to this question is going to dictate your choice in how much of your budget goes toward equipment and acoustical treatments for your room. If you intend to plug your instruments directly into the mixer and you only need a microphone for the occasional vocal, you have more money to spend on synthesizers or plug-ins for your digital audio workstation (DAW) — or you just won't have to spend as much. (DAWs are covered in detail in the section "Computer-Based Digital Recording Systems," later in this chapter.)

  Conversely, if you plan to record a band live, you must allocate enough money for those pieces of gear to allow you to do that effectively, such as having enough mics and inputs, sound isolation, and available tracks of simultaneous recording.

- **How many tracks do I need?** The answer to this question is important if you're considering a system that has limited tracks, such as mobile or studio-in-a-box (SIAB) systems that come with 2, 4, 8, 16, 24 (and sometimes more) available tracks. (For the lowdown on these systems, see the sections, "Studio-in-a-Box Systems" and "Mobile-Device Recording," later in this chapter.) This question is still worth considering even if you end up with a computer-based system because, even though many recording software programs boast having "unlimited" available tracks, you're still limited by the power of your computer and the number of inputs and outputs contained in your audio interface hardware. (For more on the capabilities of computer-based systems, check out the section, "Computer-Based Digital Recording Systems," later in this chapter.)

  REMEMBER

  Having more tracks is not necessarily a better thing. The more tracks you have, the more you think that you need to fill them for every song. This can make for cluttered arrangements and hard-to-mix songs. No matter how many tracks you end up with, use only those that you need to make your recording the best that it can be.

  TIP

  With digital recorders, you can create submixes and bounce several tracks into one or two without losing sound quality, reducing the need for more tracks. (Find out more about bouncing in Chapter 10.) Remember that some great albums were made using just four or eight tracks.

- **Will I be sequencing the parts or playing the instruments live?** If you plan on *sequencing* all your music (that is, programming your part into a computer or sequencer and having it play your part for you), make sure you get a good Musical Instrument Digital Interface (MIDI) controller. You can also consider having less capability for audio tracks. But if you plan to play and record all the instruments live, make sure your recorder has enough tracks for you to put each instrument on its own track.

Detailing Your Digital Options

Even with the fast pace of today's technology, one thing is for sure in the home recording world: Digital is here to stay. Digital recording has become the standard for home recordists and most commercial studios. And the format of choice is hard drive because it has many advantages over the other forms of digital recording. Not only does digital recording create a great sound, but it's also relatively inexpensive, especially compared with an equivalent-sounding studio from 20 to 25 years ago.

In the sections that follow, I examine the main types of digital home studios: computer-based DAWs, the all-in-one SIAB systems (such as the Zoom R24 or TASCAM DP-24SD), and mobile recording on your phone or tablet. Each has its advantages. What's right for one person may not be the best choice for another. (Isn't it great to have choices?)

Regardless of the type of digital recording system you like, consider the following things before buying:

- **Editing capabilities:** Some systems allow very fine editing of audio data, while others offer less. If you want so much control that you can edit down to the waveform — which basically means being able to edit out a single note or even just a part of a note — look for a system with that capability. If such control is less important to you, take a pass on such systems.

  Along with the actual editing capabilities, find out how this editing is done. Is it on a tiny LCD screen or can it be done on a large computer monitor? Of course, if you won't be doing a lot of editing, this feature may not be important to you. If this is the case, you may be able to buy a system for less money that sounds as good as the one with full editing capability. Paying for something that you won't use doesn't make sense.

- **Compatibility:** Compatibility between the various parts of your system (the recorder and sequencer or the software and audio interface, for instance) or between your studio and other studios (your friend's or a commercial studio) is an important issue for many people and one that may come back to bite you if you don't consider it before you buy a system. For example, some plug-ins don't work with certain software programs. If you just have to have a certain soft-synth (software synthesizer) or amp simulator plug-in, make sure that you buy a system that allows you to use it. (*Plug-ins* are extra sounds, samples, and effects that you can "plug in" to your computer-based DAW's software program to increase its capabilities.) Likewise, some sound cards don't work well with certain software programs.

- **Number of simultaneous tracks:** Even though a recorder may say it has 16 tracks, it may not be able to actually record that number of tracks at one time. Most SIAB recorders, for example, record fewer tracks than they can play back at once. This usually isn't a problem because you likely record only a few tracks at a time and overdub the rest. This would be a problem if you needed to record all 16 tracks of a 16-track recorder, such as recording a band playing live at a club.
- **Realistic track count:** If you end up considering a computer-based system, the number of tracks that a computer software program is advertised to record and how many tracks you can actually record with your computer are often two very different things. Find out beforehand what a realistic track count is with the central processing unit (CPU) and random-access memory (RAM) that you have so that you're not disappointed after you've forked over your hard-earned money. The best way to do this is to go to online forums (you can find some by typing **audio recording forum** in your favorite search engine) or talk to other users in your area to see what their real-world experiences are.
- **Sample rate and bit depth:** The sample rate and the bit depth of the system determine the sound quality that it can record. (The *bit depth* is the resolution of the audio sample in binary digits, and the *sample rate* is how often the sample is taken per second — notated as kHz.) Most semipro and pro systems have a 24-bit resolution and the ability to record at several sample rates — 32, 44.1, 48, 88.2, and 96 kHz, for instance. The number of tracks may vary depending on what sample rate setting you choose.

TIP

I recommend recording at 24 bits if you can because converting to 16 bits (the CD standard) is easy and doesn't cause damage to the quality of the sound.

The sample rate you choose is a bit more complicated because sample rate conversion (SRC) doesn't always sound good. I recommend thinking ahead about your final format and choosing your sample rate accordingly. Consider these final formats:

- **CD:** The standard for CD is 44.1 kHz.
- **Video:** If you edit video and want to import audio into your session, choose 48 kHz.
- **Extensive audio processing:** If you have a powerful computer and lots of storage space and do a lot of audio processing with plug-ins, you may find using 96 kHz or 192 kHz produces the best results.

Ever since I stopped releasing physical CDs and instead release all of my music online and rarely do much processing of my tracks, I use 48 kHz. I am happy with the quality of the sound.

- **Expandability:** As you learn and grow as a musician and recording engineer, your needs also grow. Knowing this, your best bet is to plan ahead and choose a system that can grow with you. Can you add more tracks by syncing another machine or increasing available RAM? Can you easily synchronize the system with other machines? For example, if you want to record 24 tracks now and you use a stand-alone recorder, can you add another recorder and have it sync properly? Or, if you buy an SIAB and you want to add more inputs later, can the system you're looking at do that by syncing with other devices, for instance? Some can and some can't, so do your research and think about your future needs.

  You'll find that almost all the new semipro and pro systems available are expandable, but explore these questions carefully if you look at purchasing used gear.

Computer-Based Digital Recording Systems

Computer-based DAW systems are hardware and software options that you can connect to your computer. These systems can be pretty straightforward, such as simple two-track recording freeware that you install on your home computer using a stock sound card. Or, you can go for a sophisticated system, like built-from-the-ground-up computers optimized to do one thing and one thing only: record, mix, and play back audio. (Okay, that's three things, but you get my point.)

To set up a computer-based DAW, you need the following items:

- A computer (preferably with a speedy processor)
- A bunch of memory and dual hard drives
- An audio interface
- The software

Finding the right computer setup

No matter which computer platform you choose (see the nearby sidebar "Mac or PC?"), the stuff you find inside your computer plays a major role in determining how smoothly (or how less-than-smoothly) your DAW runs.

MAC OR PC?

Whether to buy a Mac or a PC is a hotly debated topic among home recordists. Most professional studios used to favor Macintosh computers for recording audio. PCs were thought to have too many bugs to work well for audio. Even if this were true in the past, it's not true anymore. Your decision between a Mac- or PC-based recording system should be based more on your personal preferences in computer platforms and the particular software you intend to use rather than which one is more stable. Either platform may or may not be stable, depending on what you're trying to do.

Choose the software you want to use, and buy the computer that has the best track record for running that software. Some programs are available only for one platform or another. For example, Logic Pro X and Digital Performer are Mac-only programs, and Sound Forge and Sonar are available only for Windows PC users. Other programs, such as Nuendo and Pro Tools, are available for both Mac and Windows computers.

If you already have a computer or if you prefer one platform over another (PC or Mac), be sure to determine whether a program works on that platform before you buy it.

TIP

I suggest buying a computer that you can dedicate solely to recording audio, because running other types of applications (home finance software, word processors, or videogames) can cause problems with your audio applications and reduce the stability of your system.

The following list clues you in on the various pieces of hardware that you find in your computer:

- **CPU:** The CPU is the heart of your computer studio. The speed of your CPU ultimately dictates how well a program runs on it. As a general rule, for audio, get the fastest processor you can afford. For most audio software, you need at least a dual-core CPU. But honestly, these requirements are the absolute minimum you'll need to use the software programs. If you want a system that can handle the demands of recording or mixing many tracks (24 or more), you'll need to step it up a notch or two and get a computer with a dual or quad core processors (Mac or PC — it doesn't matter).
- **Memory:** Computer-based audio programs and all the associated plug-ins are RAM hogs. Here's my advice: Buy a lot of RAM. Okay, that's not very specific, but how much you need depends on your recording style. If you record a lot of audio tracks and want reverb or another effect on each track, you need more RAM (and a faster processor). If you record mainly MIDI tracks with instruments that already have the effects that you want, you can get by with less RAM (and a slower processor).

For most software programs, the recommended minimum amount of RAM is around 16GB; 32GB is recommended for typical use, and 48GB or more enables the program to run much more smoothly. RAM is relatively inexpensive, so get as much as you can. I'm currently using 40GB of RAM, and I'm at the low end of what's comfortable.

REMEMBER

Regardless of the platform that you choose (PC or Mac), keep in mind that you can never have a processor that's too fast or have too much RAM.

» **Hard drives:** To record audio, make sure you get the right type of hard drives. Notice that I said hard *drives* (plural). Yep, you should get more than one if you want to record more than a few tracks of audio. You need one hard drive for all the software and the operating system and another drive for the audio data. Having this setup greatly increases the likelihood that your system remains stable and doesn't crash, especially if you try to run 16 or more tracks. As for the drives themselves, here are some things to consider:

  - **Size:** For hard drives, bigger is better, at least for the drive where you store your music. For the core system drive, you can get by with an 256GB drive; for the audio drive, having even 500GB is pretty conservative because audio data can consume a ton of space. For example, a five-minute song with 16 tracks recorded at 24 bits and a 44.1 kHz sample rate takes up about 600MB of hard drive space (that's about 7.5MB per track minute). If you choose to record at 96 kHz, you can double this figure.
  - **Interface type:** Most external drives contain ports for a variety of interface types, such as USB 3.0, eSATA, and Thunderbolt. All of these provide ample speed for recording large track accounts of audio. Choose based on what ports you have on your computer.
  - **Drive type:** Hard drives come in two basic types: HDD (hard disk drive) and SSD (solid state drive). HDDs are often less expensive than SSDs but are more prone to failure. They are also slower. In the past, I offered a detailed analysis of the various HDDs to help you choose the best one for you, but because SSDs are more reliable, faster, and are priced close enough to HDDs, this decision process is unnecessary. Get SSD drives for both the system and for your audio.

My current favorite SSDs for recording audio are the SanDisk Extreme Portable External SSD and the WD My Passport Go SSD. Both can be found for around $100 for 500MB.

TIP

You may also want to add a third hard drive so you can back up your data. I usually buy a duplicate to my recording drive and transfer my work each day. As computer experts often say, "Your data doesn't exist if it doesn't exist in at least two places." If you prefer not to have a third hard drive, you can burn your data to DVDs or even use an online backup or storage service, such as ADrive, Backblaze, Carbonite, or Dropbox. You can find more services like these by searching for "online data storage" in your favorite search engine.)

Getting the sound in and out

After you have a computer with enough speed and muscle (see the preceding section), you need the appropriate hardware to transfer the sound into and out of it. This requires a device called an *audio interface.* Audio interfaces are available with three types of connection methods: PCIe, Thunderbolt, and USB. Here's a quick rundown on the three types (the details are spelled out in the following sections):

- **PCIe:** PCIe interfaces are inserted into one of the PCIe slots located inside your desktop computer's case.
- **USB:** USB 2.0 and 3.x interfaces are the most common types of audio interfaces, with options starting under $100.
- **Thunderbolt (USB-C):** Thunderbolt has gone through several iterations since its inception. The current version is Thunderbolt-3 or USB-C. Thunderbolt offers speeds that are considerably faster than PCI and USB options.

PCIe interfaces

Peripheral Component Interconnect (PCI) is the old standard for getting audio into and out of a computer. This technology consists of a slot into which you place a card containing the audio transfer components. PCI Express (PCIe) replaced the original PCI slot in computers starting in 2004 and it has essentially replaced them in any computer you'll find working today (or at least any computer capable of recording music). PCIe had an advantage over the other interface types because of the fast transfer speed of PCIe technology. This type of interface isn't without its problems, though:

- Many computers (for example, laptops and all Macs except the Mac Pro) don't have a PCIe slot.
- Because PCIe technology is changing, all cards don't fit in all computers, so make sure that the PCIe interface that you're considering can fit into your computer.

PCIe interfaces come in the following varieties:

- **Separate sound card with no analog inputs and outputs:** In this case, you need to buy separate preamps, direct boxes, and analog-to-digital (AD) and digital-to-analog (DA) converters. For most home recordists, the separate-sound-card route isn't the best solution. In fact, even for the pros, this isn't the most popular choice — so much so that this option is quickly falling from the marketplace. Figure 2-1 shows examples of PCIe sound cards.

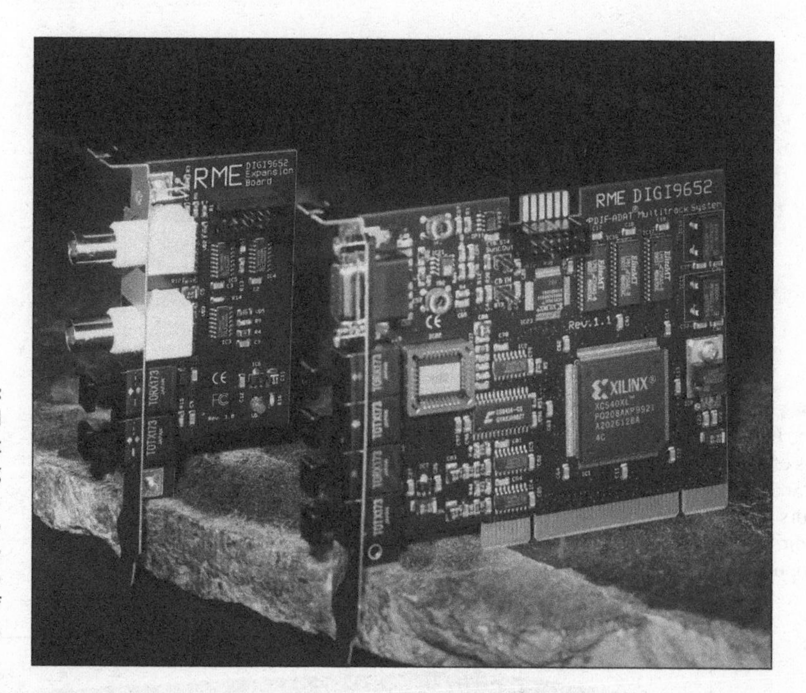

FIGURE 2-1: A PCIe sound card doesn't contain analog inputs or outputs, so you need to buy separate components to use this type of card for audio recording.

- **Analog inputs and outputs within the card:** Having the analog connection located in the card used to cause interference with the other components in the computer's housing (such as fans and hard drives), which caused low-level hums in the recorded audio (not a sound you would want, I can assure you). This is generally no longer the case unless you buy a really inexpensive card, but the bad rap led buyers to shy away from this approach and it has become uncommon as a result. You can find some less expensive audio interfaces configured this way, but the higher end of the market has generally abandoned it. Figure 2-2 shows an example of a PCIe card with analog connections.
- **Analog inputs and outputs housed in a separate box:** This box is called a *breakout box.* Because of the low-level hum problems in the early interfaces, most manufacturers of PCIe-based audio interfaces put their analog circuitry in a separate box with a cord attached to the PCIe card. One advantage to this — besides eliminating the hum in early models — is that you can tweak the input and output levels without having to use a software menu. The dials for the levels are placed on the breakout box within easy reach, as shown in Figure 2-3.

TIP

If your preferred audio recording computer doesn't have a PCIe slot, don't worry (or don't bother adding one). Thunderbolt and USB are both excellent technologies to use for recording music.

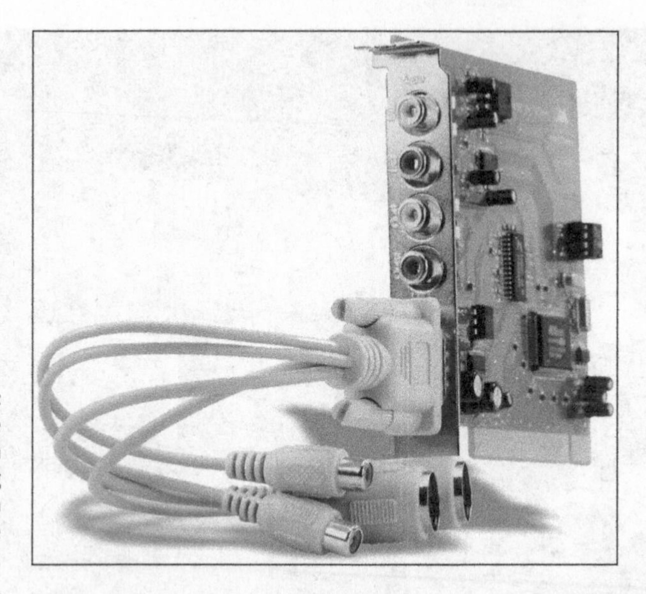

FIGURE 2-2: Some PCIe interfaces often come with analog connectors run from the computer.

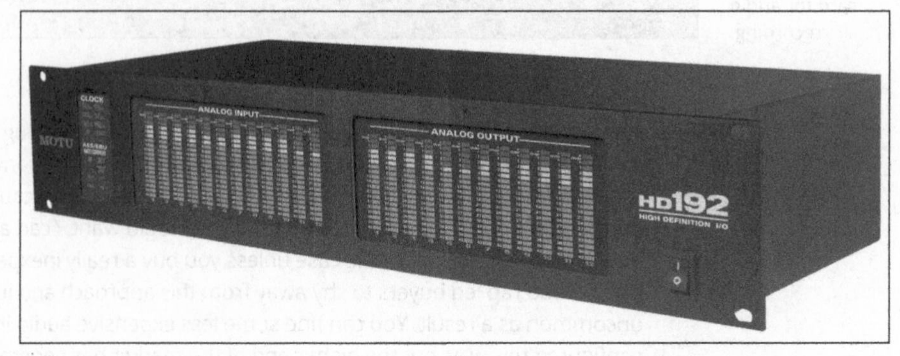

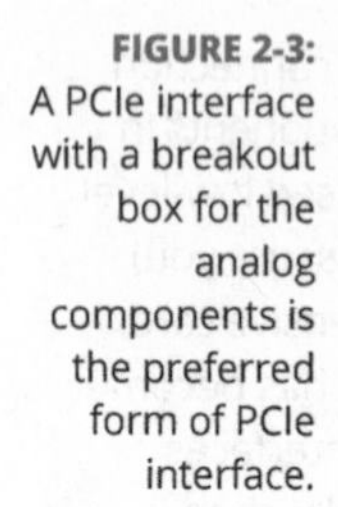

FIGURE 2-3: A PCIe interface with a breakout box for the analog components is the preferred form of PCIe interface.

USB interfaces

USB interfaces (see Figure 2-4) come in two varieties: those using USB 2.0, and those using USB 3.0. Most computers have at least one USB port. USB is a great option for your audio interface. They can be inexpensive and offer a variety of input/output configurations.

WARNING

Beware of used USB 1.1 interfaces. The *latency* (delay between the sound entering the interface and exiting your speakers) is too great to keep from being frustrating. You can find decent USB 2.0 and USB 3.0 interfaces for very little money, often starting at about $100 (USB 2.0), though they can run as much as $1,000 (USB 3.0), depending on the manufacturer and the number of tracks and other options they include.

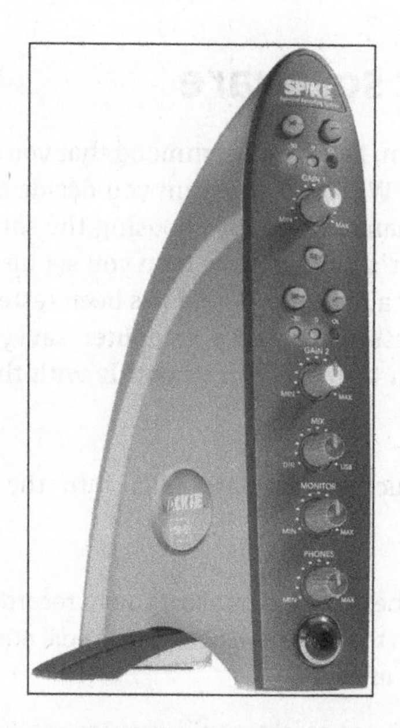

FIGURE 2-4: A USB interface connects to your computer's USB port.

Thunderbolt interfaces

For the last two revisions of this book, I had hoped that I could talk at length about the super, most awesome Thunderbolt interface and how it changed recording in the same way that moving from tape to digital did, but, alas, I wasn't able to. However, now I can. Though it would be a stretch to say that Thunderbolt has reinvented audio recording, it does offer some benefits that makes it better than either PCIe or USB.

Compared to USB, Thunderbolt offers eight times faster transfer speed and the ability to chain a variety of devices through the same port without any loss of speed. This means you can have more analog inputs and outputs than USB.

Compared to PCIe, Thunderbolt connectivity is more available — you can find them on laptops as well as on desktop computers. There are also many more interface options to choose from.

Thunderbolt audio interfaces tend to be more expensive than USB, not because of the technology, but because these interfaces often include better analog components, such as preamps, and more inputs and outputs. Expect to spend at least $500 for two input channels and $1,000 and more (often much more) for higher counts.

TIP

Quite a few audio interfaces have both Thunderbolt and USB 3.0 ports. If you're unsure of which to choose, or you plan to upgrade your computer from USB to Thunderbolt, these interfaces are excellent options.

Choosing the right software

TIP

When setting up a recording system, I always recommend that you start by exploring the software you want to use. Whatever program you decide to use will work better on one type of computer than another. By choosing the software first, you can use the software manufacturer's guidelines to help you set up your computer. Most software is written for either a Mac or a PC and has been tested with a variety of hardware configurations. Unless you're very computer savvy, I recommend starting with a system that's been tested to run smoothly with the program that interests you.

For the most part, audio production software falls into the following two categories:

- **Audio-recording programs:** These programs allow you to record numerous tracks (the number depends on the program) and let you edit, equalize, and mix those tracks as well as add effects.
- **MIDI-sequencing programs:** These programs allow you to record MIDI performance data (without the sounds) and edit and mix the data. The difference between audio and MIDI recording is covered in detail in Chapter 11.

REMEMBER

Most audio production programs offer both audio and MIDI recording and generally do a good job of both (and they're getting better all the time), but some entry-level programs allow you to only record audio or do MIDI sequencing. If your budget is limited and you want to record using both audio and MIDI, make sure that your chosen software allows you to do so. That said, choose the program based on its features and whether it fits with your working style.

Researching a program you're interested in

If you already own a computer and you want audio-recording or sequencing software to go with it, do the following research on the software that interests you:

- **Find out the product's compatibility with your system.** Visit the software manufacturer's website for information about whether your system will work with that program, as well as what additional hardware you may need in order to get the software up and running.
- **Find out what other users are saying.** On the Internet, you can find an online discussion board for each of the major audio-recording software programs. Before you buy a program, go to the sites of the programs that interest you and see what people are saying about them. Ask questions and explore the issues that other people are having with the programs. Doing so can save you lots of time dealing with bugs in your system and allow you to record a lot more music.

TIP

You can find these sites by using the product name as the keyword in your favorite search engine and checking out the Internet forums.

One great way to see whether a particular program is right for you is to find out what people who play your type of music are using. For instance, a lot of people who compose with synthesizers and MIDI use Logic Pro X because using MIDI and software synthesizers is quick and easy in this program. They also don't need a bunch of hardware synthesizers to get the sounds they want, which saves space in their studio and saves money, because they can bypass the hardware to get their synthesizer sounds.

Checking out some popular programs

You can choose from numerous music-production software programs. In this section, I include some free ones, full-featured, professional-level ones, and online collaboration-friendly ones. I'm sure at least one of these will meet your needs.

FREE PROGRAMS

There is a huge amount of free audio recording programs available if you are on a tight budget. Here are a few I recommend:

- **Audacity:** Audacity is the most popular free multi-track recording program. It is compatible with Windows, Mac, and Linux computers.
- **GarageBand:** GarageBand is extremely easy to use. It is only available for Macs, but it's so popular I can't not include it in this list.
- **Pro Tools First:** This is a free version of one the most popular and powerful professional programs. You are limited to 16 tracks and four inputs, which may be plenty, depending on your music. It can be used with both Windows and Mac computers.

COLLABORATION PROGRAMS

For many people, making music is a collaborative process. You can find a variety of websites online that make this process easy with full-featured recording programs and active communities of artists you can connect with. Here are some popular options (you can find many more with an Internet search):

- **BandLab:** BandLab is a free and is compatible with Windows, Mac, iOS, and Android devices.
- **Soundtrap:** Soundtrap has several pricing tiers, including a free tier. It is compatible with Mac, Windows, iOS, and Android devices.

- **Pro Tools:** Avid has made it easy for you to collaborate with Pro Tools software on Mac and Windows. There is no extra cost to use the tool. All you need to do is enable collaboration in your Pro Tools session.

PROFESSIONAL-LEVEL PROGRAMS

Though there are numerous high-quality audio recording programs, some have been around long enough and used by enough professionals that they stand out. Here are a handful of companies that make some of the best:

- **Apple:** Makes Logic Pro Audio and GarageBand. These programs run only on Mac systems. Logic Pro X has been around for a while and is one of the top programs available. The downside is that it's for Macs only. Like all the programs, Logic has its way of working — some people like it, while others have a hard time grasping the way the user interface functions. (I love it.)
- **Avid:** Makes Pro Tools, Pro Tools HD and HDX, and Pro Tools First. These programs work on both Mac and PC systems. Avid's Pro Tools HD and HDX systems are arguably the standard for digital audio in pro studios, although many pro studios are using any one (or more) of the other programs I list in this section.
- **Mark of the Unicorn:** Makes Digital Performer. This program runs only on a Mac up to version 10, and now works on Windows as well. Digital Performer is a powerful program that does MIDI and audio equally well. One advantage of this program is that Mark of the Unicorn makes very good audio interfaces that are designed to work well with its software. You end up with a better chance of having a stable system.
- **Steinberg:** Makes Cubase, Cubasis, Nuendo, and WaveLab. These programs run on both Mac and PC platforms. Nuendo is Steinberg's best program, and it's excellent for recording audio. Nuendo isn't very strong in MIDI sequencing, so if this feature is important to you, this may not be the best program to use. In that case, if you like the Steinberg line, you may want to try Cubase, which is a great program that's on par with Logic and the others, and is stronger in MIDI sequencing than Nuendo.

Most of these manufacturers offer program demos that you can download for free to see whether you like them. These demos work just like the full versions except that you generally can't save or print your work.

TIP

Some of these manufacturers also make audio-interface/sound-card hardware optimized for their systems; this hardware can generally work on other systems (check with the manufacturer to make sure). You may find an easy and great-sounding solution by choosing a software and hardware setup from a single manufacturer. If you do, you're likely to have fewer compatibility problems.

Studio-in-a-Box Systems

Integrated mixers/recorders/effects processors were once quite common (computer-based systems have overtaken them in the last few years). Cassette porta-studios, first introduced in the 1970s, enabled the home recordist to compose music at home without spending a fortune on equipment. But it wasn't until the Roland VS-880 came out in 1997 that great-quality recordings could be made at home using a single piece of equipment. Okay, you still needed an instrument and microphone to plug into it, but everything else fit into this one little box, which is now referred to as a studio-in-a-box system.

Taking a look at the benefits

One of the biggest advantages of using a SIAB system is that you don't need to be computer literate — just turn it on and start to record. SIAB systems are also portable — you can take them almost anywhere to record, so you're not limited to your studio room. (You can get a view of an SIAB system in Figure 2-5.) Think about this for a second: If you want a big drum sound and all you have is a small converted bedroom for a studio, you can load up your SIAB system, a few microphones, and your drummer's drum set (don't forget the drummer) and go to an empty warehouse, gymnasium, or church, for example. (Of course, you can do this with a laptop computer system, too, but it'll cost you more.) In fact, with many of these recorders you don't even need to have electricity to do this. Some of these recorders draw very little power and can operate on batteries.

Early versions of SIAB systems were somewhat limited in what they offered and weren't very user-friendly when it came to sharing files between systems. The newer generation of SIAB systems is being designed to import and export audio files in formats that you can open on other manufacturers' recorders, freeing you to transfer files between different systems.

Examining some popular SIAB systems

Many of the major recording manufacturers make SIAB systems. Check out these companies and compare the specifications of each unit:

- **TASCAM:** TASCAM has been in the home recording market for a long time, first with cassette porta-studios in the 1970s and now with digital systems. You can find several units, including the DP-005 six-track recorder, which records at 16 bits, and the DP-32SD 32-track recorder, which records in 24 bits.

- **Zoom:** Zoom is a relative newcomer to the SIAB market and offers innovative solutions that can be used as a stand-alone studio, computer audio interface, and computer software controller. Zoom's two recording systems include the R16 and R24, 16- and 24-track units, respectively. They both record in both 16 and 24 bits and integrate seamlessly with a computer. This means you can record on location and connect to a computer to overdub and/or mix.

FIGURE 2-5: A studio-in-a-box system contains everything you need to make great recordings.

Mobile-Device Recording

Smartphones and tablet computers are gaining ground, both in the number of people using them and in their ability to be used for creating music. As recently as a couple years ago, when I last updated this book, you couldn't do much with your phone or tablet. Perhaps you could record a couple tracks at 16 bits or maybe mix tracks in other software within your computer with a mixer app, but that was about it. Nowadays, you have quite a few ways you can use a smartphone or tablet to record and mix music, though your options are still mainly limited to Apple devices.

This section outlines the basics for the two most popular mobile system types: Android and Apple iOS.

TIP

Mobile development is happening at a blistering pace, and new apps and system upgrades are constantly appearing, so I recommend checking out the two main app stores for what's new:

- **Android**
- **Apple iOS**

Android

Android is, by far, the most popular mobile platform. However, it's pretty slim on apps and hardware that can be used for music composing, recording, editing, or mixing. That said, this section offers some hardware and app options to get you recording on your Android device.

Hardware

Dedicated hardware options for Android are currently limited. The basic voice-recorder apps all use the internal microphone, while some other apps, such as the USB Audio Recorder, are able to use certain USB audio interfaces.

Here is the first of what I expect will be many USB-based hardware manufacturers that will offer Android-supported devices:

- **IK Multimedia:** IK Multimedia offers a handful of hardware options for your Android device. These include mics, a mic preamp, a guitar input, and a mixer, all at pretty low prices.

Apps

Here are some audio recording apps for Android phones and tablets:

- **iRig Recorder:** This is an enhanced version of a voice recorder that allows you to record up to 16-bit/44.1-kHz audio and edit and enhance it with various tools and effects. You can also share your recordings in a variety of ways.
- **J4T Multitrack Recorder:** A four-track recorder with effects and mixing abilities. Works with the internal mic and a variety of USB audio interfaces (though it doesn't list which interfaces are compatible).
- **USB Audio Recorder Pro:** This app opens your Android device to a variety of USB audio interfaces. Be sure to check the device compatibility list before trying to use a USB interface.

Apple iOS

Apple was the first company to make apps available for mobile users, and with its head start, it has managed to provide a fairly broad selection of mobile apps and hardware that can allow you to use an iPhone or iPad to record your music. As of this writing, here are some hardware and software options that can get you creating music on your Apple device.

Hardware

Because the Apple devices have been around a while, there has been support for USB audio with the iOS software — just about any USB interface will work with your iPhone, iPad, or iPod touch. However, I strongly recommend that you choose an app first and then see what hardware is supported.

That said, here are hardware options that have proven to be reliable for iOS devices:

- **Apogee:** Apogee makes high-quality audio interfaces that are used in the better studios. It has several studio-quality interfaces for iOS devices, including One, Duet, and Quartet. These devices are more expensive than others, but they're worth it if you want to record at the highest possible level.
- **Blue Microphones:** Blue makes some nice mics, and it has two dedicated to iOS devices: Spark Digital and Mikey. Both plug right in and work flawlessly.
- **IK Multimedia:** IK Multimedia offers a fairly large selection of interfaces for the iPhone, iPad, and iPod.

Apps

There are a growing number of audio recording apps for iOS devices. Each of the hardware manufacturers that I list in the preceding section has its own apps, but here are a few that are hardware agnostic (you can find them in the iTunes App Store):

- **Auria:** This is my favorite audio recording app. Maybe it's because I've been using it a while, but after playing with other apps, I think it's because it works well. At $25, Auria is more expensive than the cheapest apps, but less expensive than the spendy ones.
- **Cubasis:** This app is based on the Cubasis computer recording program and is very powerful. It costs a bit more ($50), but for people used to professional recording software, it's a nice program.

- **GarageBand:** This is a free app made by Apple, and it's pretty much the same as the Mac GarageBand program. It's easy to use but somewhat limited in its capabilities. Still, it's stable and free, so it's worth giving it a shot.
- **MultiTrack DAW:** This app isn't as feature rich as some others, but for $10 it does a lot. And it's stable.
- **Music Studio:** This app isn't free ($14.99), but it's nice. I find it easy to use and fairly powerful.

This list could go on, so I highly recommend doing some searches for audio recording and music app in the App Store. Also, tons of instrument apps (for drums, piano, guitar, synths — you name it) are available for the iPad or iPod to allow you to make music in a variety of ways.

TIP

If you want to use more than one music app at a time and have them sync, such as audio-recording with a synth, I highly recommend Audiobus. This app opens worlds that you can only imagine until you try it. It only works with compatible apps, but at this point, there are over 400 of them, so it's not like you're limited.

TIP

If you want an inexpensive, no-fuss gadget to record two tracks, you may want to consider a *linear recorder*, a two-track recorder (sometimes called a *voice recorder* or *field recorder*). Many linear recorders come with mics built in, and some even have effects. The cool thing about a linear recorder is that it can fit in your pocket and record with surprisingly high quality, such as 24 bits (although many are 16 bits). Check the specs of the various models if the bit depth is important to you.

Exploring Sample Setups

In the following sections, I help you start thinking about the best system configuration for your needs. Whether you're an electronic musician who only needs a sequencer, some MIDI instruments, and a two-track recorder, or you're a purist who wants 16 tracks of simultaneous recording and needs dozens of microphones to record your whole band live, I help you figure it out.

Because I don't know what type of recording you want to do, I outline three basic systems to give you an idea of what may work for you. You can see a system that works well for both live recording and MIDI sequencing, a system for MIDI sequencing and the occasional instrument or vocal overdub, and a live rig that contains little or no MIDI instrumentation. This is only a starting point, but as you shop around for a system, you'll be able to find a setup that best meets your needs.

REMEMBER

You can configure your home recording system in almost unlimited ways. Part of what will influence your decisions is your initial budget and how you like to work. Look around and talk to other people who have a home studio. Join an Internet forum and discover the different ways that people are recording — find out what works for them and what doesn't. Then jump in and don't look back. The most important component in your studio is you!

Live and MIDI studio

The live and MIDI studio is your best choice if you want to incorporate both MIDI-sequenced parts and live instruments (such as guitar, electric bass, and drums). For this type of system, you need a recorder, a mixer, and a MIDI controller. You also need a few microphones and any instruments that you plan to record — generally at least one synthesizer or sound module, an electric guitar and bass, and a drum machine or real drum set. Figure 2-6 illustrates a setup that's centered around an SIAB recorder with a computer for sequencing. Of course, you could use a stand-alone recorder instead (you need a separate mixer), or you can incorporate the whole system into a computer if you choose.

You want a system with a fair number of tracks (at least eight) that allows you to record at least two tracks of MIDI instruments as well as several tracks of guitar, bass, drums, and vocals.

MIDI-intensive studio

Are you a one-man band? Do you prefer to program a performance rather than to play it? If so, you may want to have a MIDI-intensive studio. The advantage of the MIDI studio is that one person can "play" many instruments at the same time. A disadvantage is that the music can sound somewhat stiff. (See Chapter 15 for advice on how to overcome this.) And you may lose touch with what it feels like to play with other musicians — which is not always a bad thing, especially if you're into that whole reclusive artist thing.

Because MIDI instruments can be programmed to play the part perfectly, with all the dynamic variations that you want, you can spend your time working on the parts (composing, setting levels, and creating effects) without actually having to record them. As a result, you can get by with fewer audio tracks in your system, but you need to have more MIDI tracks available. An advantage to this approach is that MIDI tracks take less CPU power and RAM to run compared to the same number of audio tracks. So, you can get by with a less-expensive computer (or use the one you already have) and save your bucks for more synthesizers or plug-ins.

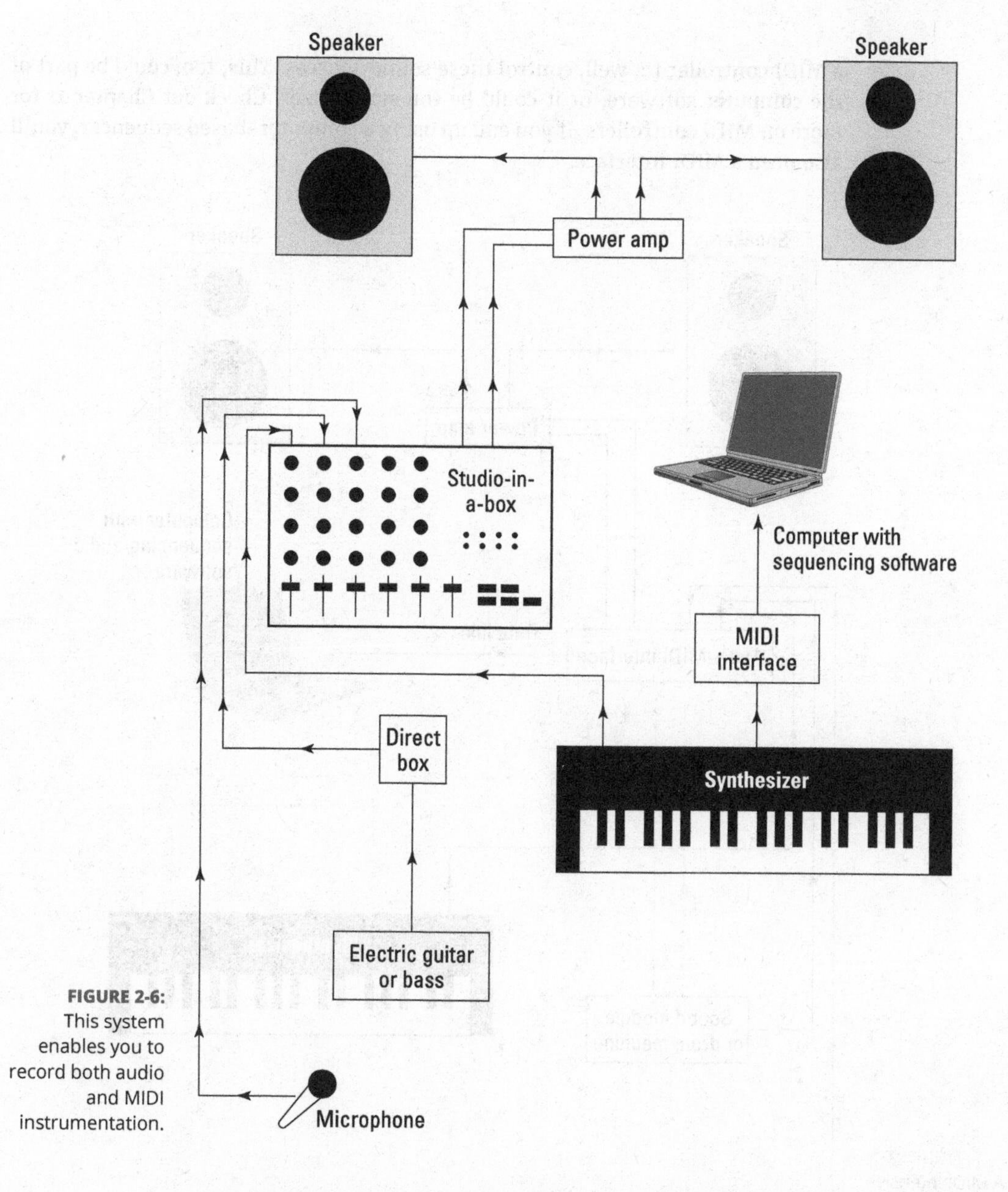

FIGURE 2-6: This system enables you to record both audio and MIDI instrumentation.

For a MIDI-intensive studio, such as the one shown in Figure 2-7, you need a sequencer (a device that allows you to record and play back MIDI performance information) and at least one sound source. This can be a keyboard synthesizer, a sound module, a sampler, or a computer equipped with sounds, called *soft-synths.* You also need a drum machine or drum sounds in your computer if you intend to make any music other than ambient or classical-type music. In addition, you need a MIDI controller to, well, control these sound sources. This, too, could be part of the computer software, or it could be the synthesizer. Check out Chapter 11 for more on MIDI controllers. If you end up using a computer-based sequencer, you'll also need a MIDI interface.

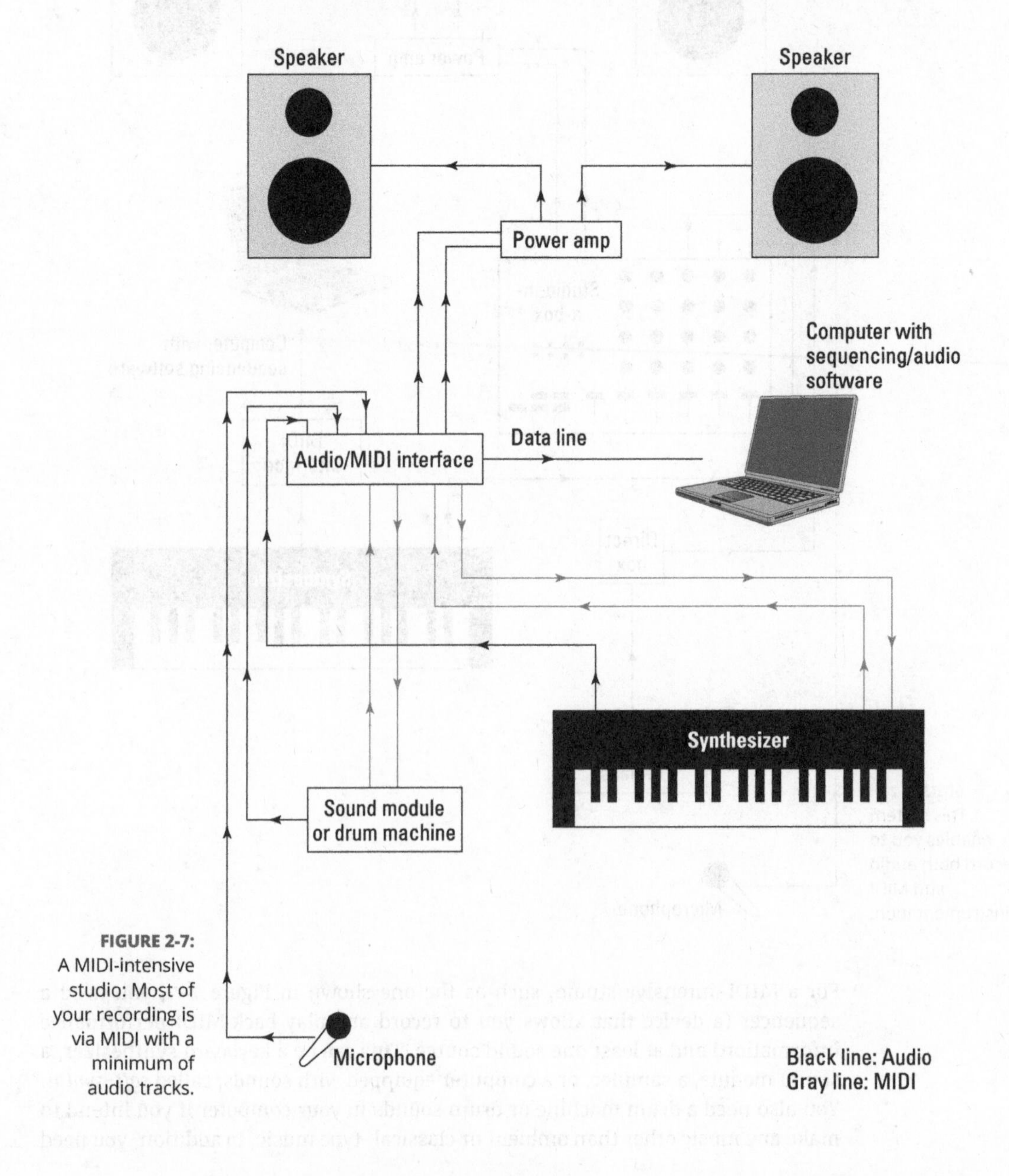

FIGURE 2-7: A MIDI-intensive studio: Most of your recording is via MIDI with a minimum of audio tracks.

In addition to the MIDI stuff, you need some sort of recorder. Again, this can be included in your computer setup. If you plan to sequence all the parts and don't want to include any vocals, you could get by with a decent two-track recorder. On the other hand, if you see yourself including vocals or any non-MIDI instruments — such as an electric guitar, for example — you need a microphone (for the vocals) and the ability to record more tracks.

Live studio

Thirty years ago, when a band wanted to record, the members all went into a studio together, set up their gear in one large room (with maybe a few dividers between them), and played as if they were at a concert. Then they would overdub a guitar solo, backup vocals, and maybe a few percussion instruments.

The beauty of this type of recording for a band is that you have a better chance of capturing the magic of a live performance. The disadvantage is that it takes a little more recording skill to get a good sound. (Of course, you discover many of these skills in this book.)

For the live studio, you need a recorder with at least as many available simultaneous tracks as you think you need for your band. Eight tracks are usually enough for most bands. The tracks would break down as follows:

- **Rhythm guitar:** One track
- **Bass guitar:** One track
- **Piano, organ, or synthesizer:** One or two tracks
- **Rough vocals:** One track

  You generally record this track over again after the rest are done to get a cleaner track.
- **Drums:** Two to four tracks

  The number of tracks varies depending on the type of sound that you want. You may need a separate mixer to create a submix of the drums if you're only using two tracks.

Aside from the simultaneous track count, you probably want extra tracks available to record a guitar solo, background vocals, and maybe percussion instruments. In this case, a 16-track recorder is a great solution. If you want more flexibility in getting your band's sound, you could get a recorder that can record as many as 16 simultaneous tracks.

If you're one of those many people who like to record one or two tracks at a time but still want to play all the instruments live (with no MIDI sequencing), your need for lots of simultaneous tracks is reduced. A computer-based system with a couple of analog inputs is probably your best solution because it costs less and takes up less space.

You can also use a computer-based system to record all the instruments live. Just make sure that you have both the inputs and available tracks that you need.

REMEMBER

If you record all the instruments live (all at once or one at a time), you also need to have enough microphones and mic stands. And you must contend with making your room conducive to recording live instruments. (I discuss this more in Chapter 3.)

With the many ways to configure a home recording system, you'll probably lean more toward one type of system than another (computer-based, SIAB, or standalone). Then it's just a matter of weeding through the options until you find one that resonates with you (and your budget).

Podcasting studio

A studio for podcasting can be as simple as your phone and a free audio recording app or as complex as what you use for live and MIDI recording. How sophisticated you decide to go depends on how much you want to add to your voice, such as intro, outro, or background music, sound effects, and the number of people you want to record at the same time.

If you are podcasting by simply recording yourself and not adding intro and outro music or interviewing guests, your phone with a free audio recording app will get you started. Add an external mic and you can get professional-quality sound (see Figure 2-8). If you want to be able to mix music, sound effects, or other vocals, you will need the ability to do multitrack mixing. In either case, I recommend you prepare for the following track counts:

- **Voice:** One mic and one input and audio track for each person.
- **Music you play while doing your podcast:** At least one track and microphone if you are recording acoustic instruments such as a guitar. Possibly more if you want to record in stereo or with more than one instrument at a time.

FIGURE 2-8: A basic podcasting studio.

If you are using music, sounds effects, or multiple voices, you also need software that lets you mix all the parts together.

Audio-for-video studio

Video cameras can record sound at a quality high enough for most videos where you are talking directly to the camera, especially if you plug in a shotgun or lavalier mic to your camera. The limitation with this is that it is more difficult to optimize the sound of your voice. Professional video production always uses separate video and audio recording processes. Doing this is not difficult. I recommend (and use) a setup with the following capabilities:

- **Voice:** One track and lavalier mic for each person talking, or one shotgun mic and one audio track for all voices.
- **Ambient:** An optional stereo mic or a matched pair of mics and two audio tracks for ambient sounds.

Aside from these tracks, you probably want extra tracks available to record background music or sound effects. Of course, you also need the software that will allow you to mix multiple tracks.

Mobile on-location studio

Mobile on-location recording can be as simple as a stereo mic plugged into a two-track field recorder or as complex as the live recording setup I describe earlier in this section.

When I record live on location, I like use a four-track Zoom recorder and two sets of mics, either stereo or matched pairs. This allows me to capture the same performance twice and gives me a backup in case something goes wrong with one set of tracks. It also gives me the opportunity to place each set of mics in a slightly different location to give me options when I mix the performance.

IN THIS CHAPTER

» Getting to know the various types of connectors

» Plugging in your equipment

» Creating an efficient workstation

» Making your room sound great (or at least decent)

Chapter 3
Getting Connected: Setting Up Your Studio

Okay, so you're ready to turn that spare bedroom or basement into a recording studio. You need to unpack all your shiny new gear and get it plugged in properly, and your room needs to work for you. This involves creating an efficient place to work, but above all, it means following tips in this chapter to make your room sound good. This can be tricky — after all, pro studios spend tons of time and money so that their studios sound great. You may not need to spend a ton of money (as if you could), but you do need to spend some time.

After you decide on a space for your home recording system, the next steps involve setting up the system and preparing your space to work for you. In this chapter, I help you make sense of all those analog or digital connectors and help you plug them all in properly.

This chapter also shows you how to find the best way for you to work in your environment, with a fair measure of tips and tricks thrown in to make your room sound as good as possible.

Understanding Analog Connections

You've probably had a chance to see and use a variety of analog connectors. If you play a guitar or keyboard (synthesizer), for example, you're familiar with a ¼-inch analog plug. Some microphones use an XLR analog plug. Keeping all these connectors straight can be a little confusing: Why do you have to use one plug for one thing and another for something else? And what's a TRS plug, anyway?

Read on to discover the most common analog connectors: ¼-inch (mono/TS and stereo/TRS), XLR, and RCA.

The ¼-inch analog plug

The ¼-inch plug is the most common audio connector and one of the most versatile. These plugs come in two varieties: mono/TS and stereo/TRS.

Mono/TS

The plug on a cord that you use for your guitar or synthesizer is an example of a mono ¼-inch plug. The *mono* part of the name refers to the fact that you have only one channel through which to send the signal. This type of plug is also referred to as a *TS* plug (short for tip/sleeve). The tip is the end of the plug, and the sleeve is the rest of the metal part. A plastic divider separates these two sections. Check out Figure 3-1 to see this familiar plug.

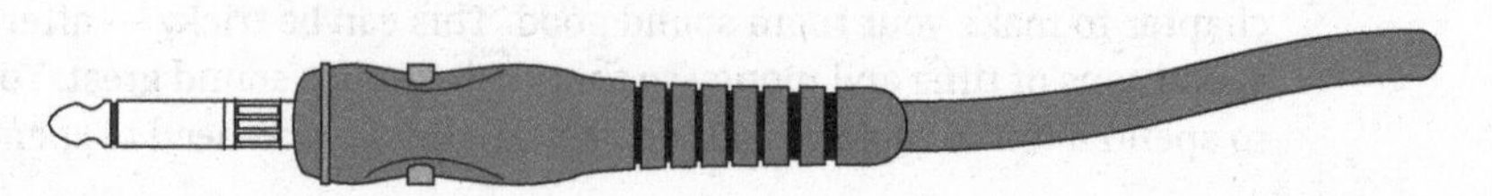

FIGURE 3-1: A typical ¼-inch plug used for guitar and other electric instruments.

TS plugs are used for a variety of purposes — to go from your guitar to your guitar amplifier (amp), from your synthesizer to your mixer, from your mixer to your power amp, and from your power amp to your speakers. You would expect that one cord could work for all these applications. After all, a TS plug is a TS plug, right? Well, not really. The same plug can be wired differently, and it can carry different levels of power. For example, here are the differences between instrument and speaker cords:

- **Instrument cord (the one you use for your synthesizer or guitar):** This cord contains one wire and a shield — the wire is connected to the tip, and the shield is connected to the sleeve. You need the instrument cable's shield to minimize noise. If you use a speaker cord (discussed next) for your instrument, you may end up with some noise (that is, you may hear a hiss or a buzz — or even a radio station — coming out of your amp or coming from where you've plugged in your instrument).

Instrument cords are often called *unbalanced lines* because of the way they're wired. An unbalanced cord has one wire surrounded by a braided shield; the wire is connected to the tip of the TS plug, and the shield is connected to the sleeve. The signal is sent through the wire, and the shield is used for the ground. (It keeps the noise down.) You can also find balanced lines, which I explain in the next section of this chapter.

- **A speaker cord:** This cord contains two wires and no shield — one wire is connected to the tip and the other to the sleeve. Because the speaker cord carries a lot more current (power) than the instrument cable, the speaker cord doesn't have a shield. The signal level covers noise that's present in the cord. Because you have much less current present in an instrument, you don't want to use a speaker cord for your instrument.

When buying cords with TS plugs, first be sure to look at (or ask about) what purpose the cord is designed for. Then, when you take the cord home, be sure to note what type it is so that you use it correctly. You can mark your cord in a number of ways: You can put colored tape on it (red for speaker or blue for instrument, for example), put a tag on it, or — gasp — dot it with nail polish.

You generally don't need to worry about which end of the cord you plug into your instrument — the signal can travel equally well in either direction. However, you can buy cords that are designed to send the current in one direction. (This cord has an arrow on it, designating in which direction the signal should flow.) I call these *designer cords*, and two of the most common brands are Monster and Planet Waves. The theory behind these cords is that they do a better job of preserving the sound qualities of the instrument for which they're designed. These cords are specifically designed for almost every instrument and application known to man.

Stereo/TRS

A stereo/TRS (short for tip/ring/sleeve) 1/4-inch plug looks like a stereo headphone plug (take a look at Figure 3-2). The tip is the end of the plug, the ring is the small middle section located between the two plastic dividers, and the sleeve is the rest of the metal part of the plug. A TRS plug can be used for the following three types of cords:

- **Stereo cord:** A stereo cord is used for signals that contain two separate portions: one for the right channel and the other for the left channel. This type of cord is generally wired with the left-channel signal attached to the tip, the right-channel signal connected to the ring, and the shield wired to the sleeve. This type of cord is typically used for headphones.

FIGURE 3-2: Use a balanced (TRS) plug to connect professional audio gear.

- **Balanced cord:** A *balanced cord* is used on professional audio gear to join the various pieces of equipment (to connect the mixer to the recorder, for example). The advantage with a balanced cord is that you can have longer cord runs without creating noise.

TECHNICAL STUFF

Why are balanced cords so conveniently noise free? The balanced cord has two wires and a shield inside and has the same signal running through both wires. One signal is 180 degrees out of phase with the other (that is, their waveforms are opposite one another), and when the signals get to the mixer (or whatever they're plugged into) one of the signals is flipped and added to the other. When this happens, any noise that built up in the signal is canceled out.

- **Y cord:** A *Y cord* consists of a TRS plug on one end and two TS plugs on the other, forming — you guessed it — a nice representation of the letter *Y*. This cord allows you to insert an effect processor — a compressor or equalizer, for example — in the line of a mixer (more specifically, into the insert jack of the mixer). Check out Chapter 4 for details on mixers. The TRS plug both sends and receives a signal. This cord is wired so that the tip sends the signal and the ring receives it (see Figure 3-3). The sleeve is connected to the shield of each cable.

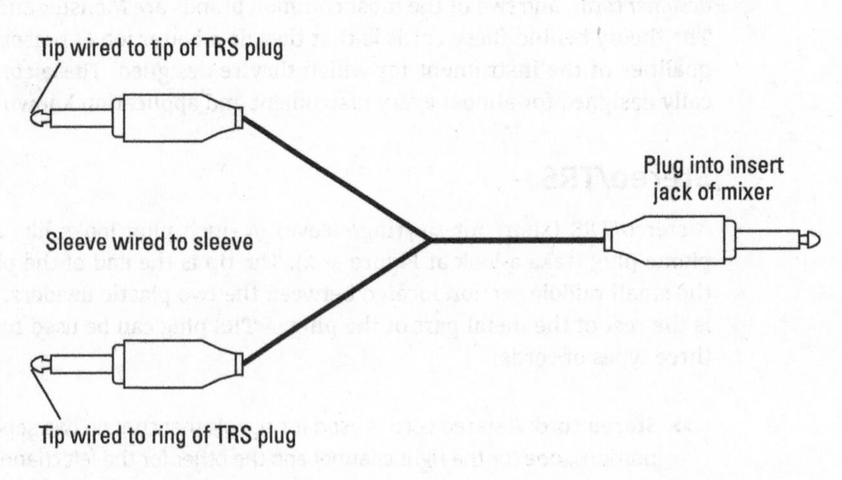

FIGURE 3-3: Use a Y cord to send and receive a signal.

XLR

The XLR connector is used for microphones and some line connections between professional gear. This cable has a female and a male end (see Figure 3-4). The cord is wired much like a TRS connector and is balanced to minimize noise. The XLR microphone cable is also called a *low Z cable* because it carries a low-impedance signal.

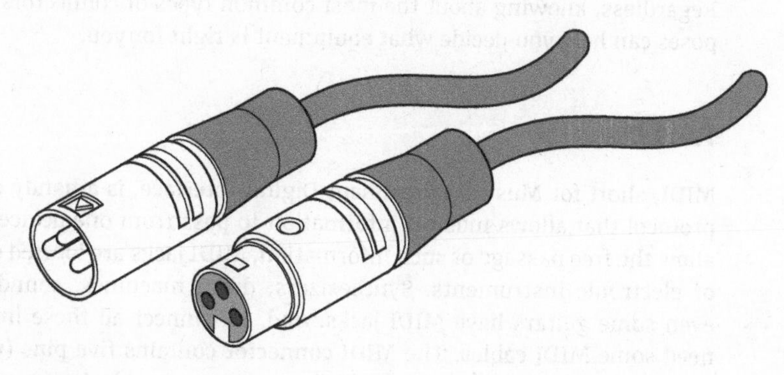

FIGURE 3-4: An XLR connector: One end is male (left) and the other is female (right).

RCA

RCA plugs — named for good old RCA and also called phono plugs — are common on home stereos and on some semipro audio gear (see Figure 3-5). They function much like a TS plug but aren't very common in professional audio equipment. However, you find them on some mixers so that you can connect a CD player, turntable, iPod, or other media device. They're also used for digital S/PDIF signals (see the next section for more details on these babies).

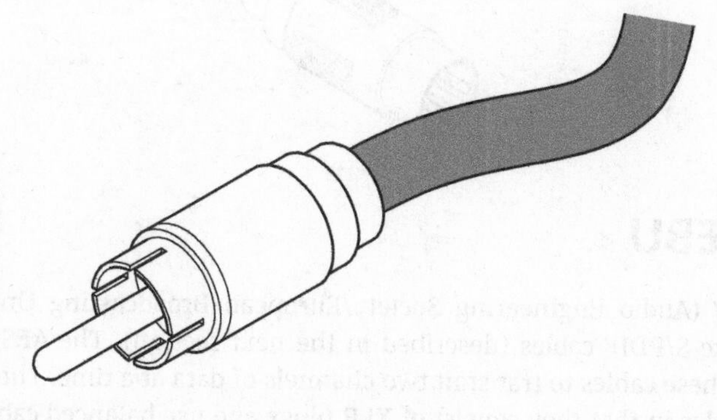

FIGURE 3-5: An RCA plug is used mainly on consumer stereo and some semipro audio equipment.

Delving into Digital Connections

If you're going to record using a digital recorder or mixer, you're going to run into digital connectors (plugs and cables/cords). Digital audio equipment is a recent invention, and as such, no one standard has emerged. Because of this lack of standardization, a variety of digital connection methods are on the market, only a few (or one) of which may be on the equipment that you own or intend to purchase. Regardless, knowing about the most common types of connectors and their purposes can help you decide what equipment is right for you.

MIDI

MIDI, short for Musical Instrument Digital Interface, is a handy communication protocol that allows musical information to pass from one device to another. To allow the free passage of such information, MIDI jacks are located on a whole host of electronic instruments. Synthesizers, drum machines, sound modules, and even some guitars have MIDI jacks. And, to connect all these instruments, you need some MIDI cables. The MIDI connector contains five pins (male) that plug into the female MIDI jack (port) on the instrument or device (see Figure 3-6).

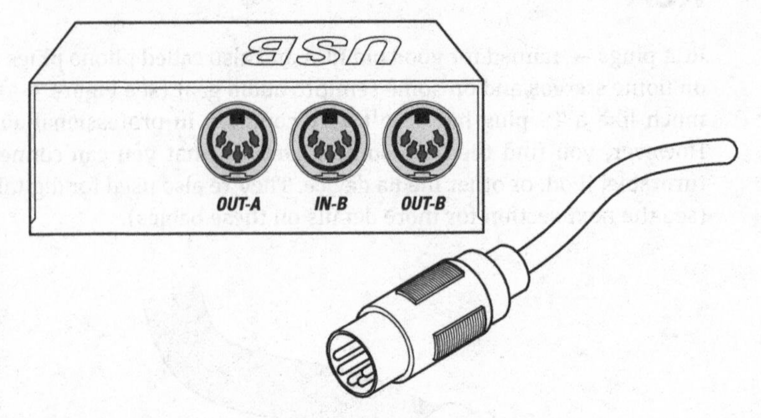

FIGURE 3-6: MIDI connectors have two male ends. The device contains the female jack.

AES/EBU

AES/EBU (Audio Engineering Society/European Broadcasting Union) cables are much like S/PDIF cables (described in the next section). The AES/EBU standards require these cables to transmit two channels of data at a time. They differ from S/PDIF cables in that they consist of XLR plugs and use balanced cables. (Figure 3-7 shows what the inputs look like on the recording equipment.) AES/EBU was developed to be used with professional audio components (hence, the use of balanced cords — the kinds used in professional-level equipment).

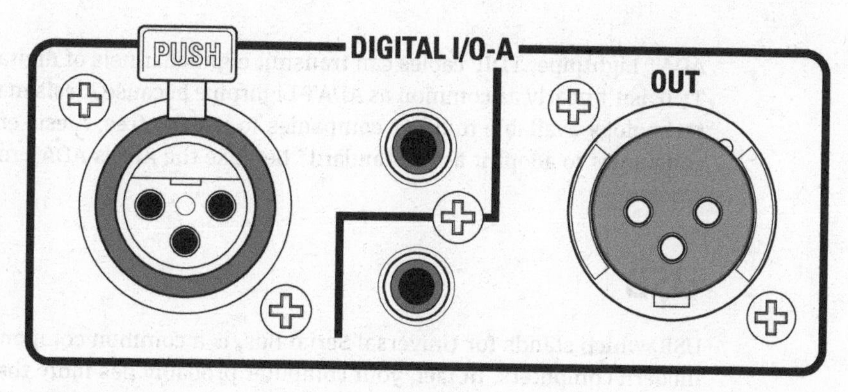

FIGURE 3-7: S/PDIF and AES/EBU connectors look the same as analog RCA (S/PDIF) and XLR (AES/EBU) but are marked as digital on the machine.

S/PDIF

S/PDIF (short for Sony/Phillips Digital Interface Format) cables consist of an unbalanced coaxial cable (one wire and a shield) and RCA plugs. (Figure 3-7 shows what the inputs look like on the machine.) These cables can also be made from fiber-optic cable and a Toslink connector. The S/PDIF format can transmit two channels of digital data at one time. S/PDIF protocols are similar to AES/EBU standards, except that S/PDIF was originally designed for the consumer market — which explains why unbalanced cords are used. In spite of being developed for the consumer market, S/PDIF connectors are found on a lot of pro recording gear along with (or instead of) AES/EBU.

TIP

If you want to use cords that are longer than 3 to 4 feet when using an S/PDIF connector — or about 15 feet for AES/EBU connectors — your best bet is to use video or digital audio cables. Regular audio cables degrade the sound at longer distances because they can't transmit the type of signal that digital produces without affecting the quality of the sound. If you use audio cables for longer distances, you lose some of the sound's definition. Some people describe this sound as "grainy."

ADAT Lightpipe

The ADAT (Alesis Digital Audio Tape) Lightpipe format allows eight tracks of digital audio to be sent at once. Developed by Alesis, ADAT Lightpipe (or simply Lightpipe for short) has become a standard among digital audio products. It consists of a fiber-optic cable that uses a special connector developed by Alesis.

TDIF

TDIF (Teac Digital Interface Format) is Teac's return volley to the ADAT Lightpipe format. TDIF uses a standard computer cable with a 25-pin connector. Like the

ADAT Lightpipe, TDIF cables can transmit eight channels of digital data at a time. TDIF isn't nearly as common as ADAT Lightpipe because Alesis made its Lightpipe technology available to other companies to use for free. Alesis encouraged these companies to adopt it as a "standard" because the Alesis ADAT recorders were so common.

USB

USB, which stands for Universal Serial Bus, is a common component in nearly all modern computers. In fact, your computer probably has more than one USB port. USB connectors are directional and contain two end types (see Figure 3-8 for an example):

- **A Connector:** This is used for a receiving device such as your PC or USB hub.
- **B Connector:** This is used for a sending device, such as your USB audio interface or printer.

FIGURE 3-8: USB uses two types of connectors: the "A" connector (left) and the "B" connector (right).

USB connectors come in three sizes:

- **Standard:** This size is used for computers and peripheral equipment, such as printers.
- **Mini:** This size is generally used for larger mobile or portable devices.
- **Micro:** This size is used for phones and thinner mobile devices.

Aside from having two different types of jacks and plugs, USB also has different standards. These are the ones that matter for audio recording (see Chapter 2 for USB interface options):

- **USB 1.1:** This standard (the original) can handle a data rate of up to 12 Mbps (megabits per second). You'll still find some USB 1.1 audio interfaces on the used market, but I recommend skipping them because you'll be disappointed in their performance.
- **USB 2.0:** Also called High-Speed USB, this standard can handle 40 times the data flow of the earlier standard — 480 Mbps. This is the most common connection for audio interfaces and can meet most home recordists' requirements.
- **USB 3.x:** This is also referred to as SuperSpeed or SuperSpeed+ USB. This connection transfers data ten times faster than USB 2.0 and will allow you to record a full symphony without a problem (you would need an audio interface with a lot of inputs and this will cost you).
- **USB C:** USB-C is twice as fast as USB 3. Though it uses the same connector as Thunderbolt (see the Thunderbolt section later in this chapter), it is considerably slower. It is fast enough, however, for any audio you may want to record.

FireWire

Developed by Apple, FireWire (also known as IEEE 1394 or iLink) is a high-speed connection that is used by many audio interfaces, hard drives, digital cameras, and other devices. You won't find FireWire ports on any new computers, but you will still find some audio interfaces with them. Luckily, all these audio interfaces also have USB ports.

Like USB, FireWire comes in two flavors, which are described as follows:

- **FireWire 400:** This standard supports data transfer speeds of up to 400 Mbps. Many audio interfaces currently use FireWire 400 as a way to connect with your computer. These interfaces can handle quite a few inputs and outputs.
- **FireWire 800:** Yep, you guessed it — this standard can handle data transfer rates of 800 Mbps. Several FireWire 800 devices are available.

Thunderbolt

Thunderbolt is the fastest connectivity format to date, with speeds between 20 gigabits per second (Thunderbolt 2) and 40 gigabits per second (Thunderbolt 3). Audio interface manufacturers are excited about this amazing speed, and many experts see Thunderbolt as the next format that the pros will embrace.

Unfortunately, things got confusing when Thunderbolt 2 was quickly replaced by Thunderbolt 3 just as audio interface manufacturers rolled out a variety of Thunderbolt 2 interfaces. Each has a different type of connector (see Figure 3-9) and a different protocol, which I outline here:

- **Thunderbolt 2:** Thunderbolt 2 uses the mini DisplayPort and can transfer data at speeds up to 20 gigabits per second (Gbps). This was available on computers between mid-2013 and late 2015.
- **Thunderbolt 3:** Thunderbolt 3 employs the USB-C connector and doubles the speed of Thunderbolt 2 to 40 Gbps. You can find Thunderbolt 3 ports on computers and peripherals made after late 2015.

FIGURE 3-9: Thunderbolt is a high-speed data-transfer protocol that comes in two varieties: Thunderbolt 2 (left) and Thunderbolt 3 (right).

Working Efficiently

I hope that you'll spend many hours in your studio creating great music (possibly to the dismay of the rest of your family). One important thing to keep in mind is that you need to be comfortable. Get a good chair and set up your workstation to be as easy to get around as possible. Figure 3-10 shows a classic L setup. Notice how everything that you need is within arm's reach. If you have enough room, you may want to consider a U-shaped setup instead, which is shown in Figure 3-11.

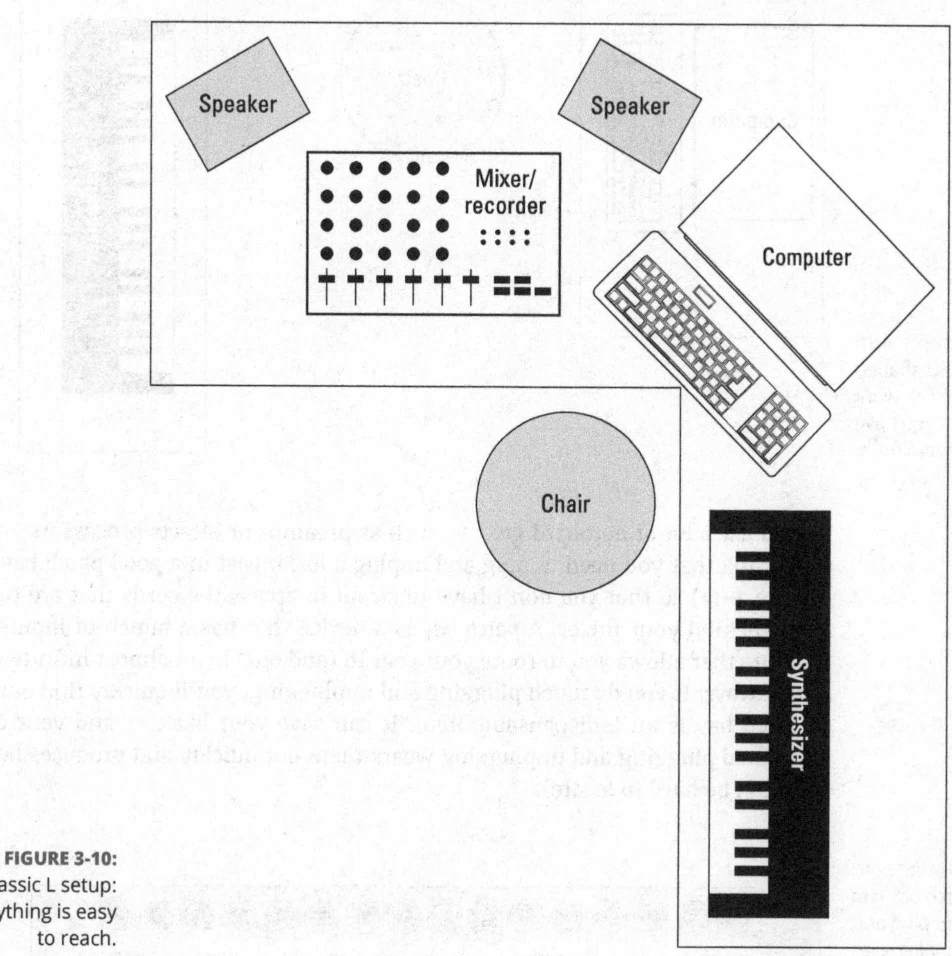

FIGURE 3-10: A classic L setup: Everything is easy to reach.

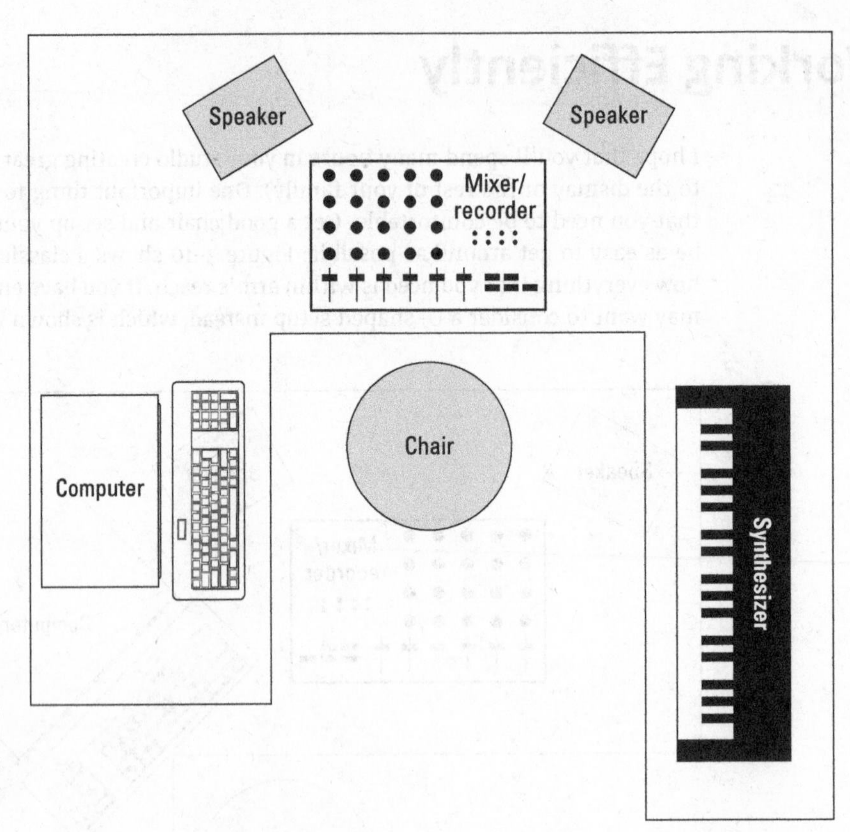

FIGURE 3-11: The U-shaped setup can work great if you have the room for it.

If you use a lot of outboard gear — such as preamps or effects processors — and you think that you need to plug and unplug a lot, invest in a good patch bay (see Figure 3-12) so that you don't have to strain to access the cords that are tucked away behind your mixer. A *patch bay* is a device that has a bunch of inputs and outputs that allows you to route your gear in (and out) in an almost infinite variety of ways. If you do much plugging and unplugging, you'll quickly find out that a patch bay is an indispensable item. It can save your back — and your cords (repeated plugging and unplugging wears them out quickly and produces buzzes that can be hard to locate).

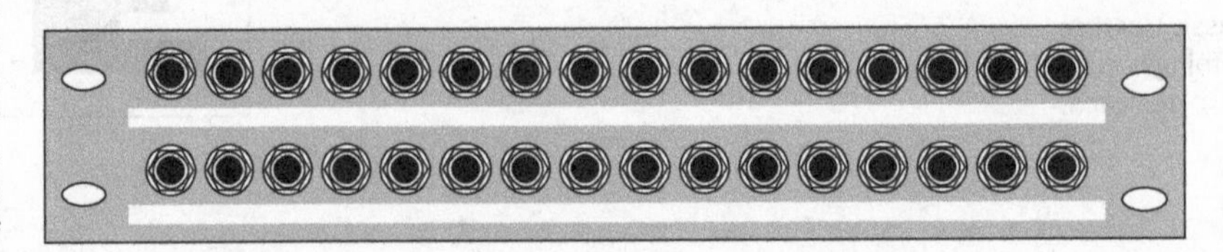

FIGURE 3-12: A patch bay lets you plug and unplug gear without having to crawl behind each piece of gear.

Taming heat and dust

The number-one enemy of electronic equipment is heat. Dust is a close second. Try to set up your studio in a room that you can keep cool and fairly dust-free. Air conditioning is a must for most studios. Be careful with a window air conditioner, though, because it can make a lot of noise, requiring you to shut it off when you record. Depending on where you live, this can quickly warm your room. Regarding dust, try to cover your equipment when you're not using it, especially your microphones. A plastic bag placed over the top of a mic on a stand works well.

TIP

You can also just put away your mics when you're not using them. However, if you use a particular mic a lot, you're better off leaving it on a stand rather than constantly handling it — some types of mics are pretty fragile. (You can find more details on caring for your mics in Chapter 6.)

Monitoring your monitors

If you have a set of near-field monitors (speakers) — the kind that are designed to be placed close to you — they should be set up so that they are the same distance from each other and from you, forming an equilateral triangle (see, high school math has some real-world applications). The monitor's speakers should also be placed at about the height of your ears.

Figure 3-13 illustrates the best placement for your monitors. Placing your monitors this way ensures that you hear the best possible sound from them and that you can accurately hear the stereo field. (For more on the stereo field, see Chapter 16.)

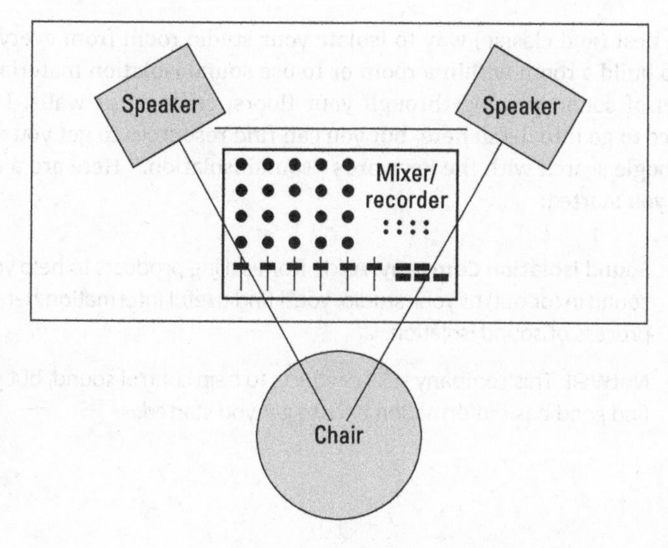

FIGURE 3-13: Your monitors (speakers) sound best when placed at equal distances from each other and from you.

Optimizing Your Room

Your studio probably occupies a corner in your living room, a spare bedroom, or a section of your basement or garage. All these environments are less than ideal for recording. Even if you intend to record mostly by plugging your instrument or sound module directly into the mixer, how your room sounds has a big effect on how well your music turns out.

As a home recordist, you probably can't create a top-notch sound room. Professional studios spend serious cash — up to seven figures — to make their rooms sound, well, professional. Fortunately, you don't need to spend near that much money to record music that sounds great. All you need is a little understanding of the way sound travels, some ingenuity, and a little bit of work.

Isolating sound

When you start recording in your home, both you and your neighbors are probably concerned about the amount of sound that gets into and out of your room. Sound waves are nasty little buggers. They get through almost any surface, and you can't do a lot to stop that from happening.

You've probably noticed this phenomenon when somebody with a massive subwoofer in his car drives by your house blasting obnoxious music. (Ever notice how someone else's music is obnoxious whereas your music never is, no matter how loud you play it?) Your windows rattle, your walls shake, and your favorite mug flies off the shelf and breaks into a thousand pieces. Well, this is one of the problems with sound.

The best (and classic) way to isolate your studio room from everything around it is to build a room within a room or to use sound isolation materials to reduce the level of sound passing through your floors, ceilings, or walls. I don't have the space to go into detail here, but you can find resources to get you started by doing a Google search with the keywords "sound isolation." Here are a couple places to get you started:

- **Sound Isolation Company:** Aside from selling products to help you keep the sound in (or out) of your studio, you'll find useful information here about the process of sound isolation.
- **NetWell:** This company sells products to help control sound, but you'll also find good basic information here to get you started.

If you don't have the money or space to build a room within a room or to add expensive sound isolation barriers to your recording space, the best thing you can do is to try to understand what noises are getting in and getting out and deal with those noises. For example, if you live in a house or apartment with neighbors close by, don't record live drums at night. You could also consider using a drum machine or electronic drum set instead.

Another idea is to choose a room in your house or apartment that is the farthest away from outside noise (an interior room, for instance). Basements also work well because they're underground, and the ground absorbs most of the sound. Placing a little fiberglass batt insulation (the typical house insulation that you can find at your local home center) in the ceiling can isolate you pretty well from your neighbors. Detached garages are generally farther away from other buildings, so sound has a chance to dissipate before it reaches your neighbors (or before your neighbors' noise reaches your garage).

Also, keep the following points in mind when trying to isolate your studio:

- **Dead air and mass are your friends.** The whole concept of a room within a room is to create mass and dead air space so that the sound is trapped. When you work on isolating your room, try to design in some space that can trap air (dead air) — such as a suspended ceiling or big upholstered furniture — or use double layers of drywall on your walls (mass).
- **Don't expect acoustical foam or carpet to reduce the noise.** Using these items helps reduce the amount of sound that bounces around inside the room, but acoustical foam or carpet does little toward keeping the sound in or out of the room.
- **Isolate the instrument instead of the room.** Isolating the sound of your guitar amp can be much less expensive than trying to soundproof your whole room. Most commercial studios have one or more isolation booths that they use for recording vocals and other acoustic instruments. You can use that concept to create your own mini isolation booths.

TIP

One idea for a truly mini isolation booth is to make an insulated box for your guitar (or bass) amp. If you just *have* to crank your amp to get the sound that you want, you can reduce the amount of noise that it makes by placing it inside an insulated box. Check out Figure 3-14 to see what I mean.

You can also create an isolated space in a closet by insulating it and closing the door when you record, or you can put your guitar amp (or drums) in another room and run a long cord from there to your recorder. If you do this, remember that for long cord runs, you need to use balanced cords; otherwise, you may get a bunch of noise and your signal may be too low to record well.

Top is 2 x 4 frame wrapped by 3/4-inch plywood and filled with fiberglass insulation
Amp sits inside
3/4-inch plywood inner shell
Hole for mic cable
2 x 4 frame
Fiberglass insulation
3/4-inch plywood outer shell

FIGURE 3-14: An amp-isolator box reduces the amount of noise you hear from your amp, even when it's cranked.

Controlling sound

After you create a room that's as isolated from the outside world as possible, you need to deal with the way sound acts within your room.

Sound travels through the air in the form of waves. These waves bounce around the room and cause *reflections* (reverberations or echoes). One of the problems with most home studios is that they're small. And because sound travels very fast (about 1,130 feet per second — the exact speed depends on the humidity in the environment), when you sit at your monitors and listen, you hear the reflected sound as well as the original sound that comes out of your speakers. With big rooms, you can hear the original sound and reflections as separate sounds, meaning that the reflections themselves become less of a problem. For a good home studio, you need to tame these reflections so that they don't interfere with your ability to clearly hear the speakers.

TECHNICAL STUFF

How all these reflections bounce around your room can get pretty complicated. Read up on *acoustics* (the way sound behaves) to discover more about different room modes: *axial* (one dimension), *tangential* (two dimensions), and *oblique* (three dimensions). Each relates to the way that sound waves interact as they bounce around a room. Knowing your room's modes can help you come up with an acoustical treatment strategy, but very complicated formulas are used to figure out your room's modes, especially those dastardly tangential and oblique modes.

You can find out more on room modes, as well as discover some room mode calculators, by searching the Internet for "room modes." I recommend that you research these modes; this topic alone could fill an entire book.

At the risk of offending professional acoustical engineers, I'm going to share some tricks that I've been using in my studios. My main goal has been to create a room with a sound I like that gives me some measure of control over the reflections within the room. Because I (and most home recordists) both record and mix in one room, it's helpful to be able to make minor adjustments to the acoustics to get the sound I want.

Sound control plays a major role in two aspects of recording — tracking and mixing — and each requires different approaches for you to get the best possible sound from your recordings. I cover both of these aspects in the sections that follow.

Sound control during tracking

Tracking is what you're doing when you're recording. Two things that can make a room a bad environment for tracking are not enough sound reflection and too much sound reflection.

When tracking, your goal is to have a room that's not so dead (in terms of sound reflection) that it sucks the life out of your instrument and not so alive that it over-colors the sound. The determining factors in how much reflection you need in your room are the instrument that you record and the way it sounds in the room. If your room is too dead (with not enough sound reflection), you want to add some reflective surfaces to liven things up (the room, that is). If your room is too alive (with too much sound reflection), you need to add some absorptive materials to tame those reflections.

You could buy a bunch of foam panels to catch the reflections or install a wood floor or attach some paneling to the walls to add some life, but then you would be stuck with the room sounding only one way. It may end up sounding good for recording drums or an acoustic guitar, but it would probably be too alive for getting a great vocal sound — which requires a deader space. One solution that works well is to get (or make) some portable panels that can either absorb or reflect the sound.

TIP

Figure 3-15 shows an absorber/reflector that I've used and found to work well. One side has an absorptive material (dense fiberglass insulation), and the other has a reflective surface (wood). They're assembled in an attractive frame and designed to stack easily. Even with minimal woodworking experience, you can crank out a set of them in a weekend for very little money (about $50 per panel). I guarantee that if you make them (or hire someone to make them for you), you'll find dozens of uses for them around your studio.

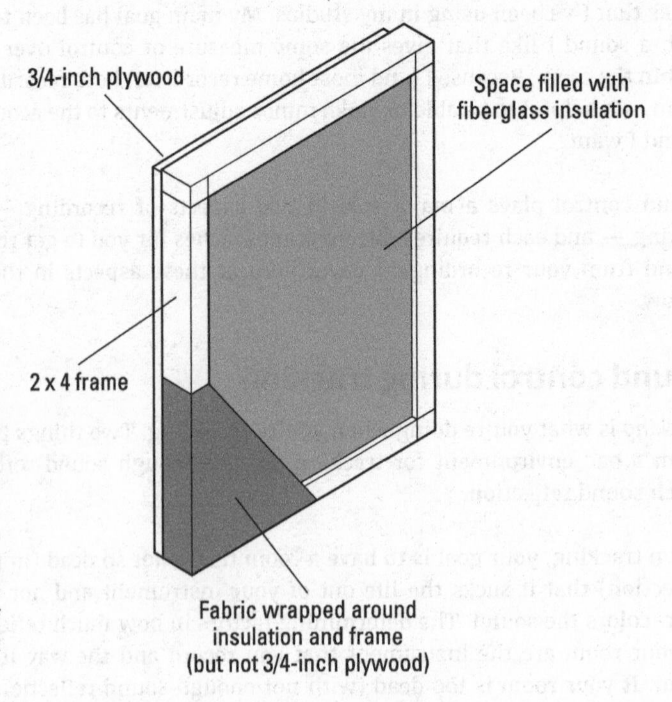

FIGURE 3-15: Portable absorbers/reflectors make changing the sound characteristics of your room quick and easy.

Here are two great video tutorials that explain how to make acoustic panels:

- **Vo Tech Guru:** How to Build Acoustic Panels (www.youtube.com/watch?v=GBHYiWIJhUA)
- **Recordeo:** How to Make Your Home Studio Sound Amazing With a Low Budget (www.youtube.com/watch?v=qBy63yKkoqQ)

Sound control during mixing

The following sections detail the steps that can help you control the sound of your (probably less-than-perfect) room during mixing.

TIP

You can skip (or delay) the following steps if you have a good pair of headphones. Headphones also allow you to cross-reference your mix's sound when you do mix with speakers in a good room.

GET A GOOD PAIR OF NEAR-FIELD MONITORS

Near-field monitors are designed to be listened to up close (hence, the *near* in their name) and can lessen the effects that the rest of the room has on your ability to accurately hear them and to get a good mix.

MIX AT LOW VOLUMES

I know, mixing at low volumes takes the fun out of it, right? Well, as fun as it may be to mix at high volumes, it rarely translates into a great mix. Great mixing engineers often listen to their mixers at very low levels. Yes, they occasionally use high levels, but only after the mixing is almost done and even then only for short periods of time. After all, if you damage your ears, you'll end up with a short career as a sound engineer (hey, that rhymes!). I don't want to sound like your mother, but try to resist the temptation to crank it up. Your ears will last longer and your mixes will sound better.

USE PANELS TO TAME SOUND

Even with these two things (near-field monitors and low mixing levels), you still need to do something to your room to make it work better for you. The secret to getting a good mixing room is to tame the sound reflections coming out of your speakers. Dealing with high-range and midrange frequencies is pretty easy — just put up some foam panels or the absorptive side of the panels from Figure 3-15. (See, I told you that you would have a use for those panels.) Here's a rundown on how to place absorption panels in your studio:

- **Start by hanging two panels on the wall behind you (or by putting them on a stand or table) at the level of your speakers.**
- **Put one panel on each side wall, right where the speakers are pointed.** This positioning, shown in Figure 3-16, gets rid of the higher frequencies and eliminates much of the echo.
- **You may need to put some type of panel on the ceiling right above your head.** This is especially important if you have a low (8 feet high or less) or textured ceiling (you know, one with that "popcorn" stuff sprayed on).

TIP

You may not want to mount one of the absorber panels over your head because they're fairly heavy. A couple of 2-x-4-foot dense fiberglass panels (the same ones that you used in the absorber/reflectors) wrapped with fabric would work perfectly. In fact, you can easily make overhead diffusers like the ones shown in Figure 3-17.

» **You can also place a set of fiberglass panels in the corners of your room behind the speakers.** Just hang the panels at the same height as your speakers so that they cut off the corner of the room. If you don't have enough room to fit the panels at an angle in the corner, you can eliminate the backing from the fiberglass and bend the fabric-covered panel to fit right in the corner. Either approach absorbs sound that may bounce around behind the speakers.

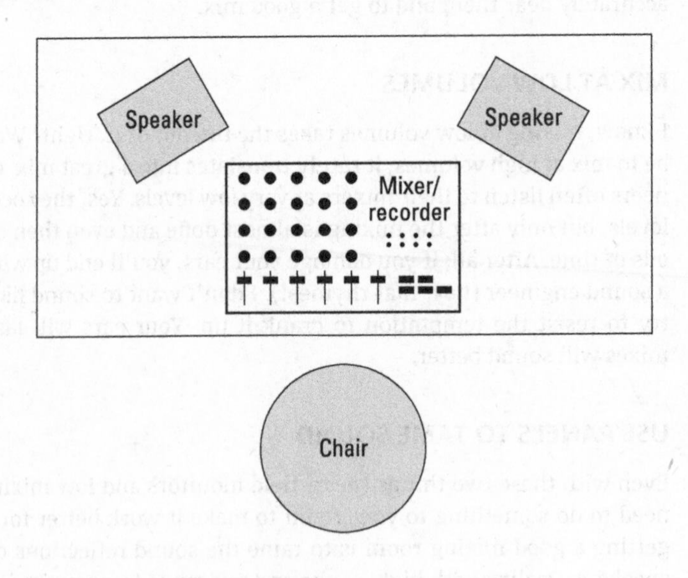

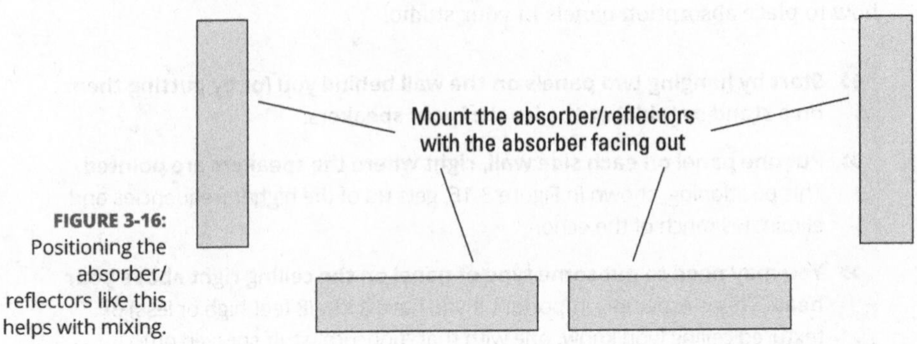

FIGURE 3-16: Positioning the absorber/ reflectors like this helps with mixing.

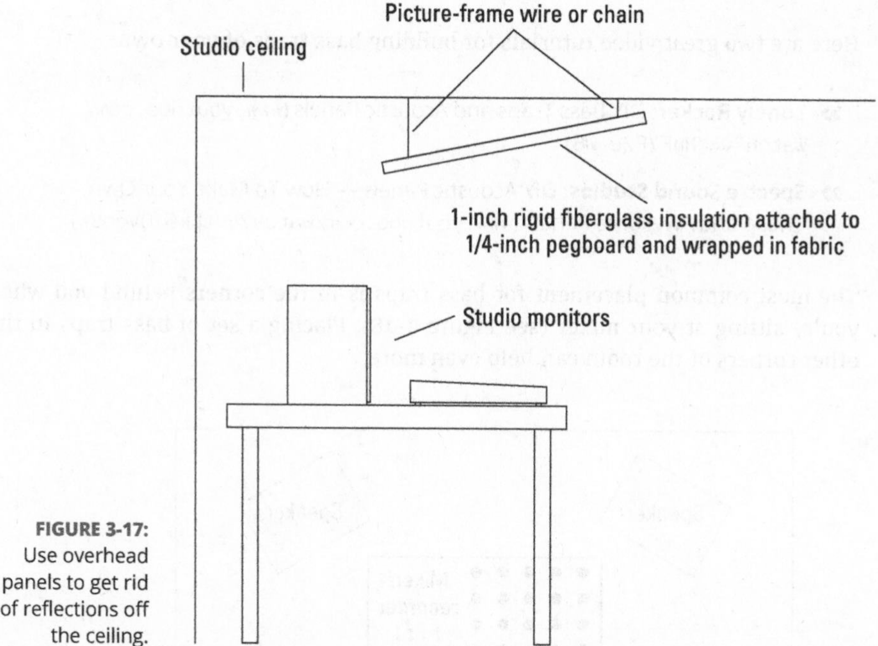

FIGURE 3-17: Use overhead panels to get rid of reflections off the ceiling.

USE BASS TRAPS TO TAME STANDING WAVES

You also need to consider standing waves when mixing. *Standing waves* are created when bass tones begin reflecting around your room and bounce into each other. Standing waves can either over-accentuate the bass from your speakers (resulting in mixes that are short on bass) or cancel out some or all of the bass coming out of your speakers (resulting in mixes with too much bass). One problem with standing waves is that they can really mess up your mixes, and you may not know that they're there.

To find out whether you have a problem with standing waves in your studio, sit in front of your monitors and carefully listen to one of your favorite CDs. Okay, now lean forward and backward a bit. Does the amount of bass that you hear change as you move? Next, get up and walk around the room. Listen for places within the room where the bass seems to be louder or softer. You may find places where the bass drops out almost completely. If either inspection proves to be true, you're the proud owner of standing waves. Don't worry, though. You can tame that standing-wave monster with a pair of bass traps.

Bass traps absorb the energy in the lower frequencies so that they don't bounce all over your room and throw off your mixes. You can buy bass traps made of foam from some music stores or (yep, you guessed it) you can make your own out of wood or metal and insulation.

Here are two great video tutorials for building bass traps of your own:

- **Lonely Rocker:** DIY Bass Traps and Acoustic Panels (www.youtube.com/watch?v=MHnFYFZc-w8)
- **Spectre Sound Studios:** DIY Acoustic Panels — How To Make Your Own Cheap and Awesome Panels (www.youtube.com/watch?v=tLk6fQVcoSw)

TIP

The most common placement for bass traps is in the corners behind you when you're sitting at your mixer (see Figure 3-18). Placing a set of bass traps in the other corners of the room can help even more.

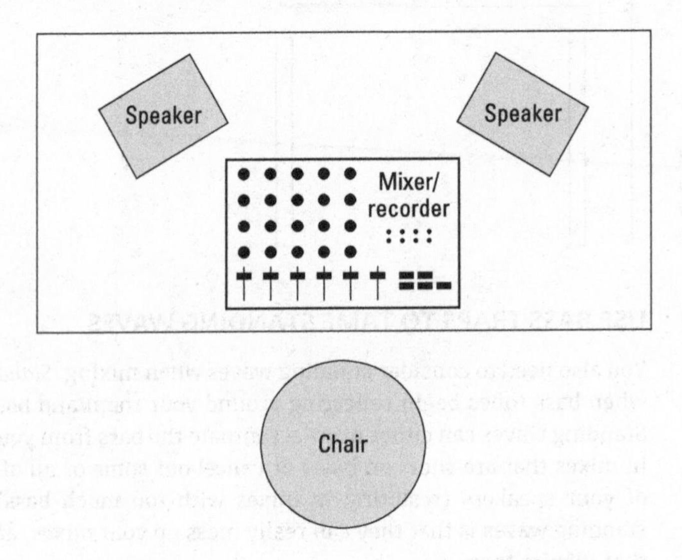

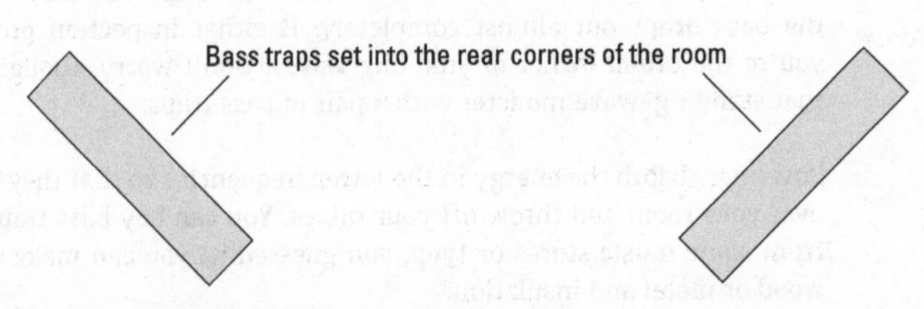

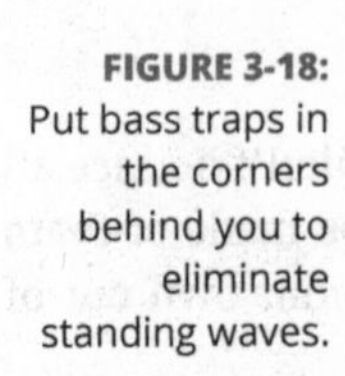

FIGURE 3-18: Put bass traps in the corners behind you to eliminate standing waves.

After you place the bass traps, do the listening test again. If you notice areas where the bass seems to get louder or softer, try moving the bass traps around a little. With trial and error, you can find a place where they work best.

REMEMBER

Try not to stress out about the sound of your room. As important as your room's sound may be, it has a lot less impact on the quality of your recordings than good, solid engineering practices. I know, I keep saying this, but it's important to remember. So, do what you can and then work with what you have.

IN THIS CHAPTER

» Understanding the different types of mixers

» Deciphering channel strips

» Exploring routing and busing

Chapter 4
Meet the Mixer

If you've ever been to a recording studio and watched a great recording engineer create a mix, you've probably been entranced by the way that he or she interacted with the mixing board: a dance around the mixer, a twist of a knob here, a push of a slider there. All this works to the beat of the music. It's like watching a genius painter paint, or a great orchestra conductor conduct, or a brilliant surgeon surge . . . er, operate. I'll even bet that one reason that home recording caught your interest is the chance to play with those knobs and sliders yourself. Go ahead and admit it — you'll feel better.

Well, you get your chance in this chapter. Not only do you discover what all those knobs and sliders do, but you also begin to understand all the functions that the mixer fulfills in the studio. You discover what makes up a channel strip and how it's used. You get a chance to see how busing and routing work and even discover what these terms mean. But first you start by examining the different types of mixers that are used in home studios.

Meeting the Many Mixers

For the home recordist, mixers come in several varieties: the analog desk, the digital mixer or computer control surface (with or without sliding faders and fader banks), and software mixers controlled by your computer mouse and keyboard.

Your choice of mixer mostly depends on the other equipment that you use in your studio and on your budget. Here's the lowdown for the four basic types of recording systems:

- **Studio-in-a-box (SIAB) system:** These all-in-one units come with a digital mixer — just plug in your instrument or microphone and you're ready to go. Most mixers in these units offer quite a bit of flexibility in routing your signal, so you'll likely be able to do quite a bit with little hassle. The features of the mixer in each SIAB system vary, so look at the specs of the unit that interests you before you buy.
- **Computer-based system:** All recording software includes a digital mixer that's controlled by your keyboard and mouse. Most of these programs also allow you to connect an external bit of hardware called the *computer control surface.* This gives you real knobs and sliders to tinker with as you work.
- **Tablet interfaces:** A number of apps are available for tablet computers that give you control over the digital mixer in a computer-based software program. These can be handy because you can use your fingertips to control the various sliders and knobs, giving you a similar tactile feel to a physical mixer instead of the singular function that exists when mixing with a computer mouse. These are also great for using as a remote control.
- **Stand-alone components:** Because everything is separate in this type of system, you need to buy a mixer before you can use your recorder. Here you can choose between an analog or digital mixer, and you need to invest in the cords necessary to make the proper connections (this alone can get expensive). The type of mixer you choose will be based partly on your budget, but mostly on your working style and whether you prefer analog or digital mixing. I talk more about analog and digital mixers in the next two sections.

Analog mixer

The *analog mixer,* shown in Figure 4-1, enables you to route the signals within the analog domain. Analog mixers tend to have many knobs, lights, and faders — a set for each channel. If you want to change from mixing inputs (your instruments) to mixing sounds recorded on the recorder, you need to plug and unplug cords, or you need to get a mixer with twice as many channels as your recorder.

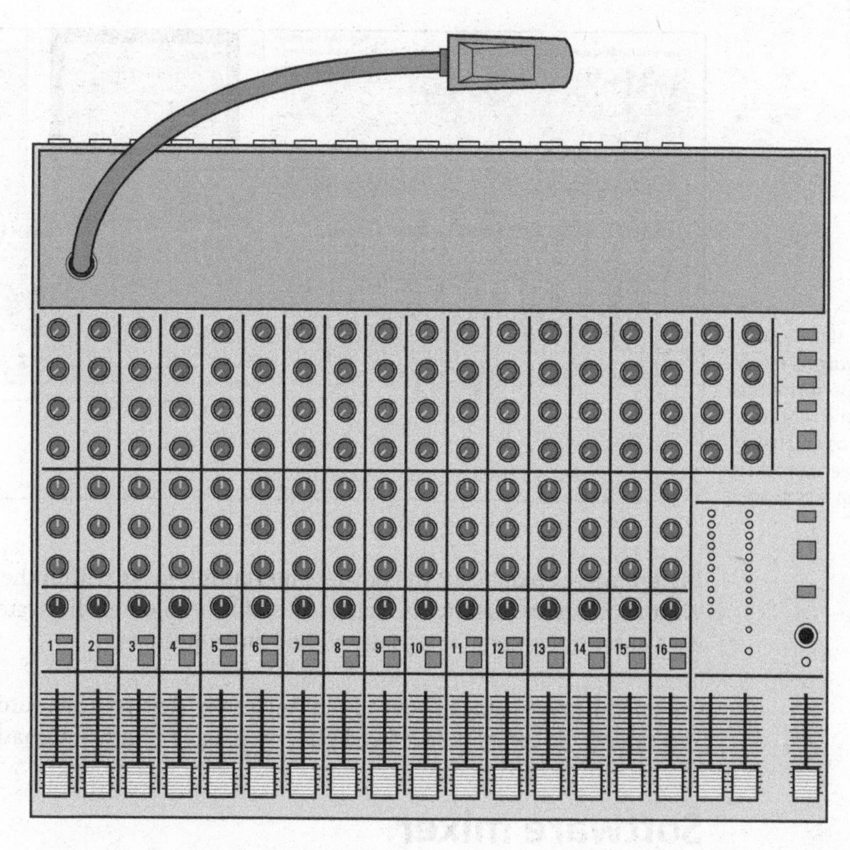

FIGURE 4-1: The analog mixer has tons of knobs, lights, and faders to play with.

Analog mixers are quickly becoming relics of the past for most home recordists. This is because digital mixers offer more functions for the price and generally sound just as good — if not better — than their analog counterparts. That said, many commercial studios still use (and prefer) large analog desks for their mixing needs. This is because top-notch analog mixers ($100,000 to over $1 million) have a sound that many pros prefer. They also look impressive, and many engineers are used to the workflow of an analog mixer.

Digital mixer

The *digital mixer*, shown in Figure 4-2, is a great option for home studio owners because it can perform the same functions as a conventional analog mixer in a lot less space. Routing — the process of sending your signals to various places within the mixer — becomes almost easy using one of these mixers. You can switch between input and track channels without having to change a single cord.

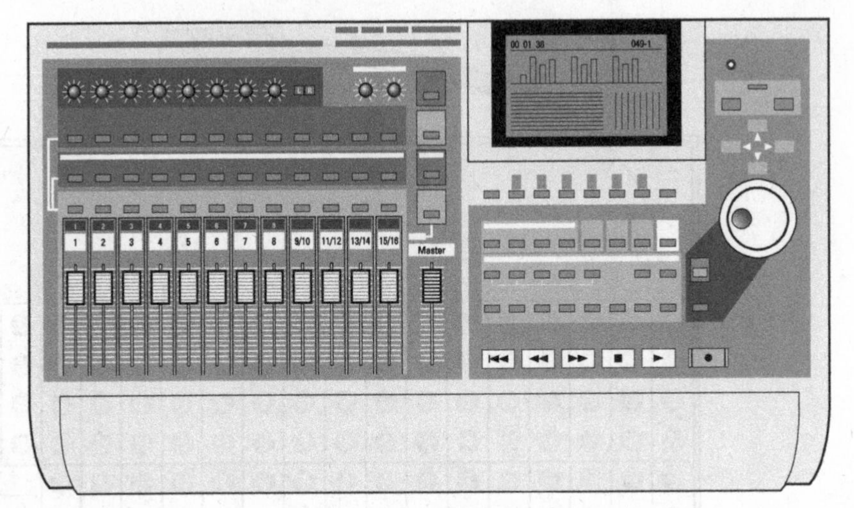

FIGURE 4-2: The digital mixer performs the same functions as an analog mixer but takes up less space.

Digital mixers handle all the busing and routing tasks within the digital domain. With no cords to mess with, noise is less likely to enter the system. And if noise does enter the system, it's easier to find and eliminate.

One of the great things about digital mixers is that you can automate your mix. You can set up complex fader and effects changes to run automatically.

Software mixer

If you want the flexibility of a digital mixer and don't have an overpowering need to physically touch the faders and knobs, a *software mixer* (shown in Figure 4-3) may work for you. The software mixer is included with any computer audio or MIDI production software program. The advantage of a software mixer is that after you have the computer and audio software that you want, you have nothing else to buy.

Software mixers work much the same way as digital mixers. Because software mixers are digital, you have an almost infinite variety of routing choices that you can make without having to patch and repatch cables. Still, some people may not be too keen on mixing with a keyboard and a mouse instead of the more traditional knobs or slide faders.

TIP

If you want the best of both worlds — high-tech computer software and tactile stimulation — you can find *control surfaces* that allow you to control the software's mixer using real faders and knobs, as described in the next section.

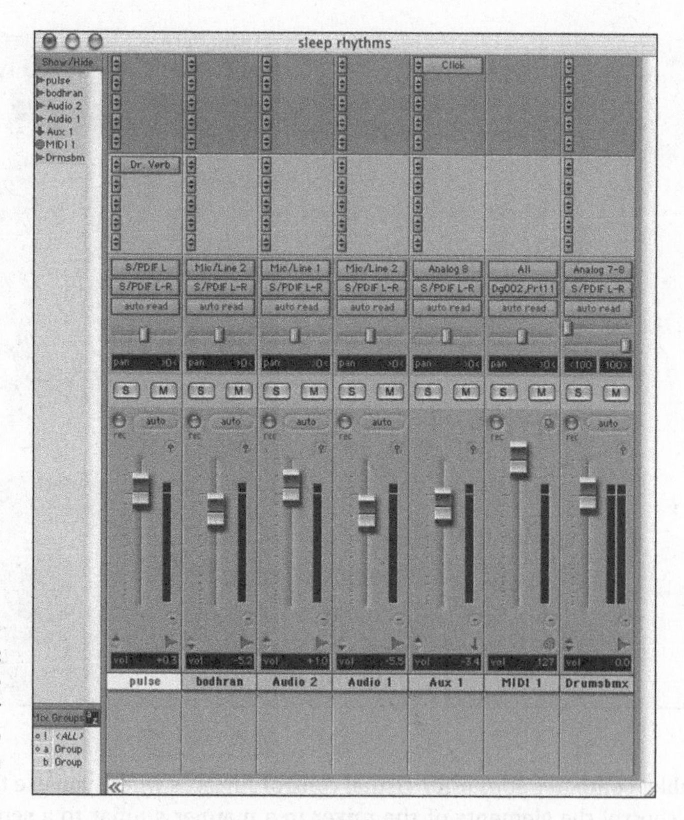

FIGURE 4-3: Use your mouse and computer keyboard to control a software mixer.

Computer control surface

If you end up with a computer-based system with a software mixer, you'll have some knobs, buttons, and faders to play around with on the *computer control surface*, as shown in Figure 4-4. Aside from being able to fiddle with knobs, you'll find that a computer control surface is a handy tool if you decide to use a computer-based digital audio workstation (DAW) and want (or need) to control the virtual mixer with some hardware.

These controllers send MIDI messages — messages encoded using the Musical Instrument Digital Interface communications protocol — to the computer. These MIDI messages tell the computer which parameters to change. Programming a computer control surface to work like a separate digital mixer is easily done.

WARNING

Not all software works with each computer control surface, so check with the software or computer control surface manufacturer before you buy to make sure that the computer control surface is compatible with your system.

FIGURE 4-4: A computer control surface acts like a digital mixer for a computer-based system.

TIP

Tablet computer apps offer virtual control surfaces where you use the touch screen to control the elements of the mixer in a manner similar to a separate hardware control surface or mixer.

Understanding Mixer Basics

The mixer is an extremely versatile piece of equipment, allowing you a staggering variety of input and output configurations. And digital mixers (both hardware and software) are even more flexible than their analog counterparts. In fact, many digital mixers can be programmed to do almost anything you can imagine. Regardless of the type of mixer that you use, some mixing aspects are universal: the inputs, the channel strip, busing (also known as routing), and the outputs. The rest of the chapter explores these functions.

TIP

Think of a mixing board as a sort of air-traffic controller for the audio world. Just as the folks in the towers near an airport communicate with all the planes in the air, making sure that collisions are avoided and that traffic moves quickly and efficiently, the mixer routes all the incoming and outgoing signals from the instruments, effects, and recording devices so that the signals reach their desired destination without any problems.

Examining inputs

To move your audio signal around within your mixer, first you need to get the signal into the system and then adjust the signal level. You perform these steps with the input jacks and the trim control.

Inputs

You find the following three basic types of inputs, which are generally located on the back of your system:

- **Microphone:** This is the XLR input (the three-pin thingy). It's used for microphones and often also has *phantom power* as part of its connection (which generally can be turned off if you want). Phantom power is necessary for condenser mics to function; Chapter 6 has details.
- **Line/instrument:** This is a ¼-inch jack (generally TS- but sometimes TRS-balanced) that accepts line-level signals from a synthesizer, a drum machine, or the line output from your guitar amp.
- **Hi-Z:** This is an input designed for the home recordist. This type of input uses a mono ¼-inch (TS) jack and allows you to plug your electric guitar (or bass or fiddle — anything with an electronic pickup) directly into your system without having to mic it or run it through a direct box first.

For more on the different connector types, check out Chapter 3.

A *direct box* (or DI box, short for direct injection) is traditionally used to connect your guitar or bass directly to the mixer without having to run it through your amp first. A direct box's purpose is twofold:

- To change the guitar's impedance level so that the mixer can create the best sound possible (otherwise, the guitar can sound thin or noisy)
- To change the cord from unbalanced ¼-inch to balanced XLR so that you can use a long cord without creating noise

For more on cord types and balanced versus unbalanced signals, see Chapter 3.

If you use a computer-based system, the inputs and outputs are located in your *audio interface* (the hardware you use to connect the analog world to the computer world). Chapter 2 has more on the various types of available interfaces.

Trim control

The Trim control is a knob that's used to adjust the level of the input signal as it enters the mixer. You usually find the Trim control at the top of the front panel of your hardware unit. On SIAB systems and analog and digital mixers, this control is generally located at the top of the mixer section for each channel, and on audio interfaces, it's often found on the front panel. The amount that you adjust the Trim control depends on the instrument that you have plugged into the channel strip. If the Trim control is set too high, you get distortion; if it's set too low, you get a signal that's too weak to record. So be sure to listen as you make your adjustments.

Most Trim controls have a switch or markings for Line or Mic(rophone) signals, with the Line level to the right and the Mic level to the left. Turn the knob all the way to the left for line sources — or slowly turn it to the right for microphone sources — until you get a nice, clean sound coming into the mixer. See Chapter 9 for more on setting input levels.

TECHNICAL STUFF

For microphone sources, you use the Trim control to adjust the level for recording. Turning the control up (turning the knob clockwise) activates an internal preamp in the mixer, which boosts the level of the signal coming from the mic. The internal preamp in pro mixers is usually fairly decent (it can sound pretty good). However, many professionals prefer to use an external preamp because it can often sound better or have a sound characteristic they want.

TIP

If you use an external preamp, check the owner's manual of your mixer to see whether you can bypass the internal preamp. Most professional mixers enable you to do this. Sometimes just turning the Trim control all the way down (to the Line marking) disengages the preamp from the circuit.

Checking out the channel strip

The mixer is composed of numerous channels through which you route your signal when you record or mix. The set of controls for each channel makes up what's called the *channel strip.* The channel strip contains a lot of information, and the visual position of the various functions often doesn't correspond with the actual flow of the signal. In the following sections, I explain both the elements of a typical digital channel strip and the path of the signal through this part of the mixer.

Viewing the channel strip layout

Figure 4-5 shows the channel strip in a typical analog mixer, and Figure 4-6 shows the channel strip for a software mixer. Even though the mixer may look confusing with all its knobs or buttons, lights, and sliders, you only need to understand the basic makeup of one channel to understand them all. The channel strip's job is to send the signal from an instrument or microphone to wherever you want that signal to go.

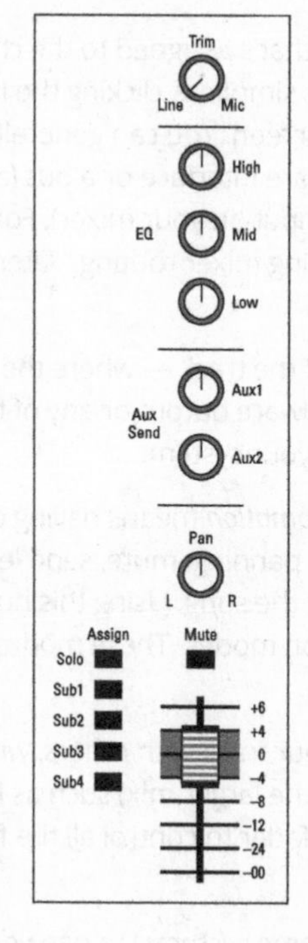

FIGURE 4-5: The channel strip in an analog mixer moves the signal through your mixer.

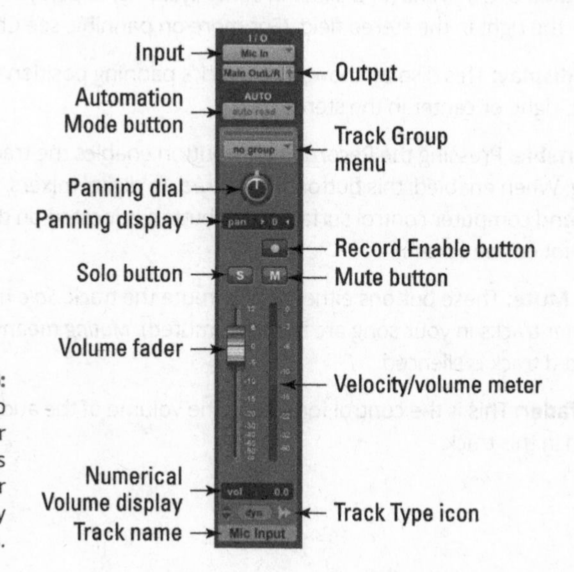

FIGURE 4-6: The channel strip in a software or digital mixer lets you control your signal in many ways.

Because most home recordists use a digital mixer of some sort — whether software or hardware — I explain the channel strip in Pro Tools to give you an idea of the functions of digital mixers in the channel strip window (as shown in Figure 4-6). Your mixer may have some different features (and a different layout), but the basic functions are pretty universal. These features are as follows:

- **Input:** This is where you choose the input that's assigned to the channel strip. In most systems, making the selection is as simple as clicking the Input button and choosing from a menu that opens onscreen. You can generally choose between a physical input from your hardware interface or a bus (an internal signal routed from a different channel or input on your mixer). For more on routing an input, see the section "Recognizing mixer routing," later in this chapter.
- **Output:** This button controls the output of the track — where the sound goes when it leaves the track. This can be a hardware output or any of the *buses* (internal signal paths) that are available in your system.
- **Automation Mode:** In digital systems, *automation* means having certain channel strip parameters (such as volume, panning, mute, send level, and insert level) adjust dynamically throughout the song. Using this button, you can choose among the different automation modes. These modes vary depending on the type of system you have.
- **Track Group:** This menu lets you group your track with others, which is handy for creating *submixes* (mixed tracks within the larger mix) such as for drums. Creating a group lets you adjust one track fader to control all the faders in the group.
- **Panning dial:** Use this dial (or a slider in some systems) to pan your track to the left or the right in the stereo field. (For more on panning, see Chapter 16.)
- **Panning display:** This display shows your track's panning position — its place to the left, right, or center in the stereo field.
- **Record Enable:** Pressing the Record Enable button enables the track for recording. When enabled, this button flashes red. In digital mixers, SIAB systems, and computer control surfaces, this button is located on the physical unit and not on the screen.
- **Solo and Mute:** These buttons either solo or mute the track. *Solo* means that all the other tracks in your song are silenced (muted). *Muting* means that only the selected track is silenced.
- **Volume fader:** This is the control for setting the volume of the audio that's contained in this track.

- **Velocity/volume meter:** This display, located to the right of the Volume Fader, shows you the volume (Pro Tools calls this *velocity*) of the track as the music plays. If you have a color display, any notes above digital 0 usually show in red at the top of the display.
- **Track Type:** This icon shows you the type of track. This is handy with systems that can record and play back audio and MIDI tracks.
- **Numerical Volume:** This display shows you the volume of the track in decibels.
- **Track name:** Many digital mixers allow you to customize the tracks' names so you can remember what's recorded on them. You see the name listed here. To change the name at any time, click it and type a new one.

Following the flow of the signal

One of the most important things to understand when recording is how the signal moves within your system. This knowledge lets you make the most of your tracks and helps you tailor the sound to match the music you hear in your head as you compose, engineer, or produce your masterpiece.

Using the ubiquitous Pro Tools as an example again, here's how the signal flows through the channel strip (shown from top to bottom in Figure 4-7):

- **Source audio or input:** This is the signal that is coming from your hardware input or that is recorded to your hard drive. The signal starts here and enters the track's channel strip.
- **Insert:** This function lets you insert effects into your track. The entire signal from your track is routed through the insert. Historically, the Insert function was used for effects, such as equalizers or dynamics processors, where you want to change the sound of the entire signal. With DAW system, you can use any effect plug-in for a track as long as it has a mix function. This allows you to mix the balance between the effected and uneffected sounds.
- **Send prefader:** The Send function lets you route part of your signal out to an aux bus, where you can then insert an effect such as reverb. With modern DAWs, you can use the Insert function for adding your effects but the Send option can be handy if you want to add the same effect to a group of tracks, such as compression or reverb to your drum tracks. This can help the sound blend better than adding the same effect to each individual track. This can also be a lifesaver if your computer can't handle running a ton of effects.

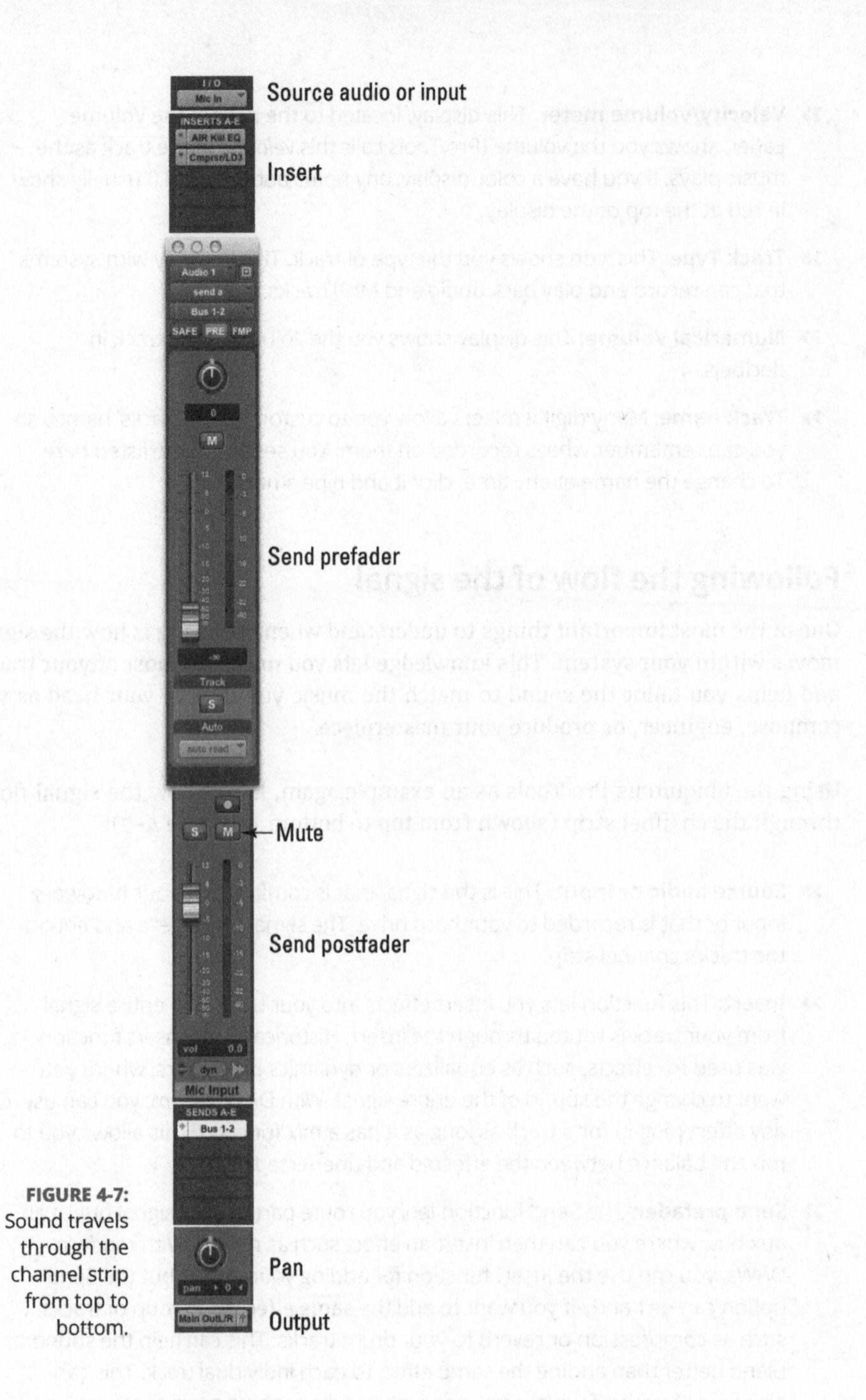

FIGURE 4-7: Sound travels through the channel strip from top to bottom.

Adjust this slider or knob to *send* as much or as little of the signal to the appropriate *auxiliary* component (aux, get it?) for effects processing, applying as much or as little of that effect to your final sound. Turning the knob to the left produces less effect, and turning it to the right gives more effect.

Along with being able to set the Effect Send level at each channel (you can send more than one channel's signal to each effect), you can also adjust the level of the affected signal that's brought back into the mixer by using the aux bus fader (which is described in the next section).

TIP

The Aux and Send functions can often be set to send the track's signal either prefader or postfader. Having this option gives you more flexibility to control the affected sound. For example, you can send the dry signal of a kick drum to a reverb (with the switch in the Pre position) and then boost the bass on the dry signal. Doing this gives you some reverb on the higher frequencies without adding it to the lower ones, which would create some mud in the final mix.

The downside to this technique is that you can't control the level of the signal being sent to the effect using the fader. (You bypassed the fader in the Pre position.) In this case, if you raise and lower the channel fader, the amount of effect that you hear in relation to the dry signal changes as well. For example, when you lower the fader, you hear more effect because less dry signal is mixed in — and when you raise the fader, you hear less effect because the dry signal is louder and the effect level is the same.

- **Solo and Mute:** These buttons let you solo (silence all other tracks) and mute (silence) the output of the track.
- **Fader:** This function lets you control the level (volume) of your signal leaving the track and going to the output(s) you've chosen in the Output section of the channel strip.
- **Send postfader:** When you have the Pre button disengaged, your Send signal is sent from your track after it passes through the track fader. Adjusting the volume of the track also adjusts the level going through your Send function.
- **Pan:** This control lets you adjust the amount of your signal that goes to the left or right channel of your stereo output.
- **Output:** This is where your signal goes as it leaves the track's channel strip. This can be the master bus (connected to one of your physical outputs) or an aux or a submix bus, where it will later be sent to the master bus.

Recognizing mixer routing

After you have an instrument plugged into the mixer channel strip, you want to send that signal somewhere. This is referred to as *routing* or *busing.* (The place where the signal ends up is, conveniently enough, referred to as a *bus.*) Most mixers offer numerous busing possibilities, as follows:

- **Auxiliary bus:** This is where you can add an effect to your signal and then move it along to the master bus.
- **Master bus:** This is where your signal goes before it leaves your system and where you mix all your tracks.
- **Submix bus:** This is where you can mix several tracks before they go to the master bus.

In the next few sections, I introduce you to some of the most-used busing options and describe some ways to make this process easier.

Master bus

The master bus is where your music gets mixed and where you choose which of the physical outputs this stereo mix goes to. The Pan knob setting for each channel strip (how far to the left or right) dictates how much signal is sent to the left or right channels of the master bus.

The master bus has a channel strip of its own where you can insert effects such as a compressor or EQ. (I'm not a big fan of this, as you find out in Chapter 17.) The master bus channel strip looks like a, ahem, stripped-down version of a regular channel strip — it doesn't have some routing options such as an Input selector, Sends, or Solo and Mute buttons. This is because it's the final stage of your signal flow, so these functions aren't necessary.

REMEMBER

Faders for each channel control how much level is sent to the master bus and how the volume of each channel relates to the other. The master fader only determines the amount of overall volume of all channels that are routed to it (for sending out to your speakers or to the stereo mix level).

Sub (submix) bus

Sometimes you have a group of instruments (such as drums) that you want to control as a group independently of the master fader. Sending these tracks to another track and submixing them there enables you to adjust the overall volume of the drums without affecting the volume of any other instruments that aren't assigned to this channel. This is called a *submix*, and signals sent this way are sent (wait for it) through the submix bus. When your signal exits this bus, it goes to the master bus, where your signal is blended with the rest of your tracks.

Software mixers, such as the one in Pro Tools, often don't have submix buses per se. Instead, you can simply route your signal to any of the internal buses, where you can adjust the level of all the signals coming to that bus by using the channel strip fader associated with the bus.

Auxiliary (aux) bus

The *aux bus* is where you send your signal when you use one of the Send functions in your channel strip. This bus often has a channel strip of its own, where you can insert the effect you want to use. From this bus, your signal goes to the master bus, where the signal is mixed with the rest of your tracks.

Opting for outputs

Most mixers have a bunch of output jacks that are located on the back of the hardware, to the left. You often find output jacks for the master bus, headphones, and monitors.

Master Out jack

The Master Out jack goes to the power amp for your speakers or goes directly to powered monitors, if you have any. This jack is generally controlled by the master fader and sends the signal that's routed through the master bus.

Phones jack

The Phones jack is for your headphones and is fed by the Phones knob on the master console. This jack carries the same signal as the master bus — only you can control the volume separately.

Monitors jack

The Monitors jack generally contains that same signal as the headphones and master outs but gives you another place to be able to plug in speakers or headphones. Oftentimes the Monitor Out jack is also used for hardware monitoring in systems that have it. *Hardware monitoring,* which is common on computer-based audio interfaces, enables you to monitor directly from the interface, rather than wait until the audio signal goes into the computer and back out again before it reaches your ears. This reduces the latency that is often heard when listening to yourself as you record.

IN THIS CHAPTER

» Understanding multitrack recording

» Setting up a song to record

» Monitoring your mix

» Saving and sharing files

Chapter 5 Multitrack Recording

As recently as the 1950s, when someone wanted to record a song, he had to assemble a band, rehearse, and then perform the song live. If one of the musicians made a mistake, the whole band had to start over and record the song again. Not so anymore. You're lucky enough to record in an age where you can not only write the song, but also record it yourself and play all the instruments. If you like, you can make lush, layered music without involving anyone else. In other words, you can *multitrack.*

In this chapter, I introduce you to the basics of multitrack recording, a process that enables you to assemble a song by recording one part at a time. You discover how to set up a new song in a variety of systems, and you find out how to set up the monitoring source and sound to help you inspire a great performance. This chapter also walks you through the process of saving files and transferring data between systems.

Understanding Multitracking

Multitrack recording is the process of recording each instrument (or group of instruments) individually and keeping those performances separate until a later date. Consider the music you play on your smartphone or hear on the radio. All the instruments are contained on a pair of stereo tracks. You can adjust the volume or equalization (EQ) of these tracks, but you can't adjust the sound qualities of the individual instruments contained on these two tracks. The multitrack recorder, on the other hand, allows you to keep all these instruments separate (see Figure 5-1). Multitrack recording lets you do the following things:

- Make adjustments to the sound of the instrument on each track.
- Adjust the levels (volume) of the instruments in relation to one another.
- Assemble a "performance" that never happened.

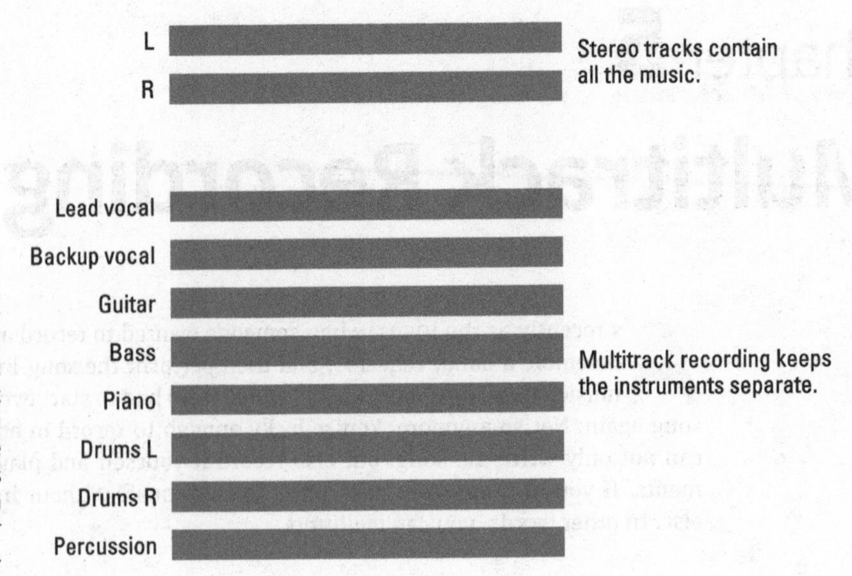

FIGURE 5-1: Multitrack recording lets you keep all the instruments separate, unlike a smartphone or the radio.

Getting Ready to Record

Before you can press the Record button on your system, you need to:

- Find and choose the instrument or sound that you want to record.
- Set the optimum volume level going to the recorder.
- Decide what you want to hear while recording your performance.

These steps are covered in detail in the following sections.

Setting up a song

If you're using a digital recording system, you need to open a new song file. When you do this, you may be asked (or prompted) to choose the sampling rate and resolution of this new song. (Some systems have you provide this information when you choose a track to record to rather than when you open a song file.)

You generally have the option to choose a *sampling rate* (the number of times every second that the digital recorder or converter takes a snapshot of the sound; check out Chapter 2 for details on sampling rates). Your options may include 32 kHz, 44.1 kHz, 48 kHz, 88.2 kHz, 96 kHz, 176.4 kHz, or 192 kHz. Some digital recorders don't allow you to make a CD if you record with anything but a 44.1 kHz sampling rate, the sample rate of CDs. Check your owner's manual if you intend to eventually put your music on a CD.

Some systems may also let you choose the *bit depth* (the size, in binary digits, of the sample that the converter or recorder takes) that you want to record in. For this parameter, I usually choose the highest bit depth available to capture the best sound possible. If you choose 20 or 24 bits, you need to convert the final mix to 16-bit if you want to put your music on a CD or want to deliver your music to a host of online download or streaming sites, but the advantages you gain from recording at a higher bit depth far outweigh the conversion factor. (Go to Chapter 2 for more on bit depth.)

Finally, name your file, and you're ready to add some tracks and organize your song.

Creating and organizing your tracks

When you set up a song, you will have a blank slate to work with. This means you will need to add some tracks and set the inputs and outputs for them. While you're at it, I recommend organizing and naming them. This section details the process.

TIP

To speed up your workflow, you can create your song from a template that has the types and number of tracks with input and output settings already created for you.

Creating new tracks

Setting up your recording project is a little like setting up a railroad: It'll take you somewhere only if you first put the tracks in place. This process is pretty simple. In this section, I show you how it's done in Pro Tools (other programs are similar).

Begin by opening the New Track dialog box (choose Track⇨New from the main menu), as shown in Figure 5-2. Then choose the following:

- **Number of new tracks:** The default here is 1, but you can pretty much create as many tracks as you need.
- **Track format:** Here you choose stereo or mono.
- **Track type:** Clicking the arrows opens a drop-down menu that lets you choose between an Audio, an Auxiliary Input, a Master Fader, a VCA Master, a MIDI, or an Instrument track.
- **Samples or ticks:** You can choose between samples or ticks (bars/beats) for your new tracks.
- **Plus sign:** Clicking this adds another tracks selection row containing all the options listed in this section so that you can add more than one type of track without having to open the New Track window repeatedly.

FIGURE 5-2: Create a new track here.

Make your selections and then click Create to create your new track. This track then appears in the Edit and Mix windows and in the Show/Hide list located on the right side of the Edit window. If the Show/Hide list isn't visible, click the double arrow at the lower-left corner of the Edit window.

Naming tracks

When you open a new track (choose Track⇨New), your DAW creates a default name for the track — something really helpful, like `Audio 1` — but you can change the name to anything you want. In most programs, you do this by double-clicking the name of the track in either the Mix or the Edit windows. A dialog box similar to what you see in Figure 5-3 opens, from which you can use the fields to both change the name of the track and add any comments you want to include about the track. After you enter your track name and comments, click OK — you're set!

TIP

I highly recommend that you name your new tracks right away; give each a name that describes what you plan to record on it. Some examples include *Vox* (or *Vocals*), *Ld Gtr*, *Snare*, *Kick*, and so on. This will save you confusion later on when you start to mix.

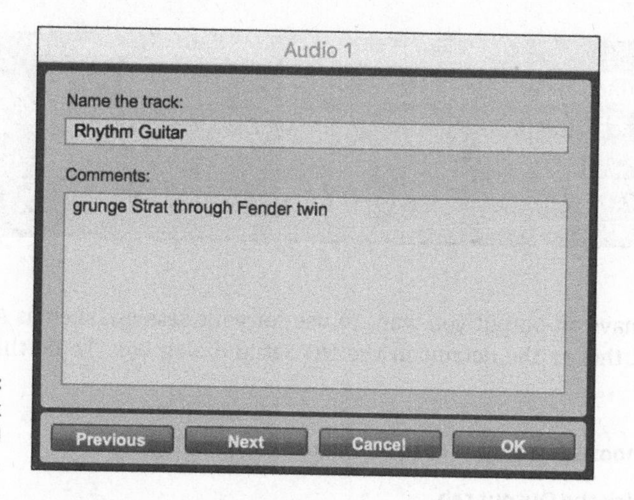

FIGURE 5-3: Choose a track name and add comments here.

Assigning inputs and outputs

To record with your new track, you need to assign an input to it so Pro Tools knows where your source sound is coming from. To hear the track play, you need to choose an output so Pro Tools can send the sound out to your monitors or to your headphone jack.

That makes sense, right? Now, to actually assign an input to your track in Pro Tools, do the following:

1. **Choose View ⇨ Edit Window Views ⇨ I/O from the main menu to open the I/O section of the Edit window.**

TIP

   The I/O section shows the inputs and outputs for each track.

2. **Within the I/O section of your track in the Edit window, click and hold the Input selector (see Figure 5-4) until the Input contextual menu pops up.**
3. **While still holding down your mouse button, move the mouse over the Input menu until it rests on the input listing you want.**
4. **Release the mouse button to select your choice from the Input contextual menu.**

   This menu closes, and the input you select appears in the Input selector.

Choosing your outputs requires pretty much the same procedure, although now you start things off by clicking the Output selector instead.

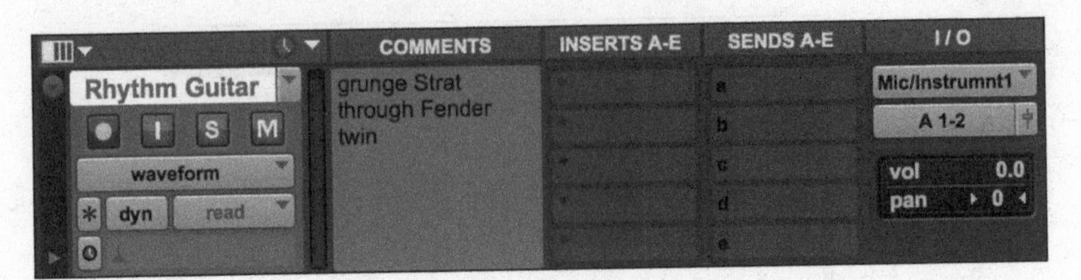

FIGURE 5-4: Assign an input or output here.

TIP

If you have an output you want to use for your session, such as Analog 1-2, you can set this as the default in the I/O Setup dialog box. To do this, follow these steps:

1. **Choose Setup ⇨ I/O to open the I/O Setup dialog box.**
2. **Click the Output tab.**
3. **Choose your output from the New Track Default Output drop-down menu.**
4. **Click OK.**

   The window closes, and all your new tracks automatically receive your chosen output upon creation.

Selecting a sound source

When you select a sound source, you simply set up your instrument or microphone so that it records to the track of your choice. Here's how to select a sound source:

1. **Turn the input trim knob and fader on the channel strip of your mixer all the way down to avoid hearing an unpleasant noise or potentially damaging your monitors.**
2. **Plug your instrument or microphone into the appropriate input jack of your system.**

   For a microphone, this may be a separate preamp or the internal preamp in your mixer, studio-in-a-box (SIAB) system, or audio interface. For an electric guitar or bass, use the Hi-Z or instrument input or a direct box, and for a keyboard or other electronic instruments (such as a drum machine or sound module), use any of the instrument inputs.
3. **Choose the track you want to record the signal to.**

   This procedure varies from system to system. Here's how to route the signal in the following systems:

SIAB systems: In many SIAB systems, you can route the signal from any mixer input to any recorder track by pressing a button. For example, on the Tascam DP-24SD, just press and hold the Input button for the input channel your instrument or mic is connected to until it flashes. Continue holding the input channel's button and press the Select button for the track channel that you want to route that instrument or mic through. Release the Status button, and you're all set.

Computer-based systems: You need to open the Input window to choose your input source. This process is pretty simple and is similar for most programs. Here's how you do it in Pro Tools:

a. **Choose Display ⇨ Edit Window Shows ⇨ I/O View.**

   The I/O section of the Edit window appears, showing the inputs and outputs for each of your tracks.

b. **Click and hold your mouse button on the Input selector until the Input menu pops up.**

c. **While still holding down your mouse button, move the mouse over the Input menu until it rests on the input listing you want.**

d. **Release the mouse button to select the input listing.**

   This menu closes, and the input you've selected appears in the Input selector.

4. **Arm the track that you want to record to (that is, set it to the Record mode).**

   This procedure also varies from system to system. Here's how to arm the track on the following systems:

   SIAB systems: A Selector button glows various colors, depending on the mode that the channel is in. Press the button on the track number that you're recording to until you see a red glow. This means that the track is ready to record.

REMEMBER

   If you're using an SIAB system and want to record to a different track number than the input channel you're plugged into, make sure you arm the track you want to record to and not the track associated with the input channel. If you don't do this, you either record your music to the wrong track (and possibly erase something else) or you don't record anything, depending on the routing of your system.

   Computer-based systems: Arm the track within the software by clicking the Record Enable button in the main window of your program. In Pro Tools, for example, this button is located in both the Edit window and the Mix window for each track.

Setting levels

Getting a sound signal to the recorder takes several steps. The path that the sound takes from the instrument or microphone to the recorder is called the *signal chain* (or the *gain structure*). For example, if you want to record your voice, you first capture your voice with a microphone and then you feed that signal to a preamp. From the preamp, you send the signal to the channel strip of your mixer, which sends the signal to the analog/digital (A/D) converter and then to the recorder. (Chapter 9 has more on signal flow.) The signal chain may have all or just a couple of these steps, however. For example, a synthesizer is connected to the mixer, which is in turn connected to the recorder.

You need to be aware of the signal level at all these steps to get the best sound possible. Too much gain at one stage forces you to reduce the gain at another. Likewise, too little gain at one point may require you to add too much gain during the next stage, which could cause distortion. Either of these scenarios reduces the quality of your sound. See Chapter 9 for more on setting optimal signal levels.

Getting the sound you want

After your levels are set, you can concentrate on fine-tuning the sound of the instrument before you record it. Here you can either adjust the EQ or apply effects to your sound.

EQ

I reserve EQ for getting rid of any seriously unwanted frequencies that I'm picking up in a mic. For example, I generally cut some low midrange frequencies on the bass guitar and kick drum because I know that these frequencies will be a problem later. Otherwise, I pretty much leave the EQ alone when tracking.

Don't get too wrapped up in perfecting the EQ of a recorded instrument at this point. All you want is a good, clean sound that approximates what you want in the final mix. You have another chance to make adjustments to the sound of your recorded instrument in the mixing phase.

REMEMBER

Check the levels going to the recorder after you've made adjustments to the EQ, because the levels may change.

Effects

The question of whether to record effects — reverb, delay, chorus, and so on — along with an instrument is a long-debated topic. Professional recording engineers caution you against recording your instruments *wet* (with effects) because this limits your options when you mix the song. On the other hand, by recording an instrument with an effect, you can use that effect processor on another instrument during the mixing process. Ultimately, you have to decide whether adding an effect to an instrument on the front end (before recording) is the way to go. (I describe effects in greater detail in Chapter 19.)

WARNING

If you record using a computer-based system, adding an effect during tracking may stress your computer's processor to the point that it affects your recording. This can cause audio dropouts, pops, clicks, or other unwanted interruptions or corruptions to your audio data. If you have a slower computer or if you record a lot of tracks at once, you may find that you can't record with effects. In this case, your headphone mix while you track has no effect added to the sound, but you can still add effects during the mixing process (as described in Chapter 19).

If you're sure about the sound you want, you can add the effect on the front end. If you're not sure, you're probably better off waiting until later. You can always *print* (record) the effect during a *bounce procedure,* a neat trick where you rerecord one or more tracks to another track. Bouncing is a common procedure if you don't have enough tracks in your system to record each of your instruments to its own track. I cover the bounce process in Chapter 10.

If you decide that you want to record your instrument with effects, you need to route the instrument through the effect processor and route the effect to the recorder. If you have an SIAB system, this is pretty easy. For example, to do this in a Tascam DP-24SD, follow these steps (most SIAB systems are similar):

1. **Select the Source button for your input channel that your instrument is plugged into and route the channel to the track that you want to record to.**

   If you have a computer-based system, you need to use the Input menu on your screen to do this. On an SIAB system, your manual spells out the specific routing procedure.

2. **Arm the recorder's track (press the recorder's Status button until the button blinks red).**

3. **Select the effect that you want to use and assign it to one of your effects buses.**

   Go to the Effect 1 menu by pressing the cursor to move to the Insert Effect function. Next, scroll through the Effects list using the jog wheel and turn on Insert Effect (the indicator will light) for the effect that you want to use. Press the Select button. Your chosen effect is now assigned to Aux Bus 1.

4. **Choose prefader or postfader on your Aux Send and turn the knob until you have the right amount of the instrument's signal sent to the effect.**

   You do this by going to the channel mixer settings menu on your screen.

5. **Start recording.**

   See Chapter 10 for the lowdown on recording.

REMEMBER

On some systems, if you want to hear your recorded track, you may have to "unroute" the effect from that track. Your owner's manual spells this out for you.

Adding an effect in a computer-based system, such as Logic Pro, involves these steps:

1. **Select one of the buses from the Send selector in each track's channel strip that you want to route to the effect.**

   You can view a track's channel strip in the Environment window (choose Windows ⇨ Environment if the window isn't open) or in the Arrange window. To open a track's channel strip in the Arrange window, click the track name in the Arrange window to highlight it. The channel strip appears on the left.

   When you release your mouse button after selecting the bus, the bus is listed, and a *trim pot* (knob) appears next to the bus number.

2. **Adjust the trim pot to a moderate level.**

   I usually start with about –15dB.

3. **Double-click the bus number.**

   You're taken to the Bus Channel strip in the Environment window, where you can choose the effect to insert into the bus.

4. **Using the Insert selector pop-up menu in the Bus Channel strip, select the Effects plug-in that you want to use from the Inserts pop-up menu.**

   The Effects Plug-In window opens. Here you set your parameters, such as predelay, reverb time, and room type (for a reverb plug-in, for example).

5. **Play your track by clicking the Play button in the Transport window.**

   Your session plays, and you hear the effect of your plug-in on your track. You can then tweak the plug-in parameters or the send level for your track as your song plays to get the sound that you want.

Choosing a monitoring source

To record effectively, you need to hear what you're doing. This requires you to set up your monitoring source so that you can hear what you want to hear. You want to monitor the sound that's going through the recorder. This way, you can hear any distortion or hiss that may be present. Here's how monitoring works on the following systems:

- **Computer-based systems:** Set the output for your track(s) to the output that you have your monitor speakers plugged into. If you use the main outputs in your interface, these are usually assigned to outputs 1 and 2 in your system. (You can assign them however you want — check your manual for the specifics on doing this.) Set your outputs to channels 1 and 2 and turn on your monitors.
- **SIAB systems:** Because SIAB systems have fader banks, make sure that you designate the track channel to monitor rather than the input channel. After you've chosen the track channel that you want to listen to, bring up the fader to a level that allows you to hear what's going to disk.

Setting a Tempo Map

Before you start to record, set a tempo map of the song within your system. You do this by entering the number of measures (on some systems), the time signature, and the tempo for each section of the song in the Tempo Map or Metronome dialog box of your system. Then, when you record, play to this metronome. I go into detail on how to create a tempo map and click track in Chapter 13.

When it's time to do your editing, having a tempo map allows you to choose the section(s) of your song that you want to edit by cueing the measure and beat that you want to work with. This enables you to choose edit points much faster and more accurately and makes quick work of producing loops or assembling a song from parts (check out Chapters 14 and 15 for editing your tracks).

Saving Your Work

After you record a track that you want to keep, you can save the song. If you use an SIAB system or a computer-based system, however, you need to save the file just like you save a file when you're working in a computer program. And like other files in other computer programs, it's a good idea to save your work often so that you don't lose any of the music that you worked so hard to record. Check your owner's manual for your system's procedures.

In addition to basic file-saving commands, most digital systems (computer-based and SIAB) allow you to save individual "scenes" or "snapshots" within each song that contain things such as mixer and effects settings.

Sharing Files with Others

Because your music is stored on a hard drive, you can transfer the data to other systems. The advantages of file sharing are far-reaching. You can collaborate with other people without ever being in the same room together. In fact, I'm working on several projects where I've never sat down with the other musicians. One such musician is even across the country from me. We just upload the files to a shared folder on a cloud service.

The disadvantage of file sharing is that there isn't yet a single standard for saving data. Some recorders use proprietary file formats that only a system from the same manufacturer can open.

If you're concerned about being able to transfer data from one system to another, look for a system that can import and export WAV or AIFF files. Nearly all computer-based programs and stand-alone systems are compatible with these file types. SIAB systems may or may not have this capability.

All is not lost if you have a system that has a proprietary file format. All digital recorders have jacks in them that enable you to transfer the data from one system to another. This means that you can send your file from your system to a computer and then use software to convert the file into a format that another person's recorder can read. (The software that you choose varies depending on the systems that you want to transfer the files to and from.) If you're doing a lot of transferring, this can be time consuming, but for the occasional transfer, it's no big deal.

If you work with a system that can save files in the WAV or AIFF format, you don't have this problem, and you can easily transfer your stuff from one machine to another. Also, if you're transferring songs from one system to another system of the same type (a Zoom R24 to another Zoom R24, for instance), you don't have to worry about file conversion either.

2

Working with Microphones

IN THIS PART . . .

Explore the process of setting the best levels for both plugged-in and miked instruments.

Get to know the fundamentals of microphone placement.

Dig into common miking approaches.

Mike a variety of common instruments to get nice-sounding tracks.

IN THIS CHAPTER

» Discovering the various type of microphones

» Positioning microphones for the best sound

» Exploring a variety of preamps

» Understanding how to care for your microphones

Chapter 6 Understanding Microphones

A microphone's job is generally to try to capture, as closely as possible, the sound of an instrument. But you can also use a microphone to infuse a specific sound characteristic into a performance. Likewise, a preamp, which boosts the signal of a microphone as the signal travels to the recorder, can be used to accurately represent a sound or to add texture and dimension to it. Microphones and preamps are the center of the sound engineer's palette. Just as a painter has his paints and brushes, you have your microphones and preamps. And just as a painter can create a stunning variety of visual textures with his tools, you too can make your creative statement with the judicious use of these two pieces of equipment.

In this chapter, I explore the two most versatile tools of your auditory craft. You look at the various types of microphones and preamps, and you gain an understanding of each one's role in capturing a performance. You also discover what types of mics and preamps work for particular situations. To top it off, this chapter guides you through purchasing and caring for your precious new friends (the mics and preamps, that is). You can find out how to use your mics in Chapter 8, where I discuss specific mic placement options.

Meeting the Many Microphone Types

When you start looking at microphones, you basically find four different types of construction methods (condenser, boundary, dynamic, and ribbon) and three basic polarity patterns (omnidirectional, cardioid, and figure-8). The following sections explore these various constructions and patterns and help you make sense out of them.

Construction types

Whether a microphone is a $10 cheapie that has a cord permanently attached to it or a $15,000 pro model with gold-plated fittings, all microphones convert sound waves to electrical impulses that the preamp or mixer can read and the recorder can store. Each of the three construction types captures this auditory signal in a different way, and as such, each adds certain characteristics to the sound. Here's how the different mics affect sound:

- **Condenser:** This type tends to have a well-rounded shape to its frequency response and a fast response, allowing it to often pick up high transient material, such as the initial attack of drum, very well. These mics can sound more natural, but they can also be somewhat harsh if placed too close to a high transient source.
- **Boundary:** Boundary mics are like condenser mics in that they can capture a broad range of frequencies accurately. Because these types of mics rely on the reflection of the sound source to a flat surface they're attached to, you need to make sure that this surface is large enough to reproduce the lowest frequency you want to capture. (***Remember:*** Sound waves get longer as the frequency gets lower.) Otherwise, you lose the low frequencies.
- **Dynamic:** Dynamic mics tend to accentuate the middle of the frequency spectrum because the thick diaphragms (relatively speaking when compared to a condenser mic) take longer to respond.
- **Ribbon:** Because the ribbon mic is relatively slow to respond to an auditory signal, it tends to soften the *transients* (the initial attack of an instrument) on instruments such as percussion and piano. The high end isn't as pronounced as with other construction types, so these mics tend to have a rounder, richer tone.

I detail these aspects in the following sections. In most cases, the type of construction dictates the general cost category in which the mics fit.

PHANTOM POWER

Phantom power is the small amount of voltage that is applied to a condenser microphone when it's connected. This power enables the mic to function properly. In most cases, the phantom power comes from your mixer or preamp and is sent to the microphone through one of the wires in the XLR cable. (I cover XLR cables in Chapter 3.) Some condenser mics have an internal battery or separate power supply that provides this power.

A switch, usually located on the preamp or mixer, enables you to turn phantom power off and on. Even though dynamic microphones don't use phantom power, this small amount of voltage doesn't damage them.

Condenser microphones

The condenser microphone is, without a doubt, the most popular style of microphone used in recording studios (home or commercial). Condenser mics are sensitive and accurate, but they can also be expensive. Recently, however, condenser mics have come down in cost, and you can buy a decent one for about $200. Very good ones start at about $500.

TECHNICAL STUFF

The condenser microphone has an extremely thin metal (or metal-coated plastic or Mylar) *diaphragm* (the part that senses the signal). The diaphragm is suspended in front of a metal plate (called a *backplate*). Polarizing voltage is applied to both the diaphragm and the backplate, creating a small electrical charge in the space between them. When the diaphragm picks up a sound, it vibrates into the field between it and the backplate. This produces a small signal that can then be amplified. Figure 6-1 shows how a condenser mic is constructed.

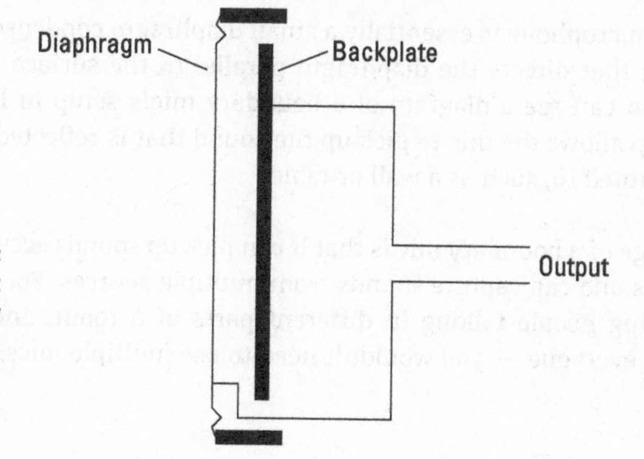

FIGURE 6-1: A condenser mic consists of a very thin diaphragm suspended parallel to a backplate.

Condenser mics need a small amount of voltage (from 9 to 48 volts) to function. If you use a condenser mic, make sure that either it has its own internal battery or you have a preamp or mixer equipped with *phantom power*, which is described in the nearby sidebar.

Here are a few additional decisions you need to make when selecting a condenser mic:

- **Tube or solid-state?** Condenser mics can be made with either vacuum tubes or transistors (known as solid-state). As with all the tube or solid-state gear, base your decision on the sound characteristics that you prefer. For the most part, tube condenser mics have a softer high end and a warmer overall tone. Solid-state mics, on the other hand, are often more *transparent* — they capture the sound with less coloration.

  Tube mics also are less reliable because they have a tube that can wear out or malfunction.

- **Large or small diaphragm?** Condenser mics come in two broad categories: large diaphragm and small diaphragm (see Figure 6-2). Large-diaphragm mics are more popular than their smaller-diaphragm counterparts, partly because large-diaphragm condenser (LDC) mics have a more pronounced bottom end (low frequencies). Large-diaphragm mics also have a lower *self noise* (noise created by the microphone).

  Before you buy only large-diaphragm mics, consider this: Small-diaphragm condenser (SDC) mics often have an even frequency response and can more accurately capture instruments with a pronounced high-frequency component (violins, for instance).

Boundary microphones

A boundary microphone is essentially a small diaphragm condenser mic mounted in a housing that directs the diaphragm parallel to the surface onto which it's mounted. You can see a diagram of a boundary mic's setup in Figure 6-3. The parallel setup allows the mic to pick up the sound that is reflected off the surface that it's mounted to, such as a wall or table.

The advantage of a boundary mic is that it can pick up sounds accurately in reverberant rooms and can capture sounds from multiple sources. For example, if you were recording people talking in different parts of a room, one boundary mic could record everyone — you wouldn't need to use multiple mics.

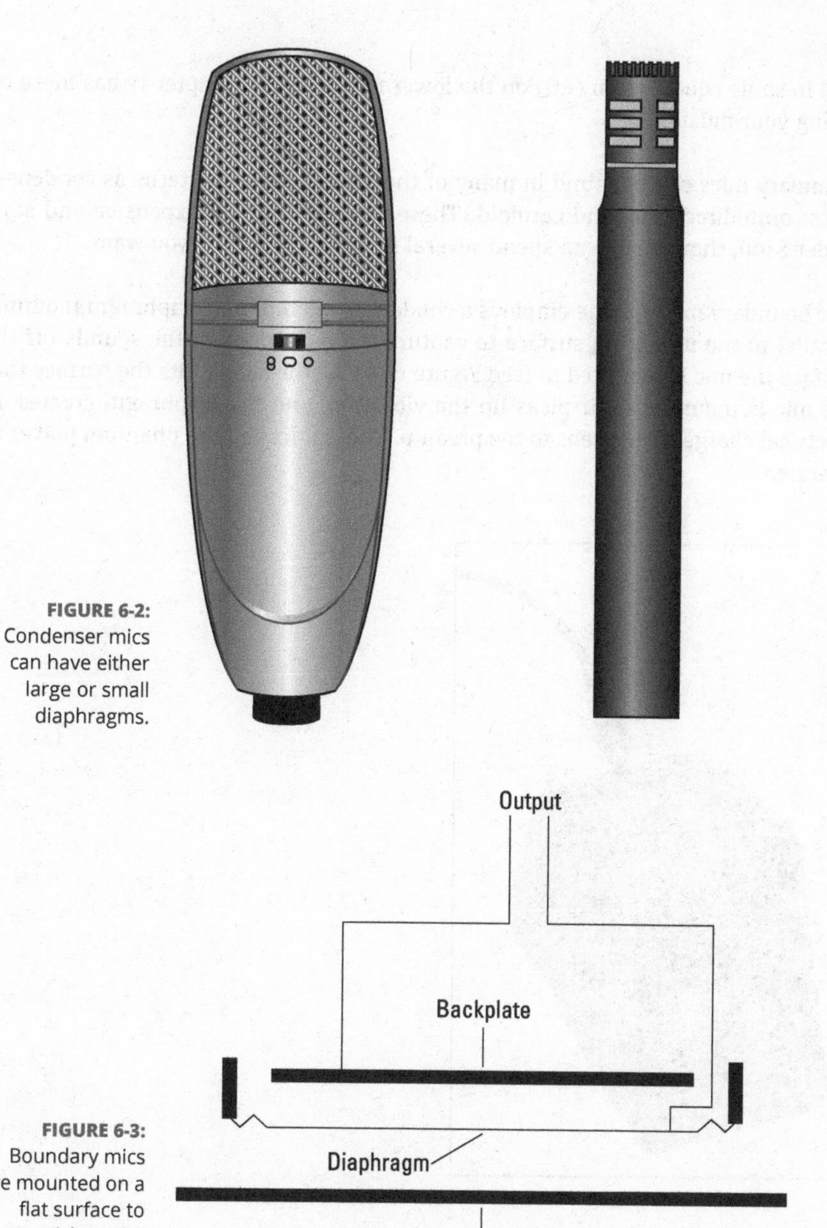

FIGURE 6-2: Condenser mics can have either large or small diaphragms.

FIGURE 6-3: Boundary mics are mounted on a flat surface to pick up the sound.

Boundary mics are often mounted on the floor of a stage, a table in a conference room, or a lectern of a church or large hall. Because it's hard to find a surface large enough to vibrate to the lowest frequencies, it's more common to use these mics for vocals, pianos, and other instruments that don't have a super-low pitch. If you do record something like a kick drum with a boundary mic, you'll likely need to dial in some equalization (EQ) on the lower frequencies. (Chapter 17 has more on EQing your music.)

Boundary mics can be found in many of the same polarity patterns as condenser mics: omnidirectional and cardioid. These mics are fairly inexpensive and start under $100, though you can spend several hundred or more if you want.

TECHNICAL STUFF

The boundary microphone employs a condenser microphone diaphragm mounted parallel to the mounting surface to capture the reflections of the sounds off the surface the mic is mounted to (see Figure 6-4). As the sound hits the surface that the mic is mounted to, it picks up the vibration, and the diaphragm creates an electrical charge that is sent to the preamp. These mics require phantom power to operate.

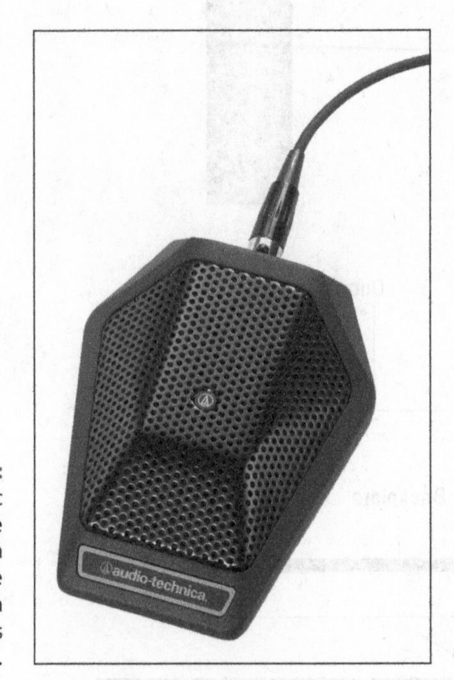

FIGURE 6-4: A boundary mic places the diaphragm parallel to the surface to which the mic is mounted.

Dynamic microphones

You've probably had the chance to use a dynamic mic. The hugely popular Shure SM57 and SM58 often characterize this type of mic. Dynamic microphones have several qualities that make them unique. They can handle a lot of volume (technically known as *sound pressure level* [SPL]), which makes them perfect for extremely loud signals, such as drums, amplifiers, and some rock vocalists. Dynamic mics are also not as transparent (they don't accurately represent high frequencies) as condenser mics, so they often impart a "dirty" or "gritty" sound to the signal.

TECHNICAL STUFF

The dynamic microphone uses a magnetic field to convert the sound impulse from the diaphragm into electrical energy, as shown in Figure 6-5. The diaphragm is often made of plastic or Mylar and is located in front of a coil of wire called a *voice coil.* The voice coil is suspended between two magnets. When the diaphragm moves (the result of a sound), the voice coil moves as well. The interaction between the voice coil's movement and the magnets creates the electrical signal.

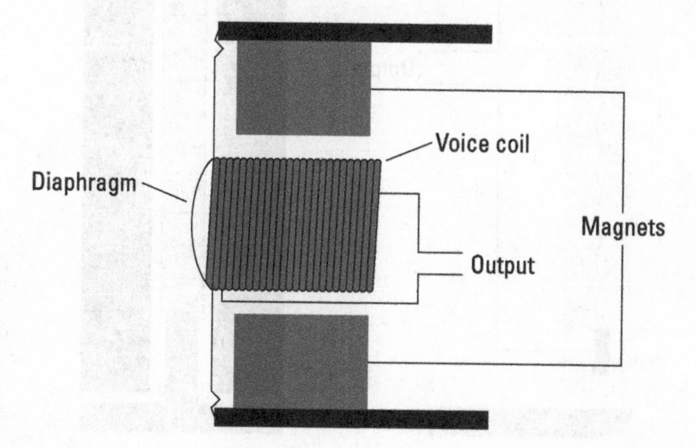

FIGURE 6-5: Dynamic mics pick up a signal using a magnetic field and a voice coil.

The sound of a dynamic mic can be described as somewhat boxy, meaning that these mics don't represent the highest or lowest frequencies of your hearing spectrum accurately (not necessarily a bad thing). Dynamic mics are also durable. Rough treatment probably won't damage them much, aside from the diaphragm, and a tough metal screen protects it. Dynamic mics are typically used for live shows and recording loud sources in the studio such as guitar amplifiers and snare drums. These mics are often very inexpensive to buy and maintain; you can get a good dynamic mic for about $100.

Ribbon microphones

A ribbon microphone produces its sound in much the same way as a dynamic mic. The diaphragm is suspended between two magnets. The ribbon mic differs from the dynamic mic in that it uses a thin ribbon of aluminum instead of plastic or Mylar (see Figure 6-6). Ribbon mics were popular from the 1930s through the 1960s but have, for the most part, taken a backseat to condenser mics in today's studios. This is mainly because ribbon mics are fragile and expensive and aren't as transparent as condenser mics. In fact, a gust of wind or a strong breath blown into the diaphragm is all it takes to break an aluminum ribbon in one of these mics. (It's not the end of the world, though; ribbons aren't that expensive to replace — they generally cost $100 to $150.)

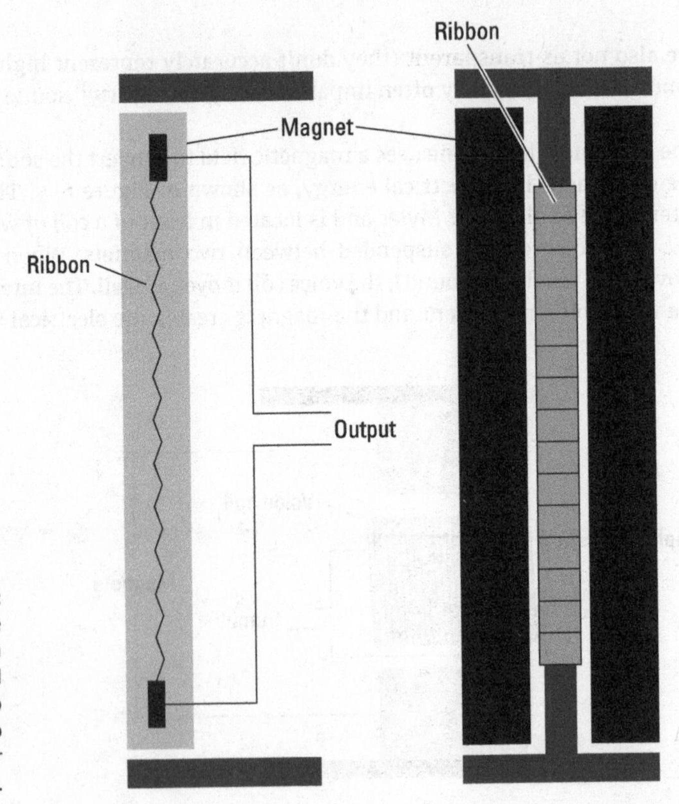

FIGURE 6-6: Ribbon mics use a ribbon suspended between two magnets to create their signals.

Ribbon mics are experiencing a renaissance because of the number of recording engineers who are searching for an old, vintage sound. Ribbon mics have a unique sound that is often described as silky or smooth. This essentially means that the high frequencies tend to *roll off* slightly (gradually reduce) and the lower frequencies smear together a bit.

Ribbon mics used to be fairly expensive (at least $1,000), but as interest in them has increased from digital recordists, you can now find some decent ones for just a few hundred dollars.

Polarity patterns

Microphones pick up sounds in different ways, which are known as *polarity patterns*. Here's how the various patterns work:

- **Omnidirectional** mics can capture sounds all around them.
- **Cardioid** (or directional) mics mostly pick up sounds in front of them.

» **Shotgun** mics are supercardioid or hypercardioid and pick up only the sound directly in front of them.

» **Figure-8** (or bidirectional) mics pick up sounds from both the front and the back.

The polarity patterns on microphones are represented on a chart that often comes with the microphone (or is part of its spec sheet). This chart is often called a *polar graph*, and the graph shows how well the microphone picks up various frequencies in front of or behind it.

Omnidirectional

The omnidirectional mic can pick up sounds coming from anywhere around it. Omnidirectional mics are useful for situations where you want to capture not only the source sound, but also the sound of the room that the source is coming from. You can find omnidirectional mics used in stereo pairs for drum overheads and groups of acoustic instruments, such as orchestras.

Omnidirectional mics are not generally used for *close miking* — when you place the mic less than a foot from the sound source — because they tend to catch too much background noise. You can see the pickup pattern of an omnidirectional mic in Figure 6-7. The round pattern shows that the mic picks up sound from all directions.

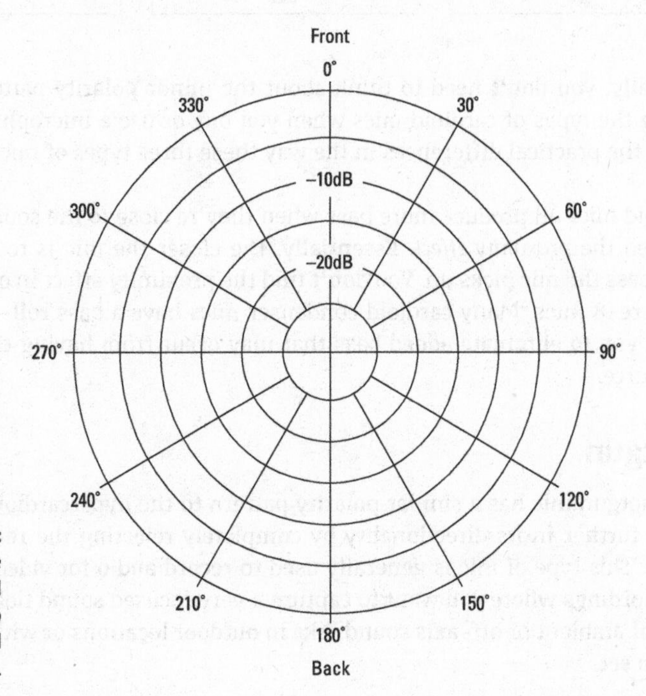

FIGURE 6-7: The omnidirectional mic picks up sounds from all around it.

Cardioid

Cardioid mics (also called directional mics) pick up the sound in front of them and reject sounds that come from behind. Cardioid mics are the most common types for live bands because you can control the sound that they pick up. If you have a cardioid mic on the tom-tom of a drum set, the mic picks up only the sound of that drum and not the sound from the other instruments around it.

TECHNICAL STUFF

The three types of cardioid mics are cardioid, supercardioid, and hypercardioid. The differences among the types of cardioid patterns of each mic aren't that great. Check out the graphs in Figure 6-8 to see how the polarity patterns of cardioid microphones differ.

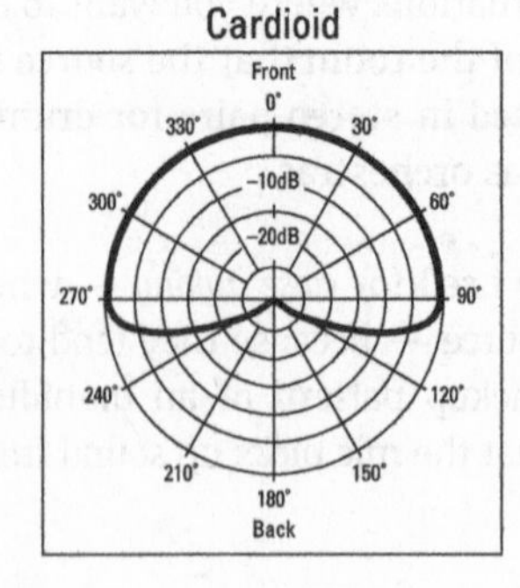

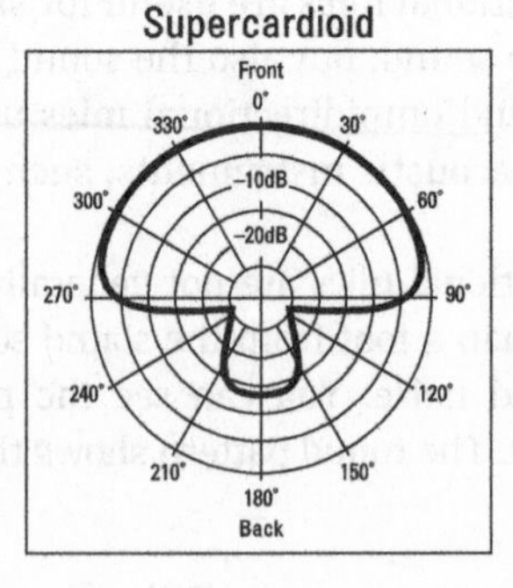

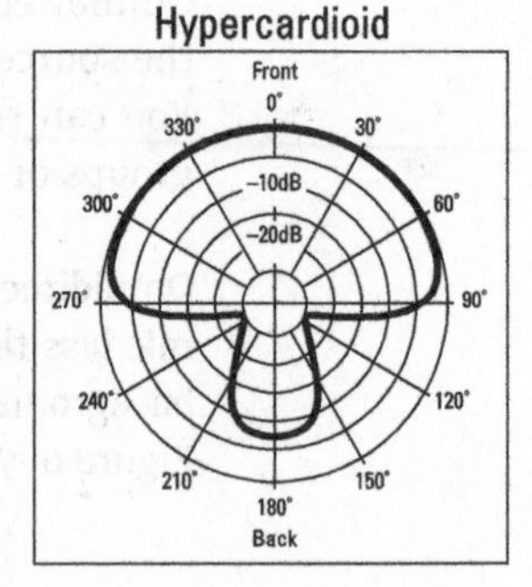

FIGURE 6-8: The three types of cardioid mics have similar polarity patterns.

Generally, you don't need to think about the minor polarity pattern differences among the types of cardioid mics when you buy or use a microphone. You won't notice the practical differences in the way these three types of mics work.

TIP

Cardioid mics all produce more bass when they're close to the sound source. This is called the *proximity effect.* Essentially, the closer the mic is to its source, the more bass the mic picks up. You don't find the proximity effect in omnidirectional or figure-8 mics. Many cardioid condenser mics have a bass roll-off switch that allows you to eliminate added bass that may occur from having the mic close to the source.

Shotgun

The shotgun mic has a similar polarity pattern to the hypercardioid mic but goes a step further in its directionality by completely rejecting the rear and off-axis sound. This type of mic is generally used to record audio for video production or for recordings where you want to capture a very focused sound field that has significant ambient or off-axis sound, like in outdoor locations or with the hi-hat on a drum set.

Figure-8

Figure-8 mics (also called *bidirectional* mics) pick up sound from both the front and back, but not all the way around. If you look at the graph in Figure 6-9, you can see that sound is not effectively picked up from areas on the sides of the microphone.

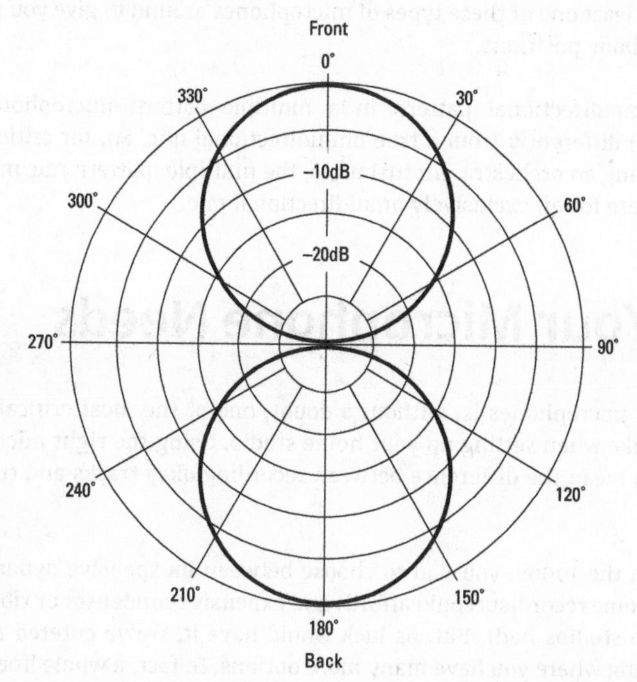

FIGURE 6-9: Figure-8 mics pick up sound from both front and back, but not the sides.

Figure-8 mics are often used to record two instruments simultaneously. For example, you can place the microphone between two horn players with the side of the mic perpendicular to the players. This allows you to capture both instruments while eliminating any sound in front of the musicians.

TIP

Most figure-8 condenser mics have the same frequency response for both the front and back sides, but some ribbon mics produce very different responses, depending on whether the sound is coming from the front or the back. For instance, a Royer r121 mic picks up more high frequencies from the back side of the mic than the front. You can use this to your advantage when recording an instrument. If the sound has too many low frequencies, just turn the mic around a little or a lot, depending on how many high frequencies you want to add (more on this in Chapter 8).

Multiple-pattern mics

Some condenser microphones can switch among various pickup patterns. These are generally large-diaphragm mics. These mics have a switch that allows you to choose from omnidirectional, cardioid, or figure-8 (refer to the left image in Figure 6-2). These mics can do this because they generally contain two sets of diaphragms and backplates, which are positioned back to back. You may want to have at least one of these types of microphones around to give you more variety in microphone positions.

REMEMBER

The omnidirectional pattern in a multiple-pattern microphone works (and sounds) differently from a true omnidirectional mic. So, for critical applications (recording an orchestra, for instance), the multiple-pattern mic may not be a fair substitute for an exclusively omnidirectional mic.

Assessing Your Microphone Needs

Buying microphones is, without a doubt, one of the most critical decisions that you make when setting up your home studio. Using the right microphone for the job can mean the difference between recording okay tracks and truly spectacular ones.

Back in the 1990s, you had to choose between inexpensive dynamic mics (what most home recordists could afford) and expensive condenser or ribbon mics (what the pro studios had). But, as luck would have it, we've entered a time in home recording where you have many more options. In fact, a whole line of project studio mics has recently emerged. This is a relatively new market in the long history of microphones that manufacturers have found to be hugely profitable, so the choices are expanding almost daily. In some cases, a $500 project studio mic can rival a $2,000-plus pro mic — at least for the home recordist's purposes.

So, the question that you're inevitably going to ask is, "What microphones should I get for my home studio?" Good question. And the answer is, "Well, it depends on what you need." Before I go into detail about what mics may be best for you, you should spend a minute assessing your needs. The following questions may help you in your assessment:

- **What type of music will you record?** If you play rock or pop music, you should probably start with dynamic mics because they're inexpensive and their limitations in high or low frequencies don't matter as much as if, for example, you wanted to record your string quartet. In this case, a pair of condenser mics would do the trick.

» **What instruments will you record?** Loud amps, drums, and screaming singers beg to be recorded with dynamic mics, whereas light percussion, vocals, and stand-up basses shine through with large-diaphragm condenser mics.

» **How many mics will you use at once?** If you need to record your whole band at once, budget constraints may dictate your choice between dynamic and condenser mics or a condenser or ribbon mic for vocals. If you need only a couple of mics to record the occasional vocal or instrument, you can invest more in each mic.

Deciding How Many Microphones and What Kind

You'll likely build your microphone collection over time instead of buying all your mics at once. This is the best way to buy mics, because it gives you time to develop an understanding of what you can do with the microphone that you have before you plunk down your money for another one. You're better off having a few mics that best fit your situation than having a whole bunch of mics that just sorta work for you.

If you're like most people, your budget dictates how many mics you can buy and what kind they may be. In the following sections, I try to help you get the best mics for your recording needs and guide you through the process of slowly accumulating microphones.

Getting started

A basic mic setup consists of a couple of dynamic mics for drums, guitar amps, or other loud instruments and a decent large-diaphragm condenser mic for vocals or other acoustic instruments. The next sections lay out the mics that I would consider if I were starting out on a budget.

Dynamic mics

A Shure SM57 is hands down the best choice for your first dynamic mic. This is a great dynamic mic for very little money (about $100). This mic works well for miking amps and drums and the occasional gritty vocal. Everyone should have at least one of these mics.

Large-diaphragm condenser mics

Your choice here depends on your voice and the acoustic sound that you're looking for. For economical options, I would check out the following mics:

- **Studio Projects B1:** This inexpensive mic is a good choice for your first large-diaphragm condenser mic. You can find one for about $120.
- **MXL 990:** This mic has a slightly different sound than the Studio Projects B1 and costs just slightly less (around $100). Buy the mic that sounds better to you.
- **Audio Technica AT2020:** This mic is in the same basic range of the Studio Projects and the MXL, with a street price around $100, but it offers a slightly different sound. I recommend auditioning all three and deciding which you prefer.
- **Blue Spark:** This mic is more expensive than the previous three (about $200), but it's several steps up from the others and worth an audition. Blue makes some awesome mics, and this is one of its least expensive ones.
- **Audio Technica AT3035:** This mic splits the difference between the Spark and the AT2020 (about $150). Check it out because it has a different flavor (sound) than the others, and you may prefer the sound of this mic over that of the Spark and AT2020.

A large-diaphragm condenser mic is the first condenser mic for most home recordists. These good all-around mics can work well for many applications.

Small-diaphragm condenser mics

If you are recording audio-for-video, your first mics will likely be small-diaphragm condenser mics in the form of either shotgun or lavalier (lapel, clip) styles.

For shotgun mics, I suggest checking out the following options:

- **Rode VideoMic:** Rode makes several versions of the VideoMic, ranging from around $100 to $300. These all sound decent and can be mounted on your video camera or portable audio recorder.
- **Audio Technica AT875R:** This mic is designed to mount directly on your camera. As with all Audio Technica mics, its sound is natural and smooth. You can find these for under $200.

- **Sennheiser MKE 600:** Sennheiser makes some great mics. This is a good mid-level option from them that I feel represents a great value, at around $350. I recommend comparing this to the AT8035 and Rode NTG5.
- **Rode NTG5:** This mic is more expensive than the previous three (about $500), but it's several steps up from the others and worth an audition.
- **Audio Technica AT8035:** This is a high-quality mic for video. It is quiet, has excellent off-axis sound rejection, and can be effectively used from farther away than a lot of other shotgun mics. This mic can be found for under $300.

Lavalier mics clip on your clothes and come as either wireless or corded versions. There are a ton of options from a variety of manufacturers. I recommend checking out these brands:

- **Audio Technica:** Audio Technica makes over a dozen lavalier mics priced from under $100 to about $200. From my experience, they all work very well. For the corded version, I recommend the Pro70 ($150). For wireless, I suggest checking out the AT831cW ($100) or the AT899cW ($180).
- **Rode:** Rode has become a popular brand for video production. They started with shotgun mics, but now have some nice lavalier mics as well, including a "pin-through" version that hides pretty well. Rode's lavalier mics costs between $80 and $250 and can be used with corded or wireless systems using their special "MiCon" connector (which will cost you extra).
- **Sennheiser:** Sennheiser has some great lavalier mics. For a basic corded mic, I recommend the MKE ($200). For wireless, the ME4 is a good place to start ($130). If you have the budget you can't go wrong with the MKE-2 corded or wireless mics ($400).
- **Shure:** Shure lavalier mics are more expensive than the other brands I list, but are definitely worth checking out. For a corded version, I like the TL47 ($400-$500). For wireless, check out the MX150B ($225).

REMEMBER

If you go for a wireless lavalier mic, you also need to buy a wireless transmitter and receiver. A decent set of these will set you back between $300 and $400. Search for "lavalier microphone wireless system" for some options.

Movin' on

After you have your basic mics, you can start to add a few more. If you intend to record your band, you need to at least mic the drum set (four mics can get you around the set). In this case, you can add a couple more dynamic mics and perhaps get one or two that are designed for particular applications. For instance, mics are made to work best on the kick drum of a drum set. At this point, you can also get a second condenser mic — maybe a small-diaphragm condenser mic this time or a large-diaphragm tube condenser mic. You may want to choose one that sounds different from the one you already have — or, if you love the one that you have, you can get a second one just like it to use as a stereo pair.

Dynamic mics

For additional dynamic mics, I would add one or two more SM-57s and try one of the following:

- **Sennheiser e609:** I like Sennheiser mics; these are some of my favorite (and inexpensive) amp or kick-drum mics. The e609 has a different sound than the venerable SM-57 and doesn't cost much more (a little over $100), so adding one of these lets you cover some more bases.
- **Audio Technica ATM25:** This is a pretty good kick-drum mic for not a lot of money (about $200), although it is more costly than some other dynamic mics. If you record drums live, this mic is worth trying.

Large-diaphragm tube condenser mics

If you're on a budget (and who isn't?), try out the following relatively inexpensive large-diaphragm tube condenser mics:

- **Rode NTK:** This is an awesome mic regardless of price, but for about $530, it's one of the best deals available. This mic is good for vocals and acoustic instruments. I've even used a pair for the overheads on a drum set.
- **Studio Projects T3:** This mic has an advantage over the Rode NTK because it has a variable polar pattern selector, allowing you to choose among omnidirectional, cardioid, and figure-8 patterns — and patterns in between. The NTK is cardioid only. This variability gives you more options when recording and increases the versatility of the mic, making this $500 mic worth checking out.

Small-diaphragm condenser mics

Though not sexy to most recordists, small-diaphragm condenser mics can come in handy. Here are a few inexpensive ones that are worth checking out:

- **AKG Perception 170:** This mic is inexpensive (about $80) and sounds good on many types of acoustic instruments — guitars, violins, cellos, double basses, drum overheads, and percussion. This is a solid starter SDC.

- **Audio Technica PRO 37:** For a few more dollars than the AKG, the AT PRO 37 ($125 street price) also offers quality sound for not a lot of money.
- **Rode M3:** The Rode M3 is pretty nice for a relatively inexpensive small-diaphragm condenser mic (around $150). I find that Rode generally offers very good mics for the money, and this mic is no exception.

Going all out

As your mic collection grows, you'll probably start looking for a vocal mic that works best for you. In this case, you may look at large-diaphragm tube condenser mics or even a ribbon mic.

REMEMBER

Choosing a vocal mic is a personal thing. If you're a singer, audition a bunch of mics by using your voice to see what sounds best to you. If you record more than one singer and each has a different type of voice (tenor or soprano, for instance), you may need to look for more than one vocal mic.

After this, consider buying a stereo pair of small-diaphragm condenser mics for drum overheads (mics placed over the drum set) or other multi-instrument applications. You may also want to start adding some higher-quality (and more expensive) mics to your collection. The following sections detail mics that offer a good bang for the buck.

Dynamic mics

Here are a couple of higher-end dynamic mics that I use:

- **Sennheiser MD421:** This is arguably the industry-standard tom mic. It's been used on tons of recordings over the years. If you intend to record drums with more than the basic three- or four-mic setup (see Chapter 9 for more details), having a couple of these tom mics is a necessity. They aren't cheap (just under $400 each), but for their purpose, they're worth every penny.
- **EV RE20:** This is a common kick-drum mic that is also used for amps and some vocals. You can get this mic for about $450.

Large-diaphragm condenser mics

You can find a ton of good large-diaphragm condenser mics, and the sky's the limit on how much you can spend on them. That said, consider the following reasonably priced options:

- **Shure KSM-44:** This is my go-to LDC. It's a multipattern mic that offers omnidirectional, cardioid, and figure-8 configurations. The sound is pretty neutral by today's standards. Many manufacturers like to boost the top and bottom ends of their mics to make them sound "sexy"; the KSM-44 doesn't have this feature, and as a result, the mic is very versatile. I often use one for drum overheads and other acoustic sources such as big percussion instruments (like surdos, congas, and djembes) and acoustic string instruments — and even as a room mic for ensembles. This mic costs about $1,000.
- **AKG C414 XLS:** This is another industry-standard mic that sounds great on a lot of sources — vocals, acoustic instruments, drums, and others. Like the KSM-44, this mic has selectable polar patterns. In this, you have five choices: omnidirectional, cardioid, wide-cardioid, hypercardioid, and figure-8. This mic sells for about $1,100.
- **Neumann TLM 103:** This is an industry-standard mic for a lot of sources, including many vocalists, percussion, and drums. (I love to use this as a room mic placed 6 to 8 feet in front of the kick drum.) This mic isn't cheap (about $1,100), but you'll never need to upgrade it.

Ribbon mics

Ribbon mics used to be very expensive and required a great preamp with lots of clean *gain* (volume) because they don't produce a very strong signal. This is changing. You can now find a ribbon mic for just a few hundred dollars, and if you don't have a high-gain preamp, you can find a mic that produces a stronger signal (called an *active-ribbon mic*). Here are some ribbon mics that I recommend:

- **MXL R40:** This is one of the least expensive ribbon mics available, and it sounds pretty good, especially for the price (under $100). For the budget-minded recordist who needs a ribbon mic, you can't go wrong with this one.
- **AEA R84:** This is one sexy mic. It looks gorgeous and sounds great. For classic "silky" vocals or to take the edge off instruments such as trumpets and other horns, this mic is awesome. Of course, awesome doesn't come cheap — it runs about $1,000, plus you need a good high-gain preamp. Still, if you like the vocals sound that you can get only from a ribbon mic or if you record a lot of horns, you need to try this mic.

» **Royer Labs 122:** This is the first active-ribbon mic. It has electronics that boost the mic's signal, so you don't need a super high-gain preamp to get a good sound. The ribbon mics from Royer Labs are known as great mics, and this one costs about $1,750.

Small-diaphragm condenser mics

If your budget allows you to get a pair of great small-diaphragm condenser mics, these boutique mics are my favorites:

» **Josephson C42:** I can't recommend this mic highly enough, especially the matched pair (model number C42mp). A pair of these mics is great for drum overheads and almost every acoustic instrument I've tried them on. I love to use a single mic on double bass, a pair on piano, and a pair on a live ensemble. These mics run about $500 each ($1,000 for a matched pair), but you'd be hard-pressed to find a mic at double the price that sounds better.

» **Peluso CEMC6:** The CEMC6 mic is a nice unit, especially for under $350 each ($700 for a matched pair). These mics rate almost as highly as the Josephsons. But if you're on a tight budget, try one or a pair of these mics.

TIP

You won't find either of these mics at the big music retailers, so if you're interested in them, you'll need to look around a bit. I suggest searching online to find an Internet retailer. A bunch of reputable dealers carry them.

Finding the Right Mic for the Situation

Certain mics work better than others for particular situations. In this section, I present some typical applications to give you an idea of what types of mics are traditionally used for various purposes. (You can find more ideas about mic usage in Chapter 8, where I discuss specific miking techniques.)

TIP

When you consider a mic, think about the frequency spectrum that the instrument encompasses. If you use a dynamic mic for a symphonic orchestra performance, for example, you'll be disappointed by the results because it lacks an accurate high-frequency response. On the other hand, using a small-diaphragm condenser mic on the tom-toms of a drum set makes them sound thin and is a waste of money because you can get by with a much less expensive dynamic mic for this purpose.

Microphone choice is fairly subjective. The following list contains basic suggestions based on what is typically used:

- **Vocals:** Most people prefer the sound of a large-diaphragm condenser mic for vocals for both singing and speaking. If you have the budget, you may also want to audition some ribbon mics for your voice. A dynamic mic is best when you're going for a dirty or raw sound (excellent for some harder rock, blues, or punk music) or if your singer insists on screaming into the mic. A small-diaphragm condenser mic is rarely the first choice for most singers, but it's not out of the question for some vocalists if you don't mind a bright, present (high-frequency) sound.
- **Vocals for video:** Audio recording for video production generally uses either a shotgun or lavalier mic. A general guideline is to choose a mic based on how many people you are recording. I usually use a lavalier mic when one person is talking and a shotgun when recording two or more people in conversation. If you are using a multitrack recorder and have the ability to use lavalier mics on each speaker and you don't mind mixing the balance between the speakers in post (the mixing stage), then you may find that you get better sound than with a shotgun mic. If you want to go all out, there is no reason you can't use both individual lavalier mics and a shotgun mic if you have the gear. This gives you the most flexibility when mixing.
- **Electric guitar amp:** A dynamic mic or a small-diaphragm condenser mic works well on an electric guitar amp. Some people use large-diaphragm condenser mics on guitar amps and like the added low frequencies that can result. A ribbon mic can sound great, but take care in placing the mic so that you don't overload it and blow the ribbon. Move the mic back a bit or off to the side and you should be fine.
- **Electric bass amp:** Your first choice when miking an amplified electric bass is either a large-diaphragm condenser mic or a dynamic mic. Either one can capture the frequency spectrum that the bass guitar encompasses. Small-diaphragm condenser mics aren't a good choice because of their inherent high-frequency focus. I like ribbon mics for electric bass, but you need to take the same care as you would with a guitar amp.
- **Acoustic guitar and other stringed instruments:** A large- or small-diaphragm condenser mic or a ribbon mic works well in most instances. A dynamic mic has too limited a frequency response to create a natural sound (but may create an effect that you like). Choose the large- or small-diaphragm type based on the overall frequency spectrum of the instrument. For example, to capture the depth of a guitar's tone, choose a large-diaphragm mic, but for an instrument with a higher register, such as a violin or mandolin, a small-diaphragm mic works great. I'm partial to small-diaphragm condenser mics for these instruments because I can get more clarity and I don't have to fight the low-end bump that often occurs with a large-diaphragm condenser mic.

- **Horns:** I'm partial to ribbon mics for horns. These types of mics can soften the tone slightly and make the horns sound more natural, especially if you mic closely (within a couple feet or so). My second choice is a large-diaphragm condenser mic in a figure-8 or omnidirectional pattern placed off to the side of the instrument a bit. For this, you need a large-diaphragm condenser mic that has multiple patterns, such as the AKG C414B or the Shure KSM-44. Some people like a tube condenser mic, so if you're on a budget, the Studio Projects T3 is a good place to start.
- **Piano:** Both large- and small-diaphragm condenser mics are generally used for piano. Your choice depends on where you place the mics and how the room sounds. For example, a great-sounding room begs for a pair of omnidirectional small-diaphragm mics placed away from the piano a bit. I'm not a fan of ribbon or dynamic mics for this instrument.
- **Drum set:** The tom-toms, snare drum, and kick (bass) drum all sound good with dynamic mics because they don't contain high frequencies. You can also use large-diaphragm condenser mics, but be careful where you place them because if your drummer hits them, they're toast.
- **Cymbals:** For the cymbals of a drum set, a pair of small-diaphragm condenser mics works well, although some people prefer to use a large-diaphragm mic instead. A ribbon mic also sounds pretty good and can take some of the harshness of cymbals when recorded digitally. A dynamic mic would lack the high-frequency response to make the cymbals shine through in a mix.
- **Miscellaneous percussion:** Now, here's a broad category. By miscellaneous, I mean shakers, triangles, maracas, and other higher-pitched percussion toys. For these instruments, either small- or large-diaphragm condenser mics can work well. If it's a very quiet instrument, a large-diaphragm mic would be preferable because of the higher self-noise of the small-diaphragm mic.

You may choose a different type of mic, especially if you try to create a certain effect. For instance, using a ribbon mic on a metallic shaker rather than a small-diaphragm condenser mic softens the highest frequencies of the instrument and gives it a mellower sound.

TIP

If you intend to record loud instruments — drums, amplified guitars, or basses, for example — look for a mic with a high SPL rating. This is a rating of how much volume (listed in decibels) the microphone can handle before distorting. A high SPL is above 130 decibels.

Some professional condenser mics have a pad switch that allows you to reduce the sensitivity of the mic, thereby increasing its ability to handle high sound pressure levels.

Partnering Mics with Preamps

One of the most important relationships in your home studio is the one between your microphones and the *preamp* (the nice bit of hardware that boosts the mic's signal so it can be recorded). The greatest microphone in the world run through a cheap preamp won't sound good. By the same token, a cheap mic plugged into a great preamp sounds only as good as the bad mic.

REMEMBER

If your mixer includes XLR inputs (low-impedance microphone inputs), you already have internal preamps in the channels with the XLR jacks. For the most part, these preamps are of lesser quality than the external variety, but they may work for you. For instance, some home recordists swear by the internal preamps in the Mackie VLZ-Pro mixers.

Plug in your mic and listen to the sound that you get. If you like it, you may not need to buy external preamps right away. If not, you may have to allocate some of your gear money for an external preamp.

You can find three types of preamps in the marketplace — solid-state, vacuum tube, and hybrid — and each has its own characteristics. In the following sections, I explore preamp styles and discuss how each relates to the sounds that are produced by the types of microphones I discuss earlier in the chapter. This can help you understand the relationship between the microphone and preamp in your studio.

Solid-state

Solid-state preamps use transistors to boost the signal of the microphone. These preamps can be designed to produce as clear and detailed a sound as possible (often referred to as "transparent") or can be designed to add a pleasing level of distortion (warmth) to your music. Solid-state preamps cost from a couple hundred to several thousand dollars.

A clean and clear solid-state preamp (such as the Earthworks, PerSonus or Focusrite brands) is a great choice if you want as natural a sound as possible on your recording of an instrument or if you're using a microphone that has a sound quality that you want to hear as clearly as possible. For example, I particularly like the way that a solid-state preamp works in conjunction with a tube condenser or ribbon mic. The warmth and smoothness of these types of microphones shine through clearly with a clean solid-state preamp.

On the other hand, a more aggressive (warm or pleasingly distorted) solid-state preamp, such as those modeled after the classic Neve designs, can add just a touch of "grit" to certain instruments. These types of preamps are great with dynamic, ribbon, or condenser mics, especially when recording drums, guitar, and some vocals.

Vacuum tube

These preamps use vacuum tubes to process and amplify the microphone's signal. This generally adds some coloration to the sound of your mic (how much and what kind of coloration depends on the particular preamp). As you've undoubtedly discovered after reading any other chapter in this book, digital recording aficionados love the sound of tube gear, especially tube preamps. The advantage of a tube preamp is that it can add a warm sound to your mics. The disadvantage is that you often can't get rid of this colored sound. Professional recording engineers often have several tube preamps in their studios to give them different coloration options.

TIP

The preamps that are included in your mixer are solid-state. If you find that you want the colored sound of a tube preamp, you need to buy an external one.

Tube preamps are great for imparting a subtle low-frequency addition to the sound of the microphone signal. Tube preamps also seem to slightly soften the higher frequencies. If you're like most people, you'll like the addition of a tube preamp, especially if you intend to record rock, blues, or acoustic jazz music. The downside is that all-tube preamps tend to be expensive (brands like Manley Labs, for instance). Recently, however, there are a growing number of companies making less expensive preamps such as Warm Audio.

I prefer to use tube preamps with drums and any "woody" instrument (acoustic guitar, for instance). In this case, I often reach for a large-diaphragm condenser mic, and in extreme cases, I may even use a large-diaphragm *tube* condenser mic with the tube preamp (for an extra dose of "tubiness").

Hybrid

A hybrid preamp contains both solid-state and tube components to boost the mic's signal. Most of the inexpensive (under $1,000) "tube" preamps that you find in the marketplace are actually hybrids. An advantage to this design approach is that the preamp can often be adjusted to have varying degrees of that warm tube sound. The disadvantage is that these relatively inexpensive tube preamps don't have as clear a sound as a great solid-state preamp, and they don't have quite the same pleasing character as an expensive all-tube preamp.

For most home recordists, this type of preamp offers a lot of flexibility and can allow you to get either the fairly clear, open sound of a solid-state preamp or the warm, colored sound characteristic of a classic tube preamp. If you can afford only one external preamp, one of these hybrid versions may be right for you.

The countless hybrid preamps on the market vary widely in price and sound quality. (In fact, most of the hybrid preamps are marketed as tube preamps.) Your best bet in choosing a hybrid — or any preamp for that matter — is to do some research. Talk to people, read reviews, visit Internet forums, and then audition the two or three that stand out to you. Choose the one that you think sounds best for your needs.

Considering Compressors

A compressor enables you to alter the *dynamic range* (the difference between the softest and loudest sound) of an instrument. Along with the microphone and preamp, the compressor is often added to the signal chain before it goes to the mixer. The advantage of using a compressor in the signal chain before it hits the mixer is that you can control the transients and have a hotter (higher) signal level going into the converters or recorder. This hotter level used to be necessary when recording at 16 bits, but with 24-bit recording, you don't need to worry as much about getting the highest signal into your system. I discuss setting optimal levels in more detail in Chapter 9.

If you record a lot of vocals or real drums, a decent external compressor may be a good idea — just go easy with it (again, check out Chapter 9). You can find some great-sounding compressors for as little as $200. My favorite is the FMR Audio RNC-1773, a really nice unit for the money.

As long as you're looking at preamps and compressors, take a look at some *channel strip devices,* which are integrated preamp, compressor, and equalizer combos. For some people (and maybe you), a channel strip device is the way to go. It allows you to have just one unit, reducing the amount of cords, and it's designed to make the three parts function well together. Quite a few great-sounding channel strip devices are available for under $500.

Analyzing Some Microphone Accessories

Along with your new mics, you're going to need a few accessories. These include mic cords, mic stands, and pop filters.

Microphone cords

Microphone cords can cost from about $10 to several hundred dollars. You're probably asking yourself, "Is there really a difference between a $30 or $40 mic cable and one that sells for hundreds of dollars?"

My answer is, "Supposedly — but chances are, you'll never hear it." Let me qualify this answer a little. Unless you have a *very* good mixer, recorder, microphones, preamps, analog/digital and digital/analog converters, monitors, and ears, you're wasting your money on expensive microphone cords. I know only one sound engineer (not me, though — I've spent too many years behind the drums) who claims that he can hear the difference between an average mic cord and one of the expensive ones. And even he says that the difference is very subtle. (It would have to be; otherwise, I would hear the difference, too.)

TIP

Don't waste your money on the most expensive mic cord (or any cord) until the cord is the weakest link in your signal chain. Don't buy the cheapest cord either. They tend to fail because they use thin wire and cheap connectors.

Microphone stands

A sturdy mic stand is essential for your studio. Mic stands are relatively inexpensive, so resist the temptation to buy a flimsy one. A good mic stand has a sturdy base and can securely hold your mics.

Good mic stands cost about $60 and have either a round cast iron base (great for getting into tight spaces) or a heavy tripod base. Either one works well. Brands such as Atlas, Hercules, or K&M offer good quality stands.

Pop filters

A *pop filter* is a nylon screen that eliminates the "pops" (technically called *plosives*) that singers make when they sing. Plosives are the result of sudden bursts of air projected into the mic (from singing words starting with P's and T's, for example). If you record vocals, a pop filter is a must-have.

TIP

Pop filters are relatively inexpensive (starting at about $20), but if you want to make your own, use a pair of tights or pantyhose and a coat hanger. Bend the coat hanger into a circle and stretch the tights or pantyhose over it. You can attach the coat hanger to the mic stand by using duct tape. Adjust the coat hanger so that the pop filter is 4 to 6 inches away from the microphone, and then have the vocalist sing through it. Check out Figure 6-10 to see a homemade pop filter.

FIGURE 6-10: You can make a pop filter out of a coat hanger and a pair of tights or pantyhose.

Caring for Your Microphones

After investing hundreds, if not thousands, of dollars in microphones, you probably want to know how to take care of them properly. Caring for or storing your microphones isn't rocket science. Just follow the general guidelines and ideas that follow, and you'll keep your mics in tip-top shape.

REMEMBER

A good microphone lasts a lifetime. Take care of your mics, and they'll give you years of service.

Daily care

The most important thing to keep in mind when using your mics is to resist the temptation to blow into them. I know you've probably seen someone on stage blow into a mic and yell "Test" to see whether it's working. And you figure that's how the pros must check their mics. Well, it isn't. Blowing into a mic is a sure way to literally blow out the diaphragm in some mics, especially those expensive ribbon mics. To determine whether a mic is working, just speak into it in a normal voice.

REMEMBER

You don't need to blow or yell into any mic unless, of course, your singer's style is to yell into the mic and you're trying to set the input level. In this case, offer him your trusty dynamic mic and keep that expensive ribbon mic hidden.

Another thing to remember when handling your mics is that they can be fragile. Condenser and ribbon mics don't survive rough handling well. In fact, if you drop a condenser or ribbon mic, you may break it (this is another good reason to have a sturdy stand). Dynamic mics, on the other hand, are more durable, which is why they're often used for live applications and on drums. (It's not uncommon for an overzealous drummer to whack them by accident — as a drummer, I know about this firsthand.)

Try to keep your mics away from dust and high humidity. Dust is probably the number-one enemy of a microphone because the dust can settle on the diaphragm and reduce the sensitivity of the mic — and even alter its frequency response. Always cover your mics or put them away when you're not using them.

Storage

Most professionals have mic lockers, where they can safely keep their mics when they're not in use. Mic lockers come in several varieties. You can make a special locked box fitted with foam padding that has a cutout for each mic, or you can keep your mics in their pouches or cases (if the mic came with a case) in a closet or cabinet.

Regardless of the type of storage cabinet you have, try to handle your mics as little as possible. In fact, if you have a mic that you use a lot, I recommend leaving it on a secure stand rather than repeatedly dragging it out of its case or storage cabinet.

TIP

If you do leave your mic out on its stand, cover the mic with a plastic bag and close the open end around the mic when it's not in use (see Figure 6-11). This keeps out the dust.

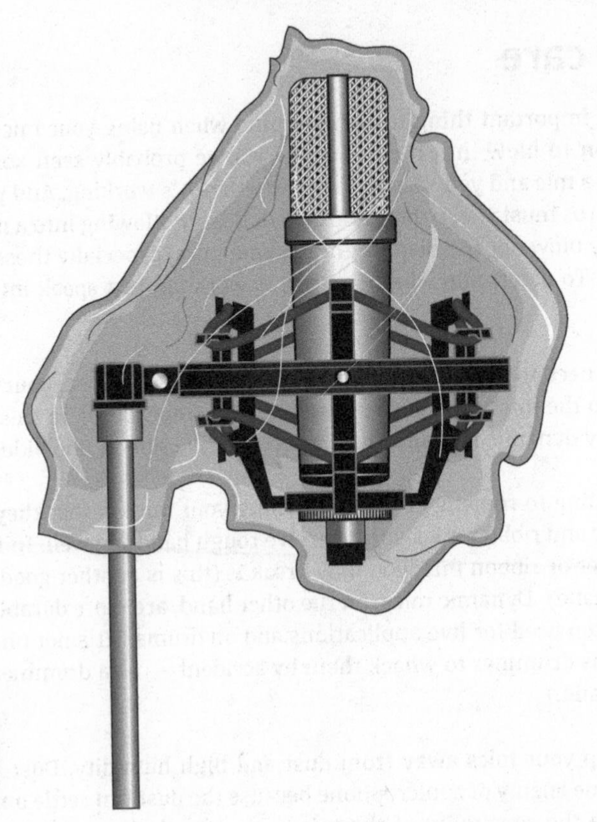

FIGURE 6-11: Covering your microphone with a plastic bag keeps out the dust.

Humidity can also be a problem for microphones. If you live in a humid environment, store your mics with a bag of silica gel next to them. (Silica gel, which absorbs moisture, is the stuff that comes in the packaging of a lot of electronic gear.) You can find silica gel listed as desiccant packets online — if you do an Internet search by typing **desiccant packets** or **desiccant sacks/sachets** into your favorite search engine, you'll find plenty of options.

IN THIS CHAPTER

» Exploring spot miking

» Discovering distant miking

» Examining ambient miking

» Exploring stereo miking

» Combining miking techniques

Chapter 7
Taking a Look at Microphone Techniques

To record acoustic instruments — that is, any instrument that doesn't have an electronic output — you need to use a microphone. The resulting sound can vary considerably based on where you place the mic in relation to the instrument and the room that you record in. I spend quite a bit of time — three chapters, in fact — talking about microphones because they're so important to the quality of your final recordings. (See Chapters 6 and 8 for more miking details.)

In this chapter, I take a look at some of the most common microphone techniques that are used in professional recording. You get a chance to see, up close, how spot miking works. You also get a broad view of distant miking and take a look at the big picture on ambient miking. In addition, this chapter explores common stereo miking techniques and explains what to look for when combining these various approaches.

Regardless of the style of microphone you use or the type of instrument you record, you can use one or more of the following mic-placement techniques to capture the sound you want:

- **Spot (or close) miking:** Put your microphone within inches of the sound source.
- **Distant miking:** Pull your mic back a few feet from the sound.
- **Ambient (or room) miking:** Place your mic way back in a room.

» **Stereo miking:** Set up two mics at various distances from one another.

» **Combined miking:** Use a combination of the four traditional placement strategies listed here.

This chapter introduces you to the four traditional mic-placement strategies that are used in recording. You discover the characteristics and purposes of each of these four methods and gain an understanding of how each relates to a particular tonal or sound quality. I also discuss how you can combine these strategies.

Singling Out Close Miking

Close miking (also called *spot miking*) involves placing your microphone within a couple feet of the sound source. Home recordists use this technique most often because it adds little of the *room* (the reverb and delay) to the recorded sound. Figure 7-1 shows the close miking placement.

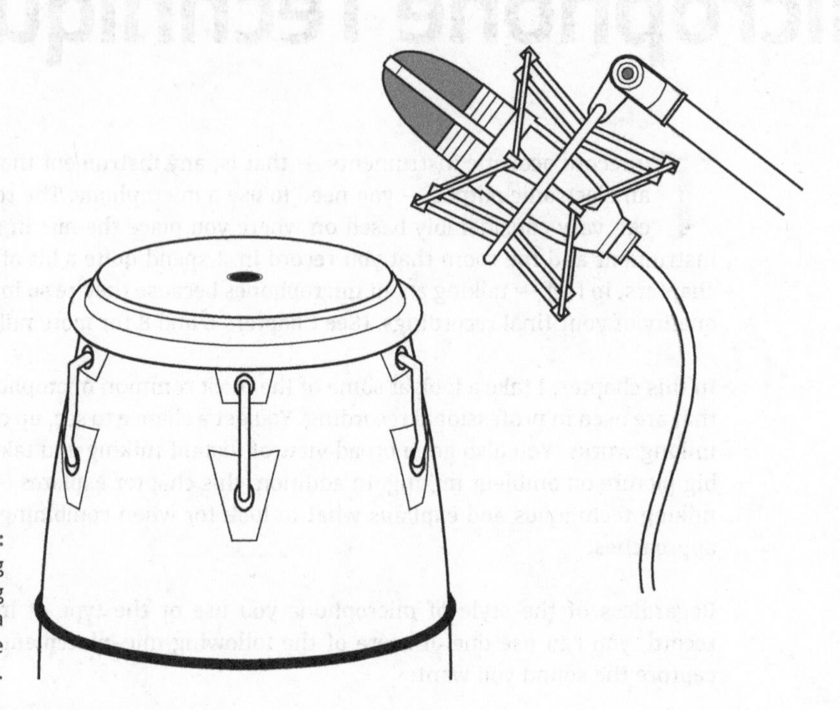

FIGURE 7-1: Close miking involves placing the mic within a couple feet of the sound source.

Close miking tends to create a less natural sound and can compromise the quality of your recordings if you're not careful. It can also offer advantages if you record multiple instruments in one pass or if your room doesn't sound good. Here are some things to consider when using spot miking:

- **Transients are more extreme.** Distance from a sound source tames the initial attack of an instrument. Spot miking picks up more transient material, which can make the sound of the instrument seem harsh and can overload your mic, preamp, or converter without your seeing it on your level meters. You need to listen closely to your recorded sound to make sure that you don't have distortion. A solution to this problem is to move the mic back a bit or point it slightly away from the instrument.
- **The room isn't part of the recording.** This can be good or bad, depending on the sound of your room:

  On the plus side, it can keep a bad-sounding room from ruining the sound of your track by putting it so far in the background of the recording that it isn't really heard on your tracks.

  On the downside, you lose the natural ambience of an instrument that gives it its character, so if you have a nice-sounding room, this technique may not be the best choice (depending on how many instruments are playing at once — see the next bullet point).
- **You can isolate each instrument.** Spot miking can help you keep multiple instruments separated in your tracks, so if you record your band live, you can create some isolation among instruments. (This assumes that you use a microphone with a cardioid polar pattern. Chapter 6 has more details on this.) This makes mixing a lot easier. Because of the downside that I list in the previous bullet, I'm a big fan of using room mics (using the ambient technique described in the section "Assessing Ambient Miking," later in this chapter) in conjunction with spot mics to create a more realistic sound.
- **Even minor adjustments in mic placement can have a huge impact on your recorded sound.** Because the mic is so close to the sound source, small adjustments to the mic's placement make a noticeable difference, and the mic may not capture the complete sound of the instrument. Finding the spot that sounds the best may take you awhile.
- **The closer you put your mic, the more bass you record.** I mention this in Chapter 6, but it bears repeating here. As you move a mic with a cardioid polar pattern in close to the sound source, the mic picks up more bass energy. This is called the *proximity effect.* It can be an advantage for some applications — rounding out the sound of a vocal, for instance — but it can also cause problems with some instruments such as acoustic strings, where you don't want the extra bass muddying the sound. To counter this effect, use an omnidirectional or figure-8 mic or move the cardioid-pattern mic away from the sound source until the bass is more manageable. (See Chapter 6 for a rundown of the different types of mics.)

Detailing Distant Miking

When you use *distant miking*, you place mics about 3 or 4 feet away from the sound source, as shown in Figure 7-2. Distant miking enables you to capture some of the sound of the room along with the instrument. An example of a distant-miking technique is the overhead drum mic. With it, you can pick up the whole drum set to some extent. Coupling the distant mic with a few select spot mics, you can record a natural sound.

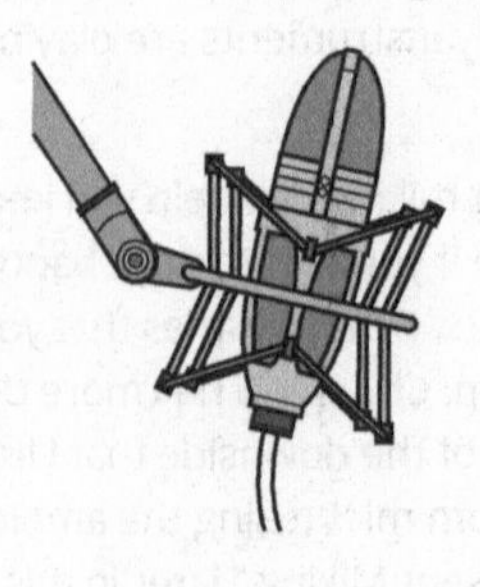

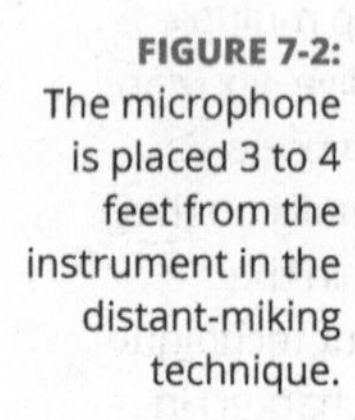

FIGURE 7-2: The microphone is placed 3 to 4 feet from the instrument in the distant-miking technique.

Distant miking has its pluses and minuses. Here are some things to remember if you use this technique:

- **You can get a more natural sound.** By moving the mic back a few feet from its source, you give the instrument a chance to breathe a bit and allow the sound to blend a little with the room in which it's played. You also eliminate the impact of the proximity effect (see the previous section) and correct the balance between the body of the instrument's sound and the transient from the initial attack. This often creates a more pleasing, natural sound.
- **Other instruments may bleed into your track.** If you record more than one instrument at the same time, distant miking increases the bleed of other instruments into the track of the instrument that you want to record. The solution to this is to use the spot-miking technique instead, move the instruments farther apart, adjust the mics so that the blind spot of the mic is facing the instrument you don't want to record, or place *gobos* (acoustic baffles) between the instruments.

» **The sound of the room is important.** With the mic farther away from the instrument, more of the *room sound* (the reverb and delay) is picked up in relation to the instrument. As a result, you hear more of the room in your tracks. This can be nice if your room sounds good, but it can get in the way if your room doesn't.

» **Multiple mics can cause phase problems.** Whenever you use more than one mic on a source such as a band or drum set, the relationship of these mics to the source and to one another plays a significant role in the sound you get. If the mics are not placed properly, some frequencies may drop out. Called *phase cancellation,* this is the result of the recorded waveforms reaching each mic at slightly different times. The section "Overcoming problems with stereo miking" and the section "Creating Miking Combinations," later in this chapter, explain this phenomenon in more detail.

Assessing Ambient Miking

Ambient miking is simply placing the mic far enough away from the sound source so that you capture more of the room sound than the sound of the actual instrument (see Figure 7-3). You may place the mic a couple feet away from the source but pointed in the opposite direction, or you may place it across the room. You can even put the mic in an adjacent room, although I admit this is an unorthodox technique. The distance that you choose varies from instrument to instrument.

Ambient miking definitely has its place, but using this technique requires forethought. Consider the following items when you use this technique:

» **You lose the attack of the instrument.** Because the mic is so far from the sound source, it picks up more of the ambience of the room than the attack of the instrument (hence, the name of the technique). To counter this effect, use distant or spot mics for the instruments that you want to have a more pronounced presence, and blend these mics with the ambient mic when you mix.

» **You need a good room.** Ambient miking relies on the sound of the room to create a pleasing ambience. If your room doesn't sound great, you're better off using a closer miking technique instead. On the other hand, if you can find a great room in which to record — a church or auditorium, for instance — setting up a mic in the middle of the room (you must listen for the best placement by walking around the room as the music plays) can give your tracks that extra something that can set them apart from the run-of-the-mill home recordings.

FIGURE 7-3: Ambient miking involves placing the mic so that it picks up more of the room's sound than the instrument's sound.

- **Placement is key.** Just as each instrument has a sweet spot, each room has a place that sounds best. Take your time finding this location and put your ambient mic there.
- **Watch for phase problems.** Because an ambient mic is typically used in conjunction with another mic or two (or more), you must keep the relationship among the mics correct; otherwise, you'll have problems with the phase of the recorded waveforms. (I introduce the concept of phase cancellation in the preceding section, "Detailing Distant Miking.")

TIP

Ambient mic placement works well in those places where the room adds to the sound of the instrument. The sound that you record is ambient (hence, the name). If you mix an ambient mic with a spot mic, you can end up with a natural reverb. So, if your room doesn't add to the sound of the instrument, avoid using an ambient mic. You can always add a room sound by using effects in the mixing process (see Chapter 19 for more details).

Selecting Stereo Miking

Stereo miking involves using two mics to capture the stereo field of the instrument. You find a variety of stereo-miking techniques and some pretty complicated ways of using two mics to record. The three most common approaches are X-Y (coincident) pairs, the Blumlein technique, and spaced pairs. You can also find stereo mics that do a good job of capturing the stereo field of an instrument.

Stereo miking has the advantage of capturing a fairly natural stereo image, though not as good as what your ears capture. When you listen to performances that were recorded with well-placed stereo miking, you can hear exactly where each instrument performed on the stage. Of course, such wonderful stereo miking is an art. You can't just set up a couple mics in a room and automatically get a good stereo sound. Capturing a stereo image with two mics requires careful planning.

X-Y pairs

X-Y (coincident) stereo miking consists of using two mics that are placed right next to each other so that the diaphragms are as close together as possible without touching one another. X-Y stereo miking is the most common type of stereo mic setup and the one that you'll likely use if you do stereo miking. Figure 7-4 shows a basic X-Y setup. Notice how the mics in this figure are attached to a special mounting bracket. This bracket makes positioning the mics easy.

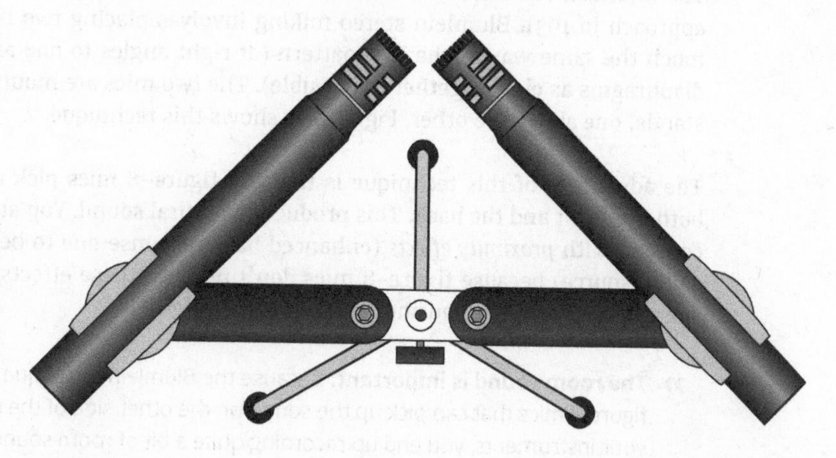

FIGURE 7-4: The X-Y stereo mic approach uses two matched microphones placed close together.

When you record using the X-Y technique, keep these points in mind:

» **The stereo image (the placement of the instruments in the sonic environment) isn't as wide or as realistic as it is in real life.** The X-Y technique is easy to set up and results in a decent sound, so (as with all things in life) you have to deal with the compromise this ease creates. No solution to this exists, so if a wide stereo image is important to you, consider using a different stereo technique, such as the spaced pair or perhaps a Jecklin disk. (See the section "Overcoming problems with stereo miking," later in this chapter for more about using a Jecklin disk.)

» **Don't use two mics when one is enough.** After you get a pair of nice mics for X-Y miking, you'll want to use them on everything. A stereo-mic approach to a classical guitar composition is nice, but honestly, recording the acoustic guitar in a rock ballad with five other instruments playing isn't necessary and just makes life more complicated when you mix the song (see the section "Creating Miking Combinations," later in this chapter).

» **Keep some distance between the mics and the sound source.** The X-Y technique has no benefit over a single mic if you place your mics within a couple feet of the sound source.

REMEMBER

You simply don't have enough space for a stereo image to develop until you're at least 6 feet from the instrument or group of instruments. In fact, I recommend being at least 10 feet from the sound source before using the X-Y stereo miking approach.

Blumlein technique

The Blumlein technique is named after Alan Dower Blumlein, who patented this approach in 1931. Blumlein stereo miking involves placing two figure-8 mics in much the same way as the X-Y pattern (at right angles to one another with the diaphragms as close together as possible). The two mics are mounted on separate stands, one above the other. Figure 7-5 shows this technique.

The advantage of this technique is that the figure-8 mics pick up signals from both the front and the back. This produces a natural sound. You also don't have to contend with *proximity effects* (enhanced bass response due to being close to the sound source) because figure-8 mics don't produce these effects. Here are some suggestions for when you should use this technique:

» **The room sound is important.** Because the Blumlein technique uses figure-8 mics that can pick up the sound on the other side of the mics than your instruments, you end up recording quite a bit of room sound with your instruments. This is one of the reasons that this technique sounds as good as it does, but your room must add to the quality of your sound, not hinder it.

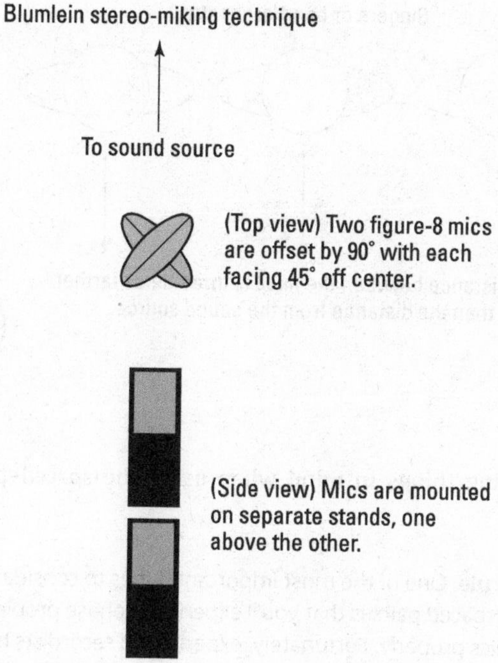

Blumlein stereo-miking technique

To sound source

(Top view) Two figure-8 mics are offset by 90° with each facing 45° off center.

(Side view) Mics are mounted on separate stands, one above the other.

FIGURE 7-5: The Blumlein technique uses two figure-8 mics placed at right angles to one another.

- **Find the best place in the room.** Take some time to find the best place to put the mics. The placement may not be in the center of the room or the front of the band. Instead, it may be off to one side or closer to the back or front. This advice holds true for all miking, but with the Blumlein technique (or when using omnidirectional mics with the other techniques), correct mic placement can make the difference between a decent recording and a truly awesome one.

TIP

- **Get a sturdy stand that can handle both mics.** Using two stands to hold both mics makes moving them around (to find the sweet spot in the room) a real pain in the you-know-what. You can easily find mic-stand adapters that hold both mics. These can be an invaluable investment.

Spaced pairs

Spaced-pair stereo miking involves placing two mics at a distance in front of the instrument(s) that you want to record and at a distance from one another. This approach can work well if you record an ensemble that takes up a lot of room. Figure 7-6 shows a top view of a typical spaced-pair stereo mic setup.

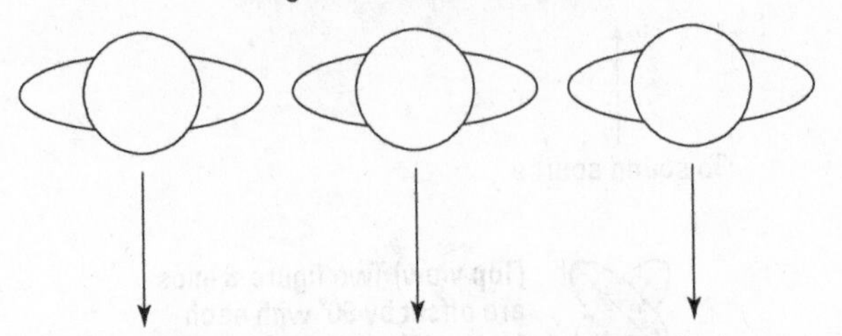

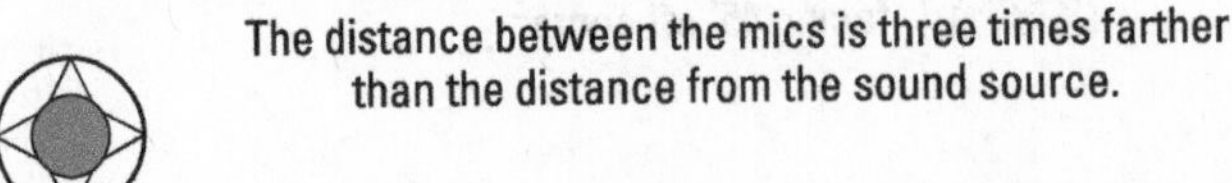

The distance between the mics is three times farther
than the distance from the sound source.

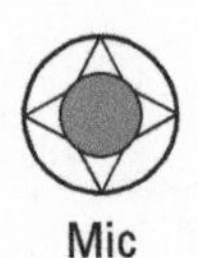

FIGURE 7-6: To use the spaced-pair approach, place two mics away from the sound source and apart from one another.

REMEMBER

Keep the following things in mind when using the spaced-pair stereo-miking technique:

- **Follow the rule.** One of the most important things to consider when stereo miking with spaced pairs is that you'll experience phase problems if you don't space the mics properly. Fortunately, experienced recordists have discovered a basic guideline that makes it easier to place the mics. Called the 3:1 rule, this guideline says that you should place the mics three times farther apart than they are from the sound source. Doing so minimizes potential phase problems.
- **Break the rule if necessary.** As handy as the 3:1 rule is, it isn't foolproof. At times, this rule doesn't produce the best sound. In the next chapter, I offer one of these instances for placing drum overheads in a three-mic technique. Use the rule as a guide, but trust your ears to determine the best place to put a spaced pair of mics (or a single mic, pair, or a group of mics).

Stereo microphones

If you want to record an instrument in stereo and don't want the hassle of learning how to set up stereo pairs, you can use a stereo mic. Stereo mics have two diaphragms in them and use a special cord that allows you to record the output from each diaphragm on a separate track. An inexpensive stereo condenser mic is shown in Figure 7-7. This type of microphone acts like an X-Y pair, so follow the guidelines and suggestions that I offer in the section "X-Y pairs," earlier in this chapter, when using one of these.

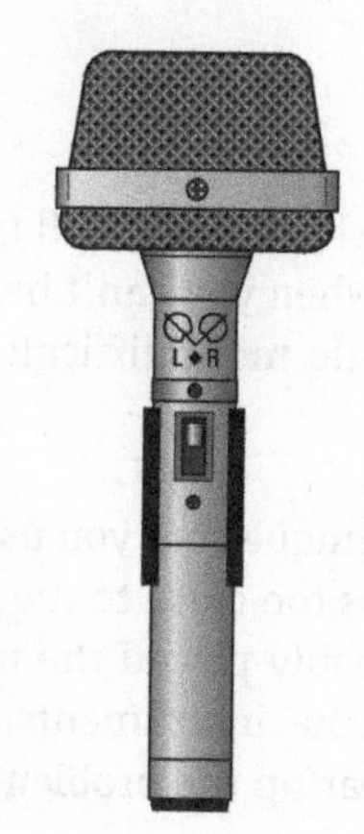

FIGURE 7-7: A stereo microphone can do a good job of capturing a natural stereo image.

Overcoming problems with stereo miking

When you do stereo miking, watch out for phase cancellation and poor stereo imaging. I describe these thorny issues and a simple solution in the following paragraphs.

Phase cancellation

Phase cancellation happens when the two microphones are placed so that each receives the sound at a slightly different time. When this occurs, you don't hear the bass as well because the low frequencies cancel each other out. Improper mic placement or two mics that are out of phase with one another can cause phase cancellation.

TIP

Most digital mixers have a phase switch that allows you to reverse the phase of the signal (even after it's recorded). To test whether two mics are out of phase, just reverse the phase on one mic (don't do both) and listen to see whether the low frequencies become more apparent:

- If they do, you've corrected the problem and you're good to go.
- If this doesn't correct the problem, try changing cords on one of the mics because some mic cords are wired differently than others. If this doesn't work either, you need to adjust the relationship between the two mics. Just move one mic around a little and listen for changes in the bass response. When the missing bass appears, you know you've solved the problem.

Poor stereo imaging

Poor stereo imaging occurs when you can't tell where things fall from left to right (or right to left, if that's the way you think), or when you can't hear a clear center point in the sound. Poor stereo imaging is a little more difficult to correct than phase cancellation, but you can fix it.

The solution depends on the stereo-miking technique that you use. If you use the X-Y technique, you've probably placed your mics too close to the sound source. If you use the spaced-pair technique, you've probably placed the mics too close to one another in relation to the distance from the instruments. In either case, adjusting the placement of your mics should clear up the problem.

TIP

A Jecklin disk is a simple device that can make dealing with these issues much easier (and give you a pretty realistic stereo image for not a lot of money). A Jecklin disk is a ¼-inch-thick round plate, approximately 12 inches in diameter, with ½-inch of foam attached to both sides (see Figure 7-8). Omnidirectional small-diaphragm condenser mics are placed on either side of the plate at precise locations and this entire unit is directed to the sound source. To learn more about the Jecklin disk, do an Internet search and you'll find plenty of hits — including some plans to build one for under $30.

FIGURE 7-8: A Jecklin disk can make stereo recording easy and capture an awesome, natural sound.

Creating Miking Combinations

Often you'll want to use more than one mic. The possible combinations are almost limitless: You can use several spot mics on one instrument, you can use a spot mic and an ambient mic, you can have a distant mic and a spot mic, or . . . well, you get my point. As exciting as these possibilities can be, keep the following points in mind to get the best sound when you combine multiple mics:

- **Be aware of phase relationships.** Each mic interacts with all the other ones when you record, and you need to take the time to set up each mic so that it doesn't interfere with any others. This means honoring the 3:1 rule for stereo mics (see the section "Spaced pairs," earlier in this chapter). The only way to ensure that your phase is good is to record a snippet of a song (or a whole song if you want) and then listen to your tracks.

  Listen to each mic individually and then together to see whether any frequencies drop out. If frequencies drop out, finding the problem mics will take some detective work. You need to play pairs of mics that you recorded until you find the problem; then you need to adjust each mic until the problem goes away. If you do this enough, you'll get pretty good at placing mics and making phase relationships work.
- **Be aware of bleed between mics.** This is mainly for bands that want to play together while still maintaining as much isolation as possible. A string quartet rarely needs isolation because all the instruments blend well together live; this blending is integral to the overall sound. However, a rock band with miked amps usually needs enough isolation so that you can do some tweaking to each instrument when you mix.

  In addition, a band that plays well together and can nail the performances can have more bleed — whereas a band with a marginal player or two (you know whether you have one in your band) who has to perform additional takes or punch-ins to fix a weak performance requires much more isolation. Doing a punch-in to a live, bleed-filled performance (for instance, if your bass player flubbed a few notes) can sound wrong in the mix.
- **Use only as many mics as you need.** Every additional mic that you add to your setup complicates your recording process considerably. To keep things simple, use as few mics as possible to get the sound you want.

REMEMBER

If you're using a digital audio workstation (DAW), it probably has a phase switch that enables you to fix the phase problems later if you missed them as you recorded. This isn't as optimal as recording without this problem, but it may allow you to save an otherwise-good set of tracks.

IN THIS CHAPTER

» Exploring microphone techniques

» Miking amplified instruments

» Miking acoustic instruments

» Miking drums

Chapter 8
Miking Your Instruments

The location of a microphone in relation to your instrument or a singer has a huge impact on the sound of your recording. In fact, just a movement of an inch or two — or even a slight turn of the mic — can bring out different characteristics in the sound. The art of placing mics is one that you will undoubtedly spend a lifetime discovering.

In this chapter, you discover the fundamentals of using microphones to get a good source sound. You explore tried-and-true miking methods along with practical miking tips and tricks that you can use right away. You also examine the use of compression and mic placement to control and eliminate *transients* — the usual peaks in the instrument's sound.

REMEMBER

In Chapter 9, I present ways to get the best sound from your mics and to keep extreme transients from ruining an otherwise-nice recording by overloading your inputs and clipping your audio, so check it out if you haven't done so yet.

Just remember, you don't need to use a compressor when tracking — simply keep your levels low enough to leave room for these unexpected signals. If you do decide to use a compressor during tracking, keep the attack and release times short (Chapter 7 has more on this). You only want to catch the initial signal and not mess with the rest of the instrument's sound. If you want to use a compressor to sculpt the sound of your instruments, you can do that easily during the mixing stage of producing your song. I cover this approach in detail in Chapter 19, where I offer a bunch of sample settings to get you started.

Getting a Great Lead Vocal Sound

Regardless of the type of home studio you have or the style of music that you record, you'll probably record vocals at some point. And unfortunately, vocals are among the most challenging sounds to do well. You have to find the right mic for the person who's singing or talking, and then you need to try different approaches to get the best sound out of him or her. Fortunately, you're in luck. In the following sections, I lead you through the (sometimes complicated) process of getting good lead vocal sounds.

Making the most of the room

To get the best possible recording of vocals, you need a dead room, which is another way of saying a room that has no reverberation. (Chapter 3 has tips on how to deaden your room.) Recording vocals in a dead room gives a sense of "presence" and allows you to add compression to the vocals without making them sound distant. (This is because the compressor raises the level of the background noise, particularly the reverberation from a live room.)

The easiest way to deaden your room for vocal recording is to hang curtains, carpet, or blankets around the room or to use the absorbent side of the reflector/absorber panels that I discuss in Chapter 3. Try to cover the front and both sides of the vocal area with absorbent materials. If you use the reflector/absorber panels that I describe in Chapter 3, you need to raise them off the ground, because the panels are only 4 feet tall.

Choosing the best mic

You have a lot of options for miking vocals. The type of mic that you use dictates where you place it.

Dynamic mic

Dynamic mics sound best when you place them close to the singer's mouth. The effect that you get is gritty. Huh? Okay, by *gritty* I mean dirty. That's no help either? Let me see . . .

- **Sound:** Dynamic mics produce a midrange sound (the high frequencies aren't reproduced well). When someone sings with the mic right in front of her mouth, the sound lacks even more high frequencies due to the proximity effect (an enhanced low-frequency response at close range). The result is a deep, bass-heavy sound that's often described as gritty or dirty. This type of sound can be great for some styles of rock and blues music.

» **Setup:** To set up a dynamic mic for this purpose, just put it on a stand so that the singer can get his mouth right up against the windscreen.

Large-diaphragm condenser mic

Large-diaphragm condenser (LDC) mics are the most common types of mics for vocals.

» **Sound:** These mics can clearly reproduce the entire audible frequency spectrum and slightly accentuate the low-mid frequencies (200 to 500 Hz) at the same time. Their sound is nice, warm, and full-bodied (that sounds like I'm describing a wine). The *proximity effect* (how close the singer is to the mic) determines how nice and warm-bodied the sound is. The closer the singer, the deeper and richer the tone.

» **Setup:** When you set up an LDC mic for vocals, you need to place the mic so that nasty *sibilances* (the sound from singing *s* and *t* sounds) and pesky plosives (pops from singing *p* syllables) don't mess up your recordings. To deal with plosives and sibilance, you can either use a pop filter (see Chapter 7) or have the singer sing past the mic.

TIP

If you want the singer to sing past the mic, you can do one of the following things:

- Place the mic above the singer and set it at an angle pointing away from him (Figure 8-1, left).
- Put the mic off to the side and face it toward the singer (Figure 8-1, center).
- Set up the mic below the singer and angle it away from him (Figure 8-1, right).

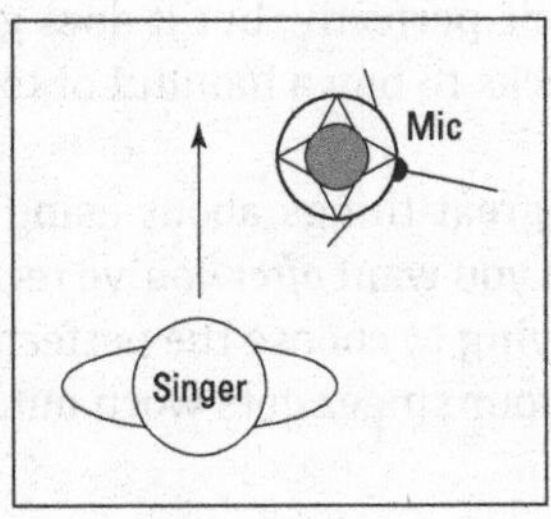

FIGURE 8-1: You can place the mic at different angles to control sibilance and plosives.

Small-diaphragm condenser mic

The small-diaphragm condenser (SDC) mic won't be your first choice in a vocal mic, unless you're recording a female vocalist with a soprano voice and you want to catch the more ethereal quality of her higher frequencies.

- **Sound:** The SDC mic creates a much brighter or airier sound than the large-diaphragm mic. This means that it doesn't accentuate the low-mid (200 to 500 Hz) warmth of its larger-diaphragm counterpart.
- **Setup:** You set up the SDC mic in the same way that you set up the large-diaphragm mic.

Ribbon mic

The ribbon mic is a good choice if you're looking for a crooner-type sound (think Frank Sinatra).

- **Sound:** The ribbon mic is thought to add a silky sound to the singer's voice. By *silky*, I mean a slight drop-off in the high frequencies (not as severe as a dynamic mic, though). To my drum-abused ears, ribbon mics have a kind of softness that the large-diaphragm condenser mics don't have. The sound is more even, without the pronounced low-mid effect.
- **Setup:** If you use a ribbon mic, you can set it up in the same way that you set up a condenser mic. Just be more careful about singing directly into a ribbon mic because the ribbon can break if you sing, speak, or breathe too hard into it.

TIP

You can find mic simulator plug-ins or software/hardware systems, from brands such as Universal Audio, Townsend Labs, Slate Digital, or Antelope, to use with your digital audio workstation (DAW). Mic simulators allow you to use a neutral-sounding mic and make it sound like a variety of much more colorful-sounding (including rare and expensive) mics. The mic simulator may not match the sound of a great mic perfectly, but it does give you more options, especially if you don't have the bucks to buy a handful of top-notch vocal mics.

One of the great things about using a mic simulator is that you can choose the exact sound you want *after* you've recorded the vocal part. This way, you can spend less time trying to choose the perfect mic and get down to the business of recording before your singer gets worn out.

Getting Good Backup Vocals

To record backup vocals, you can either track each part separately by using the same mic-placement techniques that I describe earlier or have all the backup singers sing at once into one or two mics. If you do the latter, you can use a stereo pair of mics, a figure-8 mic, or an omnidirectional mic.

If you use a stereo pair of mics, I recommend setting them up in a coincident X-Y pattern (introduced in Chapter 7). Have the vocalists stand next to each other facing the mics at 3 or 4 feet away. Large- and small-diaphragm mics work best for this setup. Check out Figure 8-2 for a neat top view of this arrangement.

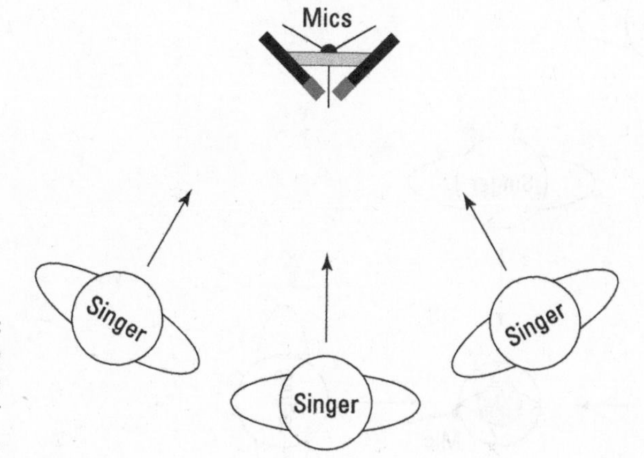

FIGURE 8-2: The X-Y stereo miking pattern can work well for backup vocals.

If you choose to use a figure-8 mic, the singers can stand on opposite sides of the mic (see Figure 8-3). The advantage of this setup is that the singers can look at each other while they sing.

An omnidirectional mic can also work well for backup vocals. In this case, the singers stand in a circle around the mic, as shown in Figure 8-4.

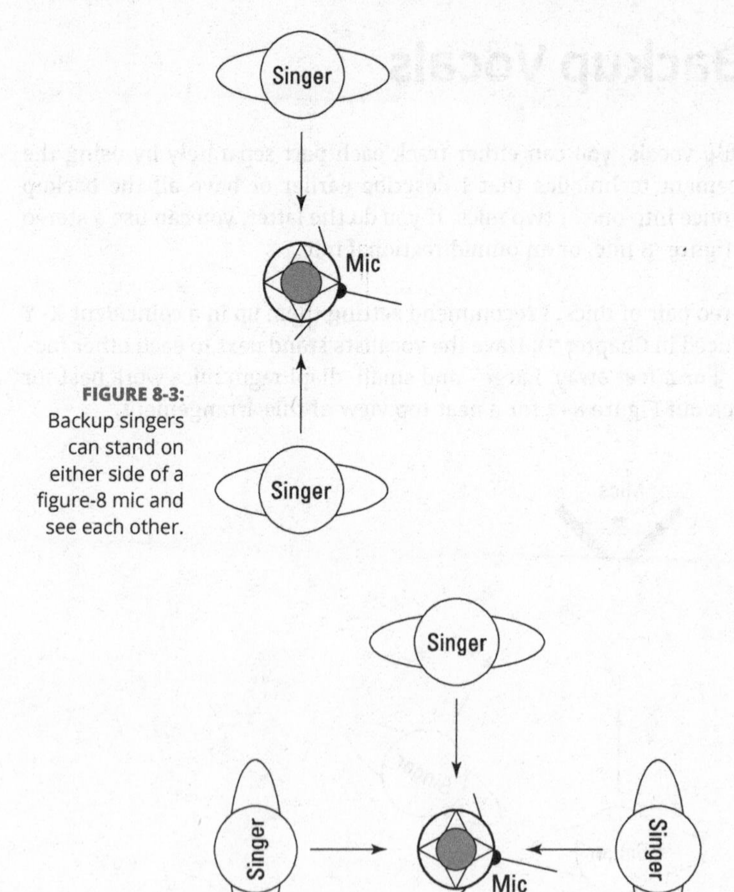

FIGURE 8-3: Backup singers can stand on either side of a figure-8 mic and see each other.

FIGURE 8-4: Singers stand in a circle around an omnidirectional mic.

Examining Electric Guitar Miking

Miking your electric guitar is a personal thing. It seems to me that every guitar player spends a lot of time getting his or her "sound" (although I don't play guitar, so what do I know?). If you're a *real* guitar player, you undoubtedly take great pride in recording your sound exactly right on tape, er, disc. You likely spend countless hours tweaking your amp and adjusting the mic to get the sound just right. On the other hand, if you're not a real guitar player, you may just want to record the part and get it over with. Either way, you can start looking for that perfect guitar sound by placing your mics in one (or more) of the ways that I describe in this section.

Guitar miking involves mostly spot mics, so your only consideration when recording a guitar using an amp is how your neighbors feel about noise, er, your most-excellent guitar playing.

Using the room

Whether you play through a small jazz chorus amp or power-chord your way through a 6-foot-tall Marshall stack, the room that you play in has less impact on your sound than it does if you play drums or sing. For the most part, look for a room that is fairly dead — a room without natural reverberation. You can always add effects later.

Getting the most out of the mics

The type of mic that you choose largely depends on the type of sound you're looking for. For example, if you're looking for a distorted rock guitar sound with effects, a dynamic mic works just fine. If you favor a clean sound, a small-diaphragm condenser mic may work better for you. If you're going for a warm, full-bodied sound, try using a large-diaphragm condenser mic.

REMEMBER

No matter which type of mic you use, you get the best sound from your amp speakers by putting a mic about 2 to 12 inches from the cabinet, with the mic pointing directly at the cone of one of the amp speakers (the dust cap is located in the center of the speaker). You can see this positioning in Figure 8-5.

You may want to experiment with how far the mic is from the amp and the angle at which you point it. Sometimes just a slight movement in or out, left or right, can make all the difference in the world. You can even try pointing the mic at different speakers if your amp has more than one, because each speaker has a slightly different sound.

TIP

I know some engineers who disconnect all but one speaker in the cabinet (assuming that you have more than one speaker) to lower the volume and still have an intense, distorted sound. This can be especially beneficial if you have one of those amp stacks with a volume knob that goes to 11, and you need to crank the amp to get your "tone" (come on, rockers, you know who you are). This way you don't overdrive the mic — creating distortion — and you can still get that nasty sound you're looking for.

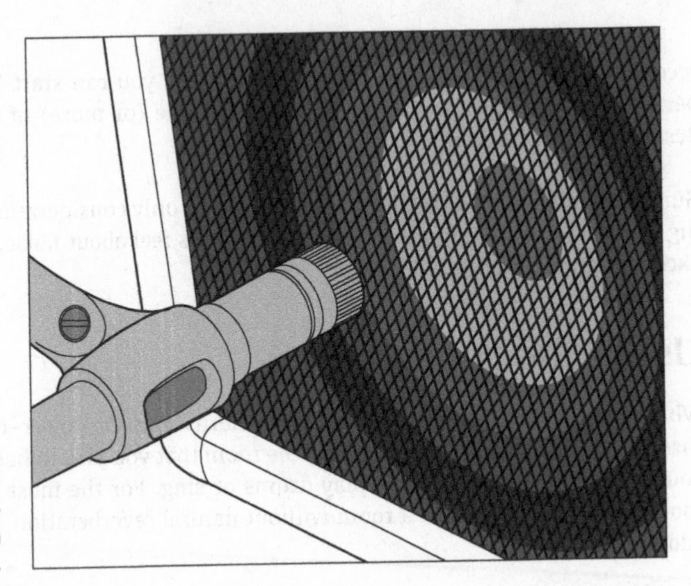

FIGURE 8-5: Start by placing a mic near the cone of a speaker in your amp.

If you can't quite get the sound that you want from your amp with the one mic pointed at the speaker cone, try adding a second mic 3 or 4 feet away. You also point this mic directly at the speaker cabinet for a more ambient sound. This may also give your sound more life, especially if you have a room with natural reverberation. If you add a second mic, remember to watch for phase differences between the mics and make adjustments accordingly. (I discuss phase cancellation in Chapter 7.)

TIP

Are you sick of the same old sound coming out of your amp? Do you wanna really shake things up (and I mean this literally)? Well, put your guitar amp in a tiled bathroom and crank it up. You can put a mic in the bathroom with your amp (a couple feet away) and maybe another one just outside the door (experiment by how much you close or open the door). The effect is, well . . . try it and find out for yourself.

TIP

On most digital recording systems, you can use an effect called an *amp simulator* to give your guitar a variety of sounds. The amp simulator can make your guitar sound like it was played through any number of popular amplifier setups. This can save you the hassle of trying to mic your guitar amp and keep your neighbors happy. Just plug your guitar into the Hi-Z jack in your mixer. If you don't have a Hi-Z jack, you can use a direct box or the line-out jack of your amp (more on this in Chapter 4).

Exploring Electric Bass Miking

When you mic an electric bass, getting a good sound can be a real bear. Your two adversaries are muddiness (lack of definition) and thinness (a pronounced mid-range tone). These seem like almost polar opposite characteristics, but they can both exist at the same time. I outline the best way to avoid these problems in the following sections.

TIP

Running your bass guitar directly into the board — via a direct box, your amp's line-out jack, or a Hi-Z jack on the mixer — gives the guitar a punchier sound. Some recorders have amp-simulator programs for bass guitar as well as guitar. So, don't be afraid to skip the amp and go directly into the mixer. Or if you're bold and have the available tracks, try using both a mic and a direct connection and mix the two mics to taste.

Managing the room

The sound of an electric bass guitar can quickly get muddy. Your best bet is to choose a room that doesn't have a lot of surfaces that reflect sound (for example, paneled walls and wooden floors). A dead room is easier to work with. Don't make your room too dead, however, or it just sucks the life out of your amp's tone. If you can get your amp to sound good in your room, placing the mic properly is easy.

REMEMBER

Don't be afraid to be creative and to try recording your bass in different rooms. Look for a room with a warm sound to it. One thing, though — the bathroom amp trick that I mention earlier in this chapter doesn't work well on bass guitar (but it can be fun to try anyway).

Getting the most from the mic

Because the bass guitar produces low frequencies, a dynamic mic or a large-diaphragm condenser mic works well. I avoid small-diaphragm condensers and ribbon mics for the electric bass, but try them if you want. Who knows — you may end up with an awesome bass track.

Mic placement for the electric bass is similar to the guitar: You place a single mic 2 to 12 inches away from one of the speakers. Sometimes with bass, angling the mic and letting the speaker's sound kind of drift past the diaphragm produces a great sound. For a bass, skip the distant mic, which generally just adds muddiness to the sound.

Miking Acoustic Guitars and Similar Instruments

At the risk of offending banjo, dobro, harp, or ukulele players, I'm lumping all strummed or picked string instruments together. I know, they all sound and play differently, but the microphone placement techniques for all these instruments are similar. Allow me to explain.

Because all these instruments have a resonating chamber, you can pretty much use the same mic placement for any of them. You use different types of mics for different instruments, and I get to that in a minute.

Making the most of the room

Because these are acoustic instruments, the room plays a role in the sound that you end up recording. Unless you have a great-sounding room, you want to minimize its impact on your instrument's sound. You can do this by recording with spot mics or by placing absorber/reflectors in strategic places around your room. Put the absorber side out if the room is too live; put the reflector side out if the room is too dead.

For example, if your home studio resides in a spare bedroom with carpeting and that awful popcorn stuff on the ceiling, you can put a couple of the reflector panels around your guitar player and the mic. This adds some reverberation to your guitar. Any unwanted reflections from the ceiling or walls are shielded from the mics, because the absorber sides of the panels are facing the rest of the room.

Using your mics

I often prefer to use condenser mics when recording acoustic instruments. The type of condenser mic you use depends on the overall tonal quality that you want to capture or accentuate. For example, if a guitar has a nice woody sound that you want to bring out in the recording, a large-diaphragm condenser mic is a good choice. On the other hand, if you're trying to capture the brightness of a banjo, a small-diaphragm mic is a better choice.

You can position your microphone in a variety of ways, and each accents certain aspects of the instrument's sound. Even a slight adjustment to the mic can have a significant impact on the sound. You may have to experiment quite a bit to figure out exactly where to put a mic.

To help with your experimentation, listen to the instrument carefully and move the mic around (in and out, left and right) until you find a spot that sounds particularly good. You need to get your ears close to the instrument to do this.

Here are some suggestions to get you started:

- **Put the mic 6 to 18 inches away from and 3 to 4 inches below the point where the neck meets the body of the instrument.** Then make minor adjustments to the direction in which the mic points. Pointing it toward the sound hole(s) often gives you a richer, deeper tone. (This can translate to muddiness on some instruments.) Turning the mic more toward the neck brings out the instrument's brighter qualities. See the image on the left in Figure 8-6.
- **Place the mic about 3 feet away from the instrument and point it directly at the sound hole.** At this distance, you capture the rich sound from the sound hole and the attack of the strings. See the center image in Figure 8-6.
- **Put the mic about 6 inches out from the bridge of the instrument.** Try pointing the mic in different directions (slight movements of an inch or less can make a huge difference) until you find the spot that sounds best to you. See the image on the right in Figure 8-6.
- **Set up the mic at about the same distance and angle from the instrument as the player's ears.** Point the mic down toward the instrument so that the mic is a couple inches away from either side of the musician's head. This is an unorthodox approach that I like because the player adjusts her playing style and intonation to correspond to what she is hearing when she plays. With this technique, you're trying to capture exactly what the musician hears.

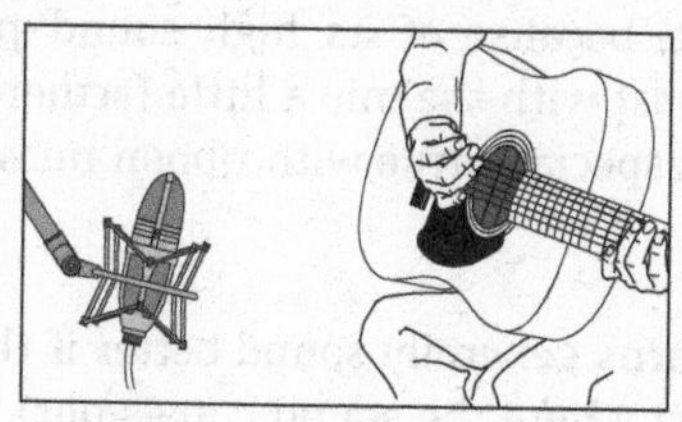
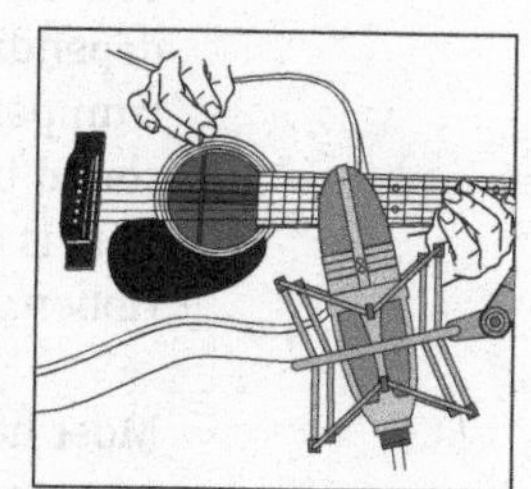

FIGURE 8-6: Positioning the mic in these ways can produce a good acoustic instrument sound.

Maneuvering Horn Mics

There's nothing like the sound of a skilled horn player. Sure, you can use a synthesizer or sampler to play horns, but it's not quite the same. Luckily, horns, such as trumpets, trombones, and saxophones, use similar miking techniques, so if you want to mic horns, you don't have to understand a ton of different techniques.

Understanding the role of the room

Because of the high volume levels of most horns and the fact that you mic them fairly closely, you don't get a ton of impact from the acoustics of the room. Unless your room sounds *really* bad (for example, a small spare bedroom with carpeting and a low ceiling), you can deal with any room sound that bleeds into the mic.

If you have a small room that adds an unwanted sound to the instrument, surround the horn player with acoustic panels; the setup is similar to what I describe in the section "Getting a Great Lead Vocal Sound," earlier in this chapter. You can experiment with using either the reflective or absorptive side of the panels to record the sound that you want. Generally speaking, err on the side of a more dead room — you can always add reverb later.

Making the most of the mics

For most horns, a decent condenser mic — large- or small-diaphragm — works well. If you want a richer tone, a ribbon mic is the way to go. In fact, whenever I mic horns, I pull out a ribbon mic first, and it usually stays out until the session is over.

You can place the mic from 3 inches to a foot or more from the instrument, depending on the instrument and the sound you're looking for. For example, a trumpet, because of its high sound-pressure levels (SPLs, or volume), would sound best with the mic a little farther away than the placement for a tenor sax. This is especially true with ribbon mics, because too much pressure can blow the ribbon.

Most horns generally sound better if the mic is placed just to the side of the *bell* (the part where the sound comes out). This keeps the SPL that the mic picks up low enough to avoid distortion and not blow your precious ribbon. For some of the louder instruments, choose a condenser mic with a high SPL rating and/or a pad switch, or move the mic away from the instrument a bit. (A *pad switch* reduces the amount of sound — usually by 10dB to 20dB — that the mic's internal circuits process, allowing you to have a louder signal without distortion.)

If you want to record more than one horn instrument at a time (a couple of trombones, for instance), you can use a figure-8 condenser mic and position each horn player on either side of the mic. As an alternative, use one or more mics a couple feet away from the players.

Placing Mics for a Piano

If you're lucky enough to have a real piano to record, you'll probably want to record it live rather than use a piano patch on a synthesizer. The following sections give you suggestions on how to effectively mic a piano.

Harnessing the sound of the room

Pianos can be tough to record if your room doesn't sound great. Because of the size of the instrument — especially if it's a grand or a baby grand piano — you need a large room with a high ceiling to get the best sound. If you have an upright piano in a living room, for example, you may find it easier to just record a piano patch (sound) on a decent synthesizer.

If your room doesn't add to the sound of the piano, use a closer mic placement than you would if your room sounded great.

Managing the mics

Condenser mics are a must for recording piano. Either small- or large-diaphragm mics work well. Your mic placement depends largely on the sound you want. Here are a couple of examples:

- **Funky rock or ragtime sound:** Place your mic close in toward the hammers. In this case, I would use two mics — one over the higher register and one over the lower, 6 to 12 inches away from the hammers.
- **Natural classical-type sound:** Move the mics out from the instrument — 2 to 6 feet is usually good, depending on how much room sound you want in the mix. The farther you move the mics outside of the lid, the higher you should place the mics because the sound moves up as it goes out. A good reference is to use the lid as a guide.

REMEMBER

The farther outside the instrument you put the mics, the more room sound you pick up.

TIP

If you don't want to use a traditional condenser mic or if you want to try another approach to piano miking, you can use a boundary mic. A boundary mic is an omnidirectional mic that attaches to the instrument. You can find a decent-sounding boundary mic for about $100 from several microphone manufacturers. I like the Audio Technica PRO44. Just mount the boundary mic to the underside of the piano's lid (consult your mic's manual for details on mounting it) to get the best sound. You can also use two boundary mics — one over the lower register and one over the higher one.

Setting Up Mics for Strings

Stringed instruments — violin and fiddle, viola, cello, and acoustic bass — can be a lot of fun to mic. They have a rich tone and produce an almost unlimited variety of textures. Each instrument has a different tonal spectrum, but because they all have the same basic shape and design (f-holes, strings, bows, and so on), they can all be thought of similarly. You can try any of the techniques that I describe for one of these instruments on the rest of them. For example, try the mic technique from the cello on the fiddle and see what you think. Your options are many, so experiment and use what you like.

Making the most of the room

As with any other acoustic instrument, the room can have profound impacts on the sound that you capture. Unless you have a really nice-sounding room, try to isolate the instrument from the room's sound. In this case, spot miking is the best choice. On the other hand, if you have access to a great-sounding room or concert hall in which to record, by all means add room mics or use a stereo-miking technique.

Making sense of the mics

My favorite type of mic for classical string instruments is a small-diaphragm condenser unit, although on occasion I reach for a large-diaphragm condenser mic. A dynamic mic may produce an interesting effect, but it doesn't capture the most natural sound.

You can place the mic for each of the string instruments as follows:

» **Violin, fiddle, and viola:** These all sound great with a mic placed 1 to 2 feet above and behind the instrument and facing down at the instrument's body.

» **Cello and double bass:** For these instruments, place the mic several feet away from the instrument (between 4 and 8 feet) and point it toward the f-hole in the instrument. This allows you to capture the sound of the entire instrument. The only drawback is that you also get a fair amount of the sound of the room. If you don't want the effects of your room recorded, you can place acoustic panels on either side of the mic.

» **Ensembles:** Ensembles sound best when miked with a stereo pair placed between 8 and 20 feet away. You can use any of the stereo-miking techniques that I describe earlier in this chapter. If you're miking soloists, you may also need to add a spot mic or two for their instruments. If so, follow the recommendations that I provide earlier in this list and watch for phase problems.

Digging into Drum Set Miking

If you're like most musicians, getting great-sounding drums seems like one of the world's great mysteries (you know, along the lines of how the pyramids were built or how to cure cancer). You can hear big, fat drums on great albums but when you try to record your drums, they always end up sounding more like cardboard boxes than drums. Fret not, for I have solutions for you.

First things first: Tuning your drums

The most important part of getting killer drum sounds is to make sure that your drums are tuned properly and that they have good heads on them (okay, those are two important things). Seriously, if you spend time getting the drums to sound good in your room, you're halfway to the drum sound of your dreams. I don't go into detail here, but if you want specific drum-tuning guidance, you can do an Internet search or check out my book *Drums For Dummies*, 2nd Edition (Wiley).

REMEMBER

You're looking for a clear, open tone on your drums. Resist the temptation to apply duct tape or other dampeners to the drumheads. Drums that are deadened and don't ring clearly definitely sound like cardboard boxes when you record them.

After you tune your drums as well as you can, the next step is to take care of rattles that may be coming from the stands or mounting hardware. Tighten any loose hardware and move any stands that may be touching one another. You may need to make small adjustments to the pitches of your drums if they're causing hardware to rattle.

If you still have ringing or unwanted overtones, you can dampen them slightly. Cotton gauze taped lightly on the edge of the head (away from the drummer) is often enough. If you want a real dry sound on your snare drum, you can use the wallet trick: Have the drummer place his wallet on the head — the drumhead, that is. (Use the drummer's wallet because it probably doesn't have any money in it.)

When your drums have been tuned perfectly, you're ready to start placing microphones. You can choose from an unlimited number of miking configurations, only a few of which I can cover here (it would take a whole book to cover them all).

Using the room to your benefit

The room influences the drums' sound more than it influences that of other instruments. If you're looking for a big drum sound, you need a fairly live room (one with lots of reflection).

I know, you're thinking, "But I just have a bedroom for a studio, and it's carpeted." No worries, you can work with that. ***Remember:*** You have a home studio, so you potentially have your whole *home* to work with. Here are a couple ideas to spark your imagination:

- Buy three or four 4-by-8-foot sheets of plywood and lean them against the walls of your room. Also, place one sheet on the floor just in front of the kick drum. The plywood adds reflective surfaces to the room.
- Put the drums in your garage (or living room, or any other room with a reverberating sound) and run long mic cords to your mixer. If you have a SIAB or a laptop computer–based system, you can just throw it under your arm and move everything into your garage or, better yet, take all this stuff to a really great-sounding room and record.
- Set up your drums in a nice-sounding room and place an additional mic just outside the door to catch an additional ambient sound. You can then mix this with the other drum tracks to add a different quality of reverberation to the drums.

Picking up the kick (bass) drum

When recording a kick drum, most recording engineers choose a dynamic mic. In fact, you can find some large-diaphragm dynamic mics specifically designed to record kick drums.

WHAT TYPE OF DRUM SET?

If you want to buy a drum set for your home studio, here are some guidelines that have worked for me:

- **Smaller drums can sound bigger.** At one point, I had two top-notch Gretsch drum sets in my studio. One was a rock kit that had a 24-inch kick; 13-, 14-, and 18-inch tom-toms; and a 6½-inch-deep metal snare drum. The other was a small jazz kit consisting of an 18-inch kick, 10- and 14-inch tom-toms, and a 5-inch deep-wood snare. Guess what? Even for the hardest rock music, the small kit sounded much bigger. You can tune the small drums down a bit and they just sing!
- **Choose your heads wisely.** Not all heads are equal. Some sound great on stage, while others are better suited to the studio. Because the heads that come with a kit are most likely not the ones that sound the best on a recording, invest some money in testing different drumheads on your kit. I prefer either Remo pinstripes (great for rock and R&B) or coated Ambassadors (great for jazz) on the top and either clear or coated Ambassadors (I choose based on aesthetics) on the bottom of the drum.
- **Use cymbals with a fast decay.** Cymbals that sound great on stage are different from those that sound great in the studio. Stage cymbals often have long decays and slow attacks. This causes bleeding, especially through the tom-tom mics, and correcting the problem can be a headache. If you buy cymbals for your studio, choose those that have a very fast attack and a short decay.
- **More expensive isn't always better.** For recording, my favorite drum sets are used kits from the late '60s and early '70s. My all-time favorite recording set is a late-'60s Gretsch jazz drum set with an 18-inch kick drum, a 10-inch mounted tom-tom, and a 14-inch floor tom. For a snare, I love old 5-inch wooden snare drums (for example, Gretsch, Ludwig, or Slingerland). The last one of these sets that I bought cost $350, including all the mounting hardware and the snare drum. It wasn't pretty, but it sure sounded great.

No matter where you place the mic, you can reduce the amount of boominess from the drum by placing a pillow or blanket inside it. Some people choose to let the pillow or blanket touch the inside head. I prefer to keep it a couple inches away from the inside head, but I find it can be beneficial to let it touch the outside head.

That said, you can place your mic in several ways:

» **Near the inside head (see Figure 8-7, left):** If you take off the outside head or cut a hole in it, you can put the mic inside the drum. Place the mic 2 to 3 inches away from the inside head and a couple inches off center. This is the standard way to mic a kick drum if you have the outside head off or if a hole is cut in it. This placement gives you a sharp attack from the beater hitting the head.

- **Halfway inside the drum:** You can modify the preceding miking technique by moving the mic back so that it's about halfway inside the drum. In this case, place the mic right in the middle, pointing where the beater strikes the drum. This placement gives you less of the attack of the beater striking the head and more of the body of the drum's sound.
- **Near the outside head (see Figure 8-7, right):** If you have both heads on the drum, you can place the mic a few inches from the outside head. If you want a more open, boomy sound (and you have the drum's pitch set fairly high), point the mic directly at the center of the head. If you want less boom, offset the mic a little and point it about two-thirds of the way toward the center.

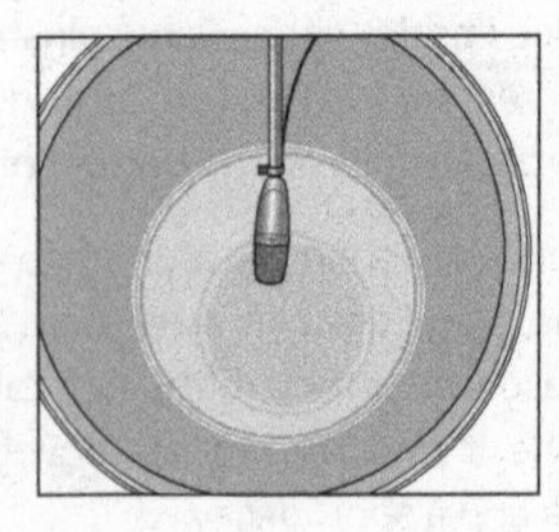

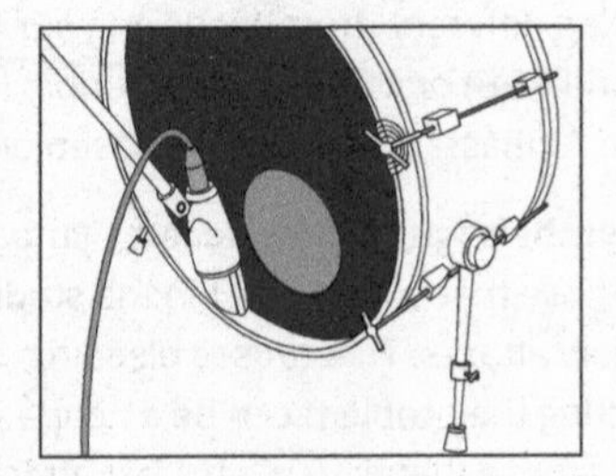

FIGURE 8-7: You can place a mic in several places to get a good kick-drum sound.

TIP

If your drum sounds thin after trying these mic placement approaches, you can try these two things:

- **Tune the drum slightly up.** In your quest for a deep bass tone, you may have tuned the drum too low. (This is especially common if you have a large bass drum.) In this case, the drum's fundamental tone may be too low to be heard clearly. Raising the pitch a bit usually solves the problem.
- **Create a tunnel with acoustic panels.** Putting the mic in the tunnel often helps if you have a room that's too dead. Place two of the panels on their sides (reflective surfaces facing in) with one end of each panel near the outside of the drum. Angle the panels out so that, where they're farthest from the drum set, the distance between them is just under 4 feet. Then lay the other two panels (reflective surface facing down) across the side panels to create a tunnel. You can also place a piece of plywood on the floor under these panels to further increase the resonance. Place the mic halfway into the tunnel, facing the center of the drum.

Setting up the snare drum

The snare drum is probably the most important drum in popular music. The bass guitar can cover the kick drum's rhythm, and the rest of the drums aren't part of the main groove. A good, punchy snare drum can make a track, whereas a weak, thin one can eliminate the drive that most popular music needs.

Because the snare drum is located so close to the other drums, especially the hi-hats, a cardioid-pattern mic is a must. The most common mic for a snare drum is the trusty Shure SM57. The mic is generally placed between the hi-hats and the small tom-tom about 1 or 2 inches from the snare drum head (see Figure 8-8). Point the diaphragm directly at the head. You may need to make minor adjustments to eliminate bleed from the hi-hats. This position gives you a nice punchy sound.

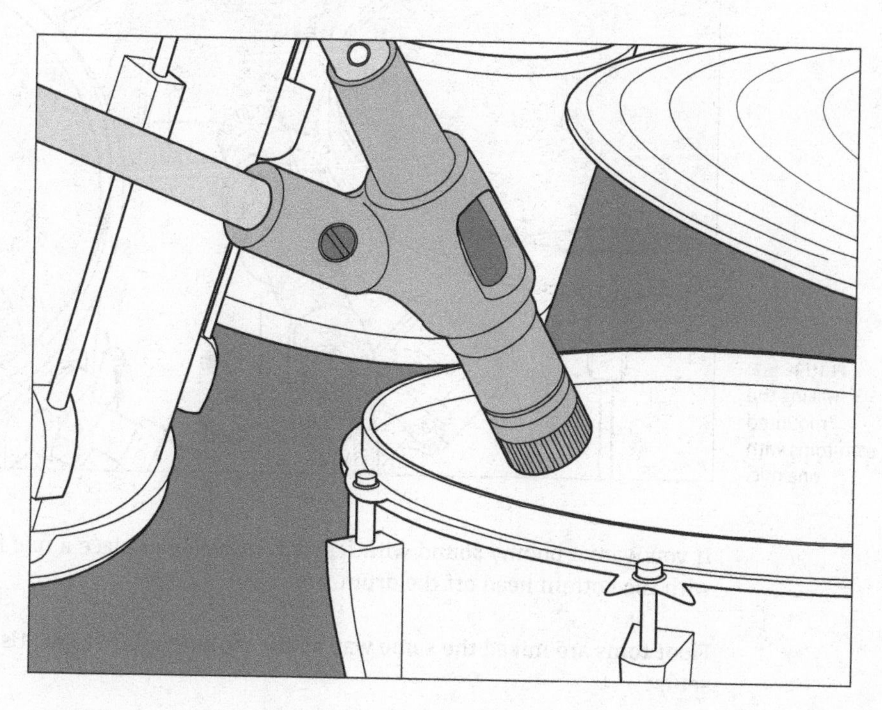

FIGURE 8-8: The proper placement for the snare drum mic.

If you want a crisper tone, you can add a second mic under the drum. Place this mic about an inch or two from the head with the diaphragm pointing at the snares. Make minor adjustments to minimize leakage from the hi-hats.

If you have the available tracks, record each snare mic to a separate track and blend the two later during mixdown. If you don't have the available tracks, blend them until you have the sound you want.

Tackling the tom-toms

The tom-toms sound best when using a dynamic mic. For the mounted toms (the ones above the kick drum), you can use one or two mics. If you use one mic, place it between the two drums about 4 to 6 inches away from the heads. (Figure 8-9 shows this placement option.) If you use two mics, place one above each drum, 1 to 3 inches above the head.

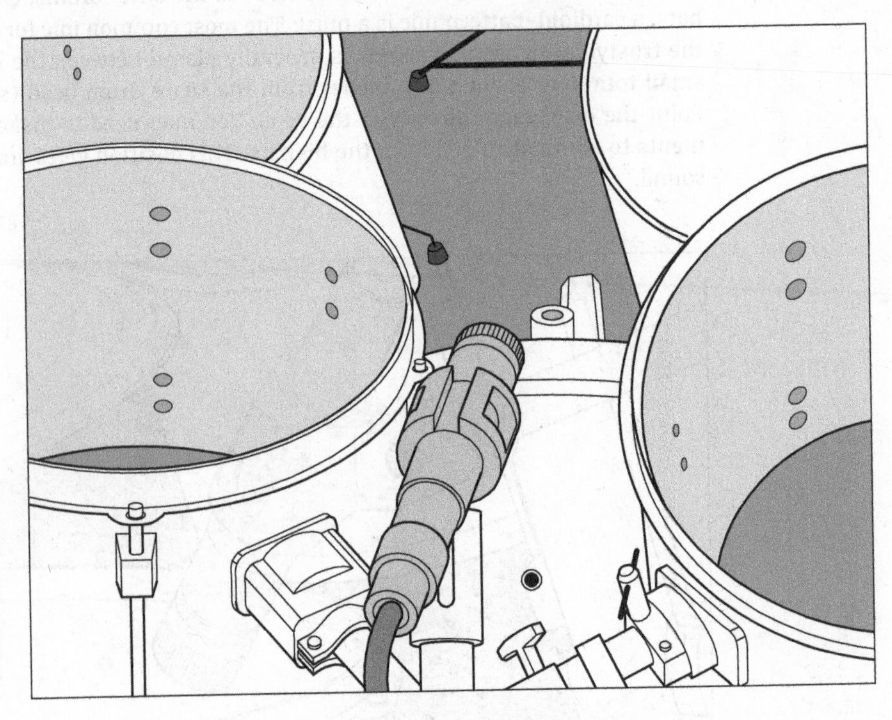

FIGURE 8-9: Miking the mounted tom-toms with one mic.

If you want a boomy sound with less attack, you can place a mic inside the shell with the bottom head off the drum.

Floor toms are miked the same way as the mounted tom-toms. Use the following setup:

- Place a single mic a couple inches away from the head near the rim.
- If you have more than one floor tom, you can place one mic between them or mic them individually.

If you want to apply compression to the tom-toms, start with the settings that I list for the snare drum in the preceding section.

Handling the hi-hats

The hi-hats are generally part of the main groove, and as such, you want to spend time getting a good sound. You may have problems with a few other mics on the drum set picking up the hi-hats, particularly the snare drum mic and overhead mics. Some people don't bother miking the hi-hats for this reason.

I like to mic hi-hats because, to me, these cymbals often sound too trashy through the snare drum mic. If you mic hi-hats, make sure that the snare drum mic is picking up as little of the hi-hats as possible by placing the mic properly and/or using a *noise gate* (a dynamic processor used to filter unwanted noise).

You can use either a dynamic mic or, better yet, a small-diaphragm condenser mic for the hi-hats. The dynamic mic gives you a trashier sound, and the small-diaphragm condenser mic produces a bright sound. You can work with either by adjusting the equalization (EQ). I usually add just a little bit (4dB or so) of a shelf EQ set at 10 kHz to add a little sheen to the hi-hats.

Place the mic 3 to 4 inches above the hi-hats and point it downward. The exact placement of the mic is less important than the placement of the other instrument mics because of the hi-hats' tone. Just make sure that your mic isn't so close that it hits the instrument.

Creating the best cymbal sound

You want to know one secret to the huge drum sound of Led Zeppelin's drummer, John Bonham? Finesse. He understood that the drums sound louder and bigger in a mix if the cymbals are quieter in comparison. (I'm guessing this is true, because I never really talked to him about this.) So, he played his cymbals softly and hit the drums pretty hard. This allowed the engineer to raise the levels of the drums without having the cymbals drown everything else out. Absolutely brilliant.

Because having the drums bleed into the overhead mics is inevitable and the overhead mics are responsible for providing much of the drums' presence in a mix, playing the cymbals softly allows you to get more of the drums in these mics. This helps the drums sound bigger.

TIP

Ask (no, demand) that your drummer play the cymbals quieter. Also, use smaller cymbals with a fast attack and a short decay. Doing these things creates a better balance between the drums and cymbals and makes the drums stand out more in comparison.

Small-diaphragm condenser mics capture the cymbals' high frequencies well, though many digital recordists like the way a ribbon mic mellows the cymbals. You can mic the cymbals by placing mics 12 to 18 inches above each cymbal or by using overhead mics set 1 to 3 feet above the cymbals (see the next section).

Miking the whole kit

Most of the time, you want to have at least one (but preferably two) ambient mics on the drums, if for no other reason than to pick up the cymbals. Assuming that you use two mics, they're called *overhead mics,* and as the name implies, they're placed above the drum set. The most common types of mics to use for overheads are large- and small-diaphragm condenser mics because they pick up the high frequencies in the cymbals and give the drum set's sound a nice *sheen* (brightness). You may also want to try a pair of ribbon mics to pick up a nice, sweet sound on the overheads.

To mic the drum set with overhead mics, you can use either the X-Y coincident technique or spaced stereo pairs. Place them 1 to 2 feet above the cymbals, just forward of the drummer's head. Place X-Y mics in the center, and set up spaced stereo pairs so that they follow the 3:1 rule (for example, the mics should be set 3 to 6 feet apart if they're 1 to 2 feet above the cymbals). This counters any phase problems. Point the mic down toward the drums, and you're ready to record. Figure 8-10 shows both of these setups.

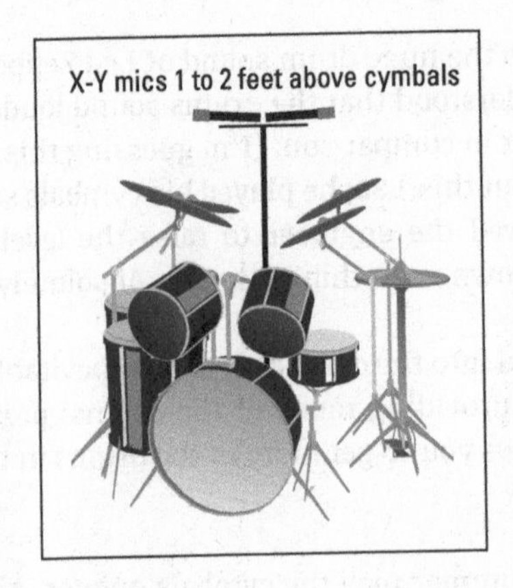

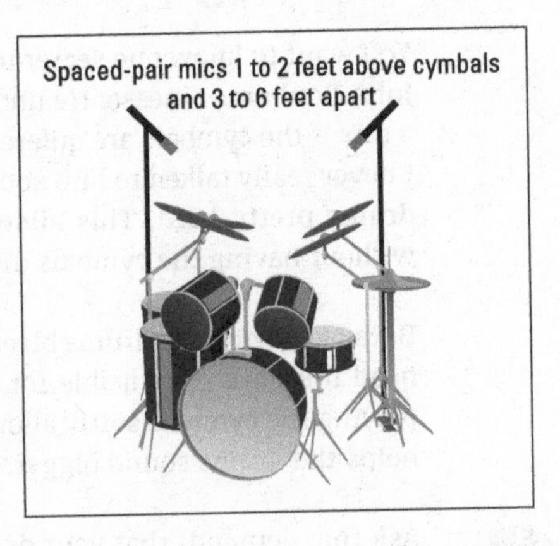

FIGURE 8-10: Overhead mics capture the cymbals and the drums.

Getting Your Hands on Hand Drums

Hand drums can be anything from the familiar conga to unusual drums, such as the North African tar. Because you may encounter many types of hand drums, this section gives you general guidelines when recording any hand drum.

Your selection in mics depends on the type of drum and its tonal characteristics. For example, conga drums occupy the middle of the frequency spectrum and produce a loud sound that a large-diaphragm condenser mic can capture well. Or, if you want a tighter, drier sound, you can use a dynamic mic. If you choose the dynamic mic, the mic colors the sound of your recording.

If you want to record any of the smaller, higher-pitched hand drums, use either a large- or small-diaphragm condenser mic and skip the dynamic mic altogether.

Mic placement also varies considerably among the various hand drums. Listen to the sound of the drum, and find a place where you like what you hear. For the most part, placing the mic 1 to 3 feet from the drum creates the fullest sound. If you want a lot of attack, you can place the mic closer. You lose some of the drum's depth, however, when you place the mic closer than a foot.

Perfecting Percussion Miking

Miscellaneous percussion instruments, such as shakers and triangles, are nice additions to many styles of music. These instruments sound best with a good condenser mic. I choose a large- or small-diaphragm mic, depending on the characteristics that I want to pick up. For instance, a shaker can sound great with a large-diaphragm mic because this mic slightly brings out the lower frequencies of the instrument and softens the overall sound a bit.

Exploring the impact of the room

Most of the time, the room doesn't have a huge impact on percussion instruments because you mic them closely. If your room does get in the way, use the acoustic panels in much the same way that I suggest for vocals earlier in this chapter in the "Getting a Great Lead Vocal Sound" section (partially surround the mic and musician with baffles).

Choosing and using the mics

Both large- and small-diaphragm mics work well for percussion. When recording percussion instruments, the main thing to remember is that they can have a high SPL, so you may need to pad the mic, move it back, or turn it sideways from the sound source.

I like to put a single mic 6 to 36 inches away from percussion instruments, depending on the size of the instrument and how much room I want in the sound. For example, because maracas are loud, I put the mic back a bit (18 inches), whereas with an egg shaker, I find that 6 to 8 inches often sounds best. But when I record an agogô bell or an Afuche, I like to have a little room in the mix to give the instrument more depth. In this case, I mic from a couple feet away.

3 Recording Live Audio

IN THIS PART . . .

Get started recording your music.

Record audio tracks, from the first track to overdubs, to punching in and out.

Record MIDI sequences and understand this often-misunderstood technology.

Record guitars, basses, and acoustic instruments with electronic pickups.

Record and edit loops.

IN THIS CHAPTER

» Setting levels properly

» Making your guitar sound great

» Getting the best sound from your keyboards

» Keeping your microphones from overloading your system

Chapter 9

Getting a Great Source Sound

The quality of your recording relies heavily on two things: how your instruments sound and how well you get that sound into your computer without messing it up. The problem is that anyone can easily mess up the sound or at least fall short of getting the best possible sound.

This chapter gives you the knowledge to keep bad sound — or sound that's not as good as it could be — from happening. In this chapter, I describe signal flow and the role it plays in shaping the sound of your instrument. I also give you tips on how to get great guitar sounds and killer keyboard sounds without hassle. To top it off, I spend a few pages getting you up to speed on miking effectively.

Making Sense of the Signal Chain

The *signal chain* is the path that your sound travels from its creation (your guitar, keyboard, or voice) to your recorder. This path often includes several steps — and pieces of gear — that need to be optimized so that you don't end up with too much or too little sound going to your system. I cover the flow of various signal chains in detail in Chapter 4, but here's an overview of the process. Figure 9-1 shows the straightforward signal chain for a mic going into a studio-in-a-box (SIAB) recorder.

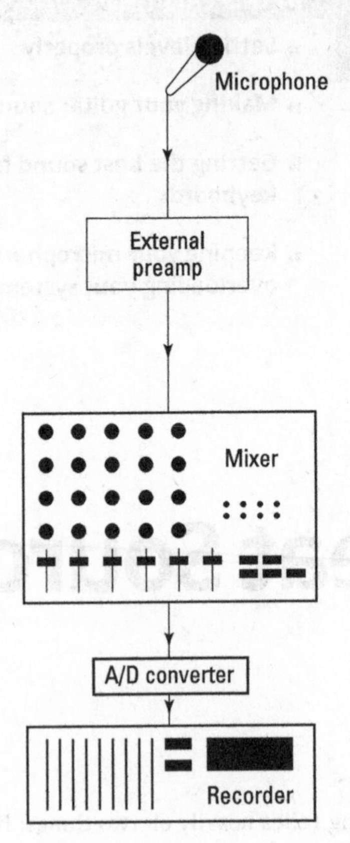

FIGURE 9-1: The signal chain is the sound-data highway.

In this example, the sound originating from your voice enters the microphone, travels to a preamp-equipped input in your device (where it's amplified), is converted into digital information by the device's analog to digital converter, and finally gets sent into the recording software section of your recorder and the hard drive (where it's stored).

The key to a good instrument or mic sound is getting each signal in the chain set to its optimal level. This particular signal chain involves just two places where you can make adjustments to your signal levels:

- **The source:** In the example shown in Figure 9-1, the microphone's placement has a huge effect on the signal level that goes into your computer. Moving the mic just a couple inches can have a significant impact on your signal level at the preamp. A good, solid level keeps you from having to crank up your preamp too far, which causes noise. If the level is too hot, though — *hot* in the sense of a solid signal between –12dB and –6dB — you risk getting distortion at the mic. This same concept holds true for keyboards or other electronic instruments, as well as guitars plugged directly into your interface.

» **The preamp-equipped input:** You adjust this level to get the right level in your recorder. I discuss the optimal signal level for different systems in the next section.

Setting Optimal Signal Levels

Getting a sound signal to the recorder takes several steps. The path that the sound takes from the instrument or microphone to the recorder is called the *signal chain* (see the previous section). You need to be aware of the signal level at all these steps to get the best sound possible. Too much gain at one stage forces you to reduce the gain at another. Likewise, too little gain at one point may require you to bump up the gain during the next stage.

Incorrect gain structuring results in a signal that's too low (which creates noise) or a signal that's too high (which causes distortion). In fact, with poor gain structuring, you can have a signal that is too quiet.

How you set the levels that you record to disk has a lot to do with how good (or bad) your performance sounds. The key to getting good recording levels is to get as hot (high) a signal as you can without going over the maximum that the converter or recorder can handle. If you use analog tape, you have some leeway in how hot your signal can get, but if you record digitally, you don't have that luxury. Anything over the baseline of 0dB is going to *clip* (distort). 0dB, by the way, doesn't mean "no sound." Instead, it refers to the highest level that a digital system can handle without clipping the signal.

How hot is hot enough, you ask? Well, it depends on who you talk to and at what bit depth you record. Because you're reading my book, here's my take on the best levels at which to record:

» **16-bit systems:** By this point in the book (assuming that you've read other sections on digital recording), you know that I'm not a fan of 16-bit recording. This is because to record with enough headroom, you need to turn the incoming level down so much that you start to lose sound quality; that is, you're using fewer than 16 bits and lowering the resolution of your system. In this case, I usually recommend setting your level higher in a 16-bit system than in a 24-bit system — usually with peaks no higher than –6dB. This allows some room for transients (check out the section "Making the Most of Microphones," later in this chapter) while preserving as much resolution as possible.

» **24-bit systems:** Because plenty of bits are available, you have more wiggle room before you start to lose sound quality. For 24-bit systems, I suggest that you record with your peak level at or below –12dB. This gives you enough room for transients to sneak through without clipping your system.

THE STRAIGHT-LINE RULE

Most professional engineers are taught to record by using the *straight-line rule.* This rule comes from the old days of analog recording. Following this rule is considered not only good engineering practice, but also a courtesy to any other engineer who may handle your tracks.

The straight-line rule basically involves setting up your input levels so that they roughly match the levels that you want when you mix the song. You do this by setting your channel fader at 0dB (also marked as Unity on some mixers) and adjusting your input gain (the trim knob on your mixer or preamp) until you have a clean signal (no distortion) on the recorder's meters. The signal's level needs to be approximately the same as the level of the instrument in the final mix. For some instruments, such as a snare drum, the level peaks close to 0dB, but on other instruments, such as the string section, the level may be near –10dB. If you follow the straight-line rule, when you're ready to mix your tracks, set all your faders at 0dB — and you'll have a rough mix.

The courtesy is that if someone then takes your recorded tracks to another system with another engineer, that engineer only has to set the faders at 0dB and everything is ready for final adjustments.

When you set your recording levels (do this by playing a section of your song), keep the following points in mind:

- **Keep an eye on the clip light on your preamp/input.** Not all inputs have a clip light, but if yours does, it's most likely located next to the trim knob. Sending too hot a signal through your preamp/input is the first way you can create distortion. Your clip light should illuminate only faintly once in a while, if at all. If your clip light is glowing red, your signal is way too hot and you may end up with distortion. (Check the owner's manual for your preamp to see when the clip light is set to activate. Some clip lights are set to go off at –6dB, others illuminate at –3dB, and still others light at 0dB.)
- **Use the meters as a guide.** Both your mixer and recorder have meters that show you the level of the signal going in. Both of these levels are important, so keep an eye on them. Make sure the meters never go above 0dB and that they peak at a maximum of –12dB to –6dB. Also, be aware of whether you're monitoring pre or post levels, which I discuss in the next section.
- **Trust your ears.** Even with the clip light and meters, you still need to listen carefully to the signal. Many of the level meters on digital recorders are fairly slow to respond and can often miss sudden, extreme transients. If you hear

any clipping or occasional harshness in the sound, turn down the level, regardless of what your meters tell you.

- **When in doubt, turn down the level.** If you can't tell whether the sound is clean, don't be afraid to turn down the level a little. Recording at –16dB instead of –12dB isn't going to ruin your track, but a clipped note can.

Understanding Pre and Post Levels

Most digital systems provide several options for monitoring meter levels. You can have prefader input levels, postfader input levels, prefader track levels, postfader track levels, and master bus levels (see Figure 9-2). Even with the same signal, different kinds of levels (prefader, postfader, input, track master bus, and so on) may end up showing different readings on your meters.

Interpreting the various levels

I try to clear up what all these different levels mean in the following list:

- **Prefader input levels:** The prefader input level shows you the level of the signal going into the mixer's channel strip before the signal hits the equalizer or fader (hence, the term *prefader*). Your sound source and trim adjustment (either on the mixer or on a separate preamp) control the level shown on this meter.

  If your signal is too low or too hot and you don't have a separate preamp, adjust the trim knob on your mixer. If you're using a separate preamp, adjust the trim knob on your outboard preamp. You can also make adjustments to this level at the sound source. This could be either the output level of your instrument or the placement of your microphone.

- **Postfader input levels:** The postfader input level shows your signal level after the signal has traveled through the input channel's channel strip — that is, after the equalization (EQ) and fader settings.

  This level is different from the prefader input level only if your fader is somewhere other than unity gain (or 0dB) or if you've made some adjustments to the EQ. To be specific, if you've removed any frequencies with the equalizer or set your fader below 0dB, your postfader level is lower than the prefader level. Likewise, if you've added frequencies with the equalizer or placed your fader above unity, your level is higher than it was going in.

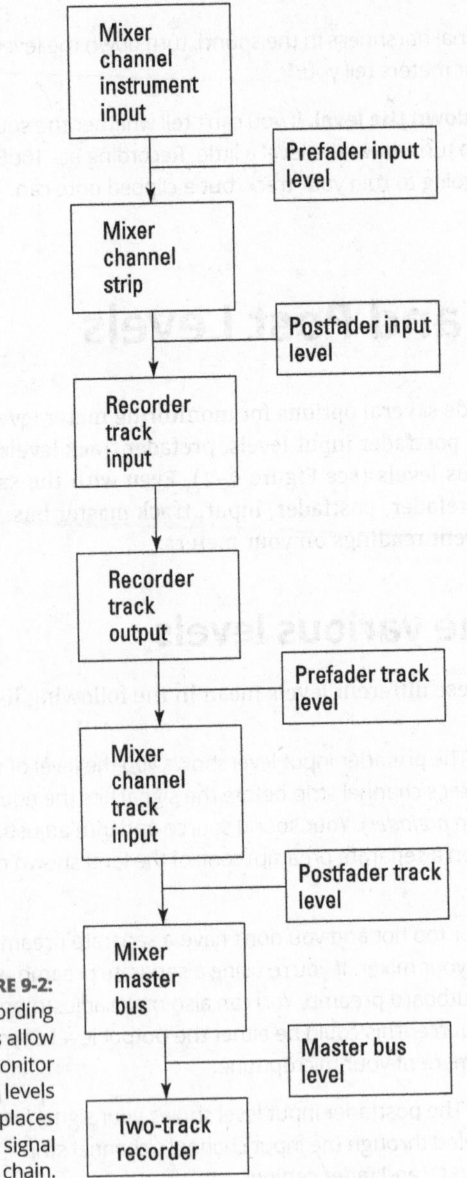

FIGURE 9-2: Most recording systems allow you to monitor your signal levels at various places in the signal chain.

TIP

» **Prefader track levels:** This is the most important level of your input signal chain (that is, if a most important level exists). This meter shows you what is actually recorded to the hard drive of the recorder.

If you're using an analog mixer and a stand-alone recorder, you see this level on the recorder, not the mixer.

This level matches the level of the postfader input channel routed to the recorder channel. If you have more than one input channel routed to a recorder track, this level is generally higher than each of the individual input postfader levels. This is because the signals combine to produce a higher overall level (called *summing*). If this is the case and the prefader track level is too high, you need to adjust the levels on all the tracks that are routed to this channel to drop the level coming in (the submix fader level, if you have these tracks run through the submix bus).

» **Postfader track levels:** The postfader track level shows you the level after you make adjustments to the track channel's fader or EQ settings. Like the postfader input level, the postfader track level is different from the prefader track level if you've made adjustments to either the EQ or the channel fader settings.

» **Master bus levels:** The master bus level shows you the sum of all the levels being routed to the master bus. Unless you have only one channel going to the master bus, this level is different from any of the individual levels going to it because all levels from all the instruments are taken into account (summed). This is the level that is most important when you're mixing because this is the level that the two-track master records.

REMEMBER

Not all types of systems have all these level-monitoring options. For example, if you have an analog mixer, you may not have meters on anything except the recorder (prefader track level) and the master bus (master bus level).

Looking at examples

You can use the various monitoring sources to find out where in your signal chain you may be introducing distortion or where you need to boost the signal. If you find the source of the signal problem, you don't have to overcompensate at a different part of the signal path. For example, perhaps you connect a microphone to an external preamp and set the trim on the preamp for a good, hot signal. The prefader track level going to the recorder, however, is too low. In this case, you can check the postfader input level to see whether something is squashing your signal. The fader may be set too low, or some EQ may be set to reduce some frequencies. To fix the problem, you can either raise the fader or adjust your EQ until your level at the prefader track meter is where you want it to be.

Another scenario is when your recorded track has even levels (as seen on the prefader track level) but you're getting distortion at the master bus (master bus level). In this case, check the postfader track level to see whether it looks different from the prefader level. It most likely will, and you can fix the problem by adjusting either the fader or the EQ until the level is tamed. If both the prefader and postfader track levels look the same, the combined levels that come from more than one track to the master bus are probably causing the distortion. In this case, you need to reduce the levels from all the tracks going to the master bus to bring the master bus level down a bit.

REMEMBER

Don't get too stressed about your levels. Use your ears and trust yourself. If you get noticeable digital clipping (distortion), just record the part again. One of the great things about digital recording is that you can erase and re-record a performance as many times as you want without compromising sound quality.

Getting Great Guitar, Bass, and Electronic String Instrument Sounds

Guitars, electric basses, and acoustic guitars (or any other instrument) with an electronic pickup can be recorded into your digital audio workstation (DAW) without having to mic your amp. This section lays out the process and offers some options for getting the best sound out of your tracks.

Connect directly

Guitars and other instruments with electronic pickups produce what is called a high-impedance (Hi-Z) signal. This signal is lower in voltage than those from keyboards or other instruments. Because of this, you need to boost the signal as you send it to your digital recorder or audio interface. You can do this in several ways:

- **Use the Hi-Z or instrument jack.** If your device has one, it will be a ¼-inch jack marked "Hi-Z." There may also be a gain knob to allow you to adjust the level of your instrument. Plug in here and adjust the level until you get a good signal.
- **Plug into the Combo jack.** A combo jack is able to receive either a microphone XLR cable or ¼-inch cord. This input runs through a preamp, which will boost your signal high enough for the recorder to handle.
- **Plug your guitar into your amp and run a cord from the line out of your amp to an instrument input in your recorded or audio interface.** The line output of an amp sends a line-level signal that doesn't need to be boosted.

» **Use a direct induction (DI) box.** A DI box will optimize the signal so that you can plug your guitar into one of the instrument inputs of your recorder or audio interface.

Many audio interfaces can handle a guitar without a DI box level-adjustment when plugged into an instrument input. Check your owner's manual to see if your device can do this.

TIP

You may not like the sound when you connect your guitar directly to your recorder — in fact, I'll bet you won't. The solution to this unfortunate state of affairs is to use a plug-in (or more than one) in your recording program to get the sound you want. This is a common way to get a guitar sound, and tons of good plug-ins can help, including plug-ins for providing distortion, delay, chorus, and even special amp simulators that are designed to sound like popular guitar amplifiers. One advantage to this approach is that you can tweak the sound of your guitar as much as you want after it's recorded.

I recommend applying some of these when you record but don't apply them to the track. This way you'll hear a decent tone, but won't be committed to it, leaving you plenty of options later during the mix process.

Process beforehand

If you are like most guitarists (or a string instrument-with-a-pickup player) you probably have a few (or more) effects pedals that you've come to rely on for your signature sound. You can use these to record your tracks. As you may expect, all you need to do is connect your guitar to your pedals and, connect your last pedal into your interface or recorder input. For the best sound, follow the advice I offer for connecting your guitar directly in the previous section.

Your recorded track will contain all the effects your pedals added to your sound. If you want to have a clean guitar sound, skip the pedals and add the effects later in the DAW.

TIP

If you want to record using your pedal but also have a clean, unaffected track to work with, you can split your guitar signal and send one through the pedals and connect the other directly to your device. To do this you will need a way to split the signal. The easiest way to do this is with a DI box, as most boxes allow you to send two signals out of the device. However, you will need two available inputs in your recorder or audio interface to make this happen.

Leverage your amp

You can use the guitar amp you've come to love the sound of in a couple of different ways beyond simply miking the speaker, such as:

- **From your guitar into your amp and from your amp's line output to your instrument input:** Recording a guitar this way is great for people who have an amp that they like the sound of but who don't want to mic a speaker. When you follow this approach, you have three volume controls to adjust to get your level into your recorder — your guitar, your amp, and your interface. You may have to take time tweaking these settings to achieve the best possible sound.
- **From your guitar into your amp with a mic picking up the speaker's sound:** This is the old standby approach because you get to record the actual sound you're used to hearing coming out of your amp. With this method, having the right mic and mic placement makes all the difference in the world. I offer some specific guitar-amping mic techniques in Chapter 8.

There is no single way to get a great guitar sound. Don't be afraid to experiment. You may just come up with a sound that really moves you.

Creating Killer Keyboard Tracks

If you have an external keyboard that contains the sounds you want to record, plug an instrument cord from the main outputs of your keyboard to the corresponding number of inputs in your system. Turn your keyboard volume up between ½ and ¾ or until you get a decent signal to register in your recorder. If your instrument input has a volume (gain) control, adjust it and the volume of your keyboard until you get a solid sound without distortion.

For the most flexibility with your sound, I recommend simultaneously recording your performance data to your computer using your keyboard's Musical Instrument Digital Interface (MIDI) ports (as long as it has MIDI ports — some old analog synths don't). If you have a MIDI-capable keyboard and a MIDI sequencer, you can record your musical performance as MIDI data and assign the sound later. In this case, connect your keyboard to your MIDI sequencer. This can be done using a MIDI cable connected to MIDI ports in each device, or it can be done with a USB connection if you have a USB-equipped keyboard and MIDI sequencer (such as a software program in a computer). Chapter 11 explains how to make the connections for this.

Because you're recording MIDI data instead of an audio signal, you don't need to worry about setting the record level. Chapter 12 explains the process of recording MIDI sequences in detail.

Recording E-Drums, Drum Machines, and Electronic Percussion

Drum machines, beat boxes, and electronic drums and percussion are basically the same to record as keyboards — they produce line-level signals that let you plug them directly into any audio interface input.

The difference between keyboards and drums for most recording is in how many outputs of the device you use. Keyboards often have two outputs so that you can record in stereo, but electronic drums often have as many as eight. For example, Roland V-Drums have six individual outputs and two stereo outputs. With this array, here is how I would assign these outputs:

Output 1: Kick drum

Output 2: Snare drum

Output 3: Hi-hat

Output 4: Toms

Output 5: Ride cymbal

Output 6: Crash cymbals

Stereo outputs: If it's possible to use these in addition to the other six outputs, I'd either arrange the entire kit in a stereo spread or assign a stereo mix of any additional percussion I plan to use.

This setup would allow you to edit and mix the drums in the most flexible way possible. If you have fewer outputs, you will need to make some compromises in this flexibility. If I only had four outputs, this is what I'd do:

Output 1: Kick drum

Output 2: Snare drum

Output 3: Hi-hat and ride cymbal. Because most these contain a similar equalization profile, you can mix them together. For more mix flexibility, you can do the copy and separate trick I list next for toms and crashes.

Output 4: Tom and crash cymbals. Once recorded, copy the track and edit out the toms on one and the crashes on the other. This essentially gives you separate tracks to equalize and mix.

Like with keyboards, if your electronic drums have MIDI outputs (most do), you can also record the MIDI data to give you more options when you mix. Chapter 12 covers this process.

Making the Most of Microphones

Finding a great sound from a mic is key to getting a great-sounding recording. To do this, you need to use the best mic for the application and place it where it can sound its best. This requires not only knowledge of the different types of mics (see Chapter 6), but also an understanding of how these mics are used for a variety of instruments (see Chapter 8). In the following sections, I give you a quick tutorial on setting optimal levels of your microphones to help you get the most out of the mics and techniques I present in the other miking chapters.

The most difficult part of getting a good sound by using a microphone is dealing with sudden, extreme increases in the sound signal. These blips are called *transients,* and they regularly happen when a drum is first struck, when a vocalist sings certain syllables (for example, those that begin with a *P*), and when a guitar player picks certain notes. In fact, because you can't always control the amount of force that you apply to an instrument, transients can happen at any time, with any instrument, and without warning. (Highly trained musicians produce fewer extreme transients because they have a greater mastery over their muscular movements.)

In digital recording, all it takes is one slight, unexpected note to cause clipping and distortion, ruining what may otherwise be a perfect musical performance. Believe me, nothing is so heart-wrenching as listening to the perfect take (recorded performance) and hearing the unmistakable sound of digital distortion. Although you can't eliminate transients (they are part of an instrument's character), you can tame extreme transients that often cause clipping. You can do this in the following three ways:

» **Set your levels with enough headroom to handle these transients.** I cover this step in the section "Setting Optimal Signal Levels," earlier in this chapter.

» **Minimize transients with proper mic placement.** I explain this process in the next section.

» **Run the signal through a compressor when recording.** The section "Compressing carefully," later in this chapter, gives you the lowdown on this process.

Placing mics properly

A microphone that's placed too close to a loud sound source or pointed too directly toward the point of attack can easily pick up extreme transients. In most cases, you just need to pull the mic away from the instrument a little or turn it ever so slightly to avoid a signal that's too high. I don't go into detail here because I cover mic placement thoroughly in Chapter 8.

REMEMBER

The main thing to keep in mind when placing your microphones is to experiment. Don't be afraid to spend time making small adjustments. After all, the track you save could be your own.

Compressing carefully

Compressors are processors that allow you to control the dynamics of a signal — and boy, are they ever versatile. You can use compressors on the front end while tracking (recording) instruments to make sure that you don't have stray transients. You can use them to level off an erratic performance. And you can use compressors to raise the overall apparent level of a mixed song. In the following sections, I discuss the first use of compression: the control of transients. (You can find out about the other ways to use compression in Chapter 18.)

TIP

If you have an SIAB system or a computer-based system, you probably have a compressor included with the effects in the unit. Although you can record tracks with this compressor, your signal has to go through the analog/digital (A/D) converter first. (The A/D converter changes your signal from analog to digital form.) Because these systems are digital, the A/D converter is the first in line after the preamp. This often defeats the purpose of using a compressor to control transients because the A/D converter is where you often get your first dose of distortion. If you're serious about using compression on the front end to tame transients, you may want to insert an external compressor into the signal chain before the A/D converter.

Getting to know compressor parameters

Compressors have a series of dials that allow you to adjust several parameters. They are as follows:

- **Threshold:** The threshold setting dictates the level that the compressor starts to act on the signal. This is listed in decibels (dB). For the most part, you set the threshold level so that the compressor acts only on the highest peaks of the signal.
- **Ratio:** The ratio is the amount that the compressor affects the signal. The ratio — such as 2:1, for instance — means that for every decibel that the signal goes over the threshold setting, it is reduced by two decibels. In other words, if a signal goes 1dB over the threshold setting, its output from the compressor will only be ½dB louder. The ratio is the one parameter that varies considerably from instrument to instrument because the level of the transient varies.
- **Attack:** The attack knob controls how soon the compressor starts, well, compressing. The attack is defined in milliseconds (ms), and the lower the number, the faster the attack. For the most part, you're trying to control transients, and they happen at the beginning of a note. Therefore, you set the attack to act quickly.
- **Release:** The release parameter controls how long the compressor continues affecting the note after the note starts. Like the attack, the release is defined in milliseconds. Because transients don't last for very long, you usually use a short release time when using compression on the front end.
- **Gain:** The gain knob allows you to adjust the level of the signal coming out of the compressor. This is listed in decibels. Because adding compression generally reduces the overall level of the sound, you use this control to raise the level back to where it was going in.
- **Hard knee or soft knee:** Most compressors give you the option of choosing between a hard knee and a soft knee (or they do it for you based on the setting that you've chosen). *Hard knee* and *soft knee* each refer to how the compressor behaves as the input signal passes the threshold. More detailed descriptions are as follows:
  - **Hard knee** applies the compression at an even rate, regardless of the level present over the threshold. So, if you choose a compression setting of 4:1, the compressor applies this ratio for any signal over the threshold limit. Hard-knee compression is used for instruments like drums, where you need to quickly clamp down on transients.

* **Soft knee** applies the compression at a varying rate depending on the amount the signal is over the threshold setting. The compressor gradually increases the ratio of the compression as the signal crosses the threshold, until it hits the level that you set. Soft-knee compression is used on vocals and other instruments where the signal doesn't have fast peaks.

Creating compressor settings

When you use a compressor to keep transients at bay, you only want to compress the highest transient levels — the ones that would overload your system or eat up your headroom — and you want to do this so that you don't hear the compressor kicking in. Even though every instrument contains different levels of transient signals and each person who plays an instrument creates different amounts of extreme transients when he or she plays, keep the following points in mind as you choose your settings:

- **Keep the threshold high.** With a high threshold setting, your compressor only kicks in as the signal gets close to distorting. For most instruments, I would use a setting of about –6dB. Some instruments with very high transients, such as percussion and drums, can handle a setting like –10dB. Set your threshold so that when the extreme transient happens, it triggers the compressor only a couple of decibels, and the nontransient material (the main sound of the instrument) doesn't trigger the compressor.
- **Adjust the ratio to the material.** For high-transient material (such as drums and percussion), choose a higher ratio, and for lower-transient material (like strummed or bowed string instruments), choose a lower ratio setting. Try to use a ratio that relates to the level of the transient over the nontransient signal. Because percussion instruments have initial signal peaks (transients) that are much stronger than the body of the instrument's sound, you can compress this peak without affecting the main sound of the instrument. By matching the ratio to the degree of the transient this way, you can create a more even level without changing the sound characteristics of the instrument.
- **Use a short attack.** Transients happen at the initial attack of the instrument. This means that if you want to compress the transient, the compressor must kick in right away when this signal happens. A setting of 1 millisecond or less is optimal.
- **Use a short release.** Transients happen quickly, and they last a very short amount of time. When you try to control these signals during tracking, you only want to catch the transient itself — and no other part of the instrument's sound. Setting a short release time — start with about 10 milliseconds — ensures that your compressor doesn't linger on to affect the body of the instrument's recorded sound.

» **Don't mess with the gain.** Because you're only catching the highest transient signals and you're only compressing them a tiny bit, you don't need to add or reduce any of the signal that's going through the compressor. Leave the gain control at 0dB.

REMEMBER

When using a compressor during tracking, keep the following two points in mind:

» **You can always add compression to a recorded track, but you can never take it away.** If you're not sure how much compression to apply to a particular situation, you're much better off erring on the side of too little because you can always run the sound through another compressor later.

» **If you can hear a change in the sound of your signal, you probably have the compressor set too high.** The reason that you use a compressor on the front end is to eliminate extreme transients, which you can't hear when you play. If your compression setting changes the sound, you should slightly reduce the compression setting (unless you're going for that effect). I talk more about the effects compressors can make in Chapter 18.

IN THIS CHAPTER

» Recording your first track

» Punching in and out

» Exploring overdubbing

» Recording a submix

» Using a bounce to consolidate tracks

» Keeping your tracks organized

Chapter 10
Recording Audio

Okay, you've plugged in your instrument, set up your routing the way you want it, gotten the levels just so, and chosen what you want to hear while you play. Congratulations, you're ready to record. Now the fun begins!

In this chapter, I walk you through the process of recording tracks for your song. You start with your first take, move on to overdubbing by adding more tracks, and punch in and out to redo some parts. You also explore the process of submixing to record multiple instruments into just a couple of tracks.

Performing Your First Take

Your palms are sweaty, your pulse rate is up, and your hands are shaking as you get ready to press the Record button. I know the feeling; I've been recording for over 35 years and I still get a little tense when the tape, er, disk starts to roll. There's something about knowing that what you're about to play is for keeps (or at least could be).

Relax. Take a deep breath and remember that you're both the artist and the producer. You can take as many "takes" as it takes you to get a good "take." (Sorry, I couldn't help myself. A *take*, by the way, is an attempt at a performance.) Anyway, it's normal to get a little nervous when you know the recorder is capturing every sound that you make.

To do your first take, follow these steps (check out Chapter 5 for how to set up a session and create and organize your tracks):

1. **Cue the beginning of the song.**

   Press and hold the Stop button while pressing Rewind on a Zoom R24 or click the Stop button twice in Logic or Cubase, for example.

2. **Arm your track by pressing the Record Enable button or, in the case of a Zoom studio-in-a-box (SIAB) system, the Status button until it blinks red.**
3. **Arm the recorder by pressing the Record button until it flashes red, and then press the Play button (or the Record button again in the case of the Zoom).**

   Presto, you're recording!

4. **When you're done, press the Stop button and then press 0 or the Stop button again to rewind.**

   To listen to your recorded track, you need to disarm the track that you recorded to and set it to play.

5. **Press the Track Status button until it turns green (or deselect the track — just click the track bar).**

   Now you're in playback mode.

6. **Adjust your channel fader on the track channel that you recorded to and press the Play button.**

Well, how does it sound? Good? Then you're ready to record a different track. If you don't like the sound, you can record the part over again by rewinding, rearming the track (by pressing the Status button until you get the red blinking light again), and pressing the Record button followed by the Play button. If you're like I am and you make lots of mistakes, you'll figure out how to do this procedure at lightning speed.

TIP

Depending on your system and the recording settings you've selected, you may be able to keep each take and decide later which one to use for your final song. This may be in the form of virtual tracks (as in the case of the Roland SIABs) or regions list (in the case of Pro Tools). I recommend checking your manual for the specifics on how to do this in your system.

REMEMBER

You don't have to save all your takes. In fact, I'm a fan of not over-cluttering my song sessions. If I know I can do a better performance, I get rid of it right away so I'm not tempted to compromise.

Punching In and Out

Punching in and out refers to being able to overdub a section of a performance (that guitar lick you keep missing, for example) while keeping the part of the performance that you like. Punching in and out can be pretty simple: Play the track and press the Record button when you want to start. Then press the Stop button when you're done. At least that's how it used to be done.

With a digital recorder, you can set up the system to punch in and out a number of ways. You can punch in and out manually either by using a nimble finger to punch buttons or by using a foot switch. You can also program the recorder to punch in and out automatically. If you go the automatic route, you usually set up your system to punch in and out once, but in some cases, you may want to rerecord over the same part of the song a certain number of times — a process known as *loop recording.*

Manual punching

Manual punching in and out is exactly what it sounds like: You manually press the Record button when it's time to start the punch, and you manually press the Stop button when you're done. This is the type of punch you do if you have enough time between when you press the Record button and when you need to start playing, as well as when you stop playing the part and when you can get to the Stop button. You may also do manual punching if you're acting as the engineer and someone else plays the instrument.

Punching with a foot switch

On most recorders, you can use a foot switch to punch in and out. This frees your hands so that you can play your instrument while you do the actual punching in and out.

Automatic punching

Automatic punching in and out is one of the many gifts from the digital recording gods. This process allows you to fully concentrate on getting your part right without having to worry about getting the punch right. With automatic punching, you can replace very small passages or get into really tight places with your punch.

For example, suppose you have one bad snare drum hit (I've been there many times) that you want to replace. With automatic punch in/out, you can set it to start recording right before that bad note and stop immediately after it, leaving the rest of the notes untouched.

Even though each recorder is a little different in its autopunch procedure, all recorders follow these basic steps:

1. **Select the track you want to punch in and out of.**
2. **Arm the track by pressing the Select button until you get the red blinking light.**
3. **Locate the punch-in point on your recorder.**

   You do this either by playing the song until you get to the point that you want to punch in or by keying in the numbers for that section of the song.
4. **Press the In Point (punch-in) button on your recorder.**
5. **Locate the punch-out point on your recorder.**

   You do this either by playing the song until you get to the point that you want to punch out or by keying in the numbers for that section of the song.
6. **Press the Out Point (punch-out) button on your recorder.**
7. **Press the Auto-Punch button on your recorder.**
8. **Rewind the recorder to just before the punch-in point.**
9. **Press the Record button followed by the Play button.**

   Some recorders don't require you to press the Record button first.
10. **Play your part.**

When you're done, your newly recorded part is neatly placed in the song.

Repeated punching (looping)

If you have a tricky part to record and you know it'll take you a few tries to get it right, you can use the repeated punching (also called loop recording) function. During the repeated punching procedure, the recorder keeps repeating the section within the loop until you press the Stop key, so you can try recording your part as many times as you want without having to set up the punch in and out procedure again.

This procedure uses the same basic steps as the automatic punch in/out procedure, except that you also need to choose the section of the song that the recorder plays before and after the actual punch times (called the *loop start* and *loop end* points). For some systems, you can do this the following way:

1. **Locate the place where you want to start the loop on your recorder.**
2. **Press the Locator or Marker button.**

   This stores the location point you chose in Step 1.
3. **Locate the place where you want the loop to end.**
4. **Press another Locator button to store this value.**
5. **Press and hold the Loop button.**
6. **While still holding the Loop button, press the Locator button that you used to store the loop start point (Step 2).**
7. **While still holding the Loop button, press the Locator button that you used to store the loop end point (Step 4).**
8. **Follow the steps for the automatic punch in/out that I list in the preceding section.**

Exploring Overdubbing

After you record one usable track, you can move to the next step: overdubbing. *Overdubbing* is simply adding another track to an already-recorded one. Overdubbing is the heart of the multitrack recording process for most home recordists and is a technique that you'll undoubtedly use and occasionally abuse.

The overdubbing process is pretty straightforward. You simply follow the procedures for recording a take while making sure that you're monitoring the recorded tracks you've already made.

TIP

When you record an overdub, hearing certain parts that you recorded earlier may throw you off. If this becomes a problem, you can turn down certain parts in a mix and only listen to those parts that help you perform the overdub. For example, if you're overdubbing the lead vocal and a dobro part breaks your concentration on your lines or on hitting a note correctly, just slide the fader for the dobro's channel down a little (or a lot).

MULTITRACK ABUSE

You have a recording system with 16 or more audio tracks, a couple dozen MIDI tracks, and countless virtual tracks (additional tracks in a digital system that are hidden behind the main tracks for recording variations of a part). What do you do? Well, you do what anyone else in your shoes would do — you try to fill all your available tracks with instruments. After all, that's how you get really lush recordings, right?

Yeah, sometimes, but this could also be a recipe for a bunch of mud. In fact, you can end up with a super-lush recording by using just a handful of tracks. Lushness is a product of the song's arrangement (how all the parts fit together) rather than just the number of tracks.

One of the most difficult things about multitrack recording is knowing how to use your tracks most effectively and having the discipline to quit when the song is done, regardless of whether you've used all your tracks. So, remember that just because you have the tracks available to you, doesn't mean you need to use them all.

Submixing

At times, you may want to record a bunch of instruments, such as the drums of a drum set, live to one or two tracks. In this case, you need to create a submix of the inputs before you commit them to disk.

Submixing is essential if you have a recorder with fewer tracks than you have instruments. The advantage of creating submixes is that you can get by with fewer tracks. The disadvantage is that you can't make many changes to the sound or volume of the individual instruments after you record them.

Recording by using submixes presents challenges that overdubbing doesn't. Here are some points to keep in mind:

- Make sure each instrument sounds the way that you want it to sound on the final mix. You can still make minor adjustments to equalization (EQ) and effects, but only to the entire submix group.
- Before you record, make sure each instrument's volume is where you want it to be relative to the volume of the other instruments.
- Decide where in the stereo field you want each instrument. This is called *panning,* and it determines how far left or right each instrument can be heard. Panning is discussed in more detail in Chapter 21.

This can take time to set up, but if you're limited on available tracks, you can record a lot of instruments on few tracks.

TIP

If you're not sure exactly how you want the final submix to sound, you can record more than one version onto separate tracks and use a bounce procedure (see the following section) after you've recorded. This gives you more time to experiment with alternative versions of your submix.

Bouncing

Bouncing is like submixing, but you do bouncing after you record the tracks. For instance, you can record all your drum mics onto separate tracks initially and then, later on, bounce (or combine) all those tracks onto one or two tracks. In most cases, you want to bounce to two tracks rather than one so that you can keep the drums in stereo and maintain panning information in your final mix.

Bouncing has advantages over submixing. You can take your time getting each instrument to sound good before you group them together. On the downside, you may not have this option if you're recording live and can only put the drums on two tracks initially. In this case, you need to create a submix.

If you have the space to record the instruments to separate tracks initially, here's how you bounce the tracks down to two:

1. **Decide which tracks you want to bounce, and route these tracks to the tracks that you want to bounce to.**
2. **Adjust the EQ of each instrument to get the sound you want.**
3. **Adjust the panning of each instrument — use the panning knob located above your mixer's channel fader — so that the instrument is where you want it in the stereo field.**

   Remember that you need to bounce to two tracks in order for panning to work.
4. **Set the levels of each instrument relative to one another.**
5. **Add any effects that you want to record with the instruments.**
6. **Press the Record button.**

You can use virtual tracks (see the next section) to record several different versions of your bounce. This gives you options later when you're mixing. For example, set the track levels differently for each bounce — raise the snare drum in one, change the EQ of the hi-hats in another, and so on.

Keeping Track of Your Tracks

One of the great things about digital recording systems is the number of tracks that are often available. Computer-based systems, for example, often have unlimited numbers of tracks (or obscenely high numbers).

Having all these tracks is great, but keeping (ahem) track of them all can be daunting. Even though many computer-based recording programs offer places to include notes in your session, I find it helpful to organize my song sessions to make it easier to keep track of everything. This process includes:

- **Name each track.** Use a descriptive name for each track, such as kick drum, lead guitar 1, lead vocal 2, and so on.
- **Include notes for each track.** Most audio programs, such as Pro Tools, include a notes section. This is where I add information about the signal chain I used for the track (for example, the mics, preamp settings, and compressor setting). This allows me to re-create the track if I need to record it again.
- **Arrange the track order.** Re-order all your tracks into a logic arrangement. I always order the tracks from the foundation on up. For example, drums are at the top of the session, followed by percussion, bass guitar, rhythm guitar, lead guitar, keyboards, other instruments, background vocals, lead vocals.
- **Color-code your tracks.** In most audio recording programs, you can select the color for your track. Do this by grouping instruments in similar color palettes.
- **Color-code the regions in each track.** Choose the same color as the track. Pro Tools allows you to do this with a single click in the Preference. Go to Set-up ➪ Preferences ➪ Display ➪ Default Region Color Coding ➪ Track Color.
- **Mark song sections.** Place a marker at the beginning of each section of your song and name it accordingly. Doing so will save you a lot of time as you navigate it during the mixing process. If you created a tempo map as I suggest in Chapter 5, you will have already done this.

An organized song session will make the editing and mixing process a lot easier and faster.

IN THIS CHAPTER

» Understanding MIDI

» Getting to know MIDI ports

» Making sense of MIDI data

» Choosing the MIDI gear you need

Chapter 11

Understanding Electronic Instruments and MIDI

My first job in a recording studio was in 1985. I can still remember the first time I walked into that studio. The owner was sitting, arms crossed, in a chair in front of the mixing console (it was called a console in those days because the mixer took up nearly the whole room). He looked at me and pressed a key on the Macintosh computer sitting next to him. Then, all of a sudden, a synthesizer started playing, then another, and yet another. This is cool, I thought. But then I heard my nemesis — the drum machine.

Drum machines made me lose my recording gigs as a drummer and drove me to expand my career to that of a recording engineer as well. However, I eventually came to love that drum machine and the many others to follow (sigh). In fact, over the years, I became so captivated by the whole MIDI/drum machine thing that I assembled a whole series of electronic drum sets using drum machines and samplers — all controlled through MIDI.

In this chapter, you find out how the Musical Instrument Digital Interface (MIDI) enables synthesizers and computers to communicate with one another — a revolutionary thing for a musician. You get your hands dirty in the world of *sequencing* — the process of recording MIDI performance information so that you can play your performance automatically. You also peruse a variety of MIDI-capable instruments and explore the ins and outs of controlling your MIDI gear.

TIP

You don't need a bunch of fancy gear to use MIDI. Whenever you use an instrument track or software instrument in your digital audio workstation (DAW), you are using MIDI. The advantage with using MIDI within your DAW is that most of the MIDI data and functions I describe in this chapter are done in the background. You may not need to connect or synchronize any hardware.

REMEMBER

Like audio recording, MIDI can be a deep subject. You can go nuts trying to understand every little nuance of MIDI. (I know some guys who are not quite the same after plunging headfirst into this stuff.) The reality is that to use MIDI effectively, you don't need to know every little thing about it. In this chapter, I focus on what you need to know to get started.

Meeting MIDI

MIDI is a protocol that musical instruments use to communicate with one another. They do this through a cabled connection and a language that allows each one to understand the other, regardless of the manufacturer or instrument. All that's required is an instrument equipped with MIDI ports (jacks).

MIDI data is different from an audio recording because it contains no sound as such; instead, it's limited to performance information. This includes information about various performance characteristics, including the following:

- **Note-on and note-off:** What note is played and when
- **Velocity:** How hard someone presses a key
- **After-touch:** Whether the key pressure changes after the initial press
- **Vibrato and pitch bend:** Whether the pitch changes while a key is pressed

This information allows the MIDI musician to potentially create a performance that is as rich in texture as those of the world's finest players.

Digital messages that are sent from one device to another across a cable (called the MIDI cable, of course) create MIDI data. The cable connects to MIDI ports on each device, and the messages are sent in the form of binary digits. Each instrument can understand and respond to these messages.

Perusing MIDI ports

Three types of MIDI ports exist:

» **Out port:** Sends messages.

» **In port:** Receives incoming messages.

» **Thru port:** Sends messages that one device receives directly to the in port of another instrument. You use the thru port when you create a daisy chain to connect more than two devices. Figure 11-1 shows a daisy-chain setup.

REMEMBER

MIDI signals travel in only one direction. Data flows from the out port of a device to an in port of another device, but not the other way around. Likewise, data going through the thru port originates from the first device in the chain and not the device whose thru port is being used. The way that data flows allows a lot of flexibility in how you can connect different devices. Here are some examples:

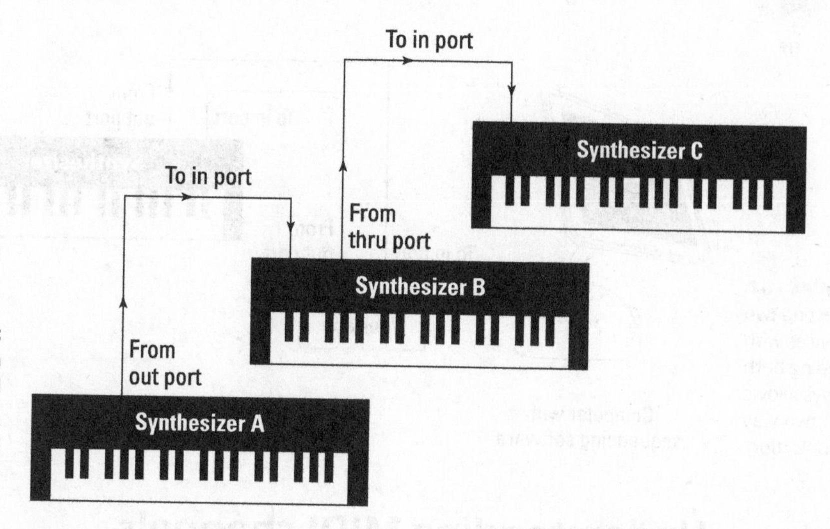

FIGURE 11-1: MIDI devices can be connected through the in, out, and thru ports on each instrument.

» **Example 1:** In Figure 11-1, three synthesizers are connected in a daisy-chain lineup. A cable connects device A's out port to device B's in port. Another cable connects device B's thru port to device C's in port. In this scenario, device A controls devices B and C. Devices B and C can't control any other device, because neither device B nor device C has a connection from its out port.

» **Example 2:** Suppose you connect device B to device C by using device B's out port instead of its thru port. In this case, device A sends messages to device B but not to device C. Device B controls device C. Device C has no control over either A or B because neither one is connected to device C's out port.

» **Example 3:** Now take a look at Figure 11-2. In this figure, two devices (a synthesizer and a computer sequencer) have MIDI cables running from the out port of each to the in port of the other. (The MIDI interface in this figure is necessary to make MIDI connections in a computer.) This allows the communication to go both ways. For example, a master synthesizer and a computer sequencer are frequently connected this way so that you can send performance information from the synthesizer to the sequencer when you're recording your part and from the sequencer back to the synthesizer when you want to play the part back.

REMEMBER

A connection to a MIDI device's in port or through a device's thru port doesn't allow the device to control another device. A MIDI device can control another device only if the cable is connected from its out port to the other device's in port.

TIP

Many newer MIDI-capable devices can connect to a computer via a USB connection. This single connection can take the place of all three MIDI connections.

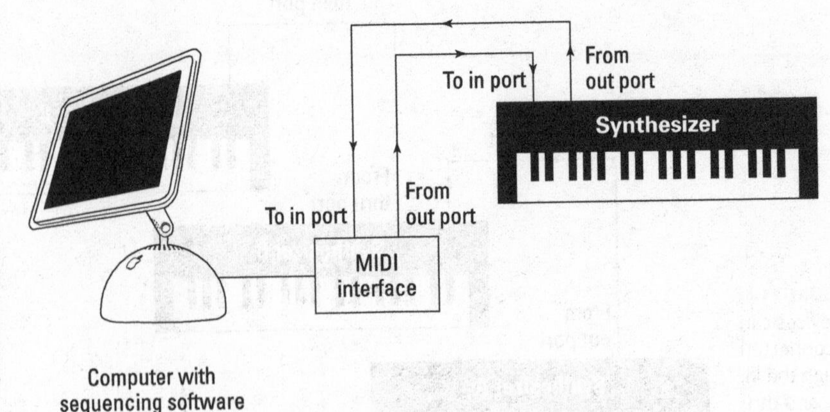

FIGURE 11-2: Connecting two devices with cords going both ways allows two-way communication.

Understanding MIDI channels

Okay, so you have a daisy chain of MIDI instruments all hooked together and you want to control them from your master keyboard or sequencer program. Now you want the drum machine to play the drum part and a sound module to play the string part. This is where the MIDI channels come in handy.

The MIDI channels allow you to designate which messages go to a particular machine. You can program each machine to receive messages on one or more of the 16 MIDI channels. For instance, you can set your drum machine to receive messages on channel 10 (the default channel for drum sounds) and set the sound module with the string sounds to receive data on channel 1. (You set the MIDI channels on your instrument by using the System Parameters menu. Check your owner's manual for specific procedures.) After you assign your channels, your master keyboard sends the performance information for both the drum machine and the sound module playing the string sounds across one MIDI cable. Each receiving device responds only to the messages directed to the MIDI channel that it's assigned to receive.

In this scenario, the sound module with the string sounds receives all the data from the master keyboard, responds to the messages on channel 1, and simultaneously sends the data from the master keyboard to the drum machine (via the sound module's thru port). The drum machine receives the same messages from the master keyboard as the sound module but only responds to those sent for channel 10.

Having 16 MIDI channels allows you to have up to 16 separate instruments playing different parts at the same time. You may use 16 different devices or 16 different parts from the same device if you have a multitimbral sound generator. (For details, see the "Synthesizer" section later in this chapter.)

You would think that each MIDI channel would be sent along its own wire in the MIDI cable, but this is not the case. Inside the MIDI cable are three wires. Two of the wires are used for data transmission, and the third is a shield. MIDI messages are sent across the two wires using a channel code, which tells the receiving device what channel the data following the code applies to. So, a MIDI channel message, called a *channel voice message*, precedes each performance command.

Appreciating MIDI messages

For MIDI instruments to communicate with one another, they need to have a common vocabulary. This is where MIDI messages come in. MIDI messages contain an array of commands, including the following:

- **Performance data messages:** These messages consist of note-on and note-off, velocity, after-touch, vibrato, and pitch-bend messages.

  Each MIDI performance data message has 128 different values. For example, each note that you play on the keyboard has a number associated with it (middle C is 60, for instance). Likewise, velocity is recorded and sent as a number between 0 and 127, 0 being the softest volume (no sound) and 127 being the loudest that you can play.
- **Control change messages:** These are a type of performance data message. These messages contain data about expression, including modulation, volume, and pan.
- **System common messages:** These messages contain data about which channel the performance data is sent to and what sound in the sound library

to play. System common messages also include information about timing data, master volume, and effects settings.

» **System exclusive messages:** These messages contain information that is exclusive to the system or device. The messages can include data transfers of new sound patches, among other things.

To use MIDI effectively, you don't need to know all (or many, really) of the MIDI messages that a device can recognize. If you hook up your gear and play, your MIDI devices generate and respond to the messages for you.

REMEMBER

Not all MIDI devices recognize all the MIDI commands. For example, a sound module generally can't send performance data messages, such as after-touch messages, because a sound module doesn't have triggering mechanisms that produce these commands.

TIP

Check your instrument's manual for a MIDI Implementation Chart. All MIDI instruments come with this chart. In it, you can find a list of all the MIDI commands that the device can send or receive. The chart also includes information on *polyphony* (how many notes the instrument can play at once) and *multitimbrality* (how many different sounds the instrument can produce at once).

Managing modes

Your synthesizer, drum machine, or other MIDI module has four operating modes that dictate how your instrument responds to the MIDI messages it receives.

Mode 1: Omni On/Poly

In Omni On/Poly mode, your instrument responds to all the MIDI messages coming across the wires (well, except the MIDI channel data). This means that your synthesizer or other device tries to play the parts of all the instruments hooked up to your MIDI controller. In this mode, your device also plays *polyphonically* (more than one note at a time).

REMEMBER

Some older MIDI devices default to Omni On/Poly mode when you turn them on. In this case, you need to reset your instrument if it's one of several in your MIDI setup. If you don't, the instrument responds to *any* MIDI messages sent from the controller, not just the ones directed toward that instrument.

Mode 2: Omni On/Mono

Omni On/Mono mode allows your device to receive messages from all MIDI channels but only lets it play *monophonically* (one note at time). This mode is rarely, if ever, used.

Mode 3: Omni Off/Poly

In the Omni Off/Poly mode, your device can play polyphonically but responds only to MIDI signals on the channels that it's set to. This is the mode you use most often when sequencing. I talk more about the magic of sequencing in the "Sequencer" section later in this chapter.

Mode 4: Omni Off/Mono

In the Omni Off/Mono mode, your instrument responds only to the messages sent on the MIDI channel that it's set to and ignores the rest. Instead of playing polyphonically, as in Mode 3, your instrument plays only one note at a time. This can be advantageous if you're playing a MIDI controller from an instrument that can play only one note at a time, such as a saxophone.

Taking orders from General MIDI

If you compose music for other people to play on their MIDI instruments or if you want to use music from another composer, General MIDI is invaluable to you. General MIDI (GM) is a protocol that enables a MIDI instrument to provide a series of sounds and messages that are consistent with other MIDI instruments. With General MIDI, you can take a Standard MIDI File (SMF) of a song that was created on one sequencer program, transfer the file to another program, and use that other program to play the exact performance — sounds, timing, program changes, and everything else.

GM instruments contain numerous sound patches that the MIDI community has standardized. Although the quality of these sounds isn't subject to a uniform standard, their sound type and location (Acoustic Grand Piano on Patch #1, for instance) are the same on all GM-compatible machines.

REMEMBER

Not all MIDI-capable instruments follow the GM standards. If this feature is important to you, be sure to find out whether the instrument that interests you is GM-compatible before you buy.

GM standards dictate not only the particular sounds of a synthesizer but also which drum sounds are located on which keys, how many notes of polyphony the instrument has, and how many different channels the instrument can receive and send instructions on. Here are the two levels of GM compatibility:

» **GM Level 1 compatibility:** Level 1 protocols were developed in 1991 and consist of a minimum of 128 instrument patches, 24 notes of polyphony, receiving and sending capability for all 16 MIDI channels, 16-part multitimbrality, and a host of controller and performance messages.

» **GM Level 2 compatibility:** Level 2 was implemented in 1999 and includes more sounds, polyphony, and features. A GM-compatible device has 32 notes of polyphony, 16-channel support, up to 16 simultaneous instrument sound patches, and a host of additional sounds (384, to be exact), including 2 channels of simultaneous percussion sounds. Also added to the GM2 standard are reverb and chorus effects.

Gearing Up for MIDI

Okay, so this MIDI thing sounds kind of interesting to you, and you want to know what you need to buy to do some MIDIing yourself. Well, I'm sorry to inform you that you can't do any of this cool MIDI stuff with your vintage Stratocaster guitar or your acoustic drum set (unless you do some fancy rigging to your gear). Here's the equipment that you need to record using MIDI:

» **Sound generator:** This device enables you to hear the music and may be a synthesizer (hardware or software), drum machine, sound module, or sampler.

» **MIDI controller:** This device controls the MIDI instruments in your studio.

» **Sequencer:** This device records and plays the MIDI performances that are programmed into it. The sequencer allows you to program your part into the synthesizer and have it play back automatically (much like the old-time player piano).

» **MIDI interface:** This interface enables your computer to send and receive MIDI data.

I know this sounds like a lot of stuff, but most of this gear performs more than one function in the MIDI studio. For example, nearly all synthesizers come with drum sounds, and some synthesizers even include a sequencer. In this case, this one synthesizer can do the job of a sound generator, drum machine, MIDI controller, and sequencer all in one. Or, you can get a computer equipped with sequencing software (part of most recording programs such as Pro Tools, Digital Performer, or Logic), a couple of software synthesizers (acting as your sound modules/ generators), and an external MIDI keyboard with its own internal interface (you can find many with USB connections that plug right into your computer). This setup gets you going with as few components as possible.

Sound generators

The sound generator is the core of the MIDI studio — it's what produces the sounds you hear. Without it, you may as well skip the rest of the stuff because, of course, you can't hear any of your work.

Sound generators can come in many different shapes and sizes: You find the fully functional keyboard synthesizer, the independent drum machine, the stand-alone sound module, samplers, software synthesizers (soft synths), and the computer sound card. Each of these devices has its strengths and weaknesses.

In the following sections, I discuss the different types of sound generators. Although you may find one piece of equipment that does everything you want, in this section, I separate all the features that different equipment may have to help you understand the function of each feature and decide how to configure your studio.

Synthesizer

A *synthesizer*, like the one shown in Figure 11-3, consists of not only sounds but also a keyboard on which you can play these sounds. Synthesizers come in a variety of sizes and configurations. For example, some keyboards come with as few as 25 keys (two octaves) while others provide as many as 88 keys — the size of an acoustic piano keyboard.

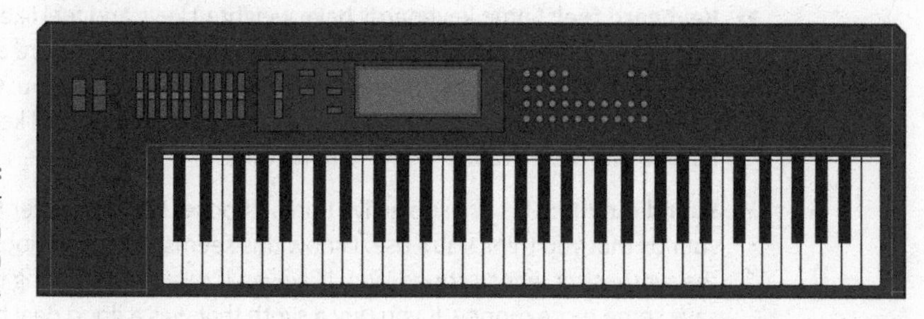

FIGURE 11-3: A synthesizer contains a keyboard and a variety of sounds.

If you're in the market for a synthesizer, you need to consider the following things:

» **Polyphony:** This is the number of keys that sound at one time. Most decent modern synthesizers have at least 16 notes of polyphony, although ones with 32 notes are not uncommon.

WARNING

Each manufacturer treats polyphony differently, and the GM standards (discussed in the section "Taking orders from General MIDI," earlier in this chapter) allow some variations on the effective use of this parameter. For instance, a synth patch may use more than one sound to create the sound that you hear. The synth patch that you love so much may, in fact, consist of four different sounds layered on top of one another. In this case, you just reduced your polyphony to one-fourth with that one patch. If your synthesizer has 16-note polyphony, it's now down to 4-note polyphony because each of those 4 notes has four "sounds" associated with it. If you use this patch, you can play only 4 notes (a simple chord) at a time, not the 16 that you thought you had to work with.

Your best bet is to buy a synthesizer (or sound module) with the highest polyphony you can afford, especially if you want to layer one sound on top of another or do multitimbral parts with your synth.

- **Multitimbrality:** Most decent keyboards allow you to play more than one sound patch at a time. This is called multitimbrality, which basically allows you to have your keyboard divided into several groups of sounds. For example, a multitimbral synth can divide a song's chords, melody, bass part, and drum-set sounds into different groups of sounds and then play all those groups at once.

TIP

If you do any sequencing, a multitimbral synth is a must-have. Otherwise you would need a separate synthesizer for each type of sound that you wanted to play. Fortunately, with the GM standards, compatible synthesizers made since 1994 have the ability to play 16 sounds at once.

- **Keyboard feel:** Some keyboards have weighted keys and feel like real pianos, while other keyboards have a somewhat spongy action. If you're a trained piano player, a spongy keyboard may feel uncomfortable to you. On the other hand, if you have no training in piano and don't need weighted keys, you don't have to pay the extra money for that feature.
- **Sound quality:** This is a subjective thing. Choose the synthesizer that has the sounds that you think you'll use. I know this seems kind of obvious, but buy the synthesizer whose sounds you like even if this means having to wait and save some more money. If you buy a synth that was a good deal but you don't love the sounds, you're wasting your money because you'll just end up buying the more expensive one later anyway.
- **Built-in sequencer:** Many keyboards contain a built-in sequencer, which allows you to program and play back your performance. These are usually called *keyboard workstations* or *MIDI workstations* because they contain everything you need to create a song. If you're considering buying one of these complete workstations, take a good, hard look at the sequencer and the user interface to make sure that you like the way it works. Each manufacturer treats the process of sequencing a little differently; you can probably find a sequencer that fits your style of working.

Drum machine

A *drum machine* contains not only the sounds of the drum set and other more exotic drums but also a sequencer to allow you to program rhythms. Figure 11-4 shows you a typical drum machine.

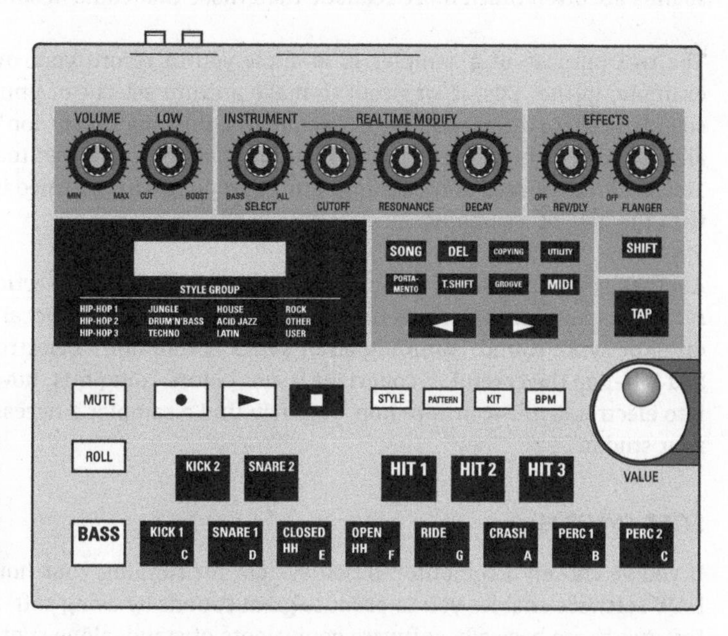

FIGURE 11-4: A drum machine has drum sounds and often a sequencer to program rhythms.

Most drum machines contain hundreds of drum sounds, numerous preset rhythm patches, and the ability to program dozens of songs. All stand-alone drum machines have pads on which you can play the part. The more advanced drum machines can give your rhythms a more human feel. Effects, such as reverb and delay, are also fairly common on the more advanced drum machines.

Sound module

A *sound module* is basically a stripped-down version of a synthesizer or drum machine. Sound modules don't contain triggering devices, such as the keys for the keyboard or pads for the drum machine. What they do contain is a variety of sounds (often hundreds) that a master controller or sequencer triggers. The advantage of sound modules is that they take up little space and cost considerably less than their fully endowed counterparts, especially in the case of software synthesizers (generally called *soft synths*).

TIP

If you already have a master keyboard, adding sound modules can be a cost- and space-effective way to add more sounds to your system.

SAMPLERS

A *sampler* is a sound module that contains short audio samples of real instruments. Most samplers come with sound libraries that contain hundreds of different types of sounds, from acoustic pianos to snare drums to sound effects. These sounds are often much more realistic than those that come in some synthesizers.

The real purpose of a sampler is to allow you to record your own sounds. For example, in the '80s, it was cool to make a drum set out of unusual percussive sounds. A snare drum could be the sound of a flushing toilet (don't laugh; I actually did this) or breaking glass. Tom-toms could be grunts set to certain pitches. You would be amazed at the strange stuff that people have turned into music — all with the help of a sampler.

Another common use of a sampler is for recording short sections of already-recorded songs. This can be a melodic or rhythmic phrase, a vocal cue, or a single drum or synth sound. Sampling other songs is common in electronic music, rap, and hip-hop (be careful of copyright issues before doing this, however). If you're into electronic music or hip-hop, you may find a sampler a necessary addition to your studio.

SOFT SYNTHS

If you've chosen a computer-based system for running your home studio, your DAW software enables you to produce great sounds by using soft-synth plug-ins. *Soft-synths* are basically software equivalents of stand-alone synthesizers, sound modules, or samplers. As you can see in Figure 11-5, a soft synth's graphical user interface (GUI) is often designed to look just like a piece of regular hardware, complete with buttons and knobs.

Countless soft-synth plug-ins are available for most DAW programs. The best way to find the soft synths for your DAW program is to do an Internet search for "instrument plug-in" or "soft-synth" with your DAW program in the search phrase.

Sound card

Most sound cards that you can install in your computer (or that come with a desktop computer) have General MIDI sounds in them. Depending on the quality of your sound card, the sound may be decent or border on the unbearable.

FIGURE 11-5: Computer-based DAW users can choose soft synths to create their synthesizer sounds.

TIP

To find out whether the GM sounds in your computer's sound card are any good, play a MIDI file on your computer. First, do an Internet search for MIDI files (just type **MIDI** in your favorite search engine). Some sites require you to pay to download a song — especially for popular or familiar tunes — but many sites allow you to choose a song to listen to without downloading or paying a fee. Click a song and it should start playing automatically. You'll immediately know whether you like the sound of your sound card.

REMEMBER

If you bought an audio interface for recording audio, you'll generally find that the sounds are pretty good. And with your audio program, you have access to soft-synth patches.

MIDI controller

A *MIDI controller* is a device that can control another MIDI device. MIDI controllers come in many different formats. In fact, a MIDI controller can be anything from a synthesizer to a drum machine or a computer to a xylophone.

When MIDI first came out, your controller choice was limited to a keyboard, but now you can choose among keyboards, wind controllers (for saxophones or other wind instruments), guitars, and drums. So, even if you don't play piano, you can find a controller that resembles an instrument that you know how to play. Look around, and you may find one (or more) MIDI controllers that allow you to create music your way.

Sequencer

Although you can get stand-alone sequencers and sequencers integrated into a synthesizer, you probably want a computer-based sequencer for your home studio. The reasons for this are many, but the overriding factor is that you can have your MIDI and audio tracks in one place, and a computer-based sequencer gives you more-powerful editing capabilities than a sequencer that's contained in a box and that uses a tiny LCD screen.

Of course, if you want to do only a minimal amount of MIDI in your studio, you don't necessarily need all the power of a computer-based sequencer program.

For example, imagine that you have a drum machine and an eight-track recorder that has synchronization capabilities (your owner's manual describes whether the recorder can synchronize with other devices) and that you play guitar-based music. Being a guitar freak, you want to use six tracks for your guitars and two for your singing. With a MIDI connection from your drum machine to your recorder, you may be able to sync these two machines and wait to record your drum parts until the final mix. This effectively gives you a lot more tracks — one for each drum sound that you're using because you can adjust the volume, pan, and sound of each instrument in your drum machine. This setup is similar to recording each instrument on a separate track in your recorder.

MIDI interface

The MIDI interface allows you to send and receive MIDI information from a computer. Many sound cards have a MIDI port, but if you end up doing a lot of MIDI sequencing and use more than one sound module or external controller, you need a separate MIDI interface, such as the one shown in Figure 11-6.

MIDI interfaces come in a staggering variety of configurations, so you need to consider several things when you buy a MIDI interface. The following questions can help you determine your needs:

- **What type of computer do you own?** MIDI interfaces are usually configured to connect to your computer using either a USB port or an audio interface, and audio interfaces use one of four available options: PCI, Thunderbolt, or USB. (Chapter 3 has more details on audio-interface connection types.) You determine which option to use by the type of port(s) you have in your computer. For example, most Macs have USB, and Thunderbolt, whereas a PC may only have a USB port (though you can add or Thunderbolt ports if you like). Having said all that, most dedicated MIDI interfaces use USB ports, which come with nearly all computers nowadays.

» **How many instruments do you intend to connect?** MIDI interfaces come with a variety of input and output configurations. Models are available with two ins and two outs, four ins and four outs, and even eight ins and eight outs. You can also buy "thru" boxes, which have one or more inputs and several outputs. If you have only one or two instruments, you can get by with a smaller interface (in this case, a 2x2 interface — two ins and two outs — would work great). If you have many instruments that you want to connect, you need a larger box.

FIGURE 11-6: You need a MIDI interface to connect your instrument to a computer.

IN THIS CHAPTER

» Synchronizing MIDI devices

» Recording your performance

» Editing MIDI data

» Saving your work

» Transferring MIDI data between systems

Chapter 12

Recording Electronic Instruments Using MIDI

Recording and editing Musical Instrument Digital Interface (MIDI) tracks are similar to the process you undertake with audio. The main difference is that MIDI tracks contain performance data instead of sound. This offers the advantage of being able to choose what sound or instrument "plays" your data after you've finished recording. Of course, this also provides the temptation not to make a decision on your sound.

In this chapter, I get you started recording MIDI by walking you through the process of synchronizing a variety of MIDI devices. Then I give you the lowdown on recording your tracks, adding to them with overdubs, and editing it all in some of the many ways that most sequencers allow you to. To top it off, I offer a little advice about saving and transferring MIDI data.

Synchronizing Your Devices

To create any kind of music with MIDI, you need to synchronize your devices to one another. The first thing you have to do is decide which device is going to send the MIDI commands (called the *master*) and which devices are going to receive them (called the *slaves*). The process for synchronizing MIDI devices varies slightly from configuration to configuration. You can get a glimpse into a few possibilities in the following sections.

Synchronizing two (or more) synthesizers

In this first scenario, you synchronize a synthesizer and a sound module (or another synthesizer). In this case, your keyboard is the master because this is the instrument that you actually play. Start by attaching the MIDI cable to the out port of the keyboard and to the in port of the sound module. Figure 12-1 shows the setup for two synthesizers. If you have more than two devices, you can run a cable from the thru port of the second device to the in port of the next one, and so on. You can connect up to 16 devices this way.

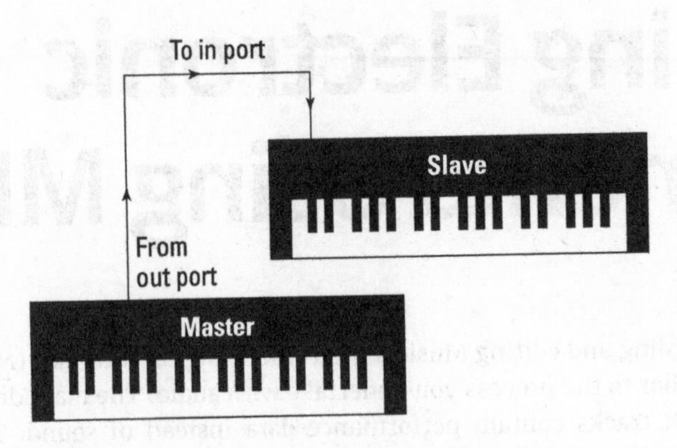

FIGURE 12-1: Synchronizing two synthesizers involves connecting the MIDI cables as shown.

The next steps involve configuring each device in the chain so that each device recognizes its place and responds only to those messages that you assign to it. Keep in mind that all devices operate differently, so I can't walk you through the exact steps for your instruments. Be sure to read your owner's manual for your device's specific procedures. The following steps give you a general idea of the process involved in synchronizing two synthesizers:

1. **Go into your master keyboard's system parameters and choose Master.**

   This is generally a dialog box located within the software of your device.

2. **Choose Slave for each of your other devices.**

   You usually do this by going into the MIDI synchronization menu in your software.

3. **Make sure that each device in your chain is set to mode 3 or 4, depending on whether you want polyphony.**

4. **Assign a MIDI channel for each device that's down line (connected to the out port) from the master.**

   You can find channel assignments within your device's system parameters. For example, in a ddrum4 sound module, you press the System button until the light next to the word *MIDI* illuminates. You then use the dial to choose the MIDI channel that you want to use.

TIP

   You can choose from 16 channels (1–16), but if you have a drum machine, set it to channel 10 because this is the default drum channel for General MIDI (GM) devices.

5. **Play the master keyboard.**

   This makes your other MIDI devices play the appropriate sounds. If you don't hear anything, make sure that you have the appropriate MIDI channel selected.

Synchronizing a computer sequencer and a synthesizer

If you're using a computer or sequencer and you want to synchronize it to a sound module or synthesizer, you need to go through some additional steps. These are as follows:

1. **Connect your synthesizer to the MIDI interface, and connect the MIDI interface to your computer.**

   Run the appropriate cable from the MIDI interface to the appropriate jack of your computer. For example, this can be a USB cable if you have a USB computer and USB MIDI interface.

2. **Connect the MIDI interface to your synthesizer.**

   You do this by connecting a cable from the MIDI out port of your synthesizer to the MIDI in port of the interface. Then connect another cable from the MIDI out port of the interface to the MIDI in port of the synthesizer. This allows the MIDI communication to go both ways, as shown in Figure 12-2.

REMEMBER

3. **If you're using a synthesizer to play your MIDI sequences from your computer, you need to set your synthesizer to local off mode. Then enable the thru function in your sequencer program so that the MIDI information that you send from the keyboard to the sequencer is sent back to the keyboard.**

   Local off mode disables the keys from the sounds and makes the sequencing process go much smoother. Enabling the thru function in your sequencer program enables you to hear what you're playing while you record your part.

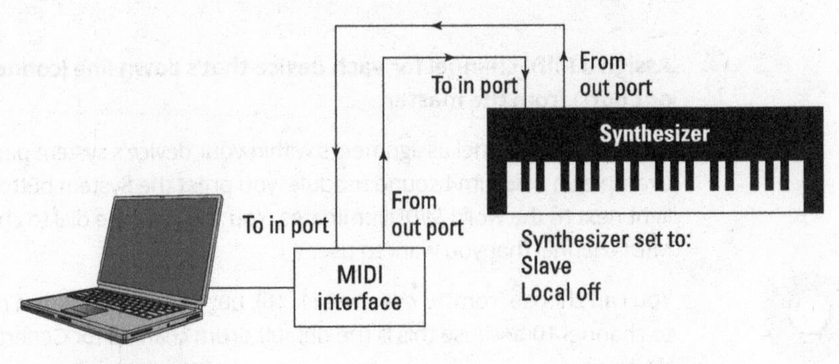

FIGURE 12-2: A computer sequencer and synthesizer are synchronized using these settings.

WARNING

If you don't set your synthesizer on local off, you create a *feedback loop*. In a feedback loop, both your synthesizer's keys and the sequencer are sending the same messages to the sound generator in your synthesizer and causing it to play each note twice. The best that can happen is that you trigger each note twice and use up your polyphony faster. The worst that can happen is echoed or stuck notes and possibly jammed messages, which may cause your system to lock.

4. **After you connect all the cables, be sure to choose the MIDI channel that you want the track recorded to and set both the sequencer and the instrument to that channel.**

   You can find the MIDI channel selector within your device's software. Sometimes, the MIDI channel selector may be a key command, such as repeatedly pressing the System button in a ddrum4 sound module. Other times, the MIDI channel selector is a pull-down menu that you access from the top of your computer screen. In Cubase, the channel selector for the sequencer is located just to the right of the track name.

After you have your channel setup and local off business out of the way, you can play your synthesizer, see it register in the sequencer, and hear it play. If you don't hear anything, check all your settings.

Synchronizing a sequencer and an audio recorder

If your system does the sequencing inside the computer and your audio tracks are recorded on either a stand-alone recorder or a studio-in-a-box (SIAB) system, like the Tascam DP-24SD, you need to synchronize them. In this case, your devices use timing data instead of communicating/responding with the help of performance data.

Both your sequencer and your recorder need to recognize the same timing data, which you ensure by determining which device is the master and which one is the slave.

The process that I describe in this section also works if you're connecting a synthesizer to a drum machine. Select the sequencer as the master device and the drum machine as the slave.

You can choose either device to be the master. In this example, I outline setting up your system with the SIAB system as the master and the sequencer as the slave, as shown in Figure 12-3. You may be able to set up your system the other way around (particularly if you have a stand-alone recorder connected to a sequencer), but I chose this way because doing so allows you to use the faders and transport functions (play, record, stop, and so on) in your SIAB system. With some systems, you may be able to use your sequencer's transport and automation functions with this setup as well, which I discuss in the section "Sequencing," later in this chapter.

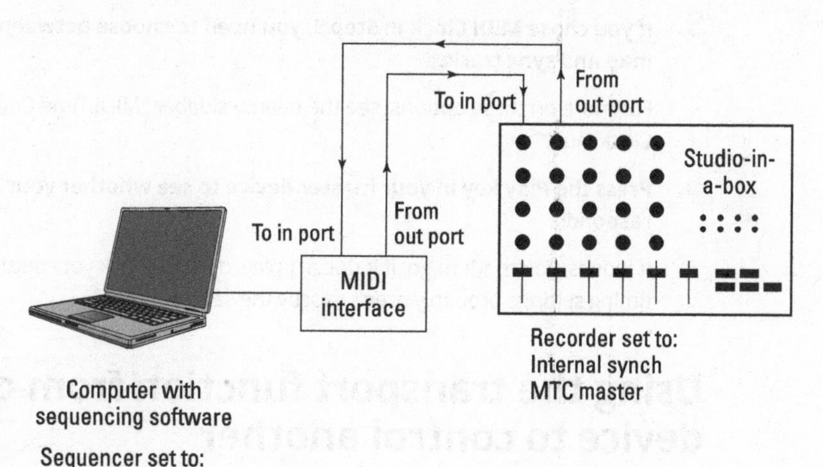

FIGURE 12-3: A system with a separate sequencer and audio recorder is set up this way.

After you've chosen which device is the master and which is the slave, you can start synchronizing your systems. These steps help you get going:

1. **Choose Internal Sync in your master device's Synchronization dialog box.**

   Each device has a different procedure for this, so read your device's manual to find out how to choose the synchronization mode. In a Tascam DP-24SD, press

SYNC/MIDI. A dialog box appears. Choose Source ➪ Internal. Click the YES/ENTER button to accept this setting and return to the main menu.

2. **Choose External Sync in your slave device.**

   This can be a dialog box within the MIDI synchronization menu. For example, in Cubase, choose Options ➪ Synchronization from the main menu on the top of your screen. The external or internal sync choice is in the upper-left corner of the dialog box.

3. **Choose either MIDI Time Code (MTC) or MIDI Clock for the timing method.**

   In Cubase, for example, this option appears directly below the external or internal sync option.

REMEMBER

   You ultimately want to choose the timing method that you prefer and the one that works best for your gear. You can find out about these timing methods in the nearby sidebar "MIDI Time Code, MIDI Clock, huh?"

4. **If you chose the MTC mode, you need to choose a frame rate to go with it.**

   For this example, set your frame rate at 24 frames per second (fps). You should be synchronized at this point.

5. **If you chose MIDI Clock in Step 3, you need to choose between tempo map and sync track.**

   For more on these options, see the nearby sidebar "MIDI Time Code, MIDI Clock, huh?"

6. **Press the Play key in your master device to see whether your slave device responds.**

   If it does, you're set to go; if it doesn't play, double-check your settings. Your timing settings probably aren't exactly the same.

Using the transport function from one device to control another

TIP

Another aspect of synchronization can enable you to use the transport function (play, stop, record, and so on) from each device to control the other. This is the MIDI Machine Control (MMC) function. The MMC function is located within the Synchronization menu of your device's software. (You can find this in the same place as the MTC sync in most systems.) MMC allows you to send machine control messages from the slave device to the master device. For example, in the setup shown earlier in Figure 12-3, you can set the sequencer to send MMC messages and the SIAB system to receive them. Your sequencer must be set as follows:

» MTC slave–External synch

» 24 fps

» MMC master

Your SIAB system in turn must be set as follows:

» MTC master–Internal sync

» 24 fps

» MMC slave

These settings enable you to use either device's transport functions to control the other. The MTC master sends the timing data, but each device sends control messages to the other. Check your system's manuals to see whether you can do this with your gear.

MIDI TIME CODE, MIDI CLOCK, HUH?

When you try to synchronize two devices using MIDI timing messages, you're met with several choices. One is between MIDI Time Code (MTC) and MIDI Clock. The other is frame rates and tempo map or sync track. This can be confusing, so this sidebar contains a brief overview of these options.

MIDI Time Code uses absolute time in its messages (the actual time on the clock from the beginning of the song or reference point in hours, minutes, seconds, frames, and subframes). This data can then be translated into SMPTE messages (the kind of synchronization data used in film and television). If you choose MTC, you also have to decide the frame rate for the time code. Several frame rates are available, and each is associated with certain mediums. They are as follows:

- **24 fps:** This rate is mainly used for films.
- **25 fps:** This rate is for audio, video, and film equipment used in Europe and other places that use the SECAM or PAL formats.
- **29.97 fps:** This rate is for color televisions used in the United States, Japan, and other places that use the NTSC format.
- **30 fps:** This rate is used for black-and-white televisions or for working with audio only in the United States (Europe's black-and-white TVs use the 25-fps rate).

(continued)

(continued)

If this isn't confusing enough, both the 29.97- and 30-fps rates also have either drop frame or nondrop frame formats. This gets pretty technical, but drop frame formats basically drop two frames every minute, except for the tenth minute, so that the timing data matches the clock exactly. These are generally used for live video feeds.

MIDI Clock is different from MTC in that it tracks the time of a song in beats and measures rather than in minutes and seconds. MIDI Clock messages are generally sent every 1/24 of a beat, but you can set most sequencer programs to much higher resolutions than that. Cubase VST version 5 can be set as high as, get this, 1,920 pulses per quarter note (PPQ).

When you choose MIDI Clock, you need to choose between using tempo map or sync track, as follows:

- **Tempo map:** This is basically a layout of the tempos and time signatures used in a song. To use a tempo map to synchronize your SIAB system and sequencer, you need to create the map itself. Every system is a little different in this procedure, so I don't go into detail here.
- **Sync track:** A *sync track* is a track (at least was a track on analog recorders) that follows along with the tempo and measures of a song. To use a sync track, you need to first record one. If you have a digital recorder, you most likely don't need to take up an actual track to do this.

So, which do you choose? Unfortunately, that question doesn't have a clear answer. The equipment that you have dictates part of your answer. (For instance, the Roland VS-1680 SIAB system can send MIDI Clock and MTC messages, but it doesn't always effectively respond to those messages.) The goals you have for your music dictate the other part. If you're composing music for film or TV, your choice is clear (24 fps and 29.97 fps, respectively).

If your equipment and musical goals don't limit your choice, choose what you like. Just make sure that both machines have the same settings.

Sequencing

Sequencing is the heart of most home recordists' MIDI studios because sequencing allows you to actually record your instrument's part and play it back. If you're like most people, the sequencing part of MIDI is what excites you the most. With sequencing, you can play as many instruments as your room can handle (or more, if you have long cords).

Sequencing is not unlike audio recording: You have the same transport functions (start, stop, record, rewind, and so on), and you have the ability to record each instrument on a separate track. This is where the similarities between audio tracks and MIDI tracks end, however. As I've mentioned before, MIDI sequencing deals with performance commands and not audio waveforms. This opens a few doors that can come in mighty handy in the following situations:

- If you aren't the greatest player in the world
- If you're not sure what key you want the song to be in
- If you don't know (or haven't decided) what sounds you want to use

With MIDI sequencing, you can make a whole host of changes to your performance after you've recorded it. You can change the placement or volume of individual notes, you can change the song's key, and you can change the instrumentation (for example, you can have a brass ensemble play a part that you originally wrote for the strings). Another great thing about MIDI sequencing is that you can capture a performance that you don't have the skills to pull off live.

Recording MIDI data

You can record a MIDI track in one of the following ways:

- **Real-time recording:** Play the part as you would for a regular audio recording.
- **Step-time sequencing:** Manually input the music one note at a time. Step-time sequencing is a great tool if you don't have the skills to perform that part in real time.

The MIDI tracks in most sequencer software programs look virtually the same as the audio tracks except for a small icon. Logic, for instance, has an M icon, and in Cubase, you find a small musical note. Each icon is located to the left of the track name. You generally engage the track that you want to record to by clicking it once.

Preparing to record

Before you start to record a MIDI track, you need to make the following adjustments to your setup:

- **Make sure that your MIDI gear is synchronized.** For details on how to do this, check out the section "Synchronizing Your Devices," earlier in this chapter.

» **Set your levels and the patch (sound) that you want to hear.** Setting levels simply means setting the volume that you hear through your monitors at a comfortable level.

  To choose the sound that you want to hear, you can select the sound in your synthesizer, in which case the sequencer recognizes this setting, or choose the sound within the sequencer program. This process is done differently for each type of sequencer, but most of them have a track menu located to the left of the screen that applies to the track you have engaged.

» **Set your metronome to the tempo that you want to record to.** You do this by opening the Metronome Settings menu (which is often located on the Options menu). Choose the tempo and time signature for your song, and you're set to go.

TIP

Within the Metronome Settings menu, you can also choose the MIDI note that the metronome sounds on, whether you have a count in before the song actually starts (called a pre-roll), and more.

REMEMBER

You don't need to set the tempo for a song ahead of time. You can always adjust this later. In fact, you can set the tempo slower than the final version so that you can play the part slower and get the notes right. This can be especially beneficial if the part is difficult or if you're not the greatest player in the world. Just be sure to set the tempo to its final speed before you start recording audio tracks, because you can't change the tempo of the audio tracks later like you can with MIDI tracks.

Real-time recording

If you're recording in real time, just press the Record button and start playing. You can find the Record button on the Transport Bar if you use a computer-based software program (this can be found on the Windows menu in Logic, for example).

If your recorded performance is the way you want it, you can move on to another instrument's part. Just set up a new track to record the sound that you want on the MIDI channel you prefer. If you don't like your performance, you have the following options:

» **Rerecord your part from the beginning.**

» **Rerecord only those sections that don't sound right.** Rerecording parts of a performance is generally referred to as punching in and out. This involves setting your recorder to just record a section of your performance, as I describe in Chapter 10.

» **Edit the performance.** I discuss the details of editing in the section "Editing your data," later in this chapter.

Step-time sequencing

Step-time sequencing involves entering your part one note at a time. This can take a long time to do, especially if it's a part with lots of notes. But step-time sequencing may be your only option if you don't have the skills to play the part live.

Most sequencer programs include a step-time sequencing mode. Select this mode and then click the Record button. You enter your part by selecting the note value (eighth note or sixteenth note, for example) for the first note or chord. Then when you play the note on your keyboard, it's entered into the sequencer. Choose your next note, press the key(s) you want to record, and so on.

TIP

Some sequencers enable you to enter notes in a score window. If you can read music, this can be much easier and faster than the traditional step-time mode. Just choose the note's duration from the menu bar and click the place where you want that note to be. After you get the hang of this method, step timing can be pretty quick. Check your sequencer program's manual for details.

Overdubbing

After you record some MIDI performances, you can easily add to or change them. The time-honored name for this kind of recording is *overdubbing.* Overdubbing MIDI performance data is similar to overdubbing your audio data. Most programs allow you to overdub in several ways: manually punching in and out, punching automatically, and loop punching. In addition, because MIDI is strictly performance information with no actual sound, most recording programs allow you to either replace or merge existing MIDI data when you overdub.

Using MIDI Merge/Replace

When you overdub to a MIDI track, many MIDI recording programs offer you the option to either replace existing material or add new data to it. For example, in Pro Tools, you make this selection by clicking the MIDI Merge/Replace button. This button is located in the Transport window, as shown in Figure 12-4. Here's how it works:

- When the Merge/Replace button is engaged (MIDI Merge mode), new material is merged with existing MIDI data on the record-enabled track(s).
- When the Merge/Replace button is disengaged (MIDI Replace mode), new MIDI data replaces existing information on the record-enabled track(s).

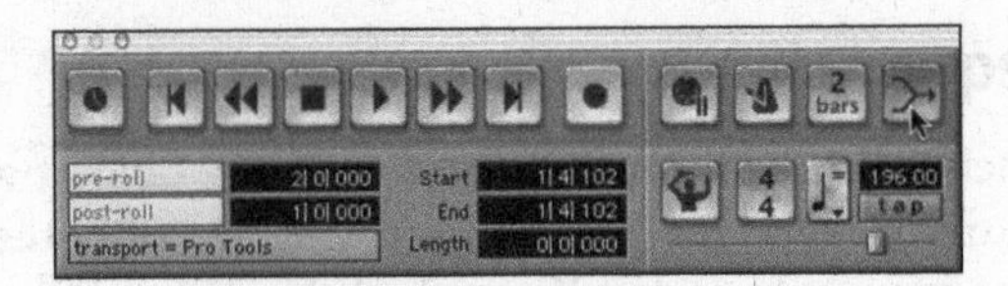

FIGURE 12-4: Add new data in a sequencer program without erasing what's there.

To engage MIDI Merge in Pro Tools, follow these steps:

1. **Open the MIDI controls section of the Transport window by choosing Display ⇨ Transport Window Shows ⇨ MIDI Controls.**

   The Transport window expands to include the MIDI controls section.

2. **Click the MIDI Merge button.**

   The button becomes highlighted.

Most MIDI sequencers have a similar function, but by default, any overdubs you do are placed in a new sequence — leaving the original intact.

Punching in and out

If you like some of your initial take and want to record over only part of it, you can set points at which to start and stop recording within the session. This is called *punching in and out.*

As is the case with audio tracks, most programs allow you to punch into MIDI tracks in several ways. These include punching in and out *manually, automatically,* and *repeatedly* (looping). With the exception of being able to choose to merge your punched data with your original performance or being able to replace it, punching into and out of MIDI tracks is the same as punching into and out of audio tracks. I detail the exact procedures for performing these punches in Chapter 10.

Saving Your Data

For the most part, saving data in your sequencer program is like saving data in any computer program. Yep, you need to click the Save button (or press ⌘+S if you have a Mac). Don't forget to save your work regularly, lest your computer crashes and you lose several hours' work.

The main thing to know about saving data in a sequencer program is that most programs have their own proprietary file format. You generally can't take a saved file from your program and play it on another one.

If you want to play your MIDI tracks on another sequencer program or make it available on the Internet for other people to play, make sure that you save your music as a Standard MIDI file (SMF). Nearly all sequencer programs allow you to save in this format. Some even do this by default. Check your owner's manual to see how to do this. Then you can give your MIDI tracks to anyone who can play an SMF, and if you recorded your stuff by using a GM standard, it sounds just how you intended it to sound, regardless of the listener's gear.

Transferring Data Using MIDI

Another great thing about MIDI is that you can use the cable and ports to send more than just MIDI performance information. Many manufacturers allow you to send sound patches through the MIDI connection by using system-exclusive messages. This can be a great tool. In fact, I own an electronic drum set; its sounds can be changed and updated by connecting a MIDI cable between the sound module (brain) and my computer. I can store gazillions of sounds on my computer without cluttering up (or overloading) my drum set's brain. But wait, it gets even better. This manufacturer makes new sounds available on its website to download for free! Yep, I can add new sounds to my drum set without having to buy anything. You gotta love it!

Performing a data transfer via your MIDI connection is easy. Just connect your device to the MIDI interface on your computer, open the data-transfer software provided by the manufacturer, and follow the directions.

IN THIS CHAPTER

» Understanding loops and looping

» Choosing loops

» Using loops in your music

» Creating and editing loops

Chapter 13 Working with Loops

The concept of looping is as old as recording with magnetic tape. Starting in the 1960s, it wasn't uncommon to include tape loops in the recording process. These were actual loops of tape that contained a short section of music, often a drum groove, that was cut from the music, its ends taped together, and then run through the machine to play an endless repeating cycle.

Modern loop technology follows this same process but substitutes digital musical segments for physical magnetic tape. Because you're not having to cut and tape the tape, you can loop on the fly. Loops can also adjust to fit the time, tempo, and key signature of your songs, which is something old-time tape loopers weren't able to do.

In this chapter, I introduce you to the world of loops and show you how to integrate loops into your compositions. First, you discover the two basic types and multiple formats of loops. Then, you explore where you can find loops for your digital audio workstation (DAW). Next, you walk through the process of actually using loops in your songs, and finally, you discover how to make loops of your own.

REMEMBER

Working with loops is different than loop recording or looping the playback of your song. Loop recording, which I cover in Chapter 10, is the process of repeatedly playing a section of your song while recording a track within it over and over again until you are happy with the performance.

Working with loops is also different from simply looping the playback of your song, which you would often do when mixing to tweak sections of your song without having to stop, rewind, and start the section again.

Understanding Loops and Loop Types

Loops are segments of a musical performance that repeat over and over in your song. They can be drumbeats, guitar riffs, synthesizer pads, or any performance that when repeated, fits into your musical arrangement.

Loops come in two main varieties: audio and MIDI:

- **Audio:** Audio loops are audio files.
- **MIDI:** MIDI loops contain MIDI data.

Each acts the same as corresponding non-loop material. You can record, edit, and mix them in the same way. Some of the more powerful looping software uses other types of loops, such as Drummer files, which are used in Logic Pro and GarageBand.

REMEMBER

Loop files include pitch, time, and tempo data that is used to allow the loop to be dropped into a song and fit its key, grid, and tempo. This means that even if the loop is in a different tempo or key, it will adjust to match your song. I go into this process later in this chapter.

Choosing Loop Formats

Because loop files contain data beyond the actual musical performance, not all loops work in all loop software. There are several different formats for loops, and you need to be sure your DAW is able to work with the format you choose. Popular formats include:

- **Acid loops:** These were developed for the Magix Acid program. They are in WAV format and are compatible with most DAWs.
- **Apple loops:** These are AIFF files created for Logic Pro and GarageBand and may not be able to be used in other DAW software, particularly Windows-based programs.
- **MIDI loops:** Because they contain typical MIDI performance data, MIDI loops are compatible with all DAWs.
- **Rex and Rex2 loops:** Developed by Propellerhead Software by Reason Studios, this format is compatible with most full-featured DAWs.
- **WAV loops:** These loops are in the WAV file format and are compatible with all DAWs.

You can add a variety of other loop file formats native to looping plug-ins to your DAW. Because these loop files use formats made for the plug-in, they often include additional features that are unique to the program and its looping functions. If you have a DAW that has limited looping abilities, such as Pro Tools, adding a looping plug-in, such as Reason, can make looping more powerful and fun.

Setting Up Your Session

Working with loops in your songs is pretty much the same as working with regular audio or MIDI files. You can edit them in the same ways, which means you're not stuck with the loop as it is. You can cut or copy sections and create something new.

In order to work with loops, however, you first need to map out your song session with your tempos, time signatures, and key signatures. You also need to enable a click track or metronome. I walk you through the process in this section in Logic Pro X (other programs have similar processes).

Setting tempo and time and key signatures

Because loops contain data for time signatures, tempo, and key signatures, you need to set them in your session so that they will play properly. It is done this way:

1. **Open the custom Transport View window from the Transport window, as shown in Figure 13-1.**

   Click the open menu icon (downward arrow) at the right side of the Transport window in Logic Pro X.

2. **Under the LCD option list, check the Tempo, Time Signature/Division, and Key Signature/Project End checkboxes and click OK.**
3. **Enter the song/section tempo in the Tempo field by either double-clicking and typing the tempo in the text field that appears, or by dragging up or down over the tempo with your mouse (the left side in Figure 13-2).**
4. **Enter the song/section time signature and division in the Tempo field by either double-clicking and typing the time signature in the text field that appears, or by dragging up or down over the time signature with your mouse (the center section in Figure 13-2).**
5. **Click and hold to open the key signature menu and scroll to select the key for the song or section (the right side in Figure 13-2).**

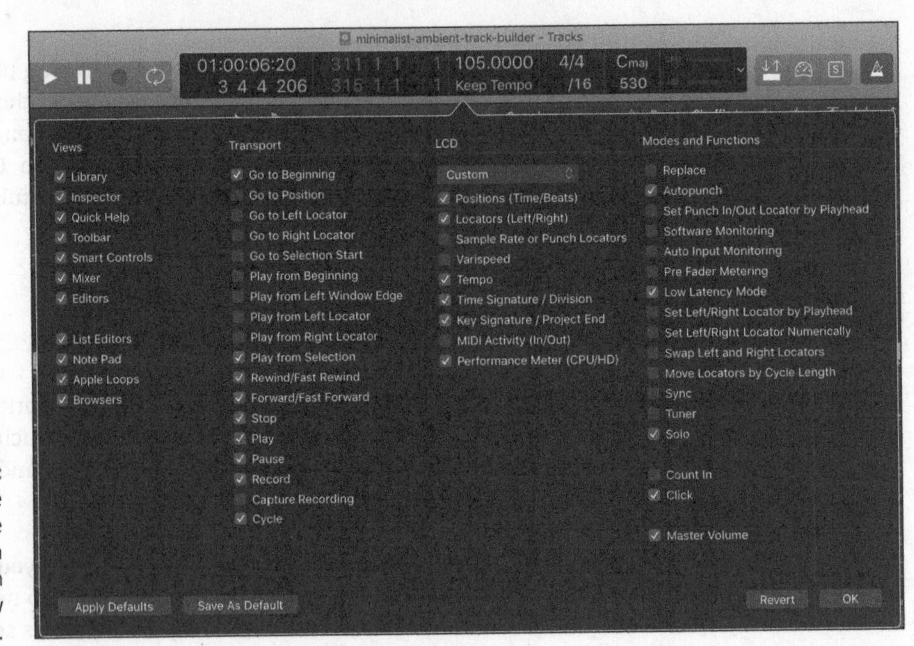

FIGURE 13-1: Tempo and time and key signature can be shown from the custom Transport view menu.

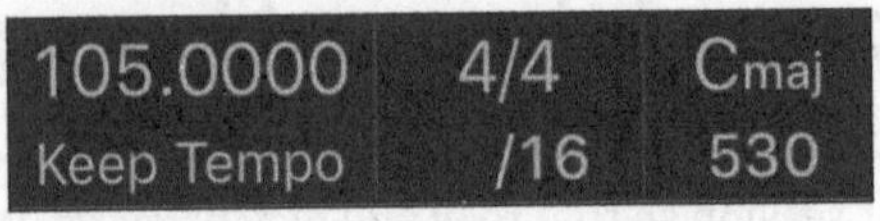

105.0000 4/4 Cmaj
Keep Tempo /16 530

FIGURE 13-2: Tempo and time and key signature settings are located in the Transport window.

Creating song maps

If your song has tempo, time signature, or key signature changes in it, you can create a song map to lay these out. This ensures your loops automatically adjust to the proper tempo, time signature, and key signatures throughout your song. This is how you do it:

1. **Open the List Editor window.**

   In Logic Pro X, this is located in the upper-right corner of the Main window.

2. **Click the Tempo tab to open the tempo menu (Figure 13-3).**
3. **Enter the position and tempo for each section of your song.**
4. **Click the Signature tab to open the time and key signature menu (Figure 13-4).**
5. **Enter the position of each time and key signature changes for your song.**

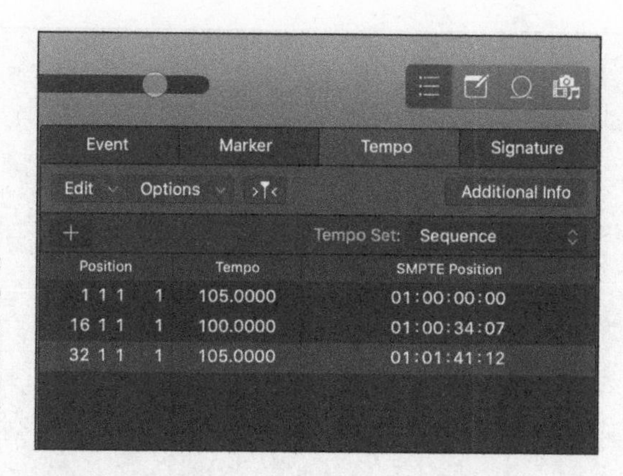

FIGURE 13-3: The tempo map menu lets you map out the tempos for each section of your song.

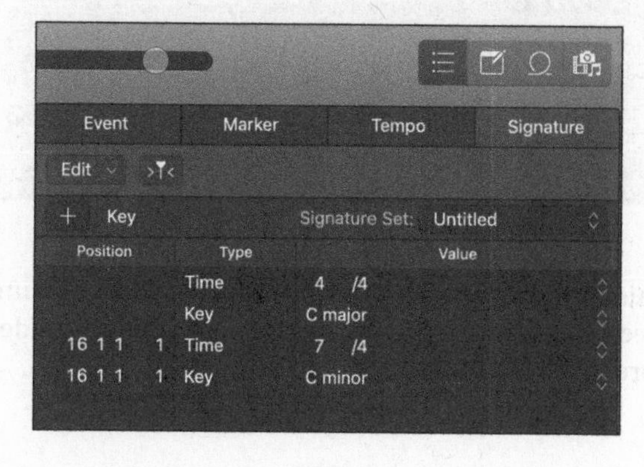

FIGURE 13-4: The time and key signature map menu lets you map out the time and key signatures for each section of your song.

Enabling a metronome

If you are going to record any live track in your song, the metronome is necessary so that your performance matches any loops you add. You enable the metronome in your song by simply clicking the metronome icon at the top of the main menu. You can then adjust the sound and behavior of the metronome by following these steps:

1. **Double-click the metronome icon to open the metronome preferences menu shown in Figure 13-5.**
2. **Under Options, check the boxes for the behavior you want.**

   At the very least, select Click While Recording.
3. **Under Source, check the boxes for when you want the metronome to make a sound and what you want the sound to be.**
4. **Close the window.**

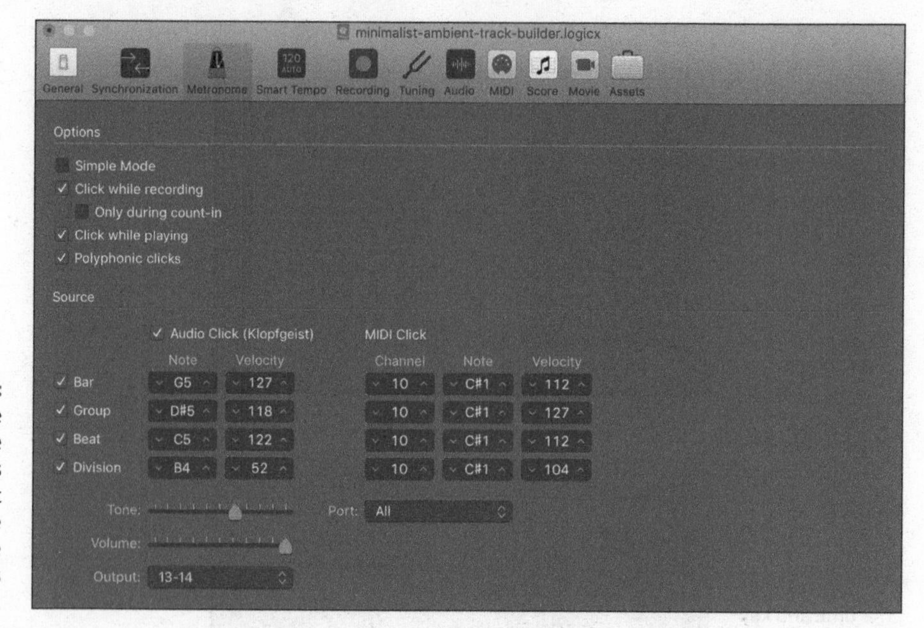

FIGURE 13-5: You can choose when the metronome plays and what it sounds like in the metronome preferences menu.

TIP

You can skip this step by adding a rhythmic loop, such as a drum groove, before you record to keep you in time. This give you a more musical guide for your tempo and may be more inspiring to play to.

Adding Loops to Your Sessions

DAWs will allow you to add loops to your sessions as easily as adding any audio or MIDI file. You can either open your media browser and select the file or drag and drop the file into your session. This section details the process.

Browsing loop libraries

Depending on your DAW, browsing can be easy (Logic Pro X) or not so easy (Pro Tools). For example, in Logic Pro X, you press O and the Loop Browser window opens (see Figure 13-6). It's intuitive and can be searched by instrument, genre, and descriptors; searched by keyword; or scrolled through a list.

Pro Tools, on the other hand, is clunky and requires you to know where your loops are located on your hard drive. You access this browser by choosing Windows ⇨ New Workspace ⇨ Default. From there you need to navigate through your folders for your loops.

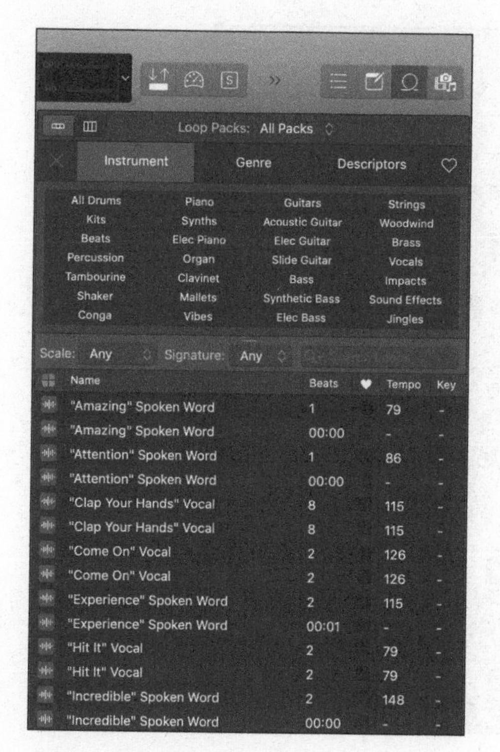

FIGURE 13-6: Logic Pro X's Loop Library Browser makes finding loops easy.

Previewing loops

To hear prospective loops before putting them in your session, click the waveform or MIDI icon that appears to the left of the loop's name in Logic Pro X's Loop Library Browser, as shown in Figure 13-7.

Adding loops to your session

Once you've chosen a loop to add to your session, you can drag it into your session in one of two ways:

1. **Drag the loop into an existing track of the same type (audio or MIDI).**
2. **Drag the loop into the song's timeline.**

   This will create a new track at the bottom of the active track list.

If the loop has a key signature associated with it, the loop automatically adjusts to the key signature of the session.

TIP

Depending on your DAW, you may need to enable tempo-matching to ensure your loop adjusts to the tempo of your session.

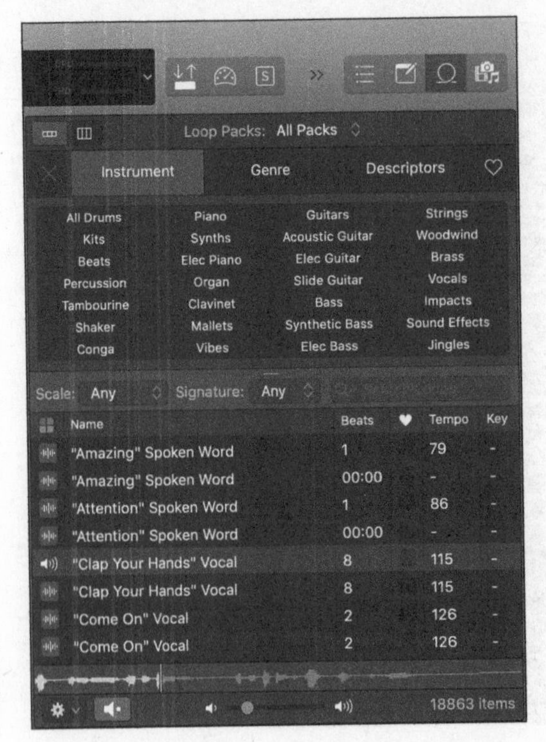

FIGURE 13-7: Click the loop's icon to preview the loop.

This option is called Smart Tempo in Logic Pro X. Located in the Transport window below the tempo setting, it offers three options:

- **Keep:** This maintains the tempo of the session. This is what I generally use.
- **Adapt:** This changes the tempo of the project to a recording or loop.
- **Auto:** This option lets Logic Pro X decide for you. You can set the preferences for this option in the Smart Tempo preferences menu.

In Pro Tools, you can make sure the loop matches the tempo of the session by enabling the Elastic Audio function at the top of the Workspace window. To do this, click the metronome icon and choose one of the algorithms to the right. This must be done before you add the loop to your session.

Editing Loops

If you're like me, you'll find it's rare that any particular loop fits what you hear in your mind perfectly. Fortunately, you can edit loops like any other audio or MIDI material and turn them into something completely new and unique. I cover the process of editing audio in Chapter 14 and editing MIDI data in Chapter 15, but there are two things I recommend doing when editing loops specifically. These are:

- **Merge the snippets (regions) of your loop into a new file.** When you edit an audio file, it breaks the file into individual regions. Merging these regions creates a new file that you can then turn into a new loop file that can be used in other projects. Merging audio in Pro Tools is as easy as selecting all the regions of the loop section and choosing Edit ⇨ Merge regions.

REMEMBER

MIDI loops don't break into separate files when you edit them, so you don't need to merge the loop section.

- **Save your edited loop as a new loop file.** Once you have a new loop you like, you can save it as an actual loop file that contains the time signature, tempo, and key signature data, allowing you to add them to your loop library to use in other projects (or share with others). I show you how to create loops in the next section.

Creating Loops

A loop can be any recording that repeats, such as a drumbeat, baseline, synth pad, or guitar riff, but what separates a looped section of a song from an actual loop file is in the meta data — the time signature, tempo, key signature, genre, and so on — contained in these files. This data helps you find a loop in a library and lets you use the loop in any song, regardless of whether these settings match.

The process and potential ease of turning your looped music into a loop file depends on the DAW you're using. For example, you are unable to convert your looped music into a loop file in Pro Tools, but it is simple in Logic Pro X. Here's how:

1. **Select the region you want to save by clicking on the region.**
2. **Press Control ⇨ Shift ⇨ O to open the Add Region to Apple Loops Library menu, as shown in Figure 13-8.**
3. **Enter a name for your loop.**

   It's best if the name evokes the feel or style of your loop.

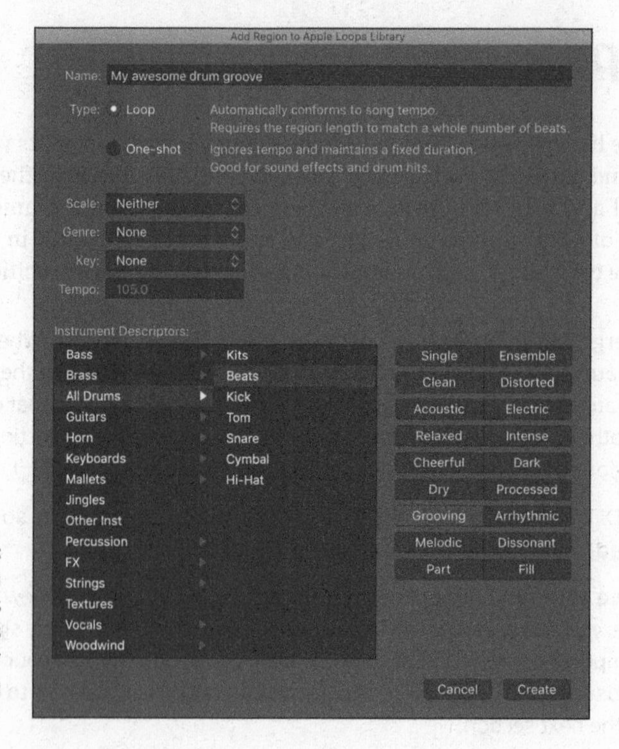

FIGURE 13-8: The Add Region to Apple Loops Library menu lets you save your loop as a loop file.

4. **Choose the type of loop it is.**

   You have two options:

   - *Loop:* This adds data about the tempo so that the loop will adjust to the song's tempo when it is added.
   - *One-shot:* This skips adding the tempo to the file data so that the loop's music plays as it is.

5. **Choose the scale that applies to your loop.**

   You have five options:

   - Any
   - Major
   - Minor
   - Neither
   - Good for Both

6. **Choose your genre from the Genre pop-up menu.**
7. **Choose the key signature from the Key pop-up menu.**
8. **Enter the tempo in the Tempo field.**
9. **Choose your Instrument Descriptors.**
10. **Click Create.**

If you use Pro Tools or another DAW that doesn't make creating a loop file possible or easy, you can use a looping plugin such as Reason Rack. If you are in this boat, do an Internet search for a loop plug-in that is compatible with your DAW software.

4 Editing and Enhancing Your Tracks

IN THIS PART . . .

Understand digital editing.

Edit your audio tracks aurally and visually and correct flaws in your performance.

Combine performances from several virtual tracks.

Edit your MIDI tracks.

Transfer MIDI data between systems.

IN THIS CHAPTER

» Understanding digital editing

» Editing aurally

» Editing visually

» Correcting flaws in your performance

» Combining your best performances from several virtual tracks

Chapter 14 Getting into Editing

Even after you put in all the time needed to get the best sound and performance, you'll most likely want to make changes to your tracks. You may want to get rid of some noise or clean up a few bad notes. Well, you can do this with editing. And if you have a digital hard-drive system, you can edit to your heart's content without sacrificing sound quality and without losing your original tracks.

In this chapter, you discover the joys of fixing a performance with editing. I cover the basics and try to help you find out whether your editing style is visual or auditory. You also explore the ways you can use the editing capabilities of your digital system to create a performance that never happened by creating loops, assembling song sections, and making composites from virtual tracks.

REMEMBER

The way you edit your tracks depends on your digital recording system. Some systems, such as computer-based digital audio workstations (DAWs), use tools similar to those in word processing programs. Other systems, such as studio-in-a-box (SIAB) systems, base their editing methods on traditional audio approaches. I can't possibly cover all the variables that exist in the many types of systems, but I can show you the basics so that you understand what possibilities exist. Hopefully, you get enough of a glimpse into the world of audio editing that you can apply these skills to the system you own.

Some people never do any editing of a recorded performance except to get rid of unwanted noise. What they record to disk is what they use. I rarely do any editing except for making the occasional loop and/or deleting a stray bad note. You may be like I am and have little use for the amazing tools available in most digital systems' editing menus. That's okay — don't feel like you have to use every capability of your system. On the other hand, if editing fits your style, don't be afraid to pull out all the stops and get creative.

Understanding Digital Editing

In the old days of analog tape, you needed to break out the razor blade and adhesive tape to do audio editing. Cutting out a performance was exactly that — physically cutting the performance from the tape that contained the audio. The problem was that after you finished the cut and taped the open ends back together, you couldn't reassemble the original performance. (Well, I suppose you could try to peel that tape off the new joint and tape the part you cut out back in again.)

And it got even worse. If you wanted to edit a single track, you had to cut a little window in the tape where that part was, but only in the track you were working on. You were left with a hole in the tape.

And then consider this: While you were cutting and taping the tape, you were touching it with your fingers and getting oils all over your precious tracks. The result: sound degradation. In all, analog tape editing was messy work that introduced unneeded stress on the tape (and perhaps the recordist) and degraded the sound of the music.

Lucky for you, there's a better way — digital editing. You can edit digitally by using your hard-drive recording system. Digital audio recording allows you to do a staggering variety of things to your recorded tracks. You can cut, copy, delete, erase, insert, move, and paste your music, among other things. And the best part is that you can do any of these procedures and still change your mind when you're done.

This aspect of digital editing is called *nondestructive editing,* which means that your original recording is kept intact (the recorder often makes a copy of the original data before it makes the edits or it simply points to the data to be played and ignores the data you chose not to have play). On the other hand, the no-returns policy of analog editing is referred to as *destructive editing,* and after it's done, you're committed to the results, regardless of whether you like them.

Editing can be done in a variety of ways, and almost every recording system does it a little differently. In the following sections, I list many of the basic editing functions that a digital system can perform.

Copy

The Copy command is universal in digital audio and does exactly what you think — it makes a copy of a selected performance. Here's how the different systems generally work:

- **Computer-based systems:** Copy can work much like the Copy function of your computer's word processing program. A copy of your selection is made and put into a clipboard section of your system. You can then take that copy and paste it somewhere else in the song.
- **SIAB systems:** These systems don't necessarily place copied material on a clipboard. Instead, you're prompted to choose a place to paste your work before you make the copy.

Many systems also allow you to choose how many times you want to copy the part and choose whether you want to override the existing material where you copy it or insert the new material into that section instead. If you insert the copy, the existing material moves over and makes room for the copied section.

Cut/Delete/Erase

The Cut, Delete, and Erase commands all do the same thing to the selected section — make it go away. The difference is what happens to that material after it disappears and what happens to the remaining material on the track; Figure 14-1 illustrates these differences. Here's the lowdown on the commands:

- **Cut:** Lifts the selected audio section and puts it on a clipboard so that you can place it somewhere else. On some systems, such as the Cubase, the rest of the audio track stays put, leaving an empty space where the cut section was. On other systems (Logic Pro X, for example), the existing material is brought forward to fill the space left by the cut material, similar to the way that your word processing software deals with the Cut command. Some systems, such as Cakewalk, allow you to choose whether the existing material moves forward.
- **Delete:** Eliminates the selected material, keeping you from placing it anywhere else. Delete acts like an analog audio cut-and-tape procedure: The

material following the deleted section is brought forward to fill the empty space.

Most computer-based systems, such as Pro Tools and Logic Pro X, have a Snap option that can treat existing material the same way as Delete, depending on how you've set your preferences. In this case, the Snap option snaps existing material back to fill any space left by a cut section.

» **Erase:** Like Delete, Erase gets rid of the selected section and doesn't allow you to put the section anywhere else. Unlike Delete, Erase leaves a hole in the audio where the selected section used to be. The remaining audio stays put.

Most computer-based systems have a Silence procedure that acts just like Erase. When material is "silenced," an empty space is left where the material used to be.

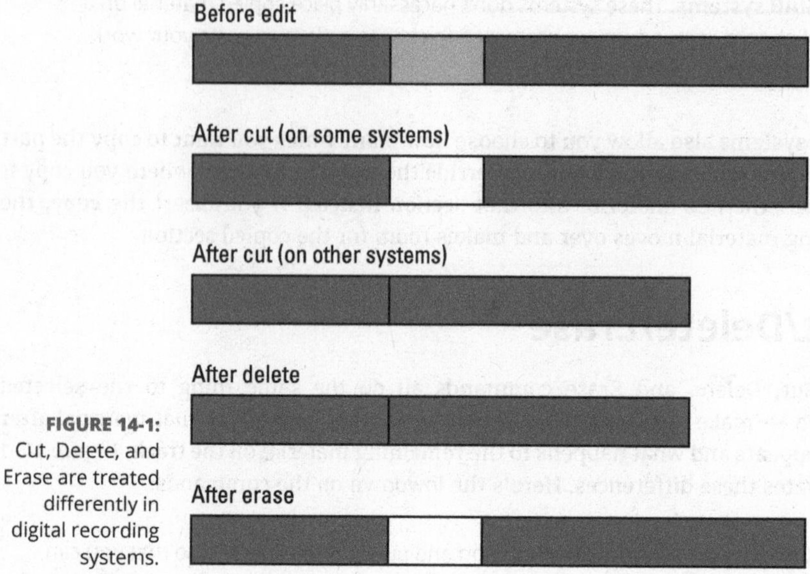

FIGURE 14-1: Cut, Delete, and Erase are treated differently in digital recording systems.

Insert

The Insert function is common among SIAB systems. It allows you to place a selected piece of music in a track (or multiple tracks) and moves the music that exists after the insert point so that there's room for the inserted material (see Figure 14-2). This is a handy feature that lets you add to a section without losing data.

Before edit

After insert

FIGURE 14-2: Insert pushes existing material back to make room for the inserted music.

For example, say you have a bridge section of a song that you wrote and recorded to be 8 bars long, but after you've finished the song, you want to add a guitar solo to the bridge and 8 bars just isn't long enough. (You guitar monster, you!) You want the bridge to be 16 bars long instead. Well, instead of having to rerecord the entire song with the new bridge section, you can copy the 8 new bars that you have for the bridge and insert them at the end of the existing bridge section, making the bridge 16 bars long. This takes only a second to do, and you don't have to plug in any mics or play any instruments.

TIP

If you have a computer-based system that doesn't have an Insert function, just select all the music immediately after the current bridge section and move it over 8 bars by using your mouse. This leaves an 8-bar space that you can then fill using the procedure I describe earlier.

WARNING

If you have a song with a lot of tempo changes and you use a *tempo map* (a function that allows you to set the tempo and time signature for each section of the song), make sure that you double-check your tempo map after you've made your edits because the tempo map won't adjust automatically. For example, if you add 8 bars to the bridge (like I describe in the earlier example), you need to add 8 bars to that section of the tempo map to make sure that the rest of the song remains accurate.

Paste

As obvious as this may sound, pasting is just placing your selected music somewhere. Like the Cut and Copy functions, this function is a staple for computer-based systems, but it isn't common among SIAB systems. In many cases, Paste overwrites the existing material where you put it, as shown in Figure 14-3, unless you have an Insert option and you use it as well. Some computer-based systems treat Paste like a word processing program does — the existing material moves over and makes room for the pasted section.

Like all computer Paste functions, whatever you put on the clipboard stays there until you replace it with something else. So, you can paste the same selection as many times as you like.

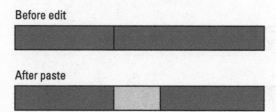

FIGURE 14-3: Paste places your selection over existing material.

Move

Nearly all digital recording systems have a Move function. In most cases, you can just choose the audio section that you want to move and choose a destination for it. If you don't have a Move function key, your system probably has the Cut, Copy, and Paste options that you can use the same way. Cut and Paste can move your music just as effectively as the Move function.

Moving audio data can be performed several ways depending on the system, but you probably move data by using a Move menu or by clicking and dragging. On the Move menu, you designate the section to be moved and where you want to move it to. This can be within a particular track or from one track to another. Within this menu, you may have the choice between overwriting the material at the destination point with your selection and moving the existing material to make space for the stuff that you moved. The latter is sometimes called a Move/Insert procedure.

If you have a system that uses a large video monitor, a mouse, and a keyboard, you may have the option to just click and drag the selection where you want it. In most cases, your moved selection overwrites the existing material in its new place, effectively erasing it (although it may still be hidden underneath — but you can't hear it when you play back the track). In other systems, the moved material is inserted in its new place, moving existing material in the process. Your system's owner's manual should spell out how this procedure is treated.

Export/Import

Exporting and importing involve moving music from one song file to another. Some systems enable you to import a single track from another song, whereas on other systems, you have to import everything in a song file.

TIP

If you can import only a whole song file but you just want a single track, just make a copy of the song that you want to import and erase everything you don't need from that song. Then when you import the song file, you import only the stuff that you want. Doing it this way rather than importing the whole song file and then erasing the unwanted stuff afterward is quicker because the computer doesn't have to import more than you need.

Undo

Undo is the most important key/function that you have in your digital system. It allows you to, well, undo what you just did. Without it, you may as well be trying to edit with analog tape, a razor blade, and adhesive tape.

How much you can undo depends on your system. Most systems give you at least 99 levels of undo — that is, you can make 99 consecutive edits and reverse them all (or just some of them). Some systems even go as far as giving you 999 undos. How's that for insurance? So, edit at will, because you can always change your mind later.

On the other hand, some systems have only one level of undo. This isn't a deficit, however, because this program gives you the option of saving your selection before you make the edit. If you choose to do this before each edit, you're essentially allowed as many undos as you want, as long as you have the hard drive space to store all those copies of your audio track.

REMEMBER

As you can see by all the different ways that various programs use and define editing procedures, you need to read your owner's manual and be familiar with your program to use these functions properly.

Finding the Section You Want to Edit

To use an editing function, you need to find the section of music you want to change. The musical section can be the whole song from one track, a short musical phrase from several tracks, or even a single note. You can find the beginning and end of the section that you want to edit in two basic ways: editing aurally and editing visually.

Each method has its advantages, and you'll probably prefer one method over the other for your working style. I'm from the old school and much prefer editing by listening to the section I work with. I trust my ears much more than my eyes. You may find that the opposite is true for you. But chances are, you'll use a little bit of both approaches for your music.

Editing aurally

The traditional way to perform an edit is to play the song on the tape deck until you reach the general area of the music that you want to edit. You then stop the tape and manually rock it back and forth against the play head to find the precise place to make the cut. You mark the back of the tape with a wax pencil and go looking for the next edit point. This process requires careful listening, and finding the exact spot to edit often takes quite a while.

For pre-digital people, such as myself, the manufacturers of digital systems make this process similar to editing analog tape (yeah). Finding an edit point aurally is often a two-step process: First you need to find and mark the general section that you want to edit using a marker (also called an *anchor point*), and then you need to identify the exact spot for your beginning and end points. You do this with the Scrub function, as detailed in the following steps:

1. **Listen to the song and place a marker (sometimes called an anchor point) on the fly as the section you want to edit passes.**

   Do this by clicking the appropriate Marker button (the Insert key on a Tascam DP24SD, for instance). Mark both the beginning and end points as accurately as you can. Your markers will be a little off, but don't worry about that now. Your next step involves refining those points using the Scrub function.

2. **Use the Scrub function that's associated with your system to zero in on the spot you need.**

   The Scrub function works much like analog tape where you can "rock" the music back and forth (this is called *scrubbing* — hence, the name) to find the precise spot that you're looking for. In some systems, such as the Tascam 2488, you can scrub using the Jog wheel. Start from the marker points that you set on the fly and dial the wheel back and forth until you find the exact spot to edit. This may take a while, so be patient. Do this for both the beginning and end points for your edit.

   There may be variation on the way scrubbing works on your device, so consult your manual if you don't have a job wheel. The Scrub feature on most digital recorders works pretty well — each just works a little differently and one approach may work better for you.

WARNING

Not all digital recorders have a Scrub feature that works as well as the old analog tape rocking technique. So, if being able to scrub is important to you, be sure to test this feature on the systems you're looking at before you buy.

TIP

If you have a computer-based system, you may find a scrub-type feature on the Tool palette. In Cubase, for instance, the Scrub tool uses an icon that looks like a small speaker. Look at your system to see whether you have this function.

Editing visually

Digital recording systems, especially those that use large video monitors, enable you to edit your music visually. This can be a great asset when you want to edit sounds down to the waveform level or if you don't want to hassle with aural searching.

In visual editing, you choose your edit points by viewing the audio waveform of a track on-screen. The audio waveform is a visual representation of the recorded sound showing its frequency (pitch) and amplitude (volume) of the sound that's recorded to disk. Check out Figure 14-4 for an example.

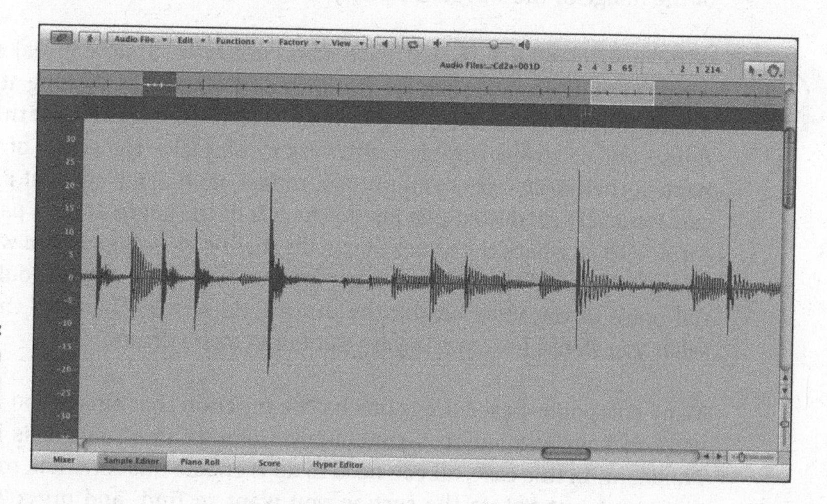

FIGURE 14-4: The waveform editor lets you see the music, making editing pretty easy.

You can use the waveform as a guide to show you where a particular sound is located. For example, if you pull up the waveform of a drum rhythm and set the track to play, you can see where the various sounds of the drum set (snare drum, kick drum, and so on) are located. Then just put a marker on the fly or stop the playback roughly where you want to be. As you get used to hearing the music and seeing the waveform pass by on your computer screen, you'll be able to tell by looking at a waveform where a sound starts and stops.

Take a look at Figure 14-4 again and find the cursor located just before the third large waveform. This is a snare drum note. You can select that section in the following ways (some systems offer you several ways, while others just have one):

- **Click and drag to create a box around the section you want to edit.** This is generally the easiest way to choose a section of audio.
- **Choose the numerical location points.** On SIAB systems, which typically don't have a cursor or mouse to work with, you can do this quickly by finding the point in the waveform and clicking a button (called the Now button in the Roland SIAB systems). The data is entered into the box, and you don't have to type the numbers.

» **Type the beginning and ending edit points in the appropriate dialog box.** This is an option if you have a computer-based system. If you have a keyboard and you're a fast typist, this may be the most efficient way for you to choose edit points.

On most systems, you can zoom in or out on the waveform graphic for a better look. You can often increase both the height (amplitude) and width (time frame) of the image of the waveform that you see.

With most instruments that have slow *attacks* — a slow initial sound, as with vocals or guitars — you can see the start of the sound by looking at the waveform. The beginning in the rise of the waves matches the beginning of the sound. But on drums and other instruments with very fast attacks, the attack of the instrument happens before the rise in amplitude. In fact, if you look again at Figure 14-4, you can see a vertical dotted line just to the left of the snare drum's part in the waveform. This is where the attack starts for that drum sound. If you were to rely only on your eyes and choose the waveform part that you see, you would miss the initial point of the stick hitting the drum (and all the character that it contains). What you would hear is a mushy-sounding snare drum.

Many computer-based programs have a function that allows you to find the start point of your audio with a simple keystroke. In Pro Tools, this is called Tab to Transient. In this case, all you need to do is enable this function, move your cursor to a point just before the section you want to find, and press Tab. The cursor moves to the beginning of the audio data. This feature is handy for making edits quickly and accurately. If this type of function is important to you, be sure to look closely at the computer program before buying to see whether it can do this.

Even though you use the waveform screen to do editing, you still need to find the beginning of that sound by using the Scrub function (described in the preceding section). Just search the space before your drum note until you hear where the attack starts. It's usually about 40 to 50 milliseconds before the waveform jumps up.

Editing to Improve the Sound of a Performance

To edit your music, you need to know a couple of useful skills. These include being able to edit individual notes and phrases, finding and replacing notes that are too loud or too soft, getting rid of noise and distortion, and correcting pitch problems.

Replacing a bad note

Replacing a bad note is one editing procedure that I use frequently. Here's an example: A few weeks ago, I played the drum part of a new song for the band I'm currently recording with. I really got into the groove — the feel was right, I made all the changes, and I even did some really cool fills and stuff. When I listened to the part after I finished recording, it sounded fine, so I went on to record other parts. But when I listened to it again a week later, I heard one snare drum hit in which I caught the rim, and it sticks out in the mix like the proverbial sore thumb. I could just punch in a new snare drum note, but I'm lazy. Besides, I had already put away my mics, and there's no way I could set them up the way I did the day I recorded the drums, not to mention tuning the drums exactly the same way I had them that day.

Well, here's a time when I'm thanking my lucky stars that I have a digital system that allows me to make minute edits (just try slicing a single snare drum note out of an analog tape). Hopefully, you won't have to do this procedure, but if you do, follow these steps:

1. **Copy the track that you want to fix.**

   This way, you can reference the original track.

2. **Place the copy on a track or virtual track that allows you to hear both the original and the copy at the same time.**
3. **Listen for a snare drum hit that you especially like and select it by using one of the techniques that I describe in the section "Editing aurally," earlier in this chapter.**
4. **Make a copy of the selection.**
5. **Find and mark the bad note.**
6. **Place the copy of the good note right where the bad note is.**

   The procedure for this varies depending on your system.

   Make sure that the Insert function is turned off. Otherwise, you add an extra note and move the bad note over, along with the rest of the music from that track.

7. **After you have the good note in the place of the bad one, turn up the volume of both versions of your track and listen to them again.**

   You should hear an exact copy of the track, except for that one note. Listen carefully at the place of the replaced note for any timing problems. The two tracks should match perfectly. If they don't, just use the Undo function and try again. Also, check the rest of the song after that note to make sure that you didn't accidentally insert the note rather than replace it.

TIP

If your system doesn't allow you to make such a fine edit or if you can't successfully select a single note, you can replace a whole measure instead of just the single note. Just follow the same steps and use a larger phrase instead of the one note.

Evening out a performance

Evening out a performance means making adjustments to the levels of a note or phrase within the song. Sometimes it can also mean changing the emphasis of certain notes to change the meaning or "feel" of a part. This section covers these areas using two functions called Normalize and Gain Change. A track often contains a stray note that is either much louder or much softer than the rest of the notes around it. In this case, you don't need to cut it out and replace it with another note, as I did in the example in the preceding section. Instead you can just make a change to the volume (or level) of that note, as follows:

- **To raise the volume of a note:** Select the note that you want to change and choose Edit ➪ Normalize. In most cases, Normalize allows you to choose the maximum dynamic level (in decibels) that you want the section to be, the amount below clipping (0dB) that you want, or the minimum headroom that you want to have left (also in decibels). These last two options are essentially the same thing.
- **To lower the volume of a note:** Select the note that you want to change and choose Edit ➪ Gain Change. This lowers the amplitude of the selected section by an amount you can choose.

TIP

You're not limited to making adjustments to single notes. You can also use Gain Change or Normalize to adjust the levels of short phrases or an entire track.

REMEMBER

Normalize and Quieten only adjust the levels of the section that you choose to work with. So, when you use these functions, be aware of how your edits relate to the music in and around your edits. For example, if you normalize or quieten a section of the waveform, the softest notes increase in volume only by the level that the highest note increases. For example, Figure 14-5 shows a percussion line before and after normalizing to maximum dB. The view on the left shows the levels before normalization. The one on the right is after the normalization procedure. The notes were raised a bit, and the overall dynamic range remains the same.

Next, take a look at Figure 14-6. This shows what happens when you choose the quietest section to normalize. As you can see, the relationship between the various notes has changed dramatically. Played back, this passage now sounds unnatural, and the original performance is altered beyond recognition.

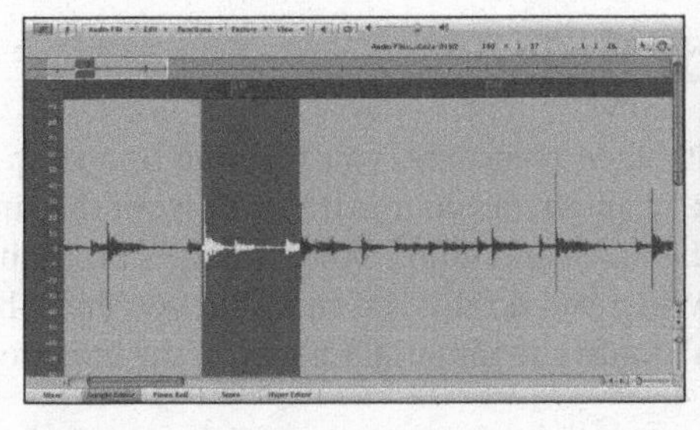
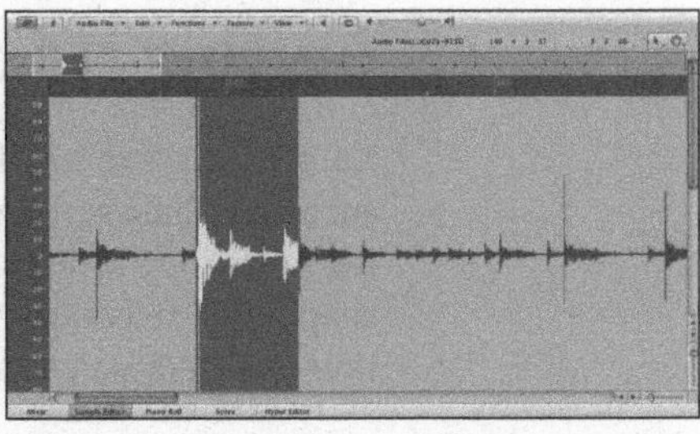

FIGURE 14-5: Normalizing keeps the dynamic range of the original section.

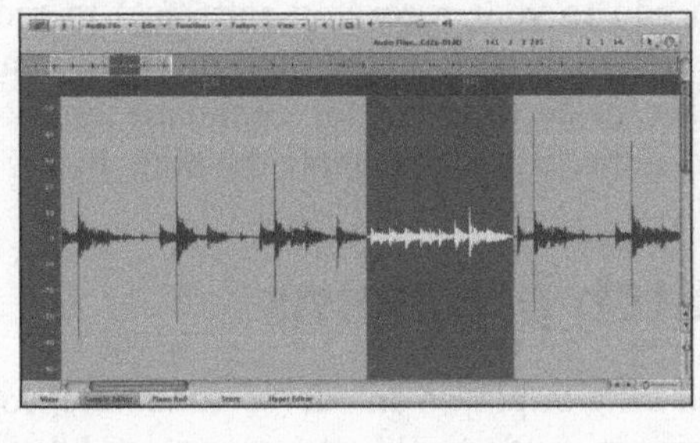
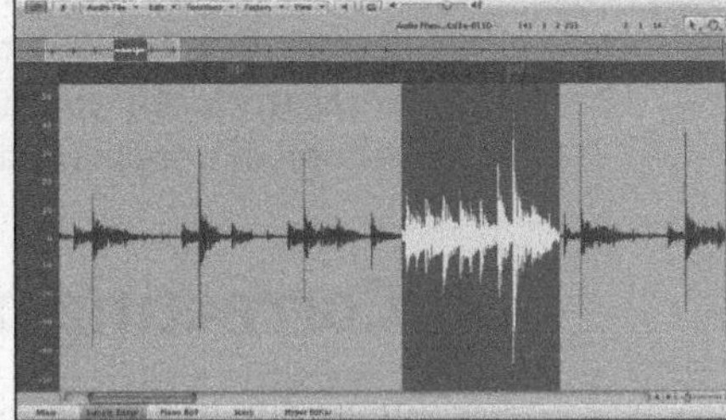

FIGURE 14-6: Choosing a quiet section of a song and normalizing it alters the dynamic range of the music.

Getting rid of distortion

In Chapter 5, I am adamant about setting your levels so that you don't get digital distortion. Even if you follow my advice and are extremely diligent in making sure that you didn't get any digital clipping, one note may have snuck through anyway. Well, it may not be the end of the world.

If you have a system that allows you to adjust the individual waves of a waveform, just reduce the level of the single clipped note. You do this by zooming in as close as you can to the distorted note and choosing only that one note to quieten. (Your system's manual should clearly explain this procedure.) If you can't adjust the waveform, you need to replace that note with a good, undistorted one (if you can find one) or reduce the level of that note until the distortion is hidden.

If this is the lead vocal, you probably don't have the option to reduce the level, and replacing a bad note in a vocal part generally sounds unnatural. If you can replace the section with another phrase from the song, that's your best bet. If you don't have that option and you can't rerecord the part, you can mask the distortion by adding a little distortion as an effect to the entire vocal track — a procedure that's performed more often than you may expect.

REMEMBER

If the performance is top-notch and if messing with it will take away some of the magic, you can always leave well enough alone and leave in the clipped note (distortion). After all, the performance is the most important part of any song.

Getting rid of noise

No matter what you do when recording, you're going to end up with extra noise, such as a chair squeak, a cough, or too much breath from the singer. To get rid of the noise, just select the noise and follow your system's procedures for erasing or silencing a selection. When you do this, be sure that you don't have a Snap function engaged; you don't want the material following the erasure to move.

Some computer-based systems also have sophisticated *plug-ins* (additional software that you can add to your recording software) to reduce noise within a track that has other material, such as the hum of an air conditioner behind a vocal track. All you have to do to reduce or eliminate this noise is choose the section of a track (or an entire track) and apply the plug-in.

Correcting pitch problems

It used to be that if you sang or played an out-of-tune note, you had to record it over again. If your singing is mediocre (like mine on a good day), you could spend hours trying to get every note just right. And after all these hours of fixing out-of-tune notes, you're often left with a performance that lacks "feel" (emotional impact). Well, those days are behind you. You can now edit your sour notes using a pitch-correction program. You can find pitch correction on nearly all digital recording systems that include effects processors (computer-based and SIAB systems in particular).

To correct pitch, choose the note(s) that you want to correct and then choose the pitch-correction option on your editing menu. In the dialog box that appears, choose the amount of change that you want. You may need to experiment a little to find just the right pitch.

Some devices, such as Antares Autotune, make the correction for you automatically. (Antares Autotune is available as both a stand-alone processor and as a plug-in for a computer-based system. You can find these components at most major musical instrument retailers.) And some pitch-correction programs, such as the one in Logic Audio, allow you to adjust not only the change in fundamental pitch but also the pitch change of that note's harmonics. This can produce a much more natural sound.

Unless you're going for a particular effect, be judicious in your use of pitch correction because it can suck the life out of a performance. Sometimes the slightly out-of-tune notes are what give a performance its character.

Pitch correction is often part of the system's editing functions, but it can be used as an effect as well. Check out Chapter 19 for ways pitch shifting can add depth to your music.

Creating a Performance That Never Happened

Editing can be much more than just fixing a bad note or phrase — editing can consist of assembling a performance that never really happened. In the following sections, I walk you through the often-timesaving process of putting together a song from small parts: one- or two-measure loops, single sections such as verses and choruses, and parts of separate performances from virtual tracks (called a *composite take*). Doing these procedures has advantages for you as a recording engineer. For example:

- By creating loops, you don't have to play the same one- or two-bar phrase over and over again for the duration of the song.
- By assembling song parts, you can alter the song's structure any way that you want.
- By making composite takes, you can create a performance that you could never play in one pass.

Creating loops

Loops are repeated phrases within a song. Looping has been around since the beginning of multitrack recording. You used to have to make an actual loop of tape containing the music that you wanted to repeat — thus, the name *loop* — and load the loop into an analog tape deck to play repeatedly. This tape deck was then connected to the multitrack deck, and the looped performance was recorded onto that deck.

Now all that looping can be done digitally. You can make loops of any instrument, but the most common ones involve drum rhythms. For example, each section of a song usually contains a short one- or two-bar rhythm that repeats many times. By using loops, you can just play the drum part once and make copies of it for the rest of the measures in that section. This saves you from having to play for the whole song. Looping can be a great feature if you play an instrument live and if keeping the part steady is fairly difficult. Chapter 13 goes into detail on how to create and work with loops.

Assembling a song

Okay, you've recorded all the parts for your new song and have the arrangement and structure the way that you thought you wanted it. But suddenly (or maybe not so suddenly), you wonder what the song would sound like if you started with the chorus instead of the first verse. (I know this isn't common, but go along with me here.) All you have to do is choose the chorus from all the tracks in the song and copy or move the tracks to the place where you want them to be.

TIP

This process is easiest if you created a tempo map of your song before you started to record and played to a metronome to keep in synch with the map. For more on creating tempo maps and using metronomes, check out Chapters 5 and 12.

Today, many musicians play just a portion of a song and assemble the song from there. For instance, except for the lead vocal, you can just record one verse and one chorus on each instrument. You then go into your editor palette and put the song together. This lets you alter the song's structure quickly and easily.

This procedure is pretty simple: Just choose your musical section and then cut, copy, or paste it to where you want it to be. If your system doesn't have the Cut and Paste functions, you can use the Copy and Move functions instead. (All these functions are described earlier in this chapter.)

Making compilations of your tracks

If you used your digital system to record several versions or takes of a part onto different tracks (also known as *virtual tracks* in some systems — tracks hidden behind a main track), you can use the editing function of your system to blend the best parts of each performance into one perfect track. Take, for example, a lead guitar part that may be used throughout the song to act as a counterpoint to the lead vocal. Now assume that you weren't sure when you recorded the part what you wanted to do for each phrase. In this case, you would have recorded several versions of this guitar part onto different tracks in your system (or onto several virtual tracks of one track). I explain this procedure in Chapter 19.

To make a composite track of the best parts of your various lead guitar takes, choose the parts that you want to use and move them all onto one more track (assuming that you have another empty track or virtual track to put them on). Keep in mind that you need to move each of the good parts one at a time because each is on a separate take or playlist.

You can move your guitar parts in one of the following ways:

- Click and drag your selection to the new virtual track.
- Use the Move function in your recorder to simply move the part from one virtual track to another.
- Use the Cut and Paste functions to cut the part from one virtual track and paste it to another.

When you're done assembling all the parts of one track, such as the lead guitar track, you can make adjustments to volume differences between the various assembled pieces using the Normalize or Quieten functions (described earlier in this chapter, in the section "Evening out a performance").

Discovering Other Ways to Use Editing

Aside from being able to fix problems in your tracks or to make changes to the structure of a song, you can use editing to simplify your other work. The following sections cover a couple ways that the editing capabilities of your digital system can be used outside the box, so to speak.

Adjusting the length of a performance

Time compression and expansion allow you to make small adjustments to the length of a section of music. This can be useful if you're trying to match your music to a video or if you want to change the feel of a vocal performance. For example, you can slow the last word in a phrase for a more crooner-type sound, or you can match certain words to rhythmic accents in the music. You can also fix a poorly performed drum fill (one that speeds up or slows down).

To compress or expand a section, you use a function called — at least on some systems — Time Machine. To use it, select the music that you want to edit and fill in the parameters in the Time Machine dialog box.

Reversing a phrase

Being able to change the waveforms of your music can open a lot of possibilities for experimentation. I'm sure you've listened to a recording and been told that a subliminal message was hidden within the music. Of course, the Beatles were famous for putting reversed vocals in the back of the mix, and you can do this easily as well. Just record a vocal phrase like "Buy Jeff Strong's CDs," select it, and then choose Edit ⇨ Reverse. Presto! You have a subliminal message. (Sit back and watch my music sales go through the roof!)

Reversing a musical phrase can be used in many more ways than to peddle my sorry music, however. For example, you can add a reversed drumbeat or cymbal crash to add anticipation. This was overused in the 1980s, but I think it can still be effective, depending on the style of music that you play.

To do this procedure, follow these steps:

1. **Select a drumbeat (be sure to get the initial attack) and copy it to an empty track.**
2. **Place the end of your selection where the drumbeat that you want to anticipate begins.**
3. **Choose Edit ⇨ Reverse to reverse the phrase.**

   If you play both tracks, you hear a reversed snare go right into a regular snare hit. Both attacks should happen at the same time. If they aren't exact, just move the reversed one over until the attacks are the same.

IN THIS CHAPTER

» Exploring MIDI windows

» Editing MIDI data

» Quantizing your performance

» Transposing your track

» Saving your work

» Transferring MIDI data between systems

Chapter 15

Editing MIDI Data

One of the best things about recording with MIDI (the Musical Instrument Digital Interface) is that, aside from being able to change the sound at any point without any compromises to the performance, you have immense control over nearly all aspects of your musical performance.

The editing capabilities for MIDI tracks are quite extensive. Not only can you perform the typical cut, copy, and paste functions, but you can also *quantize* (tighten up the rhythmic quality of a performance) and *transpose* (adjust the pitch of a note), which I cover in the sections that follow.

Understanding MIDI Windows

In most newer sequencer programs, you have two main windows from which to do your editing. These are:

» **Piano-roll graphic window:** This is the most common way to edit MIDI performances. Look at Figure 15-1. In this window, the horizontal bars in the center are the MIDI notes recorded on the track. Each of these notes can be lengthened, shortened, and moved. The top of this window contains navigation tools, editing options, and *quantization values* (the note value used to adjust the timing of a performance). Just select the note, and you can use any of these editing functions.

You can also view detailed note data including the note's start time and length, pitch, velocity (volume — both on and off), and MIDI channel by double-clicking a note in the grid.

» **Score window:** If you read music, the score window may be your choice for editing. This window looks just like a piece of sheet music (as shown in Figure 15-2). Within this window, you can move notes around in much the same way as the piano-roll window. The only difference is that you can see the musical score as you edit your performance. Some sequencers allow you to print the score as well. This can be handy if you're composing music that you want other people to play.

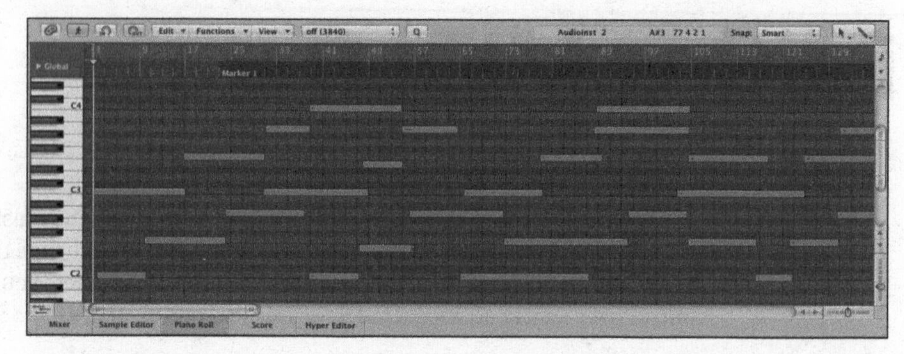

FIGURE 15-1: The piano-roll window lets you do a variety of editing functions.

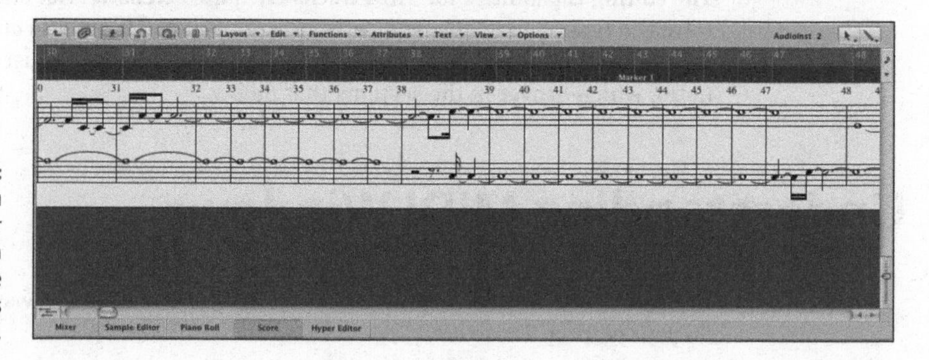

FIGURE 15-2: The Score menu shows you your MIDI data in musical score form and allows you to edit them.

Selecting track material

You can select track material the same way you select material from audio tracks — well, okay, with a few variations. The following sections tell you about those variations; Chapter 10 covers the selection stuff about audio tracks that's perfectly applicable to MIDI and instrument tracks.

Selecting notes with the Pencil tool

You select notes with the Pencil tool by clicking the notes. (No big deal, right?) To select more than one note, press the Shift key while you click each note. Selected notes become highlighted.

Using the Selector tool

When you use the Selector tool to select notes, certain conditions apply. They're pretty straightforward:

- Before a note can be included in a selection, its start point must be in the selection range.
- Notes with end points outside the selection range are still selected.
- When you select notes with the Selector tool, you also select (automatically) all the underlying automation and controller data pertaining to the notes.

Setting MIDI patches on tracks

You can change the default program (sound patch) in use with your MIDI tracks so your MIDI device automatically resets to the program you want for your track. Here's how to make it happen in Pro Tools (other programs have similar steps):

1. **Click the Program button in the Track Controls section of the Edit window.**

   The Patch Select dialog box opens.

2. **Click the patch number or name that you want from the list in the main section of the dialog box.**

   It becomes highlighted.

   Depending on your MIDI device, you might need to specify a bank along with the patch number. The bank number is entered in one of the Controller fields at the top of the dialog box. Check the specification for your device to see what to enter in this field.

3. **Click Done.**

   The Patch Select dialog box closes, and the patch number/name is displayed on the Program button of the Track Controls section.

Adding MIDI events

You can add MIDI notes or controller data (collectively called *MIDI events*) to a MIDI or Instrument track by using the Pencil tool. This section shows you how most programs perform this procedure.

Inserting notes

To use the Pencil tool to insert a note, do the following:

1. **Click and hold the Pencil icon and then choose the Pencil tool you want to use from the Pencil Tool drop-down menu that appears.**
2. **Locate the place you want to add your MIDI note in the track's playlist area.**
3. **With the Pencil tool you select in Step 1, click in the playlist to insert a note with a duration equal to the grid value.**

Drawing velocity or continuous controller data

To draw velocity or continuous controller data in a track's playlist, do the following:

1. **Click and hold the Pencil icon and then choose the Pencil tool you want to use from the menu that appears.**
2. **Locate where you want to enter your MIDI data in the track's playlist.**
3. **With the Pencil tool you choose in Step 1, click and drag in the track's playlist to sketch in the velocity or the controller level you want to draw.**
4. **Release the mouse button when you reach the end point of your edit.**

Inserting program changes

To insert MIDI program changes, do the following:

1. **From the Track View drop-down menu, set the track to Program Change view.**

2. **Click and hold the Pencil icon and then choose the Pencil tool you want to use from the menu that appears.**
3. **Click in the track's playlist where you want the change to occur.**

   The Patch Select dialog box opens.
4. **Click the patch number or name in the main section of the dialog box to select it.**
5. **Click Done.**

   The program change is inserted, as shown in Figure 15-3.

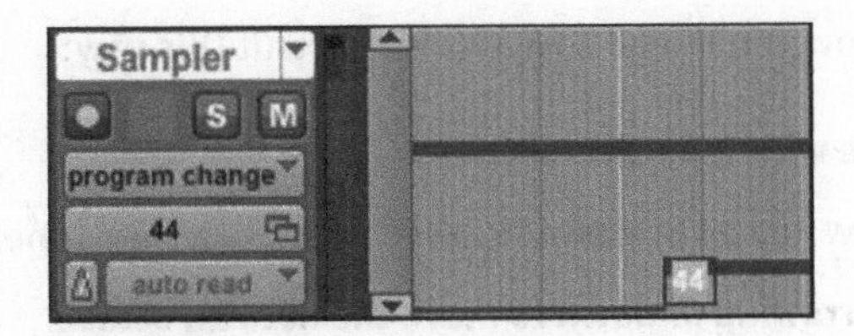

FIGURE 15-3: A program-change event appears in the track's playlist in Program Change view.

Deleting MIDI notes

To delete a MIDI note, do the following:

1. **Using the Selector tool, select the note in the playlist you want to delete.**
2. **Press Delete/Backspace on your keyboard or choose Edit ⇨ Clear from the main menu.**

REMEMBER

In some programs, deleting the note also deletes all automation and controller data.

Editing MIDI Data

Each note you play contains a plethora of information, all of which you can change. You can edit MIDI notes in a variety of ways including changing pitch, duration, velocity, and time location. This is easily done in the piano-roll window.

In this section, I show you how to make a variety of changes to your MIDI notes. All full-feature sequencing programs can perform these, though the exact process may differ.

Changing a note's pitch

To change a note's pitch, do the following:

1. **Choose the Selector or Pencil tool.**
2. **Click the note and drag it up (higher pitch) or down (lower pitch) in the playlist.**

   In some programs you can press Shift to keep the note's start point from changing while you move it.
3. **Release the mouse button when the note is where you want it.**

Some programs allow you to use a keyboard shortcut this way:

1. **Select the note with the Selector tool.**
2. **Press the arrow key up or down to move the note a semi tone.**
3. **Press Shift + Arrow up or down to move the note an octave.**
4. **Press Control + left or right Arrow (Mac) or Start + left or right Arrow (Windows) to move the note within the session's key.**

Changing a note's duration

To change a note's duration — its Start or End points — do the following:

1. **Choose the Selector or Pencil tool.**
2. **Click the note you want to change.**

   TIP

   Press Shift while you click to select more than one note.
3. **Click the Start or End point of the note and drag it left or right.**
   - *If your edit mode is set to Grid,* the note is moved along the grid boundary.
   - *If you're using the Spot edit mode,* the Spot dialog box appears; there, you can type in a location for the note and then click Done.
4. **Release the mouse button when the note is where you want it.**

Or, in some programs, you can use the following keyboard shortcut:

1. **Select the note with the Selector tool.**
2. **Press Control + left or right Arrow (Mac) or Start + left or right Arrow (Windows) to move the note's start time one grid value.**

3. **Press Option + left or right Arrow (Mac) or Alt + left or right Arrow (Windows) to move the end time of the note one grid value.**

   Adding Shift to the key command moves the note two grid values.

Changing a note's velocity

In the MIDI world, *velocity* means *volume.* To change a note's velocity, do the following:

1. **Choose the Selector tool.**
2. **Click-hold over the note.**
3. **Drag left to decrease or right to increase the volume.**

Or, in some programs like Pro Tools, you can use the following keyboard shortcut:

1. **Select the note with the Grabber or Smart tool.**
2. **Press Command + up or down Arrow (Mac) or Control + up or down Arrow (Windows) to change the note's velocity by five units.**

   Add Shift to the key command to change the velocity by 15 units.

TIP

Some programs let you color-code your MIDI notes according to their velocity. In Logic Pro, you do this by choosing View⇨ Set Note Color⇨ By Velocity.

Changing time locations

Time locations define where the Start points of your notes are placed within your session. To change a note's time location, do the following:

1. **Choose the Selector or Pencil tool.**

   In some programs, such as Pro Tools, pressing Shift will keep the note's pitch from changing while you move it.

2. **Click the note and drag it left or right.**
   - *If your edit mode is set to Grid,* the note is moved along the grid boundary.
   - *If you're using Spot edit mode,* the Spot dialog box appears; there, you can type in a location for the note and then click Done.
3. **Release the mouse button when the note is where you want it.**

Moving notes freely

To move a note freely in the track, do the following:

1. **Choose the Selector or Pencil tool.**
2. **Click the note and drag it left or right, up or down.**
3. **Release the mouse button when the note is where you want it.**

Editing Program Data

Because MIDI contains no sound in itself, you can create program change events to change the sound patches of your MIDI sound modules throughout the session. This can keep your computer processing resources optimized as well as keep you from using more tracks than absolutely necessary for your session.

Changing program patches

Program patches are the sounds available in your MIDI device. Here's how to change program patches:

1. **From the Track View drop-down menu, set the track to Program Change view.**
2. **With the Grabber tool, double-click the program change event you want to change.**

   The Patch Select dialog box appears.
3. **In the Patch Select dialog box, select the new patch name/number.**

   If the patch resides on a different bank as the current patch, select the new bank as well.
4. **Click Done.**

   The Patch Select dialog box closes, and the new program is sounded when you play your session.

Moving program change markers

Program change markers are helpful little tools because they tell Pro Tools when to change the sound of your MIDI device while your session plays. To move a program change marker, follow these steps:

1. **From the Track View drop-down menu, set the track to Program Change view.**
2. **Select the Grabber or the Pencil tool.**
3. **Click and drag the Program Change Marker left or right.**
   - *If you have Grid mode enabled,* the program change event moves to the closest grid boundary.
   - *If you have Spot mode selected,* the Spot dialog box opens; there, you can enter a new location for the marker and then click Done.

Changing Continuous Controller Data

When you deal with *continuous controller data,* you are dealing with Volume, Pan, Pitch Bend, Mono Aftertouch, and MIDI controllers. All this data is represented as a line graph punctuated by a series of breakpoints. You have a choice when you want to make changes: You can edit the line itself using the Pencil tool; or you can edit the breakpoints by using the Grabber, the Pencil, or the Smart tool.

Editing lines with the Pencil tool

To edit the line graph with a Pencil tool, do the following:

1. **From the Track View drop-down menu, select the track view that corresponds to the parameter you want to edit (Volume, Pan, Pitch Bend, Mono Aftertouch, MIDI Controller).**
2. **Click and hold the Pencil icon, and then select the Pencil tool you want to use from the menu that appears.**
3. **Click in the playlist where you want to start drawing and then drag your mouse to draw the new values.**

   The line is drawn, and breakpoints are inserted according to the resolution you set for the Pencil Tool Resolution When Drawing Controller Data option on the MIDI tab of the Preferences dialog box. (Choose Setup ⇨ Preferences from the main menu to access the Preferences dialog box.)
4. **Release the mouse button when you reach the end of your edit.**

Editing breakpoints

If you're not adept at drawing lines, you might want to work with breakpoints instead. Here's how:

1. **From the Track View drop-down menu, select the track view that corresponds to the parameter you want to edit (Volume, Pan, Pitch Bend, Mono Aftertouch, MIDI Controller).**
2. **Select the Grabber tool.**
3. **Click and drag the breakpoint.**
4. **Release the mouse button.**

Scaling breakpoints

When you *scale breakpoints*, you move a group of breakpoints while retaining the relationship between them. You can use the Trimmer tool to scale breakpoints, as in the following step list:

1. **From the Track View drop-down menu, select the track view that corresponds to the parameter you want to edit (Volume, Pan, Pitch Bend, Mono Aftertouch, MIDI Controller).**
2. **Select the Selector tool.**
3. **With your mouse, click and drag across the breakpoints you want to scale.**

   The selection becomes highlighted.
4. **Select the Trimmer tool.**
5. **Click and drag the breakpoints up or down.**

   REMEMBER

   The breakpoints move as a unit, but they don't all move the same amount. Rather, they move differently to keep the relationship between the breakpoints intact.
6. **Release your mouse button.**

Quantizing Your Performance

Quantization is simply allowing the sequencer to fix your rhythmic timing. Say you recorded a drum pattern, and because you played it on your keyboard, the timing kinda stinks. The bass drum missed the downbeat, and the snare drum is inconsistent. Don't worry — you don't need to rerecord your part. You can just move all those notes into their proper places — and you don't even have to touch each note to do it. Just choose the quantization function, choose your settings, and click a button.

All sequencing programs have a quantize function, each with its own process, and offer these basic areas to adjust. Pro Tools contains the following fields (see Figure 15-4):

- **What to Quantize:** From this section, choose which part of the note to quantize:
  - *Note On:* Selecting this check box sets the quantization to the start of the selected notes.
  - *Note Off:* Selecting this check box quantizes the ends of the notes.
  - *Preserve Note Duration:* Selecting this check box produces different results depending on whether you choose Attacks or Releases.

    With Attacks selected, Preserve Note Duration keeps the end of the note intact. With Releases selected, the start of the note is left intact. If both Attacks and Releases are selected, the Preserve Note Duration option is dimmed.
- **Quantize Grid:** Here is where you choose the resolution of the quantize grid, from whole notes to sixty-fourth notes. If you choose sixteenth notes, for example, your notes will move to the nearest sixteenth note when you quantize.
  - *Note selector:* Choose the note value of your quantize grid from this drop-down menu. Click the note to select it.
  - *Tuplet:* This check box allows you to select odd note groupings, such as triplets. When you select this option, you need to fill in the tuplet value. For example, to create a regular eighth-note triplet, enter 3 in Time 1; for a quarter-note triplet, enter 3 in Time 2.
  - *Offset Grid By:* Use this option to move the Quantize grid forward or backward in time by the selected number of ticks. This is helpful for creating a groove that lies slightly ahead of — or behind — the beat.
  - *Randomize:* Using this option adds a level of randomness to the quantizing of your selection — no, not to mess up the rhythm, but to keep it from being too rigid. You can select values between 0% and 100%. Lower values place the randomized notes closer to the grid.

» **Options:** Select these items to fine-tune your Grid/Groove Quantize operation by specifying which notes to quantize and by how much:

- *Swing:* This option and slider allows you create a *swing feel* (a dotted-quarter, eighth-note triplet). You specify a percentage (from 0% to 300%); selecting 100% provides a triplet feel.
- *Include Within:* Here you specify a range of notes to include. Selecting this option quantizes only selected notes that fall within the boundaries you set here (from 0% to 100%); the smaller the number, the narrower the range of notes affected.
- *Exclude Within:* Here you specify a range of notes to exclude from quantization. Any selected notes that fall within the boundaries you set here (between 0% and 100%) won't be quantized.
- *Strength:* This is, in my opinion, the most useful function in the Pro Tool Grid/Groove Quantize operation. You can use it to move your quantized notes *by a percentage* (from 0% to 100%) rather than just snapping them right to the grid. Higher numbers keep more strictly to the grid than do the lower values.

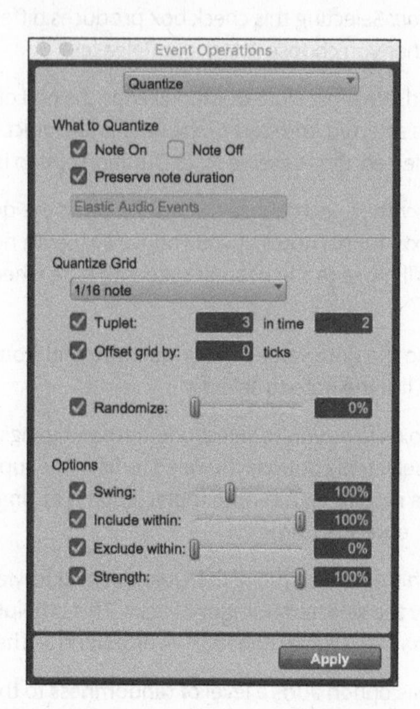

FIGURE 15-4: The Quantize function lets you align your MIDI notes to a time grid.

REMEMBER

Using the options in these four sections well helps keep a natural feel in your performance.

TIP

Many programs, Pro Tools included, allow you to assign a groove template to the notes you want to quantize. You also have the ability to create your own on many of these programs or to buy or upload professionally created ones.

TIP

Some programs, such as Pro Tools, also have an Input Quantize option. This allows you to set a quantize value that your recorded performance is adjusted to automatically as you record it. The fields you can adjust in the Input Quantize version of the Operations window (see Figure 15-5) are the same as with the Grid/Groove Quantize operation.

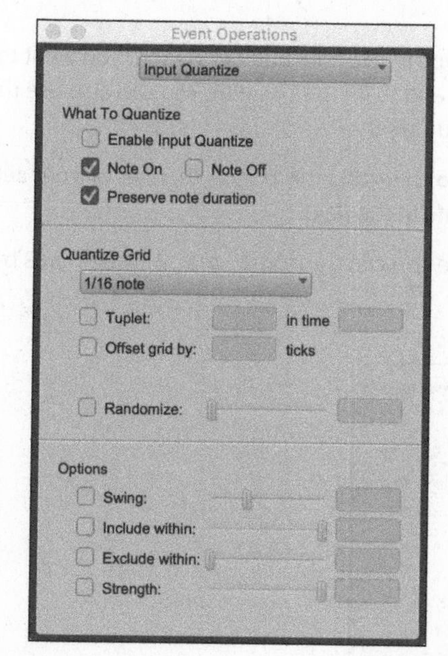

FIGURE 15-5: The Input Quantize function allows you to automatically adjust note timing while it's recorded.

TIP

Double-check your track after you've quantized it because it may have moved a misplaced note in the wrong direction. This happens if your note is farther away from where you want it to be and closer to another quantization point. If a note has moved in the wrong direction, select that note and move it to where you want it.

Transposing Your Performance

Transposing refers to changing the key of your selected notes (some programs call this *pitch quantization*). Depending on the program you use, you can do this several ways. This section explores the most common.

Use the Transpose operation to change the pitch of selected notes. Checking out the Transpose version of the MIDI Operations window, as shown in Figure 15-6, you see that the Transpose operation offers these ways of changing pitch:

- **Transpose By:** Use this setting to transpose by octaves or semitones (one half-step). You can either type in the value or use the sliders to adjust the setting.
- **Transpose:** Here you type in the note and octave that you want to transpose from (in the From field) and to (in the To field). You can also use the slider to adjust the settings if you prefer.
- **Transpose All Notes To:** Selecting this option changes all your selected notes to the note you designate in the field.
- **Transpose in Key:** Here you can transpose your selected notes by scale steps.

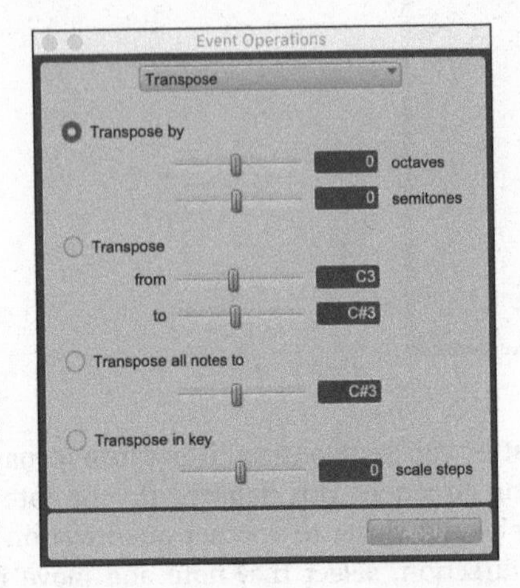

FIGURE 15-6: Use the Transpose function to change the pitch of a selection.

Transposing using this MIDI operation makes it easy to change the pitch — in effect, the musical key — of the entire song or clip. This is especially helpful if you decide that the song needs to be in a different key for your singer to sing well.

Saving Your Data

For the most part, saving data in your sequencer program is like saving data in any computer program. Yep, you need to click the Save button (or press ⌘+S if you have a Mac). Don't forget to save your work regularly, lest your computer crashes and you lose several hours' work.

The main thing to know about saving data in a sequencer program is that most programs have their own proprietary file format. You generally can't take a saved file from your program and play it on another one.

REMEMBER

If you want to play your MIDI tracks on another sequencer program or make it available on the Internet for other people to play, make sure that you save your music as a Standard MIDI File (SMF). Nearly all sequencer programs allow you to save in this format. Some even do this by default. Check your owner's manual to see how to do this. Then you can give your MIDI tracks to anyone who can play an SMF, and if you recorded your stuff by using a GM standard, it sounds just how you intended it to sound, regardless of the listener's gear.

Transferring Data Using MIDI

Another great thing about MIDI is that you can use the cable and ports to send more than just MIDI performance information. Many manufacturers allow you to send sound patches through the MIDI connection by using system-exclusive messages. This can be a great tool. In fact, I own an electronic drum set; its sounds can be changed and updated by connecting a MIDI cable between the sound module (brain) and my computer. I can store gazillions of sounds on my computer without cluttering up (or overloading) my drum set's brain. But wait, it gets even better. This manufacturer makes new sounds available on its website to download for free! Yep, I can add new sounds to my drum set without having to buy anything. You gotta love it!

Performing a data transfer via your MIDI connection is easy. Just connect your device to the MIDI interface on your computer, open the data-transfer software provided by the manufacturer, and follow the directions.

5 Mixing and Mastering Your Music

IN THIS PART . . .

Explore the process of editing audio and MIDI data to help you clean up your recorded tracks or to create new arrangements of your songs.

Get clear on mixing, the process of blending all your individual tracks into a cohesive whole.

Use signal processors to add interest and dimension to your music.

Add the final touch to your album with mastering so that it can compete with the albums you find at the music store.

Put your music in its final format for distribution, including on the Internet, vinyl, and as a physical CD.

IN THIS CHAPTER

» Getting to know the mix process

» Managing levels

» Understanding the stereo field

» Using reference music

Chapter 16
Mixing Basics

Think about all the time it took for you to record all the tracks for your song. You spent countless hours setting up mics; getting good, *hot* (high, but not distorting) levels on your instruments; and making sure that each performance was as good as you could get it. You'd think, then, that most of your work would be done.

Well, on the one hand, it is — because you no longer have to set up and record each instrument. On the other hand, you still have to make all the parts that you recorded fit together. This process can take as long as it took you to record all the tracks in the first place. In fact, for many people, it takes even longer to mix the song than to record all its parts.

In this chapter, I introduce you to the process of mixing your music. You discover how to set up external mixing aids, such as Musical Instrument Digital Interface (MIDI) control surfaces, digital mixers, and analog mixers. You also discover how to reference your music to other people's recordings as well as how to train your ears so that your mix "translates" to different types of playback systems.

REMEMBER

Mixing music is very subjective. You can relate one instrument to another in an almost infinite variety of ways. You might find that several mixes work equally well for your song. Allow yourself to experiment — and don't be afraid to record several different mixes.

Understanding Mixing

The goal of mixing is to make sure each instrument can be heard in the *mix* — the recorded whole that results from blending all your recorded parts — without covering up something else or sounding out of place. You can pull this off in several ways:

- **Choose the parts that add to the emotional impact of the music and build intensity throughout the song.** By necessity, this also means choosing to not use unnecessary parts or those that clash with parts that have a greater effect.
- **Set the *level* (volume) of each instrument relative to the others.** That way, nothing is buried so far back in the mix that you can't hear it, and no instrument is so loud that it overpowers the other instruments.
- **Adjust the equalization (EQ, or frequency response) of each instrument.** This leaves room for all instruments in the mix. You get rid of any frequencies of an instrument that clash with those of another, or emphasize certain frequencies that define the sound of an instrument so it can be heard clearly in the mix.
- **Take advantage of stereo panning (movement from left to right).** This puts each instrument in its proper place in the stereo field — toward the left or right — where it can either sound as natural as possible or produce a desired effect. Also, stereo panning allows you to make room for each instrument in the mix, especially those with similar frequency ranges.
- **Add effects (such as reverb or delay) to the instruments in the mix.** You place instruments in front or in back, relative to other instruments, or to create a desired sound.

REMEMBER

During mixing, you can get really creative in crafting your song. The stress of capturing great performances is over: All that's left for you to do is to massage all the parts of your song into a cohesive whole. Don't be afraid to try new things. Experiment with different EQ, panning, and effect settings. Take your time and have fun. The great thing about mixing is that you can make as many versions as you want — and you can always go back and try again.

Managing Levels as You Work

When you mix all the tracks in your session, the *mix bus* (which, for its part, is controlled by the Master fader) is where they end up. There the signals are *summed* (added) and result in a *level* (volume) that's higher than that of the original tracks. One danger of mixing in-the-box (within the computer) is that this level can get pretty high, and you might not recognize it unless you listen very carefully.

TIP

While you work, watch the level meter in the Master fader and make adjustments to the individual tracks to bring down the individual levels, rather than dropping the fader on the master.

TIP

Many people like to get the most volume out of a song when mixing, so they crank up the Master fader to where the levels peak right at 0 decibels (dB) or maybe –0.1dB. This used to be considered okay, but more and more professional engineers are backing off on the mix bus by as much as 6dB. This is what I recommend as well. Keep your peak levels that go to the Master fader down to about –3dB to –6dB and make this up when you master (or have someone else master) your music. Sure, the volume will be lower than it is on the commercial music you own, but you can adjust that during the mastering process. (Chapter 22 has more on mastering.)

The advantage to keeping down peak levels is that you get better levels going to the mix bus and reduce the chance that some *clipping* happens. (Clipping is also called *overs* in digital recording; it's distortion that results when the summed signals end up too hot and overload the mix bus.)

Getting Started Mixing Your Song

Before I start to mix a song, I do a few things to prepare myself for the process. My goal before I mix is to get in the headspace of mixing. This often means taking a step back from the song and approaching it as a listener rather than as the musician who recorded each track. Start the mixing process by following these steps:

1. **Determine the overall quality you want from the song.**

   At this point, I don't mean *quality* in terms of, "Is it good or bad?" Rather, I define quality here as a musical style or a feeling. Do you want it to kick? Soothe? Scream? You probably don't need to think about this too hard if you had a definite sound in mind when you started recording. In fact, most composers hear a song in their heads before they even start recording.

2. **Listen to a song or two from a CD that has a sound or feel similar to the song you're trying to mix.**

   Listen to the examples on your studio monitors if you can; try to get a sense of the tonal and textural quality of these songs. Listen to them at fairly low volume; be careful not to tire your ears. All you're trying to do at this point is get your ears familiar with the sound you're trying to produce in your music.

3. **Set up a rough mix, using no EQ or effects, and listen through a song once.**

   For this listening session, don't think like a producer; rather, try to put yourself in the mindset of the average listener. Listen to the various parts you recorded — does anything stick out as particularly good or bad? You're not listening for production quality. You're trying to determine which instruments, musical phrases, licks, melodies, or harmonies grab you as a listener.

4. **Get a piece of paper and a pen to jot down ideas while you work.**

   When you listen through the song, take notes on where certain instruments should be in the mix. For example, you might want the licks played on lead guitar throughout the song to be muted during the first verse. Or maybe you decide that the third rhythm guitar part you recorded would be best put way to the right side of the mix, while the other two rhythm guitar parts might be closer to the center. Write down these ideas so you can try them later. Chances are that you'll have a lot of ideas as you listen through the first few times.

Mixing in DAWs

Most digital audio workstation (DAW) programs, such as Logic Pro X or Pro Tools, come with a powerful software mixer, and everything you might want to do can be done via your mouse and keyboard. Even so, many people — myself included — prefer to mix by using real faders, knobs, and buttons. This can be done several ways: using a computer control surface (such as the Artist Mix or a Mackie MCU Pro), a MIDI controller, a digital mixer, or an analog mixer. These alternative types of mixers are covered in more detail in Chapter 4; for now, I just want to cover the basic setups of these various options.

Using a control surface

If you have a computer control surface such as Avid's Artist Mix (see Figure 16-1), your system is easily integrated within the software. With your system hooked up via USB, MIDI, or wirelessly, all your faders, knobs, and buttons work seamlessly with the software mixer. When you push a fader on the control surface, the corresponding track fader on the computer screen moves as well. An Internet search for "DAW controller" will bring up quite a few great options.

Using a digital mixer

If you want to use a digital mixer with your computer-based audio recording system, you need to make sure you have the proper number of digital inputs and outputs in your audio interface to connect to your mixer.

For example, if you have a MOTU 828x, you have ten outputs (eight ADAT and two S/PDIF) that you can use to send your tracks from your computer to your mixer. (Just make sure that your mixer can accept ADAT and S/PDIF signals — Chapter 3 has more on ADAT and S/PDIF — at the same time; otherwise you're down to eight.) This means you can send no more than ten tracks of material to your mixer to mix.

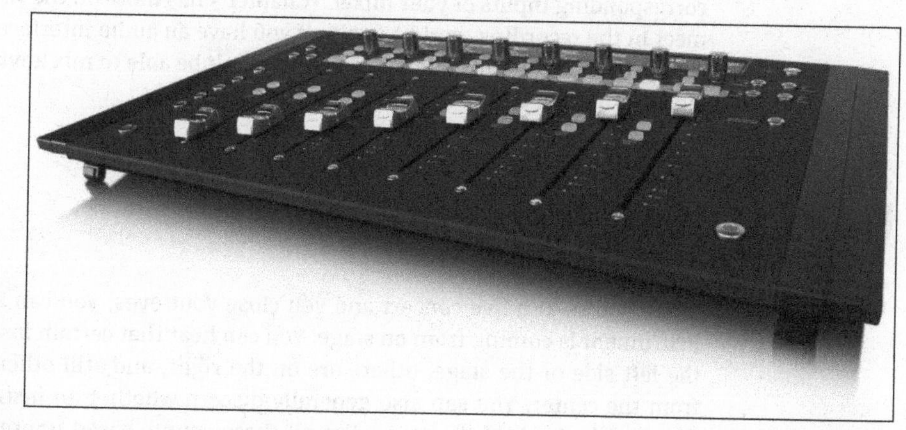

FIGURE 16-1: Mixing with Avid's Artist Mix control surface lets you use your hands to control the mix.

Courtesy of Avid

TIP

If you're equipped with an audio interface that doesn't have enough digital ins and outs, such as a Focusrite Scarlett 2i2, you have too few inputs and outputs to work successfully with a digital mixer. In this case, if you want to mix with faders you really need to go the MIDI controller route.

In this example, if you have a session with more than ten tracks, your digital mixer becomes somewhat useless unless you want to mix in stages (ten tracks at a time) or mix in the box (within your computer) *and* from your mixer.

To connect your digital mixer to your system, simply run the appropriate cables (ADAT, for instance) from the output of your audio interface to the input of your digital mixer. When you move a fader (or a button or a knob) in your mixer, the corresponding fader (or button or knob) track in the audio recording software you see onscreen won't be affected.

Using an analog mixer

Like with a digital mixer, your ability to mix in an analog mixer is limited by how many outputs your interface has. In this case, it all depends on the number of analog outputs you have. For example, the MOTU 828x provides eight analog outputs, so this is the maximum number of tracks you can mix with an analog mixer at any one time.

TIP

Mixing a session with more than eight tracks is possible, but it's not worth the hassle (in my opinion) unless you have a really expensive analog mixer. Inexpensive analog mixers (those less than $10,000, for instance) won't sound any better than mixing within your computer.

If you want to mix your session through an analog mixer, just connect each analog output from your audio interface to one of the inputs of your mixer. In the case of the MOTU 828x, you need eight TS cables running from outputs 1 through 8 to the corresponding inputs of your mixer. (Chapter 3 has more on the various cables you meet in the recording world.) Again, if you have an audio interface that only has a couple of analog inputs and outputs, you won't be able to mix anything other than simple songs (few tracks) using an analog mixer.

Using the Stereo Field

When you're at a live concert and you close your eyes, you can hear where each instrument is coming from on stage. You can hear that certain instruments are on the left side of the stage, others are on the right, and still others seem to come from the center. You can also generally discern whether an instrument is at the front or the back of the stage. Put all these sound-based impressions together, and you have a 3-D image made of sound — a *stereo field*.

What makes up the stereo field is the specific placement of sound sources from left to right and front to back. When you mix a song, you can set your instruments wherever you want them on the imaginary "stage" created by your listener's speakers. You can do this with *panning*, which sets your instruments from left to right. You can also use *effects* (such as reverb and delay) to provide the illusion of distance, placing your instruments toward the front or back in your mix. (See Chapter 19 for more on effects.) When you mix your song, try to visualize where on stage each of your instruments might be placed.

Some people choose to set the panning and depth of their instruments to sound as natural as possible, and others use these settings to create otherworldly sounds. There is no right or wrong when panning and adding effects to simulate depth — just what works for your goals. Don't be afraid to get creative and try unusual things.

Left or right

You adjust each instrument's position from left to right in a mix with the Panning control. (See Figure 16-2 for its location in Pro Tools.) Panning for most songs is pretty straightforward, and I outline some settings in the following sections. Some mixing engineers like to keep their instruments toward the center of the mix; other engineers prefer spreading things way out with instruments on either end of the spectrum. There's no absolute right or wrong way to pan instruments. In fact, no one says you have to leave any of your instruments in the same place throughout the entire song. Just make sure that your panning choices contribute to the overall effect of the music.

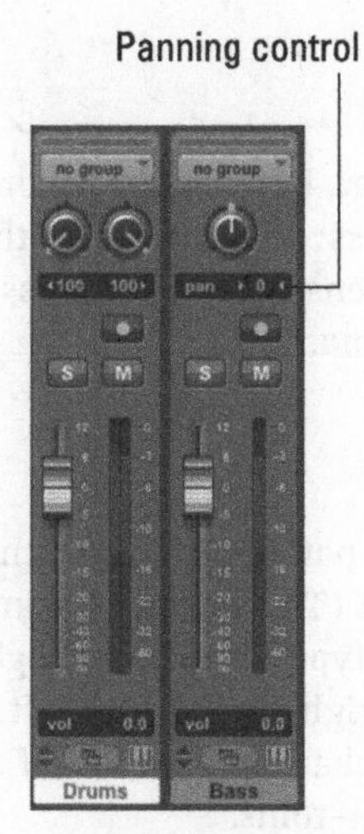

FIGURE 16-2: The Panning control in Pro Tools is located above the main fader in each track's channel strip. Left: a stereo track. Right: a mono track.

Lead vocals

Lead vocals are usually panned directly in the center. This is mainly because the vocals are the center of attention and panning them left or right takes the focus away from them. Some people will pan the vocals off center if there is more than one lead vocal (as in a duet), but this can get cheesy real fast unless you're very subtle about it. Of course, you're the artist and you may come up with a really cool effect moving the vocal around.

Backup vocals

Because backup vocals are often recorded in stereo, they are panned hard left and hard right. If you recorded only one track of backup vocals, you can make a duplicate of the track and pan one to each side, just like you can with stereo tracks. Then you can either nudge one forward or backward in time by a few milliseconds or adjust the pitch up or down a semi-tone to differentiate the two tracks.

In addition to tracks panned to each side, some mixing engineers also have a third backup vocal track panned in the center to add more depth. Your choice to do this depends on how you recorded your backup vocals as well as how many tracks are available for them.

Guitar parts

Lead guitar is often panned to the center, or just slightly off-center if the sound in the center of the stereo field is too cluttered. Rhythm guitar, on the other hand, is generally placed somewhere just off-center. Which side doesn't matter, but it's usually the opposite side from any other background instruments, such as an additional rhythm guitar, a synthesizer, an organ, or a piano.

Bass

Typically, bass guitar is panned in the center, but it's not uncommon for mixing engineers to create a second track for the bass: panning one to the far left and the other to the far right. This gives the bass a sense of spaciousness and allows more room for bass guitar and kick drum in the mix.

Drums

As a general rule, I (and most other people) pan the drums so that they appear in the stereo field much as they would on stage. (This doesn't mean that you have to, though.) Snare drums and kick drums are typically panned right up the center, with the tom-toms panned from slightly right to slightly left. Hi-hat cymbals often go just to the right of center; ride cymbals are just left of center; and crash cymbals sit from left to right, much like tom-toms.

Percussion

Percussion instruments tend to be panned just off to the left or right of center. If I have a shaker or triangle part that plays throughout the song, for instance, I'll pan it to the right an equal distance from center as the hi-hat is to the left. This way, you hear the hi-hat and percussion parts playing off one another in the mix.

Piano/synthesizers/organs

These instruments are usually placed just off-center. If your song has rhythm guitar parts, the piano or organ usually goes to the other side. Synthesizers can be panned all over the place. In fact, synths are often actively panned throughout the song: That is, they move from place to place.

Front or back

As you probably discovered when you were placing your mics to record an instrument, the quality of sound changes when you place a mic closer to — or farther away from — the instrument. The closer you place the mic, the less room ambience you pick up, which makes the instrument sound closer to you, or "in your face." By contrast, the farther from the instrument you place your mic, the more room sound you hear: The instrument sounds farther away.

Think of standing in a large room and talking to someone to see (well, hear, actually) how this relationship works. When someone stands close to you and talks, you can hear him clearly. You hear very little of the reflections of his voice from around the room. As he moves farther away from you, though, the room's reflections play an increasing role in the way that you hear him. By the time the other person is at the other side of the room, you hear not only his voice but also the room where you're at. In fact, if the room is large enough, the other person probably sounds as if he were a mile away from you, and all the reflections from his voice bouncing around the room may make it difficult to understand what he says.

You can easily simulate this effect by using your reverb or delay effects processors. In fact, this is often the purpose of reverb and delay in the mixing process. With them, you can effectively "place" your instruments almost anywhere that you want them, from front to back, in your mix.

TIP

The less reverb or delay you use with your instrument, the closer it appears on the recording; the more effect you add to an instrument, the farther away it seems.

The type of reverb or delay setting that you use has an effect on how close or far away a sound appears as well. For example, a longer reverb decay or delay sounds farther away than a shorter one.

In Chapter 19, I go into detail about the various effects processors to help you understand how best to use them. I also present settings you can use to create natural-sounding reverb and delay on your tracks, as well as some unusual settings that you can use for special effects.

Adjusting Levels: Enhancing the Emotion of the Song

After you have a rough mix and get your EQ (described in Chapter 17) and panning settings where you want them, your next step is to determine which parts of which tracks are used when — and sometimes whether a part or track is used at all. If you're like most musician/producers, you try to get all the wonderful instrumental and vocal parts you recorded as loud as possible in the mix so that each brilliant note can be heard clearly all the time. After all, you didn't go through all the time and effort to record all those great tracks just to hide them in the mix or (worse yet) mute them, right?

Well, I feel your pain. But when you get to the mixing point of a song, it's time to take off your musician's hat and put on the one that reads *Producer.* And a producer's job is to sort through all the parts of a song, choose those that add to its effect, and dump those that are superfluous or just add clutter. Your goal is to assemble the tracks that tell the story you want to tell and that carry the greatest emotional impact for the listener.

REMEMBER

This can be the toughest part of mixing your own songs because you aren't likely to be totally objective when it comes to determining what to use and what not to use. Try not to get stressed out. You aren't erasing any of your tracks, so you can always do another mix if you just have to hear the part that you muted before.

One of the great joys when listening to music (for me, anyway) is hearing a song that carries me away and pulls me into the emotional journey that the songwriter had in mind. If the song is done well, I'm sucked right into the song; by the end, all I want to do is listen to it again.

What is it about certain songs that can draw you in and get you to feel the emotion of the performers? Well, aside from a good melody and some great performances, it's how the arrangement builds throughout the song to create tension, release that tension, and build it up again. A good song builds intensity so that the listener feels pulled into the emotions of the song.

Generally, a song starts out quiet, becomes a little louder during the first chorus, and then drops down in level for the second verse (not as quiet as the first, though). The second chorus is often louder and fuller than the first chorus, and is often followed by a bridge section that is even fuller yet (or at least differs in arrangement from the second chorus). The loud bridge section might be followed by a third verse where the volume drops a little. Then a superheated chorus generally follows the last verse and keeps building intensity until the song ends.

When you're crafting the mix for your song, you have two tools at your disposal to build and release intensity: dynamics and instrumental content (the arrangement).

Dynamics

Dynamics are simply how loud or soft something is — and whether the loudness is emotionally effective. Listen to a classic blues tune (or even some classical music), and you'll hear sections where the song is almost deafeningly silent, and other sections where you think the band is actually going to step out of the speakers and into your room. This is an effective and powerful use of dynamics. The problem is that this seems to be a lost art, at least in popular music.

It used to be that a song can have very quiet parts and really loud ones. Unfortunately, a lot of music nowadays has only one level — loud. This often isn't the fault of the musicians or even the band's producer. Radio stations and record company bean counters have fueled this trend, betting that if a band's music is as loud as (or louder than) other music on the market, it'll attract more attention and sell more. (You can read more about this trend in Chapter 22.) But consider this: Whether you can hear the music is one thing; whether it's worth listening to is another.

TIP

Try recording a song with a lot of dynamic changes. I know this bucks the trend, but who knows? You might end up with a song that carries a ton of emotional impact. Also, while you mix your song, incorporate dynamic variation by dropping the levels of background instruments during the verses and bringing them up during the chorus and bridge sections of the song. You can always eliminate your dynamic variation (if you absolutely have to) by squashing your mix with compression during the mastering process.

WARNING

The biggest mistake that most people make when they mix their own music is to try to get their song as loud as commercial music. This is the mastering engineer's job, however, and not yours, so don't worry about it. Get your song to sound good with a balance between high and low frequencies and loud and soft sections. Leave it to the mastering stage to make your music as loud as it can be. Chapter 22 has more on mastering your music.

The arrangement

Building intensity with the arrangement involves varying the amount of sound in each section. A verse with just lead vocal, drums, bass, and an instrument playing the basic chords of the song is going to have less intensity (not to mention volume) than a chorus awash with guitars, backup vocals, drums, percussion, organ, and so on. Most songs that build intensity effectively start with fewer instruments than they end with.

When you mix your song, think about how you can use the instruments to add to the emotional content of your lyrics. For example, if you have a guitar lick played at every break in the vocal line, think about using it less to leave space for lower levels at certain points in your song. If you do this, each lick will provide more impact for the listener and bring more to the song's emotion.

Tuning Your Ears

To create a mix that sounds good, the most critical tools you need are your ears because your capability to hear the music clearly and accurately is essential. To maximize this capability, you need a decent set of studio monitors and a good idea how other people's music sounds on your speakers. You also need to make sure that you don't mix when your ears are tired. The following sections explore these areas.

Listening critically

One of the best ways to learn how to mix music is to listen to music that you like — and listen, in particular, for how it's mixed. Put on a recording of something similar to your music (or music with sound that you like) and ask yourself the following questions:

- **What is the overall tonal quality or texture of the song?** Notice how the frequencies of all the instruments cover the hearing spectrum. Does the song sound smooth or harsh, full or thin? Try to determine what you like about the overall production.
- **How does the song's arrangement contribute to its overall feel?** Listen for licks or phrases that add to the arrangement. Notice whether the song seems to get fuller as it goes on.
- **Where are the instruments in the stereo field?** Notice where each instrument is, from left to right and front to back, in the mix. Listen to see whether they stay in one place throughout the song or move around.
- **What effects are being used on each instrument?** Listen for reverb and delay — in particular, how they affect decay lengths — as well as for the overall effect level compared to the dry (unaffected) signal.
- **What tonal quality does each instrument have?** Try to determine the frequencies from each instrument that seem dominant. Pay particular attention to how the drums sound, especially the snare drum. You'll notice a good mix lets all the instruments fit without fighting one another. Drums can take up a lot of room in the mix if you don't narrow them down to their essential frequencies.

Even if you're not mixing one of your songs, just sit down once in a while and *listen to music* on your monitors to get used to listening to music critically. Also, the more well-made music you hear on your monitors, the easier it is to know when your music sounds good on those same speakers.

REMEMBER

A good mix should sound good on a variety of systems, not just through the speakers in your studio. Before you decide that a mix is done, copy it onto a CD or smartphone and play it in your car, your friend's stereo, and a boom box. In fact, try to listen to your music on as many different kinds of systems as you can. As you listen, notice whether the bass disappears or becomes too loud or whether the treble becomes thin or harsh. Basically, you're trying to determine where you need to make adjustments in your mix so that it sounds good everywhere.

Unless you spent a lot of time and money getting your mixing room to sound world-class, you'll have to compensate when you mix to get your music to sound good on other people's systems. If your room or speakers enhance the bass in your song, the same tracks will sound thin on other people's systems. On the other hand, if your system lacks bass, your mixes will be boomy when you listen to them somewhere else.

Choosing reference music

Reference music can be any music that you like or that helps you to hear your music more clearly. For the most part, choose reference music that has a good balance between high and low frequencies and that sound good to your ear (often referred to as *tonal balance*). That said, some music is mixed really well, which can help you get to know your monitors and train your ears to hear the subtleties of a mix. I name a few in the following list. (***Disclaimer:*** I try to cover a variety of music styles in this list, but I can't cover them all without a list that's pages long.)

- Beck, *Mutations*
- Ben Harper, *Burn to Shine*
- Bonnie Raitt, *Fundamental*
- Depeche Mode, *Ultra*
- Dr. Dre, *2001*
- Leonard Cohen, *Ten New Songs*
- Los Lobos, *Kiko*
- Lyle Lovett, *Joshua Judges Ruth*
- Macy Gray, *On How Life Is*
- Marilyn Manson, *Mechanical Animals*
- Metallica, *S&M*
- No Doubt, *Return of Saturn*
- Norah Jones, *Come Away with Me*
- Pearl Jam, *Yield*
- Peter Gabriel, *So*
- Sarah McLachlan, *Surfacing*
- Steely Dan, *Two Against Nature*
- Sting, *Brand New Day*

REMEMBER

All commercial music has been mastered. This is going to affect the sound a little: Most importantly, the music will be louder than your music in its premastered form. If you toggle between your mix and the reference music, adjust the relative levels so that each one sounds equally loud coming through your speakers. The louder song always sounds "better." And whatever you do, don't try to match the volume of your mix to the reference music.

TIP

There are plug-ins, such as Izotope Neutron, that can help you match the tonal balance of your mix or track to a reference CD.

Dealing with ear fatigue

If you've ever had a chance to mix a song, you might have found that you do a better mix early on in the process — and the longer you work on the song, the worse the mix gets. In most cases, this is because your ears get tired — and when they do, hearing accurately becomes harder. To tame ear fatigue, try the following:

- **Don't mix at the end of the day, especially after doing any other recording.** Save your mixing for first thing in the morning when your ears have had a chance to rest.
- **Keep the volume low.** I know you'll be tempted to crank the volume on your song while you work on it, but doing so only tires your ears prematurely and can cause damage, especially if you have monitors that can get really loud.
- **Take a break once in a while.** Just 10 or 15 minutes of silence can allow you to work for another hour or so. Also, don't be afraid to walk away from a mix for a day or more.
- **Try not to mix under a deadline.** This suggestion fits with the preceding one. If you're under a deadline, you can't give yourself the time you need to rest and reassess your mix before it goes to print.

Making several versions

One great thing about digital recording is that it costs you nothing to make several versions of a mix. All you need is a little (well, actually a lot of) hard-drive space. Because you can make as many variations on your song's mix as your hard drive allows, you can really experiment by trying new effects settings or trying active panning in your song and see whether you like it. You might end up with something exciting. At the very least, you end up learning more about your gear. That's always a good thing.

TIP

Print (that is, make a clear recording of) a mix early on. Most of the time, your best mixes happen early in the mixing process. Print (or save) the first good mix you make before you try making more "creative" ones. That way, if you get burned out or run out of time, you still have a decent mix to fall back on.

IN THIS CHAPTER

» Understanding equalization

» Inserting EQ in a track

» Getting to know the EQ types

» Equalizing your tracks

Chapter 17 Using Equalization

Equalization (EQ) comprises changing the frequency response of the sound in the session's track to make the track sound how you want. The main goal when EQing during mixing is to get the instruments in your song to blend together smoothly (Chapter 16 explores the process of mixing your tracks).

In this chapter, you discover the types of equalizers, and I walk you through applying EQ to your tracks. This chapter also offers some basic EQ settings for a variety of instruments to get you started EQing your songs.

Exploring Equalization

The most useful tool you have for mixing is equalization. You use equalizers to adjust the various frequencies of your instruments so that there's enough room for each of them in your stereo tracks. Four types of equalizers are used in a recording studio — graphic, parametric, shelf, and filter. Each has its strengths and weaknesses, which I outline in the following sections.

Graphic

The graphic EQ has a prescribed number of frequencies that you can adjust. Graphic EQs generally have between 5 and 31 frequency bands, each affecting a small range of frequencies. (The manufacturer determines the range, which can't be adjusted.) Graphic EQs are useful for eliminating an offending frequency from the signal or for making other adjustments to the tonal quality of the source signal. You probably won't use a graphic EQ much in the mixing process because the parametric EQ can do what the graphic EQ can do — and a whole lot more.

Parametric

The parametric equalizer allows you to choose the frequency that you want to change as well as the range of frequencies around that frequency. With a parametric EQ, you dial in the frequency that you want to change and then you set the range (referred to as the *Q*) you want to affect.

TECHNICAL STUFF

The Q is a number that signifies the number of octaves the EQ affects. Generally, you can adjust the Q setting to affect frequencies between ½ and 2 octaves wide. Not all parametric EQs use the same reference numbers for their Q settings. Some have ranges from 0.7 (2 octaves) to 2.8 (½ octave), while others, such as Pro Tools, use numbers from 0.33 to 12 without indicating what the numbers relate to in terms of octaves. The one constant among parametric EQs is that lower numbers affect larger ranges of frequencies than the higher numbers do.

REMEMBER

The fact that each brand of parametric EQ uses slightly different numbers to reference its Q settings shouldn't matter much to you, because you choose your Q setting based on what you hear in the mix. Just as you can experiment with different frequencies to adjust in the mix, you can also try different Q settings to find the best possible frequency range to use.

The beauty of a parametric EQ is that you can take a small band (range) of frequencies and boost (increase) or cut (decrease) them. This capability enables you to fit together the various instruments in a mix. (This technique is called *carving out* frequencies.) When you're mixing, the parametric EQ is the most useful equalizer because you can adjust the frequency response of each instrument so that the other instruments can be heard clearly in the mix. One downside to parametric EQs is that some systems don't offer you many bands (sometimes just one with the addition of a couple of shelf EQs), so you have to make your EQ decisions based on the type and number of EQs you have to choose from. Another downside is that parametric EQs need processing power to run. If you have a lot of EQing to do, you may end up stressing your system pretty hard.

Low-shelf/high-shelf

A shelf equalizer affects a range of frequencies above *(high-shelf)* or below *(low-shelf)* the target frequency. Shelf EQs are generally used to roll off the top or bottom end of the frequency spectrum. For example, you can set a low-shelf EQ to roll off the frequencies below 250 hertz (Hz), which reduces the amount of rumble (low-frequency noise) in a recording. You generally use the shelf EQ to adjust the lowest and highest frequencies and the parametric EQ to adjust any in-between frequencies when you mix.

Low-pass/high-pass

Believe it or not, sometimes your track just sounds better if you eliminate a few carefully chosen frequencies. You just need to know which ones to target. That's where a couple of digital audio workstation (DAW) capabilities can help with the needed audio acrobatics: *low-pass* (ducking the high frequencies you don't want) and *high-pass* (jumping over the low frequencies you don't want).

This type of EQ is actually called a *filter* because, um, it filters out frequencies either higher (low-pass) or lower (high-pass) than the target frequency. A low-pass filter is used for eliminating unwanted high frequencies, and a high-pass filter is useful for getting rid of unwanted low frequencies.

Dialing-In EQ

Before you start EQing your tracks, you need to know how to insert the EQ plug-in in a track and how to actually make those adjustments with one of the EQ plug-ins. The following sections detail these procedures in Pro Tools (other programs use a similar process).

Inserting an EQ plug-in in a track

To EQ a track, you first need to insert the Pro Tools AudioSuite plug-in in the track. To do so, follow these steps:

1. **Choose View ⇨ Mix Window ⇨ Inserts from the main menu to make sure that the Inserts section is showing in the Mix window.**
2. **Click the top arrow on the left side of the Inserts section of the track's channels strip.**

   The Inserts drop-down menu appears, as shown in Figure 17-1.
3. **To fit the type of track you have, select the Multi-Channel Plug-In or the Multi-Mono Plug-In option.**

   If your track is stereo, use Multi-Channel; if it's mono, use Multi-Mono.

4. **Select the 1-Band EQ3, 4-Band EQ-3, or 7-Band EQ 3 option.**

   Your chosen EQ plug-in window opens. (The 1-Band EQ 3 option lets you set one EQ parameter, whereas the 4-Band EQ 3 option lets you work with four parameters. I bet you can guess how many parameters you work with in 7-Band EQ-3.) For more on which option would work best for you, check out the following section.

5. **Adjust the parameters that you want to EQ.**

   You can find the particulars for each kind of EQ — parametric, low-shelf/high-shelf, and low-pass/high-pass — later in the chapter.

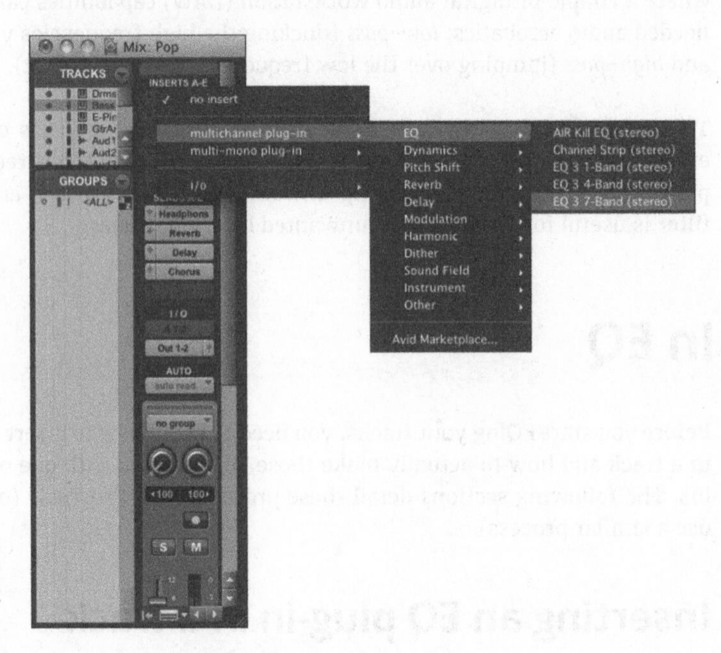

FIGURE 17-1: Select the EQ plug-in to insert into your track.

TIP

If you want to EQ a bunch of tracks at the same time and use the same settings (submixes, for example), you can do this the following way:

1. **Select one of the buses from the Output selector in each track that you want to submix.**
2. **Choose Track ⇨ New from the main menu.**

   The New Track dialog box appears.

3. **Use the drop-down menus to enter the number of tracks that you want (choose 1), the type (choose Auxiliary Input), and whether you want your track in stereo or mono.**

4. **Use your new track's Input selector to select the bus that you used for the output of the submix tracks as the input for this auxiliary track.**
5. **Insert one of the EQ plug-ins from the Insert drop-down menu in this auxiliary track.**

   The EQ plug-in window opens.
6. **Adjust the EQ settings to get the sound that you want.**

   You can find the particulars for each kind of EQ — parametric low-shelf/high-shelf, and low-pass/high-pass — later in the chapter.

Exploring EQ options

Before you start EQing your tracks, you need to know how to find the frequencies you intend to adjust and how to make those adjustments. Figure 17-2 shows an EQ plug-in for Logic Audio. Although each EQ will look a little different, they all end up performing the same basic function. In this section, I walk you through Logic's Channel EQ.

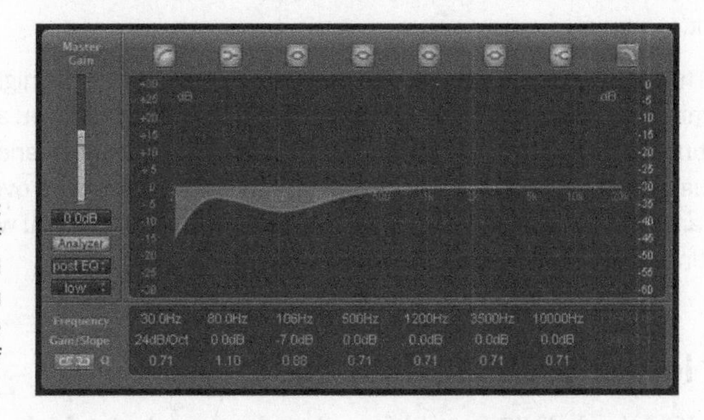

FIGURE 17-2: The EQ section of a mixer's channel strip allows you to adjust the frequencies of your track.

Logic's Channel EQ is an eight-band EQ with four parametric bands, one high-shelf EQ, one low-shelf EQ, one high-pass filter, and one low-pass filter. As you can see in Figure 17-2, the EQ types are listed at the top of the graph, but the adjustments for these bands are located under the main graph.

TIP

Logic's (and some other recording programs') EQ has a really great feature where you can see the frequency response of your track. This function is engaged by clicking the Analyzer button on the left side of the plug-in window. This is handy because, with the Analyzer button engaged, you can actually see the changes you're making to your track as you make them. This is also a potential problem because many people rely on their eyes instead of their ears. Be careful not to let what you see affect what you hear.

Using parametric EQ

The parametric EQ is the go-to EQ when mixing because it allows you to adjust specific frequencies to get each of your tracks to sit nicely in the mix. (I give you guidelines for doing this later in this chapter in Tables 17-1 and 17-2.) To use the parametric EQ, click the Peak EQ button (it looks like a circle with a line coming from the left and right sides) in the EQ plug-in window you have open. You have three settings to adjust:

» **Gain:** This is the amount of *boost* (increase) or *cut* (decrease) that you apply to the signal. In Logic and Pro Tools, to get your boost (gain) amount, either you can point your mouse over the parameter and click and drag up or down, or you can click in the EQ graph above the parameter controls and drag up or down. In Pro Tools, you can also type in the amount in a text box.

» **Freq:** This frequency is the center of the EQ. You select the range of frequencies above and below this point by using the Q setting (see the next bullet). In Pro Tools, you can either type the frequency in the text box on the left or use the slider to make your adjustment. In Logic, to get the desired frequency, you can either point your mouse over the parameter and click and drag up or down, or click in the EQ graph above the parameter controls and drag left or right.

» **Q:** This is the range of frequencies that your EQ will affect. The higher the number, the narrower the range that gets EQ'd. In Pro Tools, you adjust this setting either by moving the knob or by clicking in the text box and typing a value between 0.33 and 12. In Logic, you can point your mouse over the parameter and click and drag up or down to get the Q value you want. Your settings can be anywhere from 0.10 to 100.

Using low-shelf/high-shelf EQ

Low-shelf/high-shelf EQ is good for enhancing or reducing high or low frequencies, such as adding a sense of presence to cymbals (add a few decibels at 10 kHz). In the context of EQ, shelf means that the EQ effects are on the frequencies above (high shelf) or below (low shelf) your setting (called the *corner frequency*). To use low-shelf/high-shelf EQ, click the Low Shelf and High Shelf buttons in the EQ plug-in window. These buttons look like sideways tuning forks located second from the left and second from the right above the EQ graph shown in Figure 17-2.

When you use low-shelf/high-shelf EQ, you have three parameters to adjust in both Pro Tools and Logic:

» **Gain:** This is the amount of boost or cut that you apply to the signal. In Pro Tools, you can either type in the amount in the text box next to the shelf button or use the knob to the right. In Logic, to set the boost, you can either point your mouse over the parameter and click and drag up or down, or click in the EQ graph above the parameter controls and drag up or down.

- **Freq:** This is the starting frequency for the shelf. In Pro Tools, you can either type the frequency in the text box or use the knob to make your adjustment. In Logic, to set your desired frequency, you can either point your mouse over the parameter and click and drag up or down, or click in the EQ graph above the parameter controls and drag left or right.
- **Q:** This is the steepness of the shelf of your EQ. The higher the number, the steeper the shelf that's applied — meaning that the range of frequencies affected to get the gain change of the shelf is narrower. To adjust this parameter in Logic, you can point your mouse over the parameter and click and drag up or down to get the Q value you want. Your settings can be anywhere from 0.10 to 2. In Pro Tools, you adjust this setting either by moving the knob or by clicking in the box and typing a value between 0.1 and 2.

Using low-pass/high-pass EQ

Here's where you tell your plug-in which frequencies to avoid in the course of adjusting the EQ. (So, when you apply low- or high-pass EQ, you're telling the mixer to pass on certain frequencies.) The low- and high-pass buttons are located at the far left and far right above the EQ graph shown in Figure 17-2.

To use the low- or high-pass filter, click the appropriate button in the EQ window. In Pro Tools, you have two options: Freq and Q. The Freq setting is the frequency that the filter begins filtering. Any frequency below (high-pass) or above (low-pass) the setting is removed from the track. You can either type the frequency in the text box or use the knob to make your adjustment. The Q is the range of frequencies that your EQ will affect. With these filters, you can select among 6, 12, 18, and 24 decibels (dB) per octave. The higher the number, the more severe the filter. In Logic, you have the same three settings — frequency, gain/slope, and Q — as the rest of the EQ types. And as with the other EQ types, you adjust the settings by pointing your mouse over the column of the setting and clicking and dragging the parameter that you want to adjust. With the high-pass and low-pass EQ (filters), the gain/slope parameter adjusts the slope of the filter (how quickly it totally cuts off the frequency).

Equalizing Your Tracks

Only so many frequencies are available for all the instruments in a mix. If more than one instrument occupies a particular frequency range, they can get in each other's way and muddy the mix. When you're EQing during the mixing process, your goal is to reduce the frequencies that add clutter — and/or to enhance the frequencies that define an instrument's sound. To do this, make a little space for each instrument within the same general frequency range, which you can accomplish by EQing the individual tracks as you mix. The first part of this chapter shows you how to get up to the point of doing some EQing. The rest of the chapter gets your hands dirty with some real EQing experience.

TIP

Here's a good trick to use when initially trying to decide which frequencies to boost or cut:

1. **Solo the track you're working on by clicking the Solo button in the track's channel strip and set one band of your parametric EQ to a narrow Q setting (a high number).**
2. **Turn the boost all the way up (turn the EQ knob all the way to the right) and *sweep* the frequency setting as you listen (to sweep, just turn the EQ knob's frequency dial to the left and right).**
3. **Notice those areas where the annoying or pleasing sounds are located.**

   This can help you better understand the frequencies that your instrument produces.
4. **After you find a frequency to adjust, experiment with the Q setting to find the range that produces the best sound and then adjust the amount of boost or cut to where it has the effect that you want.**

After you determine the frequencies that you want to work with, do your EQing to the individual track while the instrument is in the mix (not soloed). You want to make the instrument fit as well as possible with the rest of the instruments, and to do this you need to know how your instrument sounds in relation to all the music going on around it.

REMEMBER

Your goal when making adjustments in EQ is to make all the tracks blend together as well as possible. In some instances, you may have to make some radical EQ moves. Don't be afraid to do whatever it takes to make your mix sound good — even if it means having cuts or boosts as great as 12dB.

REMEMBER

Boosting or cutting large amounts with your EQ will increase or reduce the output of your track, so keep an eye on your track's level to make sure that it doesn't overload the output (and cause distortion) or drop so far in the mix that you can't hear it.

General EQ guidelines

Although some instruments do call for specific EQ guidelines, you need to think about some general considerations when EQing, regardless of the instrument involved. When it comes to the audible frequency spectrum (about 20 Hz to 20 kHz), certain frequencies have special characteristics. Table 17-1 describes these frequencies.

TABLE 17-1 EQ Frequency Sound Characteristics

Frequency	Sound Characteristic
20–100 Hz	Warms an instrument or adds boominess to it
100–200 Hz	Is muddy for some instruments but adds fullness to others
350–450 Hz	Sounds boxy
750–850 Hz	Adds depth or body
1–2 kHz	Adds attack or punch to some instruments and creates a nasally sound in others
2–5 kHz	Increases the presence of instruments
5–8 kHz	Sounds harsh in some instruments
8 kHz and above	Adds airiness or brightness to an instrument

REMEMBER

To adjust frequencies via Pro Tool EQ plug-ins, use the Frequency knob to choose the frequency you want to EQ and the Gain knob to control the amount of EQ that you boost (move the knob to the right) or cut (move the knob to the left) from your track.

TIP

You're generally better off cutting a frequency than boosting one. This belief goes back to the days of analog EQs, which often added noise when boosting a signal. This can still be a factor with some digital EQs, but the issue is much less. Out of habit, I still try to cut frequencies before I boost them, and I recommend that you do the same (not out of habit, of course, but because if a noise difference exists between cutting and boosting, you might as well avoid it).

REMEMBER

The exact frequencies that you end up cutting or boosting depend on three factors: the sound you're after, the tonal characteristic of the instrument, and the relationship between all the instruments in the song. In the following sections, I list a variety of frequencies to cut or boost for each instrument (Table 17-2 shows an overview). If you don't want to follow all the suggestions, choose only the ones that fit with your goals.

TABLE 17-2 EQ Recommendations per Instrument

Instrument	Frequency	Adjustment (dB)	Purpose
Vocals	150 Hz	+2–3	Adds fullness
	200–250 Hz	–2–3	Reduces muddiness
	3 kHz	+2–4	Adds clarity
	5 kHz	+1–2	Adds presence
	7.5–10 kHz	–2–3	Cuts sibilance
	10 kHz	+2–3	Adds air or brightness
Electric guitar	100 Hz	–2–3	Reduces muddiness
	150–250 Hz	+2	Adds warmth
	2.5–4 kHz	+2–3	Adds attack or punch
	5 kHz	+2–3	Adds bite
Acoustic guitar	80 Hz	–3	Reduces muddiness
	150–250 Hz	+2–3	Adds warmth
	800–1000 Hz	–2–3	Reduces boxiness
	3–5 kHz	+2–3	Adds attack or punch
	7 kHz	+2–3	Adds brightness
Bass guitar	100–200 Hz	+1–2	Adds fullness
	200–300 Hz	–3–4	Reduces muddiness
	500–1000 Hz	+2–3	Adds punch
	2.5–5 kHz	+2–3	Adds attack
Kick drum	80–100 Hz	+1–2	Adds body or depth
	400–600 Hz	–3–4	Reduces boxiness
	2.5–5 kHz	+1–2	Adds attack
Snare drum	100–150 Hz	+1–2	Adds warmth
	250 Hz	+1–2	Adds depth or body
	800–1000 Hz	–2–3	Reduces boxiness
	3–5 kHz	+1–3	Adds attack
	8–10 kHz	+1–3	Adds crispness

Instrument	Frequency	Adjustment (dB)	Purpose
Tom-toms	200–250 Hz	+1–2	Adds depth
	600–1000 Hz	-2–3	Reduces boxiness
	3–5 kHz	+1–2	Adds attack
	5–8 kHz	+1–2	Adds presence
Large tom-toms	40–125 Hz	+1–2	Adds richness
	400–800 Hz	-2–3	Reduces boxiness
	2.5–5 kHz	+2–3	Adds punch or attack
Hi-hats	10+ kHz	+3–4	Adds brightness or sheen
Cymbals	150–200 Hz	-1–2	Reduces rumbling
	1–2 kHz	-3–4	Reduces trashiness
	10+ kHz	+3–4	Adds brightness or sheen
Drum overheads	100–200 Hz	-2–3	Reduces muddiness
	400–1000 Hz	-2–3	Reduces boxiness
High percussion	500- Hz	-6–12	Cuts boxiness
	10+ kHz	+3–4	Adds brightness or sheen
Low percussion	250 Hz and below	-3–4	Reduces muddiness
	2.5–5 kHz	+2–3	Adds attack
	8–10 kHz	+2–3	Adds brightness
Piano	80–150 Hz	+2–3	Adds warmth
	200–400 Hz	-2–3	Reduces muddiness
	2.5–5 kHz	+2–3	Adds punch or attack
Horns	100–200 Hz	+1–2	Adds warmth
	200–800 Hz	-2–3	Reduces muddiness
	2.5–5 kHz	+2–3	Adds punch or attack
	7–9 kHz	+1–2	Adds breath

The parametric EQ is the type of EQ you use most when trying to get your tracks to fit together. This EQ gives you the greatest control over the range of frequencies you can adjust. The other EQ types (high-shelf, low-shelf, high-pass, low-pass) can often be used successfully for the top or bottom frequencies listed in the sections that follow.

Equalizing vocals

For the majority of popular music, the vocals are the most important instrument in the song. You need to hear them clearly, and they should contain the character of the singer's voice and style. One of the most common mistakes in mixing vocals is to make them too loud. The next most common mistake is to make them too quiet. (The second mistake most often occurs when a shy or self-conscious vocalist is doing the mixing.) You want the lead vocals to shine through, but you don't want them to overpower the other instruments. The best way to do this is to EQ the vocal tracks so they can sit nicely in the mix and still be heard clearly. The following guidelines can help you do this.

Lead

The lead vocal can go a lot of ways, depending on the singer and the style of music. For the most part, I tend to cut a little around 200 Hz and add a couple dBs at 3 kHz and again at 10 kHz. In general, follow these guidelines:

- **To add fullness,** add a few dBs at 150 Hz.
- **To get rid of muddiness,** cut a few dBs at 200–250 Hz.
- **To add clarity,** boost a little at 3 kHz.
- **For more presence,** add at 5 kHz.
- **To add air or to brighten,** boost at 10 kHz.
- **To get rid of sibilance,** cut a little between 7.5 and 10 kHz.

Backup

To keep backup vocals from competing with lead vocals, cut the backup vocals a little in the low end (below 250 Hz) and at the 2.5–3.5 kHz range. To add clarity, boost a little around 10 kHz without letting it get in the way of the lead vocal.

Equalizing guitar

For the most part, you want to avoid getting a muddy guitar sound and make sure that the guitar attack comes through in the mix.

Electric

Electric guitars often need a little cutting below 100 Hz to get rid of muddiness. A boost between 120 and 250 Hz adds warmth. A boost in the 2.5–4 kHz range brings out the attack of the guitar, and a boost at 5 kHz can add some bite.

Acoustic

Acoustic guitars often do well with a little cut below 80 Hz and again around 800 Hz–1 kHz. If you want a warmer tone and more body, try boosting a little around 150–250 Hz. Also, try adding a few dBs around 3–5 kHz if you want more attack or punch. A few dBs added at 7 kHz can add a little more brightness to the instrument.

Equalizing bass

Bass instruments can get muddy pretty fast. The mud generally happens in the 200–300 Hz range, so I either leave that alone or cut just a little if the bass lacks definition. I rarely add any frequencies below 100 Hz. If the instrument sounds flat or thin, I boost some between 100–200 Hz. Adding a little between 500 Hz–1 kHz can increase the punch, and a boost between 2.5–5 kHz accentuates the attack, adding a little brightness to the bass.

REMEMBER

One of the most important things to keep in mind with a bass guitar is to make sure that it and a kick drum can both be heard. You need to adjust the frequencies of these two instruments to make room for both. If you add a frequency to a kick drum, try cutting the same frequency from the bass.

Equalizing drums

The guidelines for EQing drums depend on whether you use live acoustic drums or a drum machine. (A drum machine probably requires less EQ because the sounds were already EQed when they were created.) The type and placement of your mic or mics also affect how you EQ the drums. (You can find out more about mic placement in Chapter 8.)

Kick

You want a kick drum to blend with the bass guitar. To do this, reduce the frequencies that a bass guitar takes up. For example, if I boost a few dB between 100 and 200 Hz for a bass guitar, I generally cut them in the kick drum (and maybe go as high as 250 Hz). To bring out the bottom end of a kick drum, I sometimes add a couple of dBs between 80 and 100 Hz. A kick drum can get boxy sounding (you know, like a cardboard box), so I often cut a little between 400 and 600 Hz to get rid of the boxiness. To bring out the click from the beater hitting the head, try adding a little between 2.5 and 5 kHz. This increases the attack of the drum and gives it more presence.

Snare

A snare drum drives the music, making it the most important drum in popular music. As such, it needs to really cut through the rest of the instruments. Although the adjustments that you make depend on the pitch and size of the drum and whether you use one mic or two during recording, you can usually boost a little at 100–150 Hz for added warmth. You can also try boosting at 250 Hz to add some depth. If the drum sounds too boxy, try cutting at 800 Hz–1 kHz. A little boost at around 3–5 kHz increases the attack, and an increase in the 8–10 kHz range can add crispness to the drum.

If you use two mics during recording, you might consider dropping a few dBs on the top mic in both the 800 Hz–1 kHz range and the 8–10 kHz range. Allow the bottom mic to create the crispness. I generally use a shelf EQ to roll off the bottom end of the bottom mic below, say, 250–300 Hz. Depending on the music (R&B and pop, for instance), I might use a shelf EQ to add a little sizzle to the bottom mic by boosting frequencies higher than 10 kHz.

TIP

For many recording engineers and producers, their snare drum sound is almost a signature. If you listen to different artists' songs from the same producer, you'll likely hear similarities in the snare drum. Don't be afraid to take your time getting the snare drum to sound just right. After all, if you become a famous producer, you'll want people to recognize your distinct sound. And you want it to sound good anyway.

Tom-toms

Tom-toms come in a large range of sizes and pitches. For mounted toms, you can boost a little around 200–250 Hz to add depth to the drum. A boost in the 3–5 kHz range can add more of the sticks' attack. For some additional presence, try adding a little in the 5–8 kHz range. If the drums sound too boxy, try cutting a little in the 600 Hz–1 kHz range.

For floor toms, you can try boosting the frequency range of 40–125 Hz if you want to add some richness and fullness. You might also find that cutting in the 400–800 Hz range can get rid of any boxy sound that the drum may have. To add more attack, boost the 2.5–5 kHz range.

Hi-hats

Most of the time, hi-hats are pretty well represented in the rest of the mics in the drum set. Depending on which mics are picking up the hi-hats, though, you can use a hi-hat mic to bring out their sheen or brightness. To do this, try boosting the frequencies higher than 10 kHz with a shelf EQ. You might also find that cutting frequencies lower than 200 Hz eliminates any rumble created by other drums that a hi-hat mic picks up.

Cymbals

With cymbals, I usually cut anything below 150–200 Hz with a shelf EQ to get rid of any rumbling that these mics pick up. I also drop a few dBs at 1–2 kHz if the cymbals sound kind of trashy or clanky. Adding a shelf EQ higher than 10 kHz can add a nice sheen to the mix.

Overhead mics

If you use overhead mics to pick up both the drums and the cymbals, be careful about cutting too much low end because doing so just sucks the life right out of your drums. Also, if the drums coming through the overhead mics sound boxy or muddy, work with the 100–200 Hz frequencies for the muddiness and 400 Hz–1 kHz frequencies for the boxiness. Depending on your mics, you may also find adding a little between 10kHz and 12kHz can add some sizzle.

Equalizing percussion

High-pitched percussion instruments (shakers, for example) sound good when the higher frequencies are boosted a little bit — say, higher than 10 kHz. This adds some brightness and softness to their sound. You can also roll off many of the lower frequencies, lower than 500 Hz, to eliminate any boxiness that might be present from miking too closely. (See Chapter 8 for more on mic placement.)

Lower-pitched percussion instruments, such as maracas, can also have the lower frequencies cut a little: Use 250 Hz and lower. Try boosting frequencies between 2.5 and 5 kHz to add more of the instruments' attack. To brighten them up, add a little bit in the 8–10 kHz range.

Equalizing piano

For pianos, you often want to make sure that the instrument has both a nice attack and a warm-bodied tone. You can add attack in the 2.5–5 kHz range, and warmth can be added in the 80–150 Hz range. If your piano sounds boomy or muddy, try cutting a little between 200 and 400 Hz.

Equalizing horns

You find a variety of horns, from tubas to soprano saxophones, so to offer blanket recommendations for all of them would be ridiculous (although I'm no stranger to the ridiculous). So, with this thought in mind, I often start the EQ process for these instruments by looking at the 100 to 200 Hz range to add warmth to thin-sounding instruments. Next, I approach the 400 to 800 Hz range to get rid of any muddiness that occurs — unless it's a really low horn like a tuba. For really low horns, I often look for the muddiness a little lower — say, in the 200 to 400 Hz range. To add some more attack to a horn, you can tweak the 2.5 to 5 kHz range a bit, and to add some of the breath of the instrument, look toward the 7 to 9 kHz range.

IN THIS CHAPTER

» Understanding and inserting dynamics processors

» Getting to know compressors and limiters

» Introducing gates and expanders

» Examining side-chain processing

Chapter 18

Digging into Dynamics Processors

Dynamics processors allow you to control the dynamic range of a signal. *Dynamic range*, listed in decibels (dB), is the difference between the softest and loudest signals that a sound source produces. The larger the dynamic range, the more variation exists between the softest and loudest notes.

The four types of dynamics processors are compressors, limiters, gates, and expanders. This chapter gives you the lowdown on each type and how they can help you add punch to or smooth out an instrument's sound, even out an erratic performance, or eliminate noise from a track.

Connecting Dynamics Processors

Dynamics processors are Insert effects: When you insert them into a track, they become part of it, affecting the track's entire signal. To apply a dynamics processor in a track, follow these steps (I detail the process in Pro Tools, but other programs are similar):

1. **Choose View ⇨ Mix Window ⇨ Inserts from the main menu.**

   This makes sure that the Inserts section is showing in the Mix window.

2. **Click the top arrow on the left side of the Inserts section of the track's channel strip.**

   The Inserts drop-down menu opens, as shown in Figure 18-1.

3. **Select either the Multi-Channel plug-in or the Multi-Mono plug-in option, depending on whether your track is a stereo (use multichannel) or a mono (use multimono) track.**

4. **Choose the compressor you want to use from the Dynamics menu.**

   (I cover the three options in the sections that follow.) The chosen plug-in window opens.

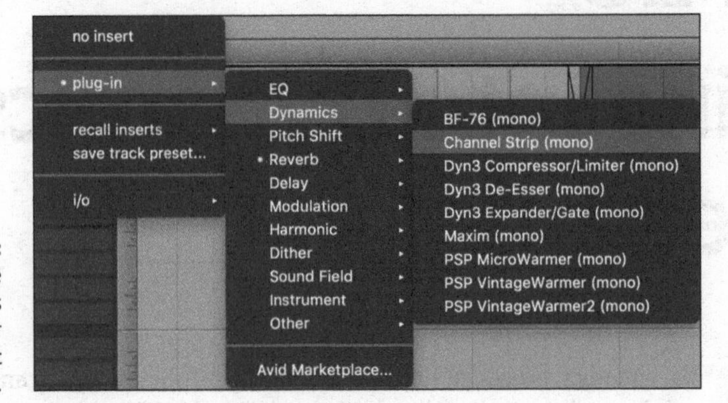

FIGURE 18-1: Choose the Dynamics processor plug-in to insert into your track.

Introducing Compressors

A *compressor*, um, compresses (narrows) the dynamic range of the sound being affected. The compressor not only limits how loud a note can be but also reduces the difference between the loudest and softest note, thus reducing the dynamic range.

Compressors are used for three main purposes (although other purposes certainly exist as well):

- **Keeping *transients* — the initial attack of an instrument — from creating digital distortion during tracking.**

  This is common with drums that have a very fast *attack* (initial signal) that can easily overload the recorder (or converters or preamps).

- **Evening any performance that shows signs of a high degree of unwanted dynamic variation.**

You do this during either the mixing or tracking stage. Some recorded passages are too loud, and others are too quiet.

- **Raising the overall apparent level of the music during mastering.**

  For example, listen to a CD recorded before 1995 and then one from the last year or so. The newer CD sounds louder.

I cover the first purpose (the first bullet in the preceding list) in Chapter 9. Likewise, I explore the third purpose in Chapter 22. So that leaves the second purpose to explore with sample settings later in this chapter.

Getting to know compressor parameters

All full-feature audio recording programs come with their own compressor plug-in, as I detail in the previous section. The compressor shown in Figure 18-2 is the Pro Tools Dyn 3 Compressor/Limiter plug-in. This compressor illustrates the many parameters that you find in typical compressor/limiter plug-ins. These include:

- **Knee:** Use the Knee knob to control how the compressor behaves while the input signal passes the threshold. The lower the setting, the more gradual the compressor acts while the signal passes the threshold.
- **Attack:** Use the Attack knob to control how soon the compressor kicks in. The attack is defined in milliseconds (ms); the lower the number, the faster the attack.
- **Gain:** Use the Gain knob to adjust the *level* (volume) of the signal going out of the compressor. This is listed in decibels (dB). Because adding compression generally reduces the overall level of the sound, you use this control to raise the level back up to where it was when it went in.
- **Ratio:** Watch the Ratio setting to see how much the compressor affects the signal. The ratio 2:1, for instance, means that for every decibel the signal goes above the threshold setting, it is reduced by two. In other words, if a signal goes 1dB over the threshold setting, its output from the compressor will be only 0.5dB louder. With ratios above 10:1, your compressor starts to act like a limiter. (See the later section, "Looking into Limiters.")
- **Release:** Use the Release knob to control how long the compressor continues affecting the signal after it drops back below the Threshold setting. Like the attack, the release is defined in milliseconds (ms). The lower the number, the faster the release time.
- **Thresh:** The Threshold setting dictates the decibel level at which the compressor starts to act on the signal. This setting is often listed as dB below peak (0dB).

In other words, a setting of –6dB means that the compressor starts to act when the signal is 6dB below its calibrated 0dB mark. In digital systems, 0dB is the highest level that a signal can go before clipping (distortions due to going over the maximum level possible).

- **Levels:** The levels section of the Compressor/Limiter processor has four basic functions:
  - **Phase Invert:** This button, located to the right of the Levels title, inverts the phase (reverses the sound wave) of your signal. Click this button to engage and disengage it. It illuminates blue when it's engaged.
  - **Input:** This meter shows the level of your signal entering the effect.
  - **Output:** This meter shows the level leaving your effect.
  - **GR:** GR stands for Gain Reduction. This meter shows you the amount, in decibels, that your input level is attenuated.

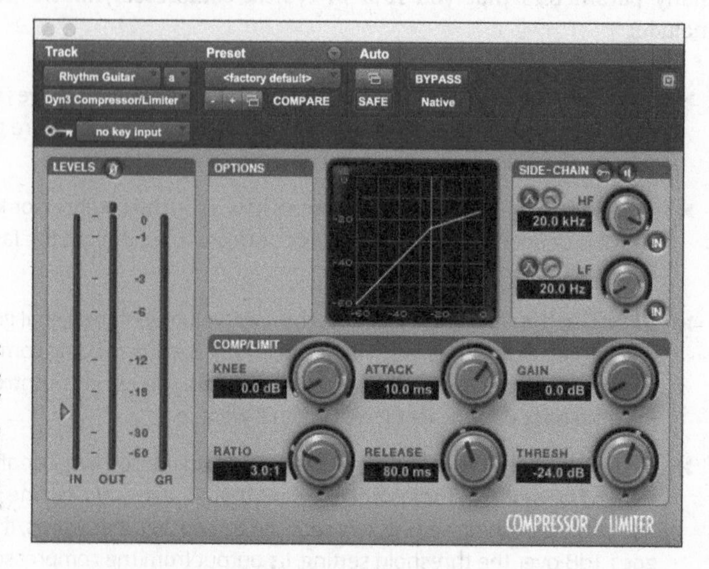

FIGURE 18-2: Use the Compressor/Limiter plug-in to adjust several parameters to even out your sound.

Also note the Side-Chain adjustments next to the graphical section of the compressor/limiter window. I cover this in detail later in this chapter in the "Setting Up Side Chains" section.

Getting started using compression

A compressor is one of the most useful — and one of the most abused — pieces of gear in the recording studio. The most difficult part of using compression is that every instrument reacts differently to the same settings. In this section, I offer you some guidelines and ideas for using the compressor effectively.

The following steps show you one good way to get familiar with the compressor. First start by playing your track (hit the Spacebar or Play button in the Transport window) and then follow these steps:

1. **Start with a high Ratio setting (between 8:1 and 10:1) and turn the Threshold knob all the way to the right.**
2. **Slowly turn the Threshold knob back to the left, watch the meters, and listen carefully.**

   While you reduce the threshold, notice where the meters are when you start hearing a change in the sound of the track. Also notice what happens to the sound when you have the threshold really low and the meters are peaked. (The sound is very different from where you started.)
3. **Slowly turn the Threshold knob back to the right and notice how the sound changes back again.**

After you get used to how the sound changes from adjusting the Threshold setting, try using different Attack and Release settings and do this procedure again. The more you experiment and critically listen to the changes made by the different compressor settings, the better you'll understand how to get the sound that you want. The following guidelines can also help you achieve your desired sound:

- **Try to avoid using any compression on a stereo mix while you mix your music.** Compression is a job for the mastering phase of your project. If you compress your stereo tracks during mixdown, you limit what can be done to your music in the mastering stage. This is true even if you master it yourself and think you know what you want during mixdown.
- **If you hear noise when you use your compressor, you set it too high.** In effect, you're compressing the loud portions enough to make the level of the softest sections of the music (including any noise) much louder in comparison. To get rid of the noise, decrease the Ratio or the Threshold settings.
- **To increase the punch of a track, make sure that the Attack setting isn't too quick.** Otherwise you lose the initial transient and the punch of a track.
- **To smooth out a track, use a short Attack setting and a quick Release time.** This evens out the difference in level between the initial transient and the main body of the sound, and results in a smoother sound.

Less is more when using compression. Resist the temptation to turn those knobs too much, which will just squash your music. On the other hand, if that's the effect you're going for, don't be afraid to experiment.

Using compression

When you first start experimenting with compressor settings, you most likely won't know where to start. To make this process easier for you, here I include some sample settings for a variety of instruments. Start with these and use the guidelines listed in the preceding section to fine-tune your settings.

Lead vocals

Some recording engineers think compression is a must for vocals. It evens out the often-erratic levels that a singer can produce and tames transients that can cause digital distortion. You can use compression on vocals to even out the performance and to create an effect.

If you use a compressor to even out a vocal performance, you don't want to hear the compressor working. Instead, you just want to catch the occasional extremely loud transient that would cause clipping. A good compression setting has a fast attack to catch the stray transient, a quick release so that the compression doesn't color the sound of the singer, and a low ratio so that when the compressor does go on, it smoothes out the vocals without squashing them. Typical settings may look like this:

Threshold: –8dB

Ratio: 1.5:1 to 2:1

Attack: Less than 1 ms

Release: About 40 ms

Gain: Adjust so that the output level matches the input level. You don't need much added gain.

If you want to use a compressor that pumps and breathes — that is, one that you can really hear working — or if you want to bring the vocals way up front in the mix, try using the following settings. These settings put the vocals "in your face," as recording engineers say:

Threshold: –2dB

Ratio: 4:1 to 6:1

Attack: Less than 1 ms

Release: About 40 ms

Gain: Adjust so that the output level matches the input level. You need to add a fair amount of gain at this setting.

As you can see, the two parameters that you adjust the most are the threshold and ratio. Experiment with these settings and check the effects of them by toggling between the affected and unaffected sound (use the Bypass switch on your compressor).

Backup vocals

What about compressor settings for backup vocals, you may ask? I recommend a setting that's midway between the invisible compressions and the pumping and breathing compressions that I describe in the previous section. Such a setting brings your background vocals forward slightly. Your settings may look like this:

Threshold: –4dB

Ratio: 2:1 to 3:1

Attack: Less than 1 ms

Release: About 40 ms

Gain: Adjust so that the output level matches the input level. You don't need to add too much gain.

Electric guitar

Generally, electric guitar sounds are pretty compressed. You don't need additional compression when you track the guitar unless you use a clean (undistorted) setting on your guitar. If you want to use a little compression to bring the guitar forward and give it some punch, try these settings:

Threshold: –1dB

Ratio: 2:1 to 3:1

Attack: 25 to 30 ms

Release: About 200 ms

Gain: Adjust so that the output level matches the input level. You don't need much added gain.

The slow attack is what gives the guitar a bit of punch. If you want less punchiness, just shorten the attack slightly. Be careful, though, because if you shorten it too much, you end up with a mushy sound (sorry — ahem — the guitar has no definition).

Electric bass

Another way to get a handle on the potential muddiness of the amplified bass guitar is to use a little compression. Compression can also help control uneven levels that result from overzealous or inexperienced bass players. Try these settings for a start:

Threshold: –4dB

Ratio: 2.5:1 to 3:1

Attack: 40 to 50 ms

Release: About 180 ms

Gain: Adjust so that the output level matches the input level. You don't need much added gain.

TIP

When using compression on bass, make sure that your attack setting isn't too short, or else the sound will become muddy.

Strummed or picked acoustic stringed instruments

You don't generally need a lot of compression on acoustic stringed instruments, especially if you want a natural sound. You can use the compressor to even out the resonance of the instrument to keep the main character of the instrument from getting lost in a mix and to avoid a muddy sound. These are good settings for strummed or picked acoustic instruments:

Threshold: –6dB

Ratio: 3:1 to 4:1

Attack: Around 150 ms

Release: About 400 ms

Gain: Adjust so that the output level matches the input level. You don't need much added gain.

The release is set very high because of the amount of sustain that these acoustic instruments can have. If you play an instrument with less sustain, like a banjo, you may find that a shorter attack and release works just fine. In this case, try the following settings:

Threshold: –6dB

Ratio: 2.5:1 to 3:1

Attack: 40 to 50 ms

Release: About 180 ms

Gain: Adjust so that the output level matches the input level. You don't need much, if any, added gain.

Horns

I rarely use a compressor on horns. The only time I may use one is if an unnatural variation exists in levels due to poor playing (although I usually prefer to ride the faders [manually adjust the level] to even the levels instead of trying to fix the problem with compression). Still, if I were to use a compressor, I would start with these settings:

Threshold: –8dB

Ratio: 2.5:1 to 3:1

Attack: Around 100 ms

Release: About 300 ms

Gain: Adjust so that the output level matches the input level. You don't need much added gain.

Piano

As with other acoustic instruments, I don't often use compression on a piano unless I'm going for a specific effect or I want to even out an erratic performance. Settings for effect can run the gamut; just dial in some settings and see what you get. Using compression to even an erratic piano performance takes a little more finesse. In this case, start with these mild settings:

Threshold: –10dB

Ratio: 1.5:1 to 2:1

Attack: 100 to 105 ms

Release: About 115 ms

Gain: Adjust so that the output level matches the input level. You don't need much, if any, added gain.

Classical strings

For the most part, adding compression to string instruments played with a bow isn't necessary. However, you'll find that using a compressor on a plucked acoustic bass and fiddle can bring them out in a mix.

A starting point for compressor settings for a fiddle would be as follows:

Threshold: –4dB

Ratio: 2:1 to 3:1

Attack: 40 to 50 ms

Release: About 100 ms

Gain: Adjust so that the output level matches the input level. You don't need much, if any, added gain.

Try these settings for the acoustic bass:

Threshold: –6dB

Ratio: 5:1 to 8:1

Attack: 40 to 50 ms

Release: About 200 ms

Gain: Adjust so that the output level matches the input level. You need a bit of added gain here.

Kick drum

The kick drum responds well to a compressor when tracking. For the most part, you can get by with settings that allow the initial attack to get through and that tame the boom a little. Sample settings would look like this:

Threshold: –6dB

Ratio: 4:1 to 6:1

Attack: 40 to 50 ms

Release: 200 to 300 ms

Gain: Adjust so that the output level matches the input level. You don't need much added gain.

Snare drum

Adding compression to the snare drum is crucial if you want a tight, punchy sound. You have a lot of choices with the snare. The following settings are common and versatile:

Threshold: –4dB

Ratio: 4:1 to 6:1

Attack: 5 to 10 ms

Release: 125 to 175 ms

Gain: Adjust so that the output level matches the input level. You don't need much added gain.

Hand drums

Compression is usually a good idea with hand drums because the drum can produce unpredictable transients. For most hand drums, start with the following settings:

Threshold: –6dB

Ratio: 3:1 to 6:1

Attack: 10 to 25 ms

Release: 100 to 300 ms

Gain: Adjust so that the output level matches the input level. You don't need much added gain.

Percussion

Because percussion instruments have high sound levels and are prone to extreme transients, I often like to use a little compression just to keep these transients from eating up headroom in the mix. Here are good starting points:

Threshold: –10dB

Ratio: 3:1 to 6:1

Attack: 10 to 20 ms

Release: About 50 ms

Gain: Adjust so that the output level matches the input level. You need a bit of added gain here.

Looking into Limiters

A *limiter* is basically a compressor on steroids. Rather than simply reducing a signal that crosses over the threshold setting, limiters put a ceiling on the highest level of a sound source. Any signal above the threshold is chopped off rather than just compressed. Using a limiter is great for raising the overall level of an instrument as well as for keeping transients from eating up all the *headroom* (maximum level) of a track.

Using the compressor/limiter in Pro Tools gives you more control than using a basic limiter in that you can adjust the ratio to be a little more subtle than just chopping off a signal.

Understanding limiter settings

Most audio recording programs contain multiple Compressor/Limiter plug-ins (which I cover earlier in this chapter), including a peak limiter. Pro tools BF-76 is shown in Figure 18-3 as an example. You insert this plug-in into a track by following the procedures listed in the "Connecting Dynamics Processors" section at the beginning of this chapter.

FIGURE 18-3: The peak limiter plug-in limits the maximum level of the signal passing through it.

The BF-76 peak limiter contains the following parameters, most of which you can find in most peak limiter plug-ins:

- **Input:** Use the Input dial to control the *threshold level* (when the limiter kicks in) as well as how much reduction the limiter applies to your signal. If you have the Gain Reduction (GR) option selected for the meter display (see its upcoming bullet), you can see how the dial relates to your gain reduction and make adjustments accordingly.
- **Output:** This is the same as Gain in most compressors. Use this dial to adjust the level (volume) of the signal going out of the compressor. You use this dial to raise the level back to where it was when it went in.

- **Attack:** Use the Attack dial to control how soon the limiter kicks in. With the BF-76 peak limiter, the dial doesn't list your setting in milliseconds. This goes back to the inspiration for this plug-in (the classic 1176 compressor made in the 1970s), but the real-world numbers for this dial are from 0.4 ms to 5.7 ms, with the shorter attack when the dial is to the left, and the longer attack times as you turn the dial to the right.
- **Release:** Use the Release knob to control how long the limiter continues limiting the signal after it drops back below the threshold setting. Like with Attack, the BF-76 uses arbitrary numbers on its Release dial. The real numbers for this setting range from 0.06 ms to 1.1 seconds. Faster release times are achieved when the dial is to the left; conversely, turning the dial to the right lengthens the release time.
- **Ratio:** Use the Ratio setting to show how much the compressor affects the signal. The ratio — 2:1, for instance — means that for every decibel the signal goes above the threshold setting, it is reduced by two. In other words, if a signal goes 1dB higher than the threshold setting, its output from the compressor will be only 0.5dB louder.
- **Meter:** You have the option to select how you want the meter to work. The BF-76 peak limiter offers you four options (which you choose by clicking the appropriate button):
  - **GR (Gain Reduction):** In this case, the meter shows you how many decibels your signal is being reduced when the limiter kicks in. This is the meter setting used most often.
  - **–18:** This option shows you the level of your output signal, calibrated such that when the needle hits 0VU (Volume Units) your level is at –18dB full-scale. Both this and the following option (–24) are used by people who want a certain amount of headroom (additional signal level higher than 0) on their meters or have other equipment that relies on either the –18 or –24 standard. The one you choose depends on how much headroom you want.
  - **–24:** This option shows you the level of your output signal, calibrated such that when the needle hits 0VU (Volume Units) your level is actually at –24dB full-scale.
  - **Off:** This turns off the meter. This is a good option if you find yourself relying too much on "seeing" what your limiter is doing and too little on actually *listening* to your music as you make your adjustments.

Setting limits with the peak limiter

The peak limiter is essentially a compressor on steroids that's designed to impart a certain sound to your music. I caution you from using too much of a peak limiter. When used judiciously, though, a peak limiter can spice up your tracks a bit.

TIP

When using any limiter, keep in mind these two tips to achieve the best results:

- **When using limiters to raise the volume of a track or mix, limit only 2dB or 3dB at a time.** This way, the limiter doesn't alter the sound of your signal but just reduces the highest peaks and raises the volume.
- **To add grunge (distortion) to a track, lower the Threshold setting so that you limit the signal 6 to 12dB.** Tweak the Attack and Release parameters to get the sound you're after. This creates distortion that might work for a particular track, such as a snare drum.

Introducing Gates and Expanders

A *gate* is basically the opposite of a limiter: Rather than limiting how loud a note can get, a gate limits how soft a note can get. A gate filters out any sound below the threshold and allows any note above it to be passed through unaffected.

An expander is to a gate what a compressor is to a limiter. Instead of reducing the volume of notes below the set threshold by a specified amount, an *expander* reduces them by a ratio. In other words, with a gate, you set a certain decibel amount by which a signal is reduced. With an expander, you reduce the signal by setting a ratio. The ratio changes the signal gradually, making the affected signals sound more natural.

Use an expander when you want to subtly reduce noise from a track rather than just filtering it out completely. A classic example is when you deal with breath from a singer. If you use a gate, you get an unnatural-sounding track because the breaths are filtered out completely. With the expander, you can set it to reduce the breath just enough so that it's less noticeable, but you can leave a little of the sound in to make the singer sound normal. (I mean, everyone has to breathe, right?)

Gates, on the other hand, are useful for completely filtering any unwanted noise in a recording environment. A classic situation for using gates is when you record drums. You can set the gate to filter any sound (other drums, for instance) except for the sounds resulting from the hits to the particular drum that you miked.

Getting to know gate parameters

You can see the expander/gate plug-in that ships with Pro Tools in Figure 18-4 (other programs are similar). The various settings that you get to play with are similar to the ones for compressors and limiters, as the following list makes clear:

- **Range:** The Range setting is similar to the Ratio setting on the compressor except that you choose the decibel amount by which the gate *attenuates* (reduces) the signal. For example, a setting of 40dB drops any signal below the Threshold setting by 40 decibels.
- **Attack:** Like with the compressor and limiter, use the Attack knob to set the rate at which the gate opens (in milliseconds). Fast attacks work well for instruments with, well, fast attacks, such as drums. Slow attacks are better suited for instruments with slow attacks, such as vocals.
- **Hold:** Use the Hold setting to control how much time the gate stays open after the signal drops below the threshold. When the hold time is reached, the gate closes abruptly. This parameter is listed in milliseconds. The Hold parameter allows you to get the gated drum sound that was so popular in the 1980s. (Phil Collins, anyone?)
- **Ratio:** The ratio dictates how much the signal is attenuated by the expander. When using a ratio of 2:1, for instance, the expander reduces any signal below the threshold by two times. In this case, a signal that is 10dB below the threshold is reduced to 20dB below it; likewise, a signal that's 2dB below the threshold is reduced to 4dB below it. Setting a ratio of 30:1 or greater turns the expander/gate effect to a gate. So, instead of lowering the levels of an effected signal, the signal is simply cut off.
- **Release:** Use the Release knob to control how long the gate is open after the signal drops back below the threshold setting. You can choose values between 5 ms and 4 seconds. Faster release times are achieved when the dial is to the left; conversely, turning the dial to the right lengthens the release time.
- **Thresh:** Use the Threshold knob to set the level (in decibels) at which the gate *opens* (stops filtering the signal). The gate allows all signals above the Threshold setting to pass through unaffected, whereas any signals below the Threshold setting are reduced by the amount set by the Range control.
- **Options: Look Ahead:** Enabling this button (click it to turn it blue) turns on the Look Ahead function for the Expander/Gate. This essentially means that the Expander/Gate will engage (open) 2 ms before the sound actually crosses the threshold value. This keeps you from losing the initial transient of an instrument, such as for drums.
- **Levels:** The levels section of the Expander/Gate processor has four basic functions:
  - **Phase Invert:** This button, located to the right of the Levels title, inverts the phase (reverses the sound wave) of your signal. Click this button to engage and disengage it. It illuminates blue when it's engaged.
  - **Input:** This meter shows the level of your signal entering the effect.

- **Output:** This meter shows the level leaving your effect.
- **GR:** GR stands for Gain Reduction. This meter shows you the amount, in decibels, that your input level is attenuated.

» **Side Chain:** This section lets you insert a side-chain into the effect. I detail this in the "Setting Up Side Chains" section, later in this chapter.

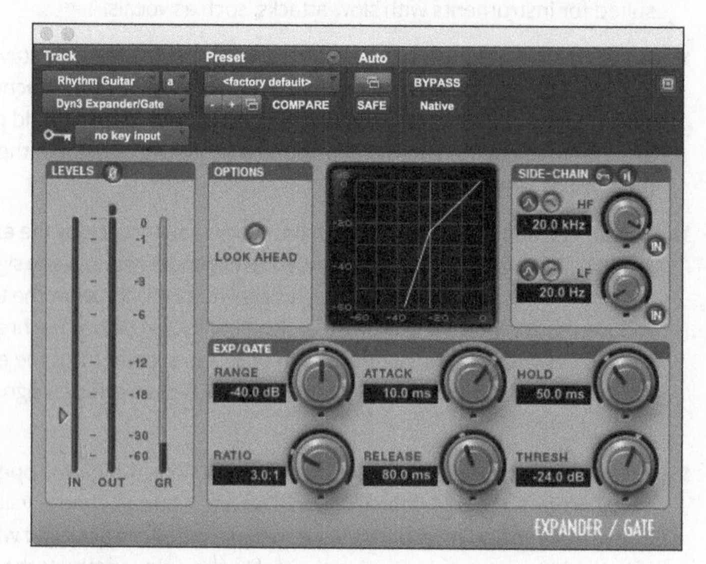

FIGURE 18-4: Use the gate plug-in to filter noise below a certain level.

Getting started using gates

Noise gates can be extremely useful for getting rid of unwanted noise. The most common use for a gate is to eliminate bleeding from drum mics. For example, you may get bleed from your snare drum into your tom-toms mics. When using noise gates, keep the following in mind:

» **When the threshold is reached, the gate allows the signal through.** If your background noise is high enough, when the gate opens, you still hear not only the intended sound but the background noise as well.

» **When gating drums, be sure to set the attack very fast.** Otherwise, the initial transient is lost, and you end up with mushy-sounding drums. You can also engage the look-ahead option to ensure that the transients are not lost.

» **When setting the release time of the gate, adjust it until it sounds natural and doesn't clip off the end of your instrument's sound.**

» **Set the range just high enough to mask any unwanted noise.** If you set it too high, the sound becomes unnatural because the natural resonance of the instrument may be filtered out.

Getting started using an expander

Because the expander works much like a gate, you can use the same basic starting points. Choose between a gate and an expander based on the type of overall attenuation that you want of the signal. For example, the expander is a good choice if you have an instrument that contains sounds that are too loud but you don't want to get rid of them completely — you just want to reduce them a little.

Adjusting for a vocalist's breath is the perfect situation for using an expander rather than a gate. In this case, you can set the expander's threshold just below the singer's softest note and start with a low ratio (1.5:1 or 2:1, for instance). See whether the breathiness improves. If it doesn't, slowly move the Ratio knob until you get the effect that you want.

WARNING

Be careful not to overdo it, though. If the breath is too quiet compared with the vocal, the vocal sounds unnatural.

Detailing the De-Esser

The De-Esser plug-in is a compressor that targets certain frequencies and is handy for getting rid of the annoying *s* sounds in a vocal track (often referred to as *sibilance*). You can also use it to get rid of any high-frequency sounds, such as the whistles or the wind across a flute. You'll find the De-Esser (Pro Tools' version is shown in Figure 18-5) in the Dynamics listing with the plug-in menu.

Pro Tools' De-Esser plug-in is simple to use, with only four basic parameters to adjust (other programs use similar parameters):

» **Freq:** Use the Frequency parameter to select the frequency range affected by the De-Esser. You'll usually set this between around 4 kHz and 12 kHz.

» **Range:** Use this knob to choose the frequency that the De-Esser is being applied to. Select a range that hits the highest note of the sibilance but not all the *s* sounds. You'll have to use your ears to assess what sounds natural.

» **HF Only:** Engaging this parameter applies the De-Esser to the frequency you set with the Frequency dial. Not selecting it applies the De-Esser evenly across the frequency spectrum. For most De-Essing tasks, I choose to have this feature enabled.

» **Listen:** Enabling this option lets you hear only the sounds that the De-Esser is removing. You want to use this to hear where the sibilance is and to help you fine-tune your settings. I generally enable this feature when I'm looking for the frequency of the sibilance.

» **Graph:** The graph shows you where the De-Esser is working, including how much gain reduction you're getting and where this reduction fits in the frequency spectrum. Try to avoid putting too much weight on the graph and use your ears instead.

» **Levels:** The levels section of the De-Esser processor has three basic functions:

- **Input:** This meter shows the level of your signal entering the effect.
- **Output:** This meter shows the level leaving your effect.
- **GR:** GR stands for Gain Reduction. This meter shows you the amount, in decibels, that your input level is attenuated by the effect.

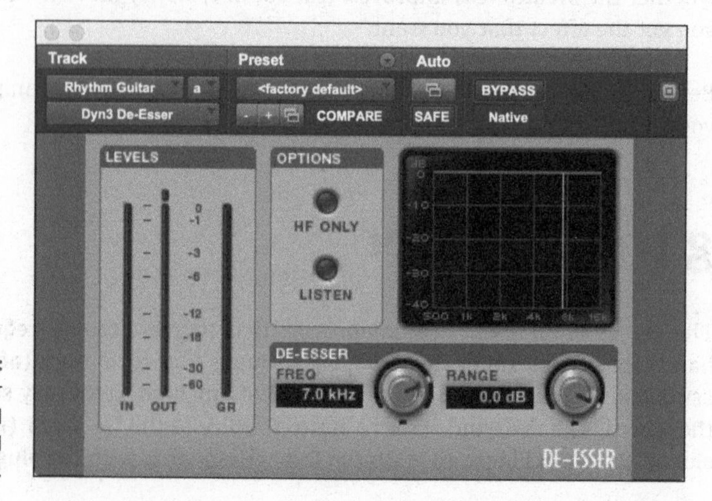

FIGURE 18-5: Use the De-Esser plug-in to get rid of unwanted sibilance.

Here's how to use the De-Esser:

1. **Insert De-Esser into your desired track after the compressor or limiter (if you're using one). Do this by clicking on the Insert drop-down menu for your track and choosing Plug-in ⇨ Dynamics ⇨ De-Esser for a mono track. For a stereo track, choose Multi-mono or Multi-channel plug-in ⇨ Dynamics ⇨ De-Esser.**

2. **Adjust the frequency to the point where the offending *s* sound is located.**

3. **Dial the range in until the *s* sound falls back far enough in the track to sound natural.**

TIP

You don't want to eliminate sibilance altogether, or your vocal will lack presence and begin to sound muddy (unclear).

Setting Up Side Chains

Using a *side chain* means that the signal from another track (through one of the buses) or from one of your interface inputs triggers your dynamics processor into action. The signal that you choose to do the triggering is the *key input.* Side chains are great for making tracks fit better in a dense mix or letting a kick drum be heard when it plays at the same time as the bass guitar. Not sure how to do this? Don't worry, I provide some examples in the following sections.

Setting up a side chain

Not all audio recording programs have a side-chain option, but those that do are pretty easy to insert. Here is the process in the Dyn3 compressor in Pro Tools (others are similar):

1. **Click to open the Key Input drop-down menu, located next to the little key icon at the top of the plug-in window.**

2. **From the drop-down menu, choose the interface input or bus that has the signal that you want to use to trigger the dynamics processor.**

   This routes the signal from that input or bus to the processor.

3. **Click the External Key button to engage the side chain.**

   The External Key button is located in the Side Chain section on the right side of the various plug-in windows. (Refer to Figure 18-2.)

4. **Click the Key Listen button — located to the right of the External Key button — to hear the signal coming through your selected key input.**

5. **Play your session and adjust the processor's parameters until you get the sound that you want.**

The Side Chain section of a compressor plug-ins generally gives you the ability to use high-frequency (HF) and low-frequency (LF) filters within the plug-in. This can be handy for keying into certain frequencies, thus making the side chain more sensitive to certain frequencies. This section offers two options:

- **HF (High Frequency):** Turn on this filter by clicking the In button to the right of the top frequency dial in the Side Chain section of the plug-in. You can control the following parameters:
  - **Band-Pass Filter:** Engaging this filter (click it with your mouse; it will glow blue) is similar to using a parametric equalizer. Whatever frequency you select with the HF Frequency Control button (see the following bullet) is the center of the filter. Frequencies on either side of this drop off at a rate of 12dB per octave.
  - **Low-Pass Filter:** Engaging this filter is the same as using a low-pass filter in one of your equalizers. Your selected frequency is the beginning of the low-pass filter, and all frequencies above this number are attenuated (reduced) by 12dB per octave.
  - **HF Frequency Control:** Use this dial to choose from frequencies between 80 Hz and 20 kHz. Turning to the right increases the frequency, and turning to the left decreases it.
- **LF (Low Frequency):** Turn on this filter by clicking the In button, next to the bottom dial in the Side Chain section of the plug-in. You have three options to select from with this filter. These are:
  - **Band-Pass Filter:** Engaging this filter (click it with your mouse; it will glow blue) is similar to using a parametric equalizer. Whatever frequency you select with the LF Frequency Control button (see the following bullet) is the center of the filter. Frequencies on either side of this drop off at a rate of 12dB per octave.
  - **High-Pass Filter:** Engaging this filter is the same as using a high-pass filter in one of your equalizers. Your selected frequency is the beginning of the high-pass filter, and all frequencies higher than this number are attenuated (reduced) by 12dB per octave.
  - **LF Frequency Control:** Use this dial to choose from frequencies between 20 Hz and 20 kHz. Turning to the right increases the frequency, and turning to the left decreases it.

Using a side chain

The uses for side chains are numerous, and only your creativity limits how you end up using a side chain. The most common use for a side chain is to create more room for your instruments in the mix. This is done by EQing the Key Input signal and then letting that EQed signal trigger a compressor or limiter.

To make room for a vocal in a dense mix, follow these steps:

1. **Route all your instruments in the mix (except the vocal) to bus 15 and 16.**
2. **Insert the compressor plug-in in this bus and set the Key Input to bus 14.**
3. **Make a copy of your vocal tracks and assign their outputs to bus 14.**
4. **Shift the copied vocal tracks ahead (to the right) a few milliseconds.**
5. **Adjust the settings on the compressor so that the volume of the instruments drops slightly whenever the vocals come in.**

   For a starting point, use the smooth vocal compressor setting that I mention in the "Lead vocals" section, earlier in this chapter.

You can also use a special trick to make the bass guitar drop slightly in the mix whenever the kick drum is played. Follow these steps:

1. **Insert the compressor plug-in into the bass guitar track and set the Key Input to bus 16.**
2. **Make a copy of the kick drum track and set the output for the copied track to bus 16.**

   The kick signal triggers the compressor that's assigned to the bass guitar track.
3. **Use fast Attack and Release settings on the compressor.**

   You want the compressor to activate only when the initial strike of the kick drum happens. The bass guitar drops in volume when the kick drum plays. This means that the kick drum creates the attack, and the bass guitar produces the sustain.

This trick works really well for music that has a kick drum and bass guitar that play similar patterns.

IN THIS CHAPTER

» Understanding and using send effects

» Getting to know reverb

» Introducing delays

» Examining offline effects processing

Chapter 19 Singling Out Signal Processors

Unless you record your songs using a live band in a perfect acoustic environment, your music will sound a little flat without the addition of some type of effects. Effects allow you to make your music sound like you recorded it in just about any environment possible. You can make your drums sound as if they were recorded in a cathedral or your vocals sound as if you were singing underwater. Effects can also make you sound "better" than the real you. For example, you can add harmony parts to your lead or backup vocals, or you can make your guitar sound like you played it through any number of great amplifiers.

In this chapter, you discover many of the most common effects processors used in recording studios. (*Signal processors* are the neat software plug-ins behind all the effects you can achieve in your studio.) You discern the difference between insert (that is, line) effects and send/return effects. You also get a chance to explore ways of using these processors, with recommendations for using reverb, delay, and chorus. To top it off, you get a glimpse into offline effects processing such as pitch shifting.

REMEMBER

The best way to learn how to use effects on your music is to experiment. The more you play around with the different settings, the more familiar you become with how each effect operates. Then you can get creative and come up with the best ways to use effects for your music.

REMEMBER

The Effects Bypass button in the effects-processor plug-in window is your friend. With a click of the Bypass button, you can quickly turn off any effect in use with your signal. Use this button to check your effect settings against your original signal. Sometimes you'll like the original sound better.

Routing Your Effects

Effects processors can be used as either send/return or insert effects. In both cases, you can work with the *dry* (unaffected) signal and the *wet* (affected) signals separately. If you use the effect in a send/return routing, you can adjust the wet and dry signals with two track faders: Aux Send (opened by clicking the effect's name in the Send list) and Auxiliary. If you use the effect in a line configuration, the plug-in window displays a Mix parameter where you can adjust the wet/dry balance.

You choose whether to insert an effect in a track or to use the Send function based upon what you intend to do. For example, if you *insert* the effect into a track (as described in the next section), that effect only alters the signal that exists on the track it's inserted into. On the other hand, using an *effect send* for your effect allows you to route more than one track through that effect. (You can adjust the individual levels going to the send at each track so you still have control over how much effect is applied to each track going to the send.)

Further, inserting an effect always puts the effect before the fader in the track (prefader); if you use a send, you can choose whether the effect does its magic before (prefader) or after (postfader) signal enters the fader that controls the track's output. If you use a send to apply the effect to more than one track at a time, you also reduce the amount of processing power the effect has to use. (Inserting the same effect into each track you want to alter ends up using more processing power.)

Inserting effects

If you want to use an effect on only one specific track, you can insert it into the track by using the Insert function. To insert an effect in Pro Tools, as an example, follow these steps:

1. **Make sure that the Inserts section is showing in the Mix window by choosing View ⇨ Mix Window ⇨ Inserts from the main menu.**
2. **Click the top arrow on the left side of the Inserts section of the track's channel strip.**

   The Insert drop-down menu appears, as shown in Figure 19-1.

3. **If your track is a stereo track, select either the Multi-Channel Plug-In or Multi-Mono Plug-In option.**

   If your track is mono, you can choose mono or mono/stereo.

4. **Choose your desired plug-in — D-Verb, Mod Delay III (mono), Mod Delay III (mono/stereo), whatever — from the menu.**

   The plug-in window opens. Here you can set your parameters. (My professional advice on what settings to actually tweak comes later in this chapter, when I cover the individual effects.)

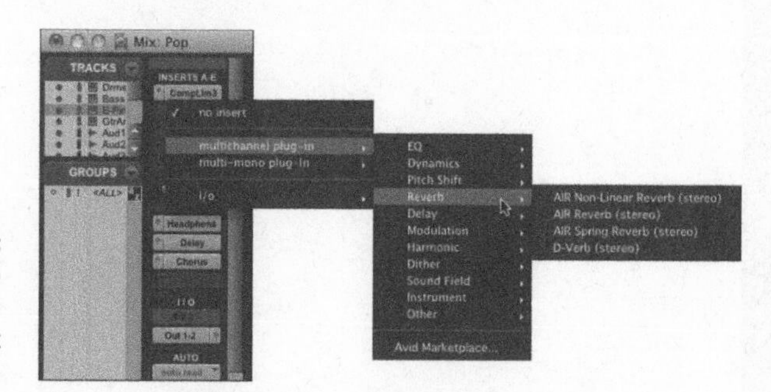

FIGURE 19-1: The Insert menu opens when you click the Insert input selector.

Sending signals to effects

Sometimes you want to route a bunch of tracks to a single effect (in the case of reverbs, for instance). In this case, you follow these steps:

1. **Select one of the buses from the Send selector in each track that you want to route to the effect.**

   The Send Output window appears, as shown in Figure 19-2. The window contains a handy channel strip for controlling the signal being sent to the selected bus.

2. **Choose Track ⇨ New from the main menu.**

   The New Tracks dialog box appears.

3. **Use the drop-down menus to enter the number of tracks you want (1), the type (Auxiliary Input), and whether you want your track in mono or stereo.**

4. **From the Input selector drop-down menu, choose the bus you used for the send of the tracks in Step 1 as the input for this auxiliary track.**

5. Choose one of the effects plug-ins from the Inserts drop-down menu and insert it into this auxiliary track.

The Effect plug-in window opens.

REMEMBER

The previous section, "Inserting effects," gives you the gory details on inserting effects.

6. Adjust the effect settings to get the sound you want.

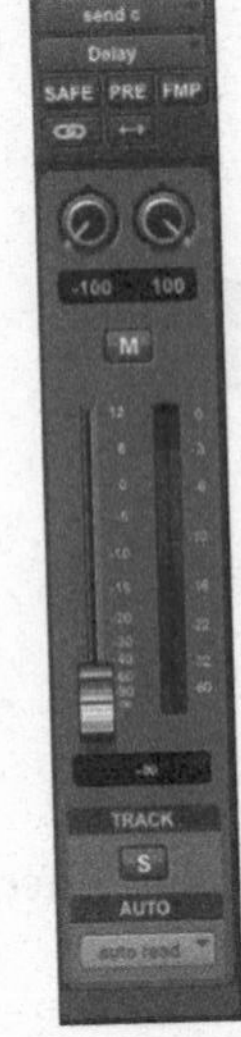

FIGURE 19-2: Use the Send Output window to control the signal going to the effect.

Rolling Out the Reverb

Reverb is undoubtedly the most commonly used effects processor. *Reverb,* the natural characteristic of any enclosed room, results from sound waves bouncing off walls, a floor, and a ceiling. A small room produces reflections that start quickly and end soon; in larger rooms, halls, or cathedrals, the sound has farther to travel, so you get slower start times and a longer-lasting reverberation.

This room effect enables you to place your track closer to the imaginary "front" or "back" of the mix. You do this by varying how much of the affected signal you include with the unaffected one. For example, mixing a lot of reverb with the dry (unaffected) signal gives the impression of being farther away, so your instrument sounds like it's farther back in the mix.

Seeing reverb settings

You can adjust several parameters when you use reverb, which gives you a lot of flexibility. Figure 19-3, which shows the Reverb plug-in, gives you a peek at the parameters you can play with.

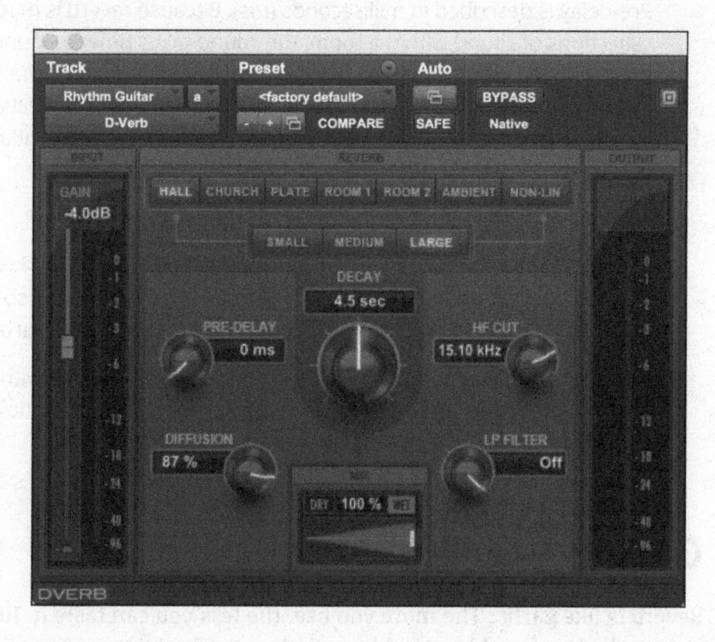

FIGURE 19-3: Reverb can add ambience to your instrument, giving it a more realistic sound.

The following list explains how the parameters — most, but not all, visible in Figure 19-3 — affect the sound of the reverb:

» **Algorithm:** This setting lets you choose the type of room that the reverb sounds like. You have the option of a hall, church, *plate* (a type of reverb that uses a metal plate to create its sound), two different rooms, *ambient* (natural room sound), and *nonlinear* (less natural) sound. Each choice also sets the other parameters for the reverb, but you can adjust those as you like to give your reverb a distinct sound.

» **Size:** This option refers to the "room" choices you have in the Algorithm setting. You have three settings to choose from: Small, Medium, and Large. Selecting one of these options adjusts the rest of the parameters in the window, except for the Algorithm setting.

» **Diffusion:** Diffusion affects the density of the reflections in the "room" you chose. A higher diffusion setting results in a thicker sound. Think of the diffusion parameter as a way to simulate how reflective or empty the room is. More reflective or crowded rooms produce a much higher diffusion. To simulate a less reflective room or emptier room, use lower-diffusion settings.

- **Decay:** *Decay* is the length of time that the reverb lasts. Larger or more reflective rooms produce a longer decay.
- **Pre-delay:** In a natural environment, direct sound waves from the instrument or voice reach your ears before the reflected waves arrive. The time after the direct sound stops and before the reflected sound starts is called "pre-delay." Pre-delay is described in milliseconds (ms). Because reverb is made up of reflections of sound within a room, the sound takes time to bounce around the room and reach your ears. By then, you've already heard the sound because it came directly to you. Pre-delay helps to define the initial sound signal by separating it from the reverb. This parameter is essential in making your reverb sound natural.

TIP

A small room has a shorter pre-delay than a large room.

- **HF Cut:** This setting allows you to control the rate at which the high frequencies decay. Most of the time the high frequencies decay faster, so being able to control this effect can result in a more natural sounding reverb.
- **LP Filter:** This filter controls the level of the high frequencies within the reverb. Setting this frequency gives the impression of a *darker* (lower-frequency setting) or *brighter* (higher-frequency setting) room.

Getting started using reverb

Reverb is like garlic: The more you use, the less you can taste it. Just as a new chef puts garlic in everything (and lots of it), many budding engineers make the same mistake with reverb. Go easy. Always remember that less is more.

Here are some other things to keep in mind:

- **Mixes often sound better when you use reverb on only a few instruments instead of them all.** For example, it's not uncommon for just the snare drum of the drum set to have reverb on it. The rest of the drums and cymbals remain dry (unaffected).
- **Try using reverb to "glue" instruments together.** Routing all your drum tracks to the same reverb, for instance, can make them sound like they were all recorded in the same room. When doing this, make sure that you adjust the Send level for each instrument so that the effect sounds natural. Also, use less reverb for all the instruments than you would for just one. This keeps the sound from becoming muddy from using too much reverb.
- **Think about how you want each instrument to sit in the mix when you choose reverb.** Make sure that the type and amount of reverb fits the song and the rest of the instruments.

» **Try putting the dry (unaffected) sound on one side of the stereo field and the reverb on the other.** For example, if you have a rhythm guitar part that you set at 30 degrees off to the right of the stereo field, set the reverb 30 degrees off to the left. This can be a nice effect.

» **To keep the vocals up front in the mix, use a short reverb setting.** A vocal plate is a great choice because the decay is fast. This adds a fair amount of the reverb to the vocal without making it sit way back in the mix.

» **Experiment with room types, sizes, and decay times.** Sometimes, a long decay on a small room reverb sounds better than a short decay on a large room or hall reverb.

Detailing Delay

Along with reverb, delay is a natural part of sound bouncing around a room. When you speak (or sing or play) into a room, you often hear not only reverb but also a distinct echo. This echo may be short or long, depending on the size of the room. The original sound may bounce back to you as a single echo or as multiple, progressively quieter delays.

Digging into delay settings

At your disposal are several types of delay effects, including a slap-back echo, tape delay, and multiple delays. Each is designed to add dimension to your instrument. To create these various effects, you adjust several parameters, as the following list and Figure 19-4 make clear. The Delay plug-ins that come with most full-feature audio programs are pretty much the same. (Okay, the default setting for each is different, but that's a pretty minor thing.) The parameters that you can adjust include the following:

» **Input:** This shows you the level of the signal entering the delay.

» **Delay:** This parameter controls the amount of time between the initial signal and the repeated sound. The time is listed in milliseconds and can be as short as a few milliseconds or as long as several seconds. This section lets you adjust the following settings:

- *FBK (Feedback):* The Feedback parameter controls how many times the echo repeats. A low setting makes the echo happen just once, and higher settings produce more echoes.

- *LPF:* The low-pass filter (LPF) lets you filter some of the high frequencies from the delay.
- *Sync:* This button synchronizes the delay to the metronomic beat of your session.
- *Meter:* This option lets you set the meter of the song and the subdivision that you want the delay to follow. When you change this parameter, the Delay parameter moves, too.
- *Tempo:* This option allows you to set the delay to beat in time with the music. The Tempo Match feature is referenced to the tempo map that you set for the song. You can set this parameter to any note division, from sixteenth notes to whole notes, if you want the delays to keep time with your song. (Quarter- and eighth-note delays are the most commonly used note divisions.)
- *Groove:* Use this parameter to adjust the rate of the delay in relation to the tempo and subdivision you chose. By changing this setting, you alter the delay (by percentages) away from the strict tempo and subdivision settings. This can be useful if you're adjusting the exact delay that you want. When you adjust this parameter, the Delay setting changes as well.

» **Modulation:** This section adds a chorus effect to the delay. You have two parameters you can tweak:

- *Rate:* This setting lets you set the amount of time that the modulation takes to cycle.
- *Depth:* This parameter controls the overall degree of the modulation. (See "Creating Chorus Effects" later in this chapter for more on chorus and flange effects.) The higher the level on this setting, the greater the modulation.

» **Gain:** This lets you set the signal level going into the delay.

» **Mix:** This parameter controls the output level of the effect. The higher you set this parameter, the louder the delayed signal is relative to the original signal.

Getting started using delay

Delay is used a lot in contemporary music, and often you don't hear it unless you listen carefully. Other times, it's prominent in the mix (for example, the snare drum in some reggae music). Here are ways you can use delay in your music:

» **One of the most effective ways to use delay is as a slap-back echo on vocals.** A *slap-back echo* consists of one to three repeats spaced very closely together, which fattens the sound of the vocals. You generally want to set your time parameter between 90 and 120 ms. Set the level so you barely hear the first echo when your vocal is in the mix and adjust it from there until you like the sound. In pop music, a slap-back echo and a vocal plate reverb are commonly used on lead vocals. (It was *really* common in the 1950s, and shows up a lot — less subtly — in rockabilly.) The Slap Delay plug-in in Pro Tools is a good place to start, although the default setting has a longer delay time than I recommend.

- **Use the Tempo Match feature to have your delay echo in time with the music.** This can add some depth to the mix without creating a muddy or cluttered sound. Be careful because if you use this too much, it can make your music sound annoyingly repetitive.

FIGURE 19-4: A Delay plug-in allows you to create various echoes.

Creating Chorus Effects

Chorus takes the original sound and creates a copy that is very slightly out of tune with the original and varies over time. This variance is *modulation*, and the result is an effect that can add interest and variety to an instrument. Chorus is used quite extensively to add fullness to an instrument, particularly guitars and vocals. Some audio programs don't contain a Chorus plug-in per se, but all Delay plug-ins can produce chorusing effects by adjusting the Depth and Rate parameters. (Check out the "Detailing Delay" section, earlier in this chapter, for more on delays.)

Most chorus effects give you several parameters with which to work, as the following list makes clear:

- **Rate:** The rate dictates how fast the modulation happens. This parameter is described as a frequency (usually 0.1 to 10 Hz). The frequency actually doesn't refer to a pitch; instead, it describes how many times per second (Hz) the oscillation happens. The oscillation is controlled by the depth parameter.
- **Depth:** The depth parameter controls the amount of pitch modulation produced by the chorus. The settings are often arbitrary (you can get a range of 1 to 100). This range relates to a percentage of the maximum depth to which the particular chorus can go, rather than an actual level.
- **Pre-delay:** The pre-delay setting affects how far out of time the chorus's sound is in relation to the original. This setting is listed in milliseconds, and the lower the number, the closer the chorused sound is to the original in time.
- **Feedback:** The feedback control sends the affected sound from the chorus back in again. This allows you to extend the amount of chorusing that the effect creates. This setting can also be called *stages* in some systems.
- **Effect level:** This could also be called *mix* in some systems. The effect level controls how much effect is sent to the aux return bus. This allows you to adjust how affected the sound becomes.

If reverb is like garlic, then chorus is like cayenne pepper. You may get away with a little too much garlic in your food without too much trouble, but if you add too much cayenne, you run the risk of making your food inedible. Such is the case with the chorus effect. Used sparingly, it can add a lot to your music; overdone, it can wreak havoc on a good song.

Try the following tips for making the best use of chorus effects:

- To fill out a vocal track, try setting the rate at 2 Hz, the depth at about 20 to 30, and the delay at 10 to 20 ms. Keep the Feedback level low.
- Use a chorus on backup vocals to make them much fuller and allow you to use fewer tracks.
- Pan the chorus to one side of the mix and the dry (unaffected) signal to the other. This can be especially interesting on guitars and synthesizer patches.

Along with chorus, your system may have other modulating effects, such as flange and phase shifting. These two effects work much like chorus, except they alter the original signal in time (flange) and in sound wave position (phase shifting) rather than pitch. The parameters you have for such effects are similar to those that you find for chorus effects. You can use the flange and phase shifters in many of the same applications as the chorus if you're going for a different effect.

Making Sense of Microphone Modeling

Mic modeling plug-ins alter your signal to make it sound like it was recorded through a different microphone than the one you used (obviously). The great thing about the mic modeling effect is that you can have a bunch of microphone sounds available to you without buying a bunch of expensive mics.

The only real drawback to mic modeling programs is that they don't sound exactly like the mics they're trying to model. I mean, making a $100 dynamic mic sound like a $3,000 large-diaphragm condenser mic is pretty hard, no matter how much computer processing you do. But this is no big deal, because all you're trying to do with a mic simulator is expand the options you have with a given mic. So, even though the modeler can't exactly match the bigger-buck mic, it can provide a pretty decent sound for your inexpensive mic.

The other possible drawback to using a mic modeling program is that the mic that you used to record the part in the first place may have an impact on how well the modeler sounds. Most mic simulator programs designate which mic was used to model the initial sound and which mic the simulator is trying to sound like. For example, in the Roland V-Studios, as you scroll through the various mic simulator patches (effects), you see them listed with one mic name followed by another ("SM57 – U87," for instance). If you want to get a sound like the second mic listed, you need to use the first mic listed. If you use a different mic than the one listed first, you get a different sound, but this isn't necessarily a bad thing; it's just different.

There are quite a few microphone modeling plug-ins on the market. Here are some worth checking out:

- **Mic Mod EFX by Antares:** Mic Mod EFX offers over 125 mics and it's easy to use.
- **T-RackS Mic Room by IK Multimedia:** T-RackS Mic Room offers over 20 types of mics.
- **Universal Audio Mic Modeling Plug-ins:** Universal Audio offer three plug-ins for modeling microphones. These include Townsend Lab Sphere, Ocean Way Microphone Collection, and the Bill Putnam Mic Collection.

There are also complete microphone modeling systems that include a reference mic along with the plug-in. This improves the quality of the modeling because the software can translate the signal better. There are currently three options:

- **Antelope Audio Verge:** Antelope Audio offers two mics, both large diaphragm condenser mics. The Solo is a single diaphragm instrument mic and the Duo is a dual diaphragm mic that captures two signals (you need two inputs in your preamp). Both of them record and model in Cardioid pattern.

» **Townsend Labs Sphere L22:** The Sphere L22 mic is also a dual diaphragm large diaphragm condenser mic that captures two signals (again, you need two inputs in your preamp) and offers a variety of polar patterns. You can also use it as a stereo mic.

» **Virtual Microphone System by Slate Digital:** The Virtual Microphone System is a complete mic processing package that includes a large diaphragm condenser mic, solid state preamp, and digital signal processing. This is not an inexpensive solution, but it produces some really nice sounds.

You can find many more by doing an Internet search for "microphone modeling plug-in."

Applying an Amp Simulator

An amp simulator effect allows you to essentially have access to a whole roomful of top-notch amps without having to buy, maintain, or store them. One of the great things about amp simulators is that they allow you to plug your guitar directly into your mixer (or direct box), which eliminates a lot of the noise that miking your guitar amp can cause. You also get to choose the sound that you ultimately want after you've recorded your part. This gives you more flexibility during mixdown.

The downside to amp simulators, as with mic simulators, is that they may not sound exactly like the amp they're trying to model, but this shouldn't matter as long as you get the sound you want. Another downside is that amp simulators use processing power, and if you have a ton of tracks with a bunch of effects and other plug-ins, you may find your computer getting bogged down a bit. The remedy for this is to print (record) the effect onto a separate track before you mix the song. This frees up power for other uses.

Dozens of amp simulators are on the market. Here are some worth checking out:

» **AmpliTube by IK Multimedia:** Several versions of AmpliTube are available, from a free version to one with 160 gear models.

» **Guitar Rig by Native Instruments:** Guitar Rig comes with 15 different amp/cabinet combos and a Control Room function that lets you mix a handful of different miked amp simulators together.

» **ReValver by Peavey:** This software includes 20 amp types, almost 800 speaker configurations, stomp box, and other effects. You can do a lot with this software.

» **Vintage Amp Room by Softube:** This program contains three vintage amp models with almost limitless virtual mic positioning.

Detailing Distortion Effects

Generally speaking, when recording audio, you want as clean and pure a sound as you can get. But as any guitar player will tell you, there is a time when adding distortion is key to the best sound for the song or instrument. In Chapters 9 and 18, I introduce you to dynamic processors and show you some settings you can use to give your tracks some character. This is done by pushing the compressor to add some distortion to your instrument.

Using compression is a common way of creating distortion, but you can also use specialized plug-ins to have more options and colors. If you are a guitar or bass player, you are probably familiar with using tools to give your sound distortion. Here are a few common types of distortion effects (you may find these combined in some plug-ins):

» **Amp modelers and pedal effects:** Multitudes of plug-ins are available for modeling bass and guitar amps and pedals. You can use these for any of your audio tracks to give them some flavor.

» **Bitcrusher:** Most DAW software has its own version of a bitcrusher plug-in. Bitcrushers create distortion by reducing the bit-depth of your audio and are not meant to offer a "pleasing" level of distortion. Instead, this is about adding grittiness and a lo-fi effect. If you want to mangle your sound, this is a great starting point.

» **Overdrive:** Overdrive traditionally happens when you push the analog circuits of an amp to the point where the harmonics of the sound change. Overdriving your sound tends to be more musical than compression and less extreme than bitcrushing it.

» **Phase Distortion:** Phase distortion combines an overdrive effect with a phase shifter.

TIP

For more plug-ins to add distortion to your tracks, do an Internet search for "audio recording distortion plug-in." You'll find a ton of options and reviews of the most popular ones.

Selecting Tape Saturation Effects

A specialized form of distortion is called *tape saturation*. Tape saturation is an artifact from old-school analog tape recorders hitting the limits of the amount of information the tape will take. Too little volume made the sound thin, whereas too high of a volume ended up with distortion, sometimes not that pleasing. Recording to tape was a delicate balance between getting the best sound from the instrument and the highest volume possible. The art to this balancing act was to push the limits of the tape to the point where you had a pleasing level of distortion. This distortion added harmonics to the instrument and, when used for mixing, acted as the glue that allowed the various instruments to blend well.

OH, HOW I YEARN FOR THAT ANALOG SOUND

An interesting trend in digital recording is the quest for analog sound. In the marketplace, you find new pieces of gear being marketed as having *warmth* or a *vintage sound.* What exactly is this sound?

This sound is . . . wait for it . . . distortion. Yep, good ol' noise and distortion. Why would someone want to duplicate that now?

When the mild distortion that's inherent in good analog recordings was eliminated in digital recordings, we missed it (sigh). In analog recording, you find a technique that's used to add something wonderful and beautifully pleasing to a recording: *tape saturation.* This is caused by recording the sound onto a tape recorder at a high enough level that the tape becomes saturated (hence, the term *tape saturation*), and certain aspects of the sound change.

For the most part, tape saturation adds *even harmonics* to the sound. Not to get too technical, but these are the tones present in the music but, for the most part, hidden behind the main tone. Tape saturation brings out those tones just a little, and people find them pleasing to listen to. Tape saturation also mellows out the high frequencies by *smearing* them together a little. Without this sound, many listeners (certainly not all) find digital recordings somewhat *harsh* or *cold.* In case you didn't know, these are highly technical terms meaning, "I don't hear that thing I'm used to hearing in an analog recording."

Digital recording can't duplicate this sound exactly, although some units come close. If you overdrive the recording level on a digital audio workstation, rather than achieving that rich analog warmth you'll end up with a harsh and horrible clipping sound. (The sound is clipped off by the digital converters, and you hear crackles and clicks.)

Digital recording doesn't offer this type of pleasing distortion. Instead, pushing the limits of the input signal just gets you noise (in the form of clipping — chopping off the audio waveform). Without the pleasing distortion inherent in analog recording, digital recording often described as sounding cold or clinical.

Many great tape emulator plug-ins are available. (I list a few below, but do an Internet search for "tape saturation emulator plug-in" for more.) All of these will offer controls to add some tape flavor to your tracks:

- **Bias:** Bias is the addition of ultra-high frequency electrical current (usually between 40 kHz and 150 kHz) to analog tape recorders to reduce the distortion of a magnetic tape recording. Tape emulators give you the ability to adjust this level to actually induce a form of distortion to your recordings.
- **Tape hiss (noise):** Tape hiss is the noise created by the magnetic particles in the analog tape. Like with bias, the goal of good analog tape machine was to reduce this noise. This noise was always present, often far in the background in good analog recordings. Digital recording doesn't have this sound, and most of us can tell it's not there. This control within tape saturation emulators allows you to add some of this noise back in.
- **Tape speed:** High quality analog tape decks allowed you to choose different tape speeds for your recordings. Slower speeds let you record more music on a spool of tape, but also introduce more tape hiss. Whereas faster speeds produced less noise at the cost of, well, more money. Creative recordists would learn pretty quickly that different speeds offered different colors of sounds as well and would choose according to their tastes. This control lets you do this to your digital recordings.
- **Wow and flutter:** Wow and flutter are measurements of the variations of frequency from the sound due to the mechanics of rolling the tape across the tape head. Being able to adjust this parameter lets you add some frequency modulation to your music.
- **Tape formulas:** Another variable in the sound in analog recording was the type of tape used in the machine. By being able to choose from typical formulations, you get another tool for adding color to your digital sound.
- **Tape machines:** Analog tape machines each had their own unique sound, and many old-school recordists have strong feelings about the subtleties in each machine. You'll find tape saturation emulators that are created based on these characteristics.

You will also be able to mix your dry and wet signals, adjust the input and output level, and view the amount of effect you are applying with meters.

Luckily, many plug-ins that allow you to add the nuances of tape saturation to your digital recordings are available. These include:

- **Softube:** Softube is a simple-to-use plug-in that provides a nice smooth saturation using a single knob (and three modes). It's free, so it's definitely worth trying.
- **Universal Audio Magnetic Tape Bundle:** Universal Audio makes high-end interfaces and plug-ins. Its tap emulators are as true as you can get representations of the effects that analog tape can impart on sound. This bundle emulates two classic tapes players: the Studer A800 and the Ampex ATR-102. These tapes players won't let you create lo-fi effects. Instead they will add a warming cohesion to whatever you run through them. These are expensive plug-ins at roughly $300, and may be worth it for your music.
- **Waves Abby Road Studio 337:** Waves makes some excellent plug-ins, and the J37 tape saturation is up there with its best. As the name suggests, this plug-in is an emulation of the J37 4-track, 1-inch tape recorder used at Abby Road Studios in the 1960s and '70s. The J37 was a very high-quality recorder and this plug-in offers a subtle glue-like quality to your sound (and it won't mangle it, even if you try). This plug-in costs about $50.

TIP

I can't offer any broad recommendations on settings because each plug-in and music track is unique. However, most of these plug-ins have decent, if not excellent, presets that will add a lot to your tracks. Play around a bit and I'm sure you'll find some setting that works for you.

IN THIS CHAPTER

» Understanding automation

» Writing automation

» Editing automation

» Playing automated tracks

Chapter 20
Automating Your Mix

You likely won't have a session without a single change in level, pan, equalization (EQ), or plug-in parameters somewhere in the song. Unless you have an external mixer or control surface, you're stuck making these changes with your mouse. The problem with all this mouse-intensive work is that you can't move more than one fader, panning knob, or plug-in setting at a time. To be honest, the only way you can really mix within digital systems is by using some kind of automation feature, which all full-featured digital audio workstations (DAWs) have.

REMEMBER

Most studio-in-a-box (SIAB) and portable system do not have automation features like the ones I list in this chapter. If you have one of these systems, and you want to mix with automation, you will need to transfer your files into a computer that has a program with automation. Fortunately, most SIAB and portable recorders make this process fairly easy. Check your owner's manual for the process.

Don't like how the guitar in the second verse sits in the mix? No problem. Just adjust your automation data and mix it again. You can even save multiple versions of these settings so you can create as many mixes as you want. (Be careful here, though: When asked, most mix engineers say that they finish a mix only when they run out of time or money to keep trying things.)

This chapter gets you going on mixing the newfangled way: automatically. Well, not exactly *automatically* — you still need to program these mixing settings, but I show you how to do that. In this chapter, I lead you through automating the various aspects of your song — volume levels, mute and panning placement, EQ, and plug-in settings. In addition, you discover how to change your automation settings and also how to play the automation data back so you're ready to do your final mix.

Understanding Automation

You can automate a variety of parameters in most audio recording programs, such as Pro Tools or Logic Pro. Each parameter has a playlist that contains its automation data. You can write this data one parameter (or more) at a time, and you can display and edit the data even while playing the session. This section describes the parameters you can generally automate in audio, auxiliary, Master fader, instrument, and Musical Instrument Digital Interface (MIDI) tracks.

Audio tracks

You can automate the following parameters in your audio tracks:

- **Volume:** Use this parameter to control the overall volume of the track.
- **Pan:** Use this to set the left/right balance of the track in the stereo field.
- **Mute:** This allows you to turn the track on and off.
- **Send:** This parameter includes volume, mute, and panning settings for the *send,* which is the routing section that lets you send part of your track's signal to an effect.
- **Plug-ins:** You adjust these parameters within the Plug-In window.

Automation data for each of these parameters resides in a playlist that's separate from the clips that contain your edits for that track. This allows you to move the clips in and out of the track's playlist without changing the automation data for that track.

Auxiliary input tracks

You can automate the following parameters when you're working with auxiliary input (aux) tracks:

- **Volume:** Use this parameter to set the overall volume of your Aux track.
- **Pan:** You can place your tracks anywhere from left to right in the stereo field.

- **Mute:** Use this to turn the track on and off.
- **Plug-ins:** You adjust these parameters within the Plug-In window.

Instrument tracks

You can automate the following parameters when you're working with instrument tracks:

- **Volume:** Use this parameter to set the overall volume of the track.
- **Pan:** Use this to set the left/right balance of the track in the stereo field.
- **Mute:** This allows you to turn the track on and off.

Master fader tracks

You can automate Volume and Plug-in settings on Master fader tracks. It sets the overall volume of the MIDI data.

MIDI tracks

You can automate the following parameters when you're working with MIDI tracks:

- **Volume:** Use this parameter to set the overall volume of the MIDI data.
- **Pan:** You can place your tracks anywhere from left to right in the stereo field.
- **Mute:** This allows you to turn the track on and off.
- **Controller data:** This includes a number of MIDI settings, including options such as the modulation wheel, breath controller, and sustain.

Accessing Automation Modes

All DAWs offer a variety of ways to automate your mixes. Called automation modes, Pro Tools and Logic Pro, for example, offer five: Auto Off, Auto Read, Auto Write, Auto Touch, and Auto Latch. You access these modes by clicking the Automation Mode selector in the channel strip of each track in the Mix window or in the Track Controls section of the Edit window, as shown in Figure 20-1. Each mode affects how Pro Tools writes or plays back automation data for a track — which I cover in this section. Other DAWs function in the same or similar ways.

FIGURE 20-1: Access the five Pro Tools automation modes here.

Now for the particulars. Here's what each mode actually does:

- **Auto Off:** This mode turns off all automation data for the selected track.
- **Auto Read:** This mode plays back the automation data for the selected track.
- **Auto Write:** This mode writes automation data for the selected parameter(s) while the session plays, thus overwriting any pre-existing automation data in the process. When you stop playback after writing automation in this mode, Pro Tools automatically switches the automation mode to Auto Touch (see the next bullet) so you don't accidentally erase this data next time you play back the session.
- **Auto Touch:** Auto Touch mode writes automation data only when you click a parameter with your mouse; it stops writing when you release the mouse button. (See the upcoming Remember icon for control-surface behavior in this mode.) At this point, your automated parameter returns to any previously automated position, according to the time that you set for AutoMatch on the Mixing tab of the Preferences dialog box. With Auto Touch, you can fix parts of your previously recorded automation data without erasing what you want to keep.

REMEMBER

Auto Touch engages differently, depending on the control surface you use. If you have touch-sensitive faders (like those on the Avis S1 or S3 or the Mackie MCU Pro), new automation data is written as soon as you touch a fader. If your control surface doesn't sport touch-sensitive faders, Auto Touch mode won't engage until you move a fader past the position it occupied in the previously written automation data (the *pass-through point*). After you hit that point, automation data is written until you stop moving the fader.

» **Auto Latch:** This mode works much like Auto Touch (see the previous bullet). After you touch or move a parameter, new automation data is written. The difference is that Auto Latch mode continues to write new automation data until you stop playback.

Writing Automation

Writing automation is easy — simply enable the parameter for which you want to write automation data, choose your automation mode, and then adjust the parameter as the session plays. The following sections detail this process.

While automation is being written, it appears in your track as breakpoints with lines (ramps) between these points. The breakpoints are placed in the track's *automation playlist:* that is, the playlist section of the track when you have the Tracks view set to one of the Automation views via the Track View drop-down menu. The number of breakpoints that appear is determined by the complexity of the changes to the automation levels and also by your setting in the Degree of Thinning drop-down menu on the Mixing tab of the Preferences dialog box.

When the Smooth and Thin Data After Pass check box is enabled, choosing None from the Degree of Thinning drop-down menu (refer to Figure 20-2 later in the chapter) creates lots of breakpoints — you might not even notice any lines between them. Comparatively, selecting Most from the drop-down menu creates many fewer breakpoints, with longer, more pronounced lines between them. Pro Tools places lines between these breakpoints to connect them. These lines follow the level from one breakpoint to another, going up, down, or staying the same. The combination of breakpoints and connecting lines represent the automation curves for your track.

TIP

To keep from accidentally erasing or overwriting automation data, suspend the writing of automation for the parameter by using one of the methods of suspending automation listed in the preceding section.

Writing automation on a track

To write automation on a track, follow these steps:

1. **Show automation for your song session.**

   For example, in Logic Pro X, you choose Mix ➪ Show Automation (or press A). In Pro Tools, you choose Window ➪ Automation from the main menu. In Pro

Tools, the automation window opens where you can choose the parameters you want to automate. In Logic Pro X, you need to click the Show/Hide automation button in the Tracks area menu to see the automation parameters for your tracks.

2. **Select the tracks and automation parameters you want to write automation data to in the Automation window by clicking the buttons of the parameters you want to enable.**
3. **Choose the Automation mode you want to use by clicking the Automation selector (Pro Tools) or pop-up menu (Logic Pro X).**
4. **Click Play in the Transport Window or press the spacebar to start your session.**
5. **Move the control for the parameters you want to automate.**

   For example, move the track's fader (located in the channel strip of the Mix window) up and down to record changes in the volume level of your track.
6. **Click Stop in the Transport window or press the spacebar to stop the session.**

   Your automation shows up as a line with breakpoints (little dots) in the track's playlist — that is, as long as you have the automation view visible. If this view isn't visible, click the Track View selector in the Track Controls section of the Edit window to open the Track View drop-down menu and then select the automation parameter — Volume, Pan, Mute, Send Level, Send Mute — you want to view.

Writing plug-in automation

Here's how to write automation data for plug-in parameters in Pro Tools:

1. **In the Mix window, click the name of the plug-in in the Insert section of the track's channel strip.**

   The particular Plug-In window appears.
2. **Click the Auto button below the word "Auto" in the Plug-in window.**

   The Plug-In Automation dialog box appears, as shown in Figure 20-2.
3. **Select the parameters you want to automate by clicking them in the column on the left and then clicking Add.**

   The selected parameters are added to the column on the right.
4. **Click OK.**

   The dialog box closes.

5. **Click Play in the Transport Window (or press the spacebar) to start your session.**
6. **Carefully move the control for the parameters you want to automate.**
7. **Click Stop in the Transport window (or press the spacebar) to stop the session.**

   Your automation shows up as a line with breakpoints (little dots) in the track's playlist as long as you have the automation view visible. If it's not visible, click the Track View selector in the Track Controls section of the Edit window to open the Track View drop-down menu and select the automation parameter — Volume, Pan, Mute, Send Level, Send Mute — you want to view.

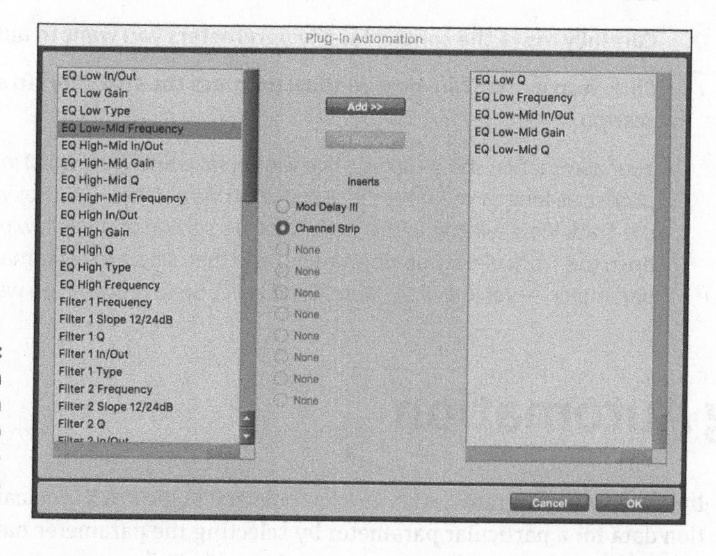

FIGURE 20-2: Use the Plug-In Automation dialog box to choose the parameters to automate.

TIP

After you finish writing the automation for the plug-in, click the Safe button in the upper-right part of the Plug-In window to make sure that you don't accidentally record over the plug-in automation.

Writing send automation

To write automation in Pro Tools data for Send Level, Mute, and Pan settings, follow these steps:

1. **Choose Window ⇨ Automation from the main menu.**

   The Automation window appears.

2. **In the Automation window, click the buttons of the Send parameters that you want to enable.**
3. **Choose View ➪ Mix Window ➪ Sends from the main menu.**

   Doing so displays the Send controls for the track(s) you want to automate.
4. **Select the Auto Write (choose Auto Touch or Auto Latch for subsequent times) in each track you want to write to by clicking the Automation selector.**

   You can find the Automation Mode selector in the Edit window.
5. **Click Play in the Transport Window (or press the spacebar) to start your session.**
6. **Carefully move the control for the parameters you want to automate.**
7. **Click Stop in the Transport window (or press the spacebar) to stop the session.**

   Your automation shows up as a line with breakpoints (little dots) in the track's playlist, as long as you have the automation view visible. If it's not visible, click the Track View selector in the Track Controls section of the Edit window to open the Track View drop-down menu and then select the automation parameter — Volume, Pan, Mute, Send Level, Send Mute — you want to view.

Viewing Automation

In many DAW programs, such as Pro Tools and Logic Pro X, you can view automation data for a particular parameter by selecting the parameter name in the Track View selector in the Edit window, as shown in Figure 20-3. For easy reference, parameters with automation data are listed with orange text in the Track View for your track.

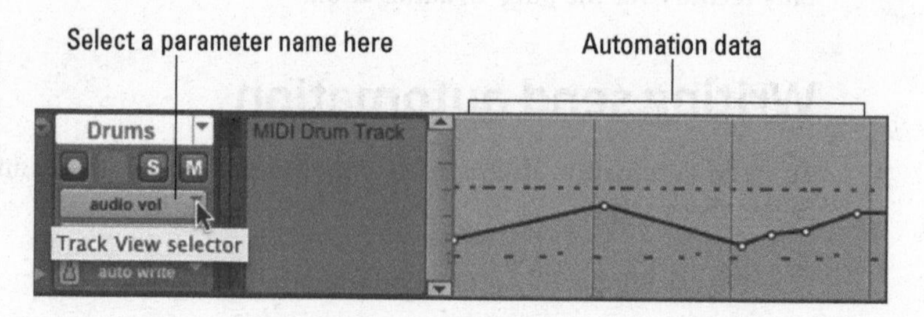

FIGURE 20-3: Select Track View for the automation parameter to display automation data in the track's playlist.

Editing Automation Data

At your disposal are many ways to edit automation data after it's written. You can use one of the Edit tools (Pro Tools, for example, offers Grabber, Pencil, or Trimmer tools); you can cut/copy/paste; and (if you want to get drastic) you can delete your automation. These options are covered in the following sections.

Using editing commands

You can use standard Edit commands (such as Cut, Copy, Delete, and Paste) to edit your automation data. To edit using these commands, though, select the data first. Here's the basic process, regardless of your DAW:

1. **From the Track View selector in either the Edit or Mix window, display the automation parameter you want to edit.**
2. **With the Selector tool, highlight the section in the playlist you want to edit.**

   If you're looking at the track in Waveform or Block view (for audio tracks) or in Block, Clip, or Notes view (for MIDI tracks), your edits affect all automation data for the selected section. To edit an individual parameter, display it in the Track view.

Cut and Delete

You get rid of unwanted stuff when you cut and delete automation data, but the Cut and Delete commands treat unwanted stuff a bit differently:

- **Cut:** When you cut a selection of automation data, Pro Tools automatically adds two new breakpoints to your remaining data and places the cut material on the Clipboard. The two new breakpoints are placed at the beginning and end of the cut section. Any slope in automation curves that exists before and after the cut section remains, as shown in Figure 20-4.

  In most DAWs, cut by choosing Edit ⇨ Cut from the main menu or by pressing ⌘+X (Mac) or Ctrl+X (PC).

- **Delete:** When you delete selected automation data, the remaining automation data connects at the nearest breakpoints. Any curves between the breakpoints and the beginning or end of the deleted selection are removed, as shown in Figure 20-5.

  In most DAWs, delete by choosing Edit ⇨ Delete from the main menu or by pressing Delete (Mac) or Backspace (PC).

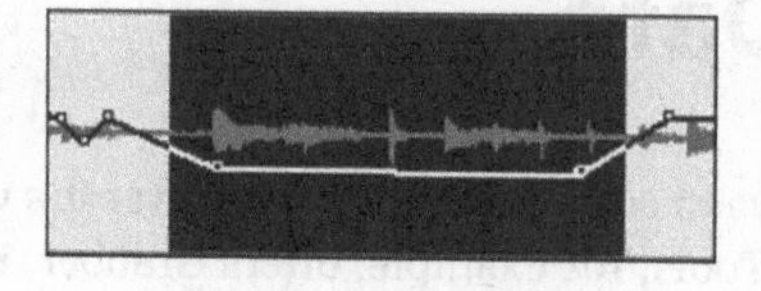

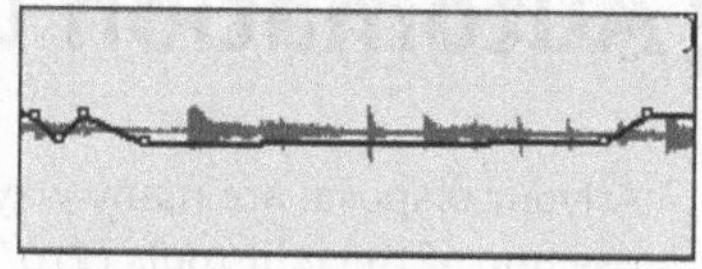

FIGURE 20-4: Before (left) and after (right) cutting automation data from a track in Pro Tools.

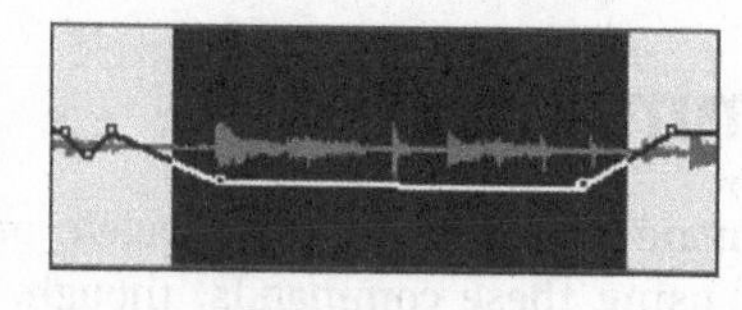

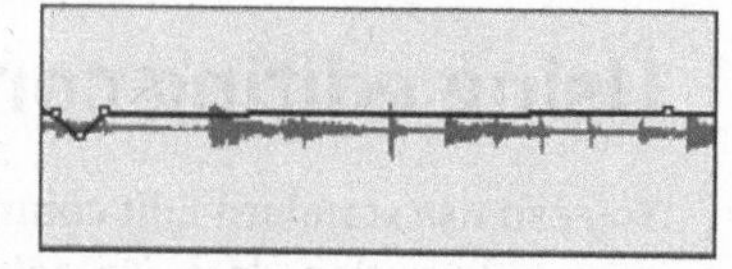

FIGURE 20-5: Before (left) and after (right) deleting automation data from a track in Pro Tools.

Copy

Choose Edit⇨Copy or press ⌘+C (Mac) or Ctrl+C (PC) from the main menu to place copied data held on the Clipboard so you can paste it somewhere else.

Paste

When you choose Edit⇨Paste or press ⌘+V (Mac) or Ctrl+V (PC) from the main menu to paste selected automation data in a new location, breakpoints are created at the beginning and end points of the selection. These breakpoints make sure that the automation levels and slope (change in level) that exist before the beginning and end points of the pasted material remain the same, as shown in Figure 20-6.

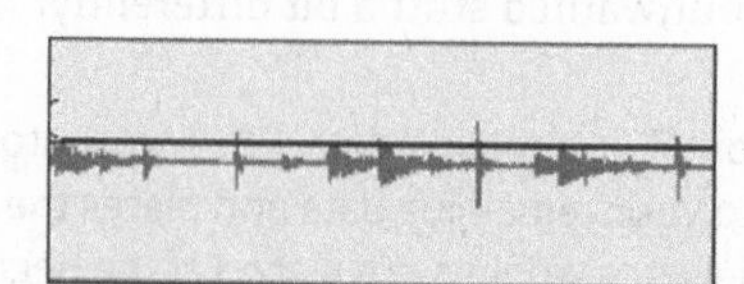

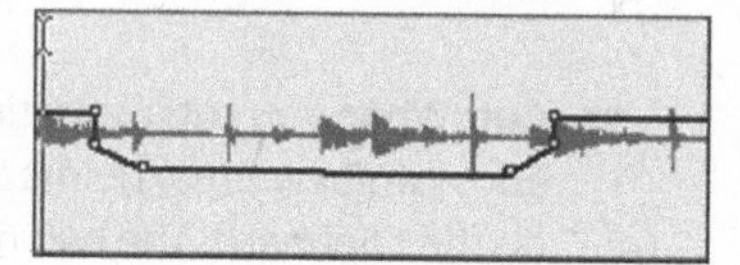

FIGURE 20-6: Before (left) and after (right) pasting automation data to a track in Pro Tools.

Editing with the edit tools

You can use the editing tools located in the Edit window to change automation data within a track. These common tools include the Grabber or Selector tool, the Trimmer tool, and the Pencil tool. These are detailed in the following sections.

Grabber or Selector

Use the Grabber or Selector tool to move, add, and delete breakpoints. To perform these operations, do the following:

» **Adding breakpoints:** To add a breakpoint with this tool, click in the automation line where you want the new breakpoint.

» **Deleting breakpoints:** To delete a breakpoint from an automation line, put this tool on it and then press Option (Mac) or Alt (PC) while you click.

» **Moving breakpoints:** To move a breakpoint, click and drag it to where you want it.

Pencil

You can add or delete breakpoints with the Pencil tool by doing the following:

» **Adding breakpoints:** To add a breakpoint with the Pencil tool, click in the automation line at the place where you want the new breakpoint.

» **Deleting breakpoints:** To delete a breakpoint, put the Pencil tool on it and then press Option (Mac) or Alt (PC) while you click.

Trimmer

Use the Trimmer tool to move selected breakpoints up or down by clicking and dragging them, as shown in Figure 20-7.

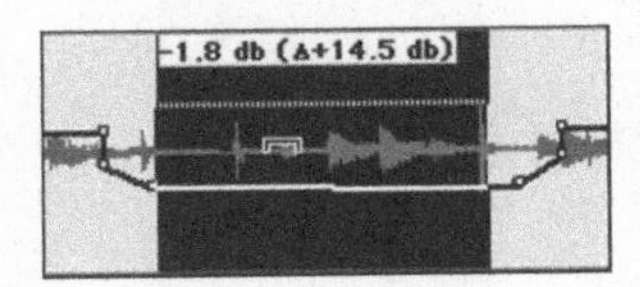

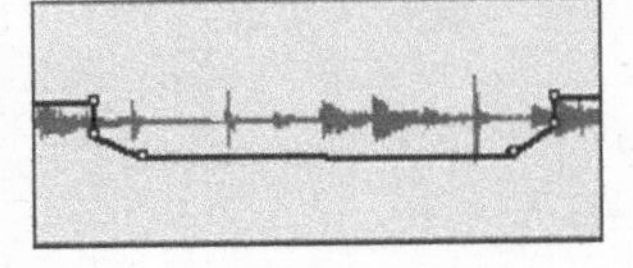

FIGURE 20-7: Before (left) and after (right) adjusting automation levels using the Trimmer tool in Pro Tools.

TIP

To move breakpoints left or right, select them with the Selector tool. Then, using the number pad on your keyboard, press the minus key (–) to move left or the plus key (+) to move right.

IN THIS CHAPTER

» Submixing your tracks

» Mixing digitally in-the-box

» Mixing to an external recorder

Chapter 21

Making Your Mix

The final step in mixing your music involves taking all your EQed, panned, processed, and automated tracks and recording them into a stereo pair of tracks. This is often called *bouncing* your mix. In the old analog days, bouncing meant sending all your tracks to two separate tracks on the same tape deck or to a different tape deck. Nowadays, with digital recording, you can create bounces several ways — all of which I cover in this chapter.

In this chapter, I lead you through making your mix either within your computer or device *(in-the-box)* or by sending your tracks to a digital or an analog two-track machine — usually a digital mastering recorder (such as the Tascam DA-3000) or (yes, even today) a reel-to-reel tape deck.

Submixing Tracks

Submixing is mixing some of your tracks down to one or two additional tracks within your session. When you record to tracks, the submixed material automatically shows up in your session. You can then turn off the voices of the tracks that you submixed and control the resulting track(s) from one (or two) fader(s). This is handy if the following scenarios apply:

» **You have more tracks than your system allows.** For example, you can reduce your track count by submixing your drums or backup vocals to two tracks and then using only those two for the final mix.

» **You have MIDI tracks and want to record the audio output from your MIDI devices to audio tracks before doing your final mix.** Your MIDI tracks are just instrument-control data; they contain no recorded sound. At some point in the process of mixing, you need to record the actual audio output from your sound source to your audio tracks.

» **You want to record your final mix in real time and still be able to move the faders and other controls while your session plays.** Some recordists get antsy when bouncing offline because it prevents them from adjusting any controls as the mix is created. See the upcoming section, "Mixing In-the-Box."

To create a submix within a digital audio workstation (DAW), follow these steps:

1. **Set your effects, panning, and EQ settings for the tracks you want to submix.**
2. **Using the Output selector, assign the outputs for all tracks you want to submix (including any auxiliary tracks that your Send effects are routed to) to one of the stereo bus paths (buses 1 and 2, for instance).**
3. **Choose Track ⇨ New from the main menu.**

   The New Track dialog box appears.
4. **Use the drop-down menus in the New Track dialog box to enter the number of tracks you want (1), the type (Audio), and whether you want your track in mono or stereo.**
5. **If you created a stereo track to submix to, set the panning of the right track to hard right and that of the left track to hard left.**
6. **Set the Input selector for the track you create in Step 4 to the same bus path that you chose for the tracks you want to submix (buses 1 and 2, in this case).**
7. **Using the new track's Output selector, select the main output for your session as the output path for the track.**
8. **Select the section of the song session that you want to submix.**

   If you want to record the entire session, be sure to put your cursor at the beginning of the session before you record it. If you want to record only part of the session, select the part you want. (Chapter 14 details this process.)
9. **Click the Record Enable button on the new track.**
10. **Click Record in the Transport window.**
11. **Click Play in the Transport window.**

    The submix process begins.

12. Press Stop in the Transport window when you finish.

If you selected part of the session to record, the session stops playing automatically when it reaches the end of your selection.

REMEMBER

Be sure to let the session play until the last bit of reverb or other effect is finished playing to avoid cutting off the effect.

Mixing in-the-Box

Mixing in-the-box refers to using the Bounce function (Bounce to Disk in Pro Tools or simply Bounce in Logic Pro, for example) to create your final mix. Bouncing processes your audio tracks either in real time (you can hear the session while it plays at normal speed) or offline (as fast as your system can process it without you hearing the mix). Either way, you can't manipulate any controls when the bounce is happening.

TIP

If you want to manually adjust any parts of your mix while it bounces, do this by submixing all your tracks to a new stereo pair. See "Submixing Tracks" earlier in this chapter for details on this process.

Your DAW creates a new file with the settings that you choose in the Bounce dialog box. What you get is a file that you can import back into your session; then you can play back your Bounced mix and evaluate how it sounds.

Examining bounce options

The Bounce dialog box (Pro Tool's version is shown in Figure 21-1) is where you choose your final mix file settings. You access this dialog box by either clicking the Bounce button in the tracks you set as your main outputs in the Mix window (in Logic Pro) or by choosing File⇨Bounce To Disk from the main menu (Pro Tools).

Pro Tools offers the following options (most other DAWs are similar):

- **Source:** Use the Bounce Source drop-down menu to select any output or bus path as your source for the bounce. (Figure 21-2 gives you a peek at some of the choices.)

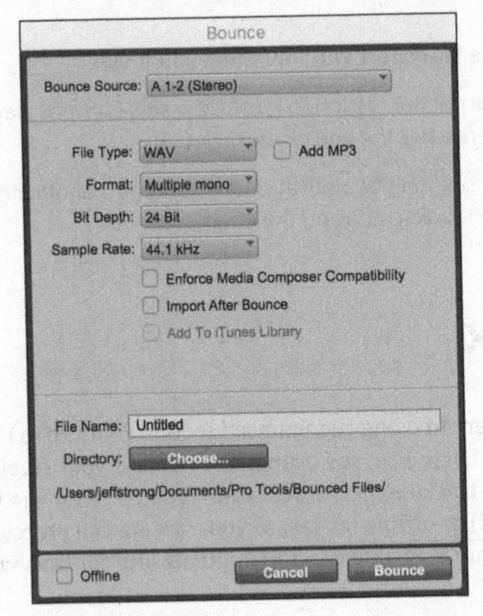

FIGURE 21-1: Use the Bounce dialog box in Pro Tools to select several bounce options.

- **File Type:** Use this drop-down menu to set the file type for the bounced file. Depending on your DAW, you have many choices for your final mix. These common file types can be found in most DAWs:
  - **WAV:** This file type, which is the standard for older, PC-based recording systems, is currently the most commonly used file type. (One big reason is that WAV files are compatible with both Macs and PCs.) This is the type I generally choose.
  - **AIFF:** Audio Interchange File Format files used to be native to Macs. AIFF files can be imported without converting into any Pro Tools session — including those on a PC — but because WAV is the standard, I skip this type. If you use a Mac and you plan to do your mastering on your Mac with Pro Tools, this file type is a fine choice.
  - **MP3:** MPEG-2 Audio Layer III is the standard for music distributed digitally. When you choose this option, a new dialog box opens. I cover creating MP3s of your music and describe this dialog box in Chapter 23.
- **Format:** This drop-down menu determines whether your bounced file is in Mono, Multiple Mono, or Stereo Interleaved. These formats do have some differences that are good to know:
  - **Mono (Summed):** Choosing this option creates a single audio file that contains all the material without any panning information.

WARNING

Because any stereo information is summed, getting too high of a combined signal is easy. This results in *clipping* (distortion). If you want to record in this format, make sure that you reduce your levels so that the left and right channels peak at no more than –3db, although –6dB is better. (Chapter 9 has more on setting levels.)

- **Multiple Mono:** This format puts the left and right channels of your stereo mix in separate files, labeling the files with the .L and .R filename extensions, respectively.

TIP

Multiple mono is the file format supported by Pro Tools, which makes it the one to use if you intend to master your music yourself within Pro Tools. If you plan to use a professional mastering engineer, call him to see what file format works with the mastering equipment (it will either be multiple mono or stereo-interleaved).

- **Stereo Interleaved:** This format contains all stereo information in a single stereo file. Panning information is retained. Any tracks set to even-numbered outputs end up on the right side of the stereo file; tracks set to odd-numbered outputs go to the left side of the stereo file.

- **Resolution:** Use this setting to choose one of three bit rates for your bounced files: 16, 24, or 32 float. (Chapter 1 has more on resolution.) For your final mix, choose 24 bit (maximum resolution). You can reduce it as needed later, either when you master your music yourself or when you have a professional do it for you.
- **Sample Rate:** You can save your file with any of several sample rates, but I recommend saving it with the same rate as the files in your session. Check out Chapter 2 for all the details about sample rates.

REMEMBER

If you intend to have your music mastered by a professional, make sure to ask her what she prefers. Some mastering engineers want the files at the highest sample rate possible while others would rather have you not change the rate.

- **Conversion Quality:** If you choose a sample rate different from the files in your session — which I don't recommend — you're prompted to choose a level of quality for the conversion. Choose the highest quality possible for your mix material, but keep in mind that the higher the quality you choose, the longer it takes to do the conversion process.

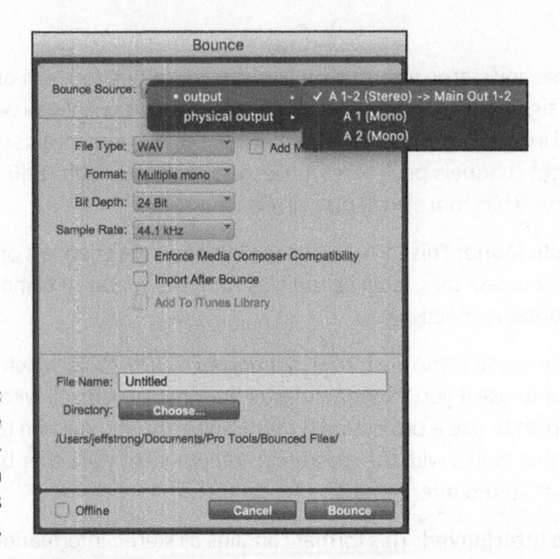

FIGURE 21-2: The Bounce Source drop-down menu in Pro Tools shows your choices.

Performing the bounce

To use the Bounce to Disk feature, first make sure that all your tracks are the way you want them. Check all routing, automation, effects, and EQ settings to make sure they're right. Then do the following:

1. **Open the Bounce dialog box.**

   In Logic Pro, click the Bounce button in the tracks you set as your main outputs in the Mix window. In Pro Tools, choose File ⇨ Bounce To Disk from the main menu.

   The Bounce dialog box appears. (Refer to Figure 21-1 for the Pro Tools version.)

2. **Set your Bounce options to the settings you want.**
3. **Click Bounce.**

   The Save Bounce As dialog box opens.

4. **In the Save As dialog box, choose a destination point for this file, enter the name of this mix, and then click Save.**

   The session plays while the bounce happens.

Using an External Master Deck

You can mix to an external device instead of mixing within your DAW. This section explains how to mix to both analog and digital recorders.

You can mix to an external digital device (such as a digital mastering recorder) or, for you "classic technology" fans, to an analog device (such as a reel-to-reel tape recorder). Just follow these steps:

1. **Connect your device to your audio interface.**

   For digital recorders, run a cable from the digital outputs of the interface to the digital inputs of your device. You'll need to use either an optical or a coaxial connection, depending on the interface.

   For analog recorders, run a cable from two of the analog outputs of the interface to the inputs of your device.

2. **(Optional) If you want to be able to monitor this device while it records, connect the device's outputs to your monitors (speakers) or plug your headphones into the headphone jack (if your device has one).**
3. **Using the Output selectors, set the output of your tracks, auxiliary inputs, and Master fader to the physical outputs of your interface.**

   These must correspond to the output you connected your device to.

4. **Enable recording in your external device.**
5. **Click Play in the Transport window of your DAW session.**
6. **Adjust your input levels on your external device.**
7. **Rewind the session.**
8. **Start recording on the external device and immediately press the spacebar or click Play in the Transport window.**

   The session plays, and you record it into your external device.

9. **Click Stop in the Transport window or press the spacebar when the music is done.**

   You have a mix recorded into your external device (look out, world, here it comes . . .).

IN THIS CHAPTER

» Understanding mastering

» Knowing when to master your music yourself

» Knowing when to send your music to a mastering house

» Taking a turn at mastering your music

Chapter 22
Mastering Your Music

You've spent a lot of time getting all your tracks recorded using the miking techniques I describe in Chapter 8. You adjusted your levels just right, EQed, panned, and added effects to each instrument with great care so that they fit perfectly in the mix. Now you have awesome-sounding music. So, all that's left is to create cool album artwork and find places to distribute — and you're ready to go platinum, right?

Well, you could do that, but you would be missing one of the most important steps in getting your music to sound its very best. This is the mastering process. Mastering can turn your already-good music into a truly great album. The only problem is that most people have no idea what mastering is. It's been presented as mysterious voodoo that only people who belong to some secret society and have access to a magical pile of gear can do.

This isn't the case. Mastering is, in fact, a pretty simple process that involves pieces of equipment that you've already used. Mastering does require specialized skills, but you don't need to go through strange initiation rites to understand them. All it takes is an idea of what to do, decent ears (you've got a couple of those, right?), and a dose of patience while you work your way through the process.

In this chapter, you get a chance to understand the "magic" that is mastering. You discover what's involved in mastering your music. You explore ways to master your music yourself and discern when it may be best to find a professional to do the job for you.

Demystifying Mastering

The mastering process of recording involves preparing your music for duplication. Several steps are involved in taking your songs from individual, mixed tunes to part of a whole album. First, you need to optimize the dynamics and tonal balance of each song. Then you need to process the songs so that they're matched to each other in volume. These steps usually involve doing some equalizing, compressing, limiting, and sometimes expanding to the songs.

You also need to sequence your music so that you have the songs in the best possible order, with the appropriate amount of time between each song. Your last step is to put your mastered music onto a format that enables you to distribute it. (This is usually a CD or digital file taken from the final CD-quality mix. I describe this process in detail in Chapter 23.)

Processing

No matter how well you recorded and mixed your music, you still need to do some processing during the mastering stage. This usually consists of adjusting levels with compression, limiting, and EQing and using additional processing if necessary.

The purpose of the processing stage is to balance the overall tonal characteristics of each song and optimize the dynamics of each song so that the songs are at their best overall volume. You can achieve these goals by using the following tools:

- **Compression:** Some music sounds best when it's smooth, and other music is much better when it has a punchy quality to it. Judicious use of compression can produce either of these effects. (I give you suggestions for compressor settings in the section "Optimizing dynamics," later in this chapter.) A good mastering engineer knows when and how to make music punchy or smooth. (Sorry, you can't have both at the same time.)

  Adding compression to the mastering process is an art. Too much or the wrong type of compression makes your music sound flat. Too little, and your music may sound weak.

- **Limiters:** If any instruments are too loud in comparison to the rest of the mix, a limiter can tame them so that the difference between the song's peak level and average level is optimal. This difference varies depending on the style of music, but it should never be less than 6dB and is usually between 12dB and 18dB.

» **Equalization (EQ):** Because you recorded and mixed each of your songs individually over a period of time (often a *long* period of time), each song probably sounds a little different. Some may be brighter than others and some may be heavier on bass, but one thing's for sure: Each has a different tonal quality.

For your compilation of songs to work as a unit, the songs' tonal quality needs to be somewhat consistent. The songs don't have to all sound the same, but they do need to work well together. The mastering engineer uses multiband equalizers on each song to make them work as separate songs and gel as a complete artistic statement.

Sequencing

Sequencing involves putting your songs in the order that you want and setting the blank space between each song so that the album flows well from one song to another. Because an album is supposed to represent a cohesive body of work, this is one of the most important aspects of mastering.

Leveling

A crucial aspect of mastering an album is getting the levels of all the songs to be the same. After all, you don't want your listener to have to adjust the volume of his stereo from one song to another. Having consistent levels from song to song helps with the cohesiveness and flow of an album. This is done with simple gain adjustments, compressors, and/or limiters.

Getting Ready to Master

When mastering your music, you can save yourself a ton of time and energy if you keep a few things in mind during the mixing stage. When you're wearing your Mixing Master hat, the following reminders can make the mastering process go a bit more smoothly:

» **Check your levels.** Listen to your mix quietly, and you can tell whether one instrument stands out too much in the mix. Also, burn a CD or create a digital file of your mixed song to test on other systems (your car, phone, or your friend's stereo system). Listen carefully. If the bass drum is even slightly too loud, it eats up the headroom of the rest of the instruments, and you can't get the volume of the song very high.

» **Check your EQ.** Even though the mastering engineer EQs the entire song, make sure that you spend the time getting each instrument EQed as best as you can in the mix. If you don't get your EQ just right during the mixing process and the bass guitar sound, for example, is muddy and needs to be EQed during mastering, you lose some of the low end on all the instruments. This makes your mix sound thin. If your bass is EQed properly in the first place, you don't have to make this adjustment to the entire mix.

» **Test your mix in mono (turn off the stereo panning on your master bus).** This helps you hear whether any instrument's volume or tonal characteristics are seriously out of balance with others. I never consider a mix finished until I monitor it in mono.

» **Apply compression to your mix before you record the two-track mix just to see what your music sounds like compressed.** Don't record the compression, though. Leave that for the mastering phase. By testing your mix with some compression, you may hear whether certain instruments are too loud in the mix because this becomes more apparent when the mix is compressed.

» **Listen for phase holes.** *Phase holes* occur when you record an instrument (for example, piano or backup vocals) in stereo and the two tracks are out of phase. To listen for phase holes, pay attention to how the instrument sounds in the stereo field. You have a phase hole if you hear sound coming only from the far right and far left and nothing seems to be coming from the center of the stereo field. If you have this problem, just reverse the phase on one of the two channels for that instrument or vocal.

REMEMBER

Even though a lot can be done to your music in the mastering stage, don't rely on mastering to fix problems in your mix. Get your music to sound as good as you can during mixing. If you do this, the mastering phase is easier and you can make your music sound even better. If you don't, you're stuck with a bunch of compromises in the mastering stage.

Paying a Pro or Doing It Yourself

Whether to master your music yourself or to hire a professional may be one of your toughest music-making decisions. If you master your music yourself, you can have complete control from start to finish and save yourself some bucks. On the other hand, if you hand your mixed music to a skilled professional, you have the added benefit of another person's ears and advice, and you can end up with a finished product that far exceeds your expectations.

So, how do you choose? Well, your first consideration is probably based on economics — do you have the money to spend on professional help (for your music, that is)? Mastering can cost from a couple hundred to thousands of dollars. A midline mastering engineer often charges around $500 to master an album (about ten songs). This may seem like a lot of money, but if you find the right engineer for your music, it can make the difference between a decent album and a truly world-class one.

Another consideration for hiring out your mastering is how well you know your equipment and how capable it is of performing the mastering procedure. To do mastering, you need at least one good (well, preferably great) multiband compressor, a limiter, and a great multiband parametric EQ. You may also need to have a CD burner of some sort and the software to create a Red Book CD master if you intend to distribute CDs.

Before you decide, take a look at other benefits of hiring a skilled professional to do your mastering:

- **You get a meticulously tuned room and top-notch monitors.** This enables you to hear what your music actually sounds like.
- **The professional has equipment that's specifically designed to handle the process of mastering.** The equalizers, compressors, and other gear that the mastering house uses can tweak your music so that it can sound its best.
- **You get a fresh set of professional ears that may be able to hear things in your mix that need fixing.** You may be so close to the project that you have a hard time hearing your mix objectively. You may not even know what adjustments to make to your music so that it sounds its best.

Hiring a Professional Mastering Engineer

If you decide to use a professional mastering engineer, the following tips can help you choose one for your project:

- **Ask around for referrals.** If you know local bands or musicians whose music you like and whose albums sound great, ask them who mastered their music. Call local studios and find out who they recommend for mastering in your area. Also check out Internet forums focusing on mastering music. Here are a few:
  - Gearslutz.com
  - ProSoundWeb
  - Recording.org

- **Listen to other recordings that the mastering house has done in a style of music similar to yours.** You're entrusting your artistic vision to someone else, and you need to be sure that this person is the right person for the job. If you like what the prospective mastering engineer has done on other people's music, you'll probably like what she does with yours. On the other hand, if she has never worked with music similar to yours or if you don't like the way she mastered someone else's music, she's probably not the right person for the job.
- **Clarify the fee for your project before you start working together.** Most mastering engineers charge by the hour and can give you a pretty good estimate of how many hours they'll need to do the job. You'll also be expected to pay for materials (reference recordings, for example).
- **If you don't like the way the engineer mastered your music, you'll probably be charged the hourly rate to redo it.** Some engineers may redo your project for free, but don't count on it. Be sure to discuss this possibility before you start the project so that you're not met with an unwanted surprise.

WARNING

TIP

Many mastering engineers can do a demo of one or two of your songs so that you can hear what kind of job they can do to your music before you hire them. Ask whether the mastering engineer you're interested in offers this service. It can save both you and the engineer a lot of time and energy if he isn't right for the job. It can also help you determine whether your mixed music is ready for mastering or whether you need to go back and make adjustments.

After you choose the mastering engineer that you think will work well for you and your music, you can make the process much easier and less stressful for both of you if you follow these guidelines:

- **Discuss your expectations and desires.** This is the best way to ensure that your mastered music turns out the way you want. People who are unhappy with the job that the mastering engineer does usually aren't clear about what they want or don't understand what's possible in the mastering process.
- **Take a few CDs or really high-quality digital files whose sound you like with you to the mastering session.** Talk with the engineer about how you can get your music to sound similar. A skilled engineer can let you know right away whether the sound you want is possible.
- **Try to be present at the mastering session.** Many people send their music to a mastering engineer and expect him to do the job without their presence in the studio. Try to go to the studio, but if you can't, be sure that the engineer clearly understands your desires and expectations.

TIP

If you're in the studio during the mastering process and things aren't going the way you want, talk with the engineer and try to get things on track again. If you're unable to communicate with the engineer, stop the session, have her burn a *ref* (reference copy), pay for the time that you've used, and listen to the ref at home. If you don't like what you hear at home, you may be better off going somewhere else with your music.

WARNING

If you're at the mastering session and the mastering engineer insists on working on your music while listening at really loud levels (although occasional checks at high volumes are okay), grab your mix album and run, don't walk, from the session. This is a true sign of an inexperienced (or incompetent) mastering engineer. Mastering needs to be done at low to moderate levels because the tonal balance of music changes at high volumes.

Mastering Your Music Yourself

If you decide that you just have to do the mastering yourself, or at least you want to try it once before you decide to spend the money on a pro, following some guidelines can increase your chances of mastering success. I describe them in this section.

In other chapters, I present specific techniques and settings to get you started. Unfortunately, I can't do that when it comes to mastering. There are just too many variables and too many ways to mess up your music when trying to master it. What I can (and do) help you with in the upcoming sections is to walk you through the process of mastering and show you the tools to use for each step. When reading these sections, keep the following points in mind:

- **Less is more when mastering.** Do as little as possible to your music. If you find that you have to make a lot of adjustments, you may want to go back to the mixing process and try again. When you master your music, you only need to optimize the dynamics and tonal balance of each song, get the levels between the songs even, and sequence your songs.
- **Mastering is all about compromise.** Each adjustment you make to your mixed music affects all the instruments. If you use EQ to get rid of muddiness on the bass guitar, you affect not only the bass guitar but also every other instrument in the mix.
- **Don't try to master a song right after you mix it.** Give yourself time and space from that song before you do anything. In fact, I recommend that you take a few days away from any of the songs for your album between the mixing and mastering stages. A little time to reflect and rest your ears can do wonders for your ability to hear what your music needs.

» **You can only master music if your monitors and monitoring environment are great.** Without a good reference for how your music sounds, trying to EQ or dynamically process your music does no good. The music may sound good through your speakers but probably doesn't through others'. Before you master, make your room sound as good as you can and get to know the strengths and weaknesses of your monitoring environment by listening to a ton of commercial CDs that have the sound you're trying to emulate.

TIP

You can add a variety of plug-ins to your digital audio workstation (DAW) that can help you master your music. Some are quite good. Even if you hire someone to do the mastering, it's worth giving at least one of these a try to see how well you can do yourself. Here are a few I recommend:

- Branworx bx_masterdesk
- Eventide Elevate Bundle
- IK Multimedia T-Racks One
- Izotope Ozone 9
- Waves Abbey Road TG Mastering Chain

For more, do an Internet search for "audio mastering plug-in."

Optimizing dynamics

Okay, this is where the magic in mastering happens — where you can make your music shine or where you can royally mess it up. (How's that for adding a little pressure?) Before you get tense (okay, breathe), remember that you can always go back and try again. Oh, did I mention that you should make backup copies of your individual tracks and your final mix? Well, if you haven't already done the backing-up business, now would be a good time to do that. I'll wait.

Are you done? Okay, now to the job at hand — getting your music to be as loud as possible. (I'm just kidding; see the nearby sidebar "Turn it up!") Seriously, optimizing the dynamics of your songs doesn't mean getting it as loud as you can, but rather giving it life and emotion. And, yes, this also means getting it loud enough to sound good.

The style of your music and the arrangements that you use determine how you optimize the dynamics of your music. For example, classical music has a much broader dynamic range than rock music does, and the infamous "wall of sound" type of arrangement has a narrower dynamic range than a song with sparse verses and thicker choruses.

When you're optimizing the dynamics of your music, be sensitive to the song and try not to get sucked into the idea that you need to get the most volume out of your music. I know I'm beating this volume thing into the ground, but you would be surprised how seductive it is to try to get just a few more decibels out of the song (no, wait; you'll soon find out).

You have two main tools to use when you work on the dynamics during mastering — a compressor and a limiter — and each has its purpose. For the most part, if you're trying to add punch or smoothness to your music, a compressor does the job nicely. On the other hand, if you're trying to squeeze a little more volume out of a song and you don't want to change the song's sound quality, a limiter is your best choice.

Here are suggestions that can help you use compression and limiting (also covered in Chapter 18) most effectively during mastering:

- **Use a mild compression ratio (between 1.1:1 and 2:1) to keep from overcompressing your music.**
- **Apply only 1dB to 2dB of compression or limiting at one time.** If you need more than that, chain more than one compressor together and use these small amounts on each. If you compress or limit more than 1dB or 2dB at a time, you end up with *artifacts* (audible changes to your music caused by the compressor or limiter).
- **Work with your attack and release times.** An attack that's too short takes the punch out of your music by cutting off the initial transients. Likewise, a release time that's too long doesn't recover quickly enough, and the dynamics of the vocals disappear. In contrast, if the release time is too short, you hear distortion.
- **Set the threshold so that your compressor's meters dance (bounce) to the rhythm of the music.** Only the loudest notes (snare drum or lead vocal accents, for example) should trigger the meters and then only by 1dB or 2dB.
- **Use a multiband compressor to bring out individual instruments in the mix.** For example, if the bass drum seems to be getting lost, you can apply mild compression to the lower frequencies (around 80 to 100 Hz). This brings the instrument forward in the mix slightly.
- **When you're not sure that what you're doing sounds better, don't use the processor.** Any dynamics processing is going to affect the quality of your song's sound to some extent. If adding this processing doesn't improve the overall sound, you're better off not using it.

A song without a significant difference between its softest and loudest notes quickly becomes tiring to listen to. Always keep the difference between the average level and the peak level greater than 6dB. In fact, try to have a peak-to-average ratio between 18dB and 24dB if you can. Your music will have a lot more life in it and sound much more interesting.

You can get a good idea of the peak-to-average ratio of your song by watching your meters and noticing where they max out and where they seem to stay most often. Some systems allow you to switch your meters between Peak and Average settings. (To find out whether your system has this option, check your owner's manual, which should be clear about your metering options.) Play the song and make note of the highest peaks using the Peak metering setting. Then listen to your song again using the Average setting on your meters and make a note of this level. When you're done, compare the two. More scientific ways to do this exist, but this technique gives you a good idea of your peak-to-average ratio.

When you're testing your compression or limiter settings (you do this by comparing the processed and unprocessed versions), be sure to have the volume of both versions exactly the same. Any difference in volume defeats the purpose of side-by-side comparison because people almost always prefer the louder version, regardless of whether it sounds better.

Perfecting tonal balance

The *tonal balance* of a song is how the various frequencies of the music relate to one another. You're not concerned with how each instrument sounds in the mix (that's the job for the mixing stage); instead, you're looking for an overall balance of frequencies within the hearing spectrum.

For the most part, a tonal balance consists of an even distribution of frequencies from 20 Hz to 10 kHz with a slight drop-off (1dB to 2dB) from 10 kHz to 20 kHz or higher. That's great, you say, but what does that sound like? Well, listen to a number of great recordings, and you'll hear it.

When you master your music, you want to constantly compare the sound of your song to that of other music whose sound you like. In Chapter 16, I list a variety of excellent reference music for mixing. These music references work just as well for mastering, so check them out.

TURN IT UP!

Everyone wants his or her music to be as loud as possible. Louder sounds better. In fact, test after test has shown that when people listen to two versions of a song, they nearly always prefer the louder one (regardless of whether it actually sounds better). Musicians, producers, and engineers seem to be in a competition to see who can make the loudest album. If you compare a CD made about 20 years ago with a recording made this year, you'll notice that the newer one is much louder. Give them both a good listen. Does the louder one really sound better?

You can test this by setting both recordings to play at the same volume and then switching back and forth. (You need to turn the volume up a bit on the older recording to match the volume of the newer one.) One way to do this is to record both songs into your DAW and set the levels of each so that they're the same. At the same volume, which song sounds better to you? I'm willing to bet that nine times out of ten, you'll prefer the older song. This is because older recordings have more dynamic range than newer ones do. The variety is pleasing to listen to, whereas the song with only a small dynamic range quickly becomes tiring.

Do yourself and your listeners a favor, and resist the temptation to compress the dynamic variability out of your music. Your mix will be much easier to listen to and have a lot more life and excitement. You can always turn the volume up on your stereo if it's not loud enough, but you can't add dynamic range after you've squashed it out.

When you adjust the overall tonal balance of your songs, listen carefully for frequencies that seem too loud or too soft. You can find these frequencies by listening to the instruments in the mix or by using a parametric equalizer and sweeping the frequency spectrum. To do this, set your Q fairly wide (0.6, for instance) and turn the gain knob all the way up. Start with the lowest frequency and slowly raise the frequency as the song plays. Adjust annoying frequencies by cutting them by a couple of decibels to see whether your overall mix improves.

Follow these general EQ guidelines:

» **If your mix sounds muddy, add high frequencies (above 10 kHz) or cut low ones (200 to 400 Hz).** Likewise, if your mix is too bright (common with digital recording), try reducing the frequencies above 10 kHz by using a shelf equalizer or a Baxandall curve.

  To use a Baxandall curve, use a parametric equalizer and set the frequency at 20 kHz with a Q setting of about 1. This gradually cuts frequencies above around 10 kHz. You can adjust the Q to reach as far down as you want. Your EQ graph shows you what's happening.

» **Use the same EQ adjustments for both the right and the left channels.** This keeps the stereo balance intact and doesn't alter the relative phase between the channels. For example, if you add some bass frequencies (100 Hz, for example) to the one channel and not the other, you may hear a wavering or pulsating sound around this frequency that goes back and forth between the speakers.

» **If you used a multiband compressor on specific frequencies, you may need to make some EQ adjustments to them.** Compression tends to mess with the frequency response.

» **If you need to adjust the EQ of certain instruments in the mix (the snare drum is buried, for example), note the overall effects of your adjustments on the rest of the mix.** If your adjustments aren't fixing the problem, go back to the mixing process and make your adjustments there. You'll be glad you took the time to do this.

REMEMBER

Any adjustments you make to the EQ during mastering impact more than just those frequencies; the adjustments alter the entire frequency spectrum and the relationship among all the instruments. So, listen carefully as you make adjustments, and back off the additional EQ if you don't like what you hear.

TIP

Some people check the tonal balance of their songs against that of their favorite music. You do this by recording a favorite-sounding song into your mastering program and taking a look at its frequency response by using a spectral analyzer. (Some programs have a built-in spectral analyzer, but you can also buy one as a plug-in for many systems.) Then do an analysis of your song and compare it to the spectral analysis of a recording you like. This technique seems to work for many people (not me, though — I like using my ears instead, but alas, I'm old-fashioned).

Sequencing your songs

Sequencing your songs consists of choosing the order of the songs on the album as well as the amount of silence between each song. When you wrote and recorded your songs, you probably had an idea about the order in which you wanted them to appear on your album. If you don't know how you want to arrange your songs, here are some things to consider:

» Consider each song's tempo in the sequencing equation. Some albums work well if songs with a similar tempo are placed together, while others work best when contrasting songs follow one another.

- Think about a song's lyrics and how they relate to the lyrics from the other songs on your album. If you want to tell your listener a story, consider how the order of the songs can best tell that story.
- Think about the chords that you used in each song and how they relate to another song that you may want to place before or after it in the sequence. The ending chord of one song can conflict with the beginning chord of another.

Aside from having to decide how your songs are ordered on your album, you also have to think about how much time you put between each song in order to create the most impact. Many people assume that you use a set amount of time between all the songs on each album. This isn't the case. You can put any amount of silence between each song that you feel is appropriate to set the mood that you want. Sometimes you may want just a second or two; other times, four or five seconds is more appropriate.

For example, if you have a mellow ballad followed by an upbeat song, you may want to leave a little more time between these two songs so that the listener is prepared for the faster song (try leaving a space that's four to six beats long at the slower song's tempo, for instance). Or, if you want two tunes to flow together, you can leave less time in between them. Use your ears and think about how you want your listener to respond when going from one song to another.

Balancing levels

For a truly professional-sounding recording, you want all your songs to be at nearly the same relative level so that your listeners (I hope you have more than one) don't have to adjust the volume on their music player from song to song.

Balancing the levels of your songs to one another is pretty easy. In fact, in most cases, you have very little to do after you EQ and optimize the dynamics of each song. You balance the levels from one song to the next by playing one song, then the next, and listening for significant volume differences. (Didn't I say that it was easy?) You can also look at your master bus meters to see whether each song is at the same level, but your ears are a much better judge.

If you notice any differences, just raise (or better yet, lower) the levels until they're all roughly the same. Don't get too finicky. Some variation from song to song is okay. In fact, minor differences can help to make your album more interesting to listen to. When you're balancing levels, just make sure that any differences aren't enough to make the listener run to her stereo to adjust the volume knob. If one or two songs seem to be much lower in volume than the rest, you may want to go back to the volume-optimizing stage and raise those songs a bit to make them more consistent with the rest of the songs on the album. This way, you don't lower the volume of the entire album based on one or two quiet songs.

Preparing for Distribution

After you have all your songs optimized, balanced, and sequenced, it's time for the final step. This last step involves saving your music in a format that enables you to distribute the music.

Distribution often involves making digital files available for music download sites or streaming services, burning CDs, or pressing vinyl records. I cover each of these options in the next chapter, so the last step you'll make in this chapter is to save your mastered music with these considerations in mind:

- **Leave some headroom.** Don't set your master gain to 0dB. I recommend dropping it to between –1dB and –3dB. Sure, it will be a little quieter than it could be, but the extra headroom is important to get the best sound out of your recordings.
- **Don't use a brickwall limiter.** This type of limiter squashes the loudest notes and limits that total dynamic range of your music and will cause distortion in low resolution MP3s and vinyl records.
- **Keep your high bit rate.** Bounce to the same rate that you used to record and mix your music. If you recorded at 24 bits, leave it there for your masters. And don't add dither. You can do this later if you intend to make CDs to distribute.
- **Don't change the sample rate.** You may choose to do a sample rate conversion later, but for now, leave it alone.

IN THIS CHAPTER

» Putting your music on CD

» Choosing settings for USB flash drives

» Encoding your music to MP3

» Preparing your music for vinyl

Chapter 23
Creating Your Finished Product

Once you have your music recorded, mixed, and mastered, you're ready for the final steps to putting it out into the world. This involves creating the final audio format for the distribution method you choose.

In this chapter, I walk you through the process of putting your music on CD whether it's for you to sell or for you to hand off to a manufacturer that creates retail-ready packages for you to distribute. This process is pretty easy, and by following a few simple steps, which I lay out in detail for you, you end up with a product you'll be proud of.

Also in this chapter, you explore the process of creating digital files to use for any kind of digital delivery option. This not only allows you to offer downloads of your music online, but also lets you put your music on streaming services such as Spotify. I walk you through the process of determining the right way to encode your digital files and preparing them for online distribution.

Last but not least, I offer insights into the fastest growing format: vinyl records! Vinyl is gaining popularity with musicians who want to use a retro technology to make a splash. I give you a few tips for making your music ready for vinyl and choosing a company to press your record.

Understanding File Formats

You can encode your music to many different file formats. They come in two varieties: lossless and lossy. This section details each type.

Not all devices or players can play all file formats. Be sure that the format you choose is able to be played where you want it to.

Lossy audio file formats

Lossy file formats allow you to reduce the file size of your music. In many cases, though, you will be able to hear the difference between your original file and the lossy one. Choose from these formats if storage is more important than sound quality. Here are the most common lossy audio file formats:

- **AAC (Advanced Audio Coding):** AAC was designed to take over MP3 files. Overall, it sounds better than MP3s at the same bit rates, but is less popular.
- **MP3:** MP3 is the most common file format for digital delivery of music online. The files are small compared to lossless formats, but the sound quality isn't as good as other comparable lossy formats.
- **OGG (Ogg Vorbis):** OGG is an open source format that sounds better than MP3 at the same file size. Like many of the other better-sounding formats, OGG is more limited on where you can play it.
- **WMA (Windows Media Audio):** WMA was developed for Windows computers to compete with MP3s. As you might imagine, you are limited on where these files will play.

Lossless audio file formats

Lossless file formats retain the sound quality of your music. They can also be *big*. Choose a lossless format if storage is less important than sound quality. Here are the most common lossless audio file formats:

- **AIFF (Audio Interchange File Format):** AIFF was developed by Apple to compete with WAV files. It is less popular than WAV, but it offers better support for metadata such as song titles and authorship.
- **FLAC (Free Lossless Audio Codec):** FLAC is an open source format that is compressed, like the lossy formats, but has no loss of sound quality. FLAC files are about one-half the size of WAV or AIFF files, but are able to be played on fewer devices.

» **MQA (Master Quality Authenticated):** MQA files are smaller than any of the other lossless formats and sound great. Unfortunately, this format is only able to be played on a limited number of devices.

» **WAV:** WAV was designed by IBM and Microsoft for PCs and is the most popular lossless file format. If you have the space and are wanting to be sure your audio will play in your device, this is the format to choose.

» **WMA Lossless (Windows Media Audio Lossless):** WMA Lossless is a lossless version of the lossy WMA format. Like with WMA, you don't find a lot of players that can use this format.

TIP

The distribution channels I list in this chapter are all able to take more than one audio file format. In general, I suggest choosing a lossless format if you are able to and let the distributor reformat the files for you. (The exception is with CDs, for which I recommend you format to CD audio quality of 16-bit/44 kHz WAV.)

Putting Your Music on CD

From the early 1980s until about 2000, CDs were the standard format for any music sold. Cassettes and vinyl records were on their way out and digital music files were just coming online. Over the next 20 years, online digital distribution took over, vinyl reemerged, but CDs still hung on — at least for independent artists who could produce them inexpensively and sell them at their shows. Arguably, CDs are on their last legs, but you may find them to still be a part of your revenue stream.

If you want to make and sell CDs, you have three options:

» **Print on demand:** Unless you have your own CD recorder and packing printer, this involves uploading your files to an online service that will do this work for you and take a cut of your sale.

» **Short-run duplication:** This process is often something most artists can't do, but any number of companies can do for a fairly reasonable fee. Short-run quantities are 10 to 300 copies. These can be produced and shipped to you so you can sell them from your shows.

» **Large-quantity replication:** If you want more than 300 CDs to sell, you need to go the replication route. The production process is slightly different than duplication, making the cost per CD lower.

TIP

Regardless of which route you choose for making CDs, your process is the same:

- **Choose how many copies you want and who will manufacture them.**
- **Master your music.** If you don't want to master your song yourself, most full-service CD manufacturers offer mastering services. In this case, send your music in the full resolution you recorded it at. For most people, it will be 24-bit/44.1 kHz or higher.
- **Bounce your music to CD quality.** Unless you have the CD manufacturer master your music, send your music in the CD quality of 16-bit/44 kHz in WAV format. This way what you hear is what your CD will sound like.
- **Organize your CD quality files.** Be sure to double-check the order you want your songs recorded on the CD on the form you complete for your CD order.
- **Copyright your songs.** Take a look at the "Protecting your rights" sidebar later in this chapter for details.
- **License any cover tunes.** If you recorded any songs from other artists, you need to get a mechanical license for each song. Do an Internet search for "cover song licensing" for companies that can make this happen.
- **Design your packaging.** Download the templates for your CD design files from the company you chose to make your CDs and lay out the design according to the specs.
- **Upload the audio and design files.** Some manufacturers will take CD-R (a CD burned by your computer) if you want to mail one, but uploading is the preferred way. Keep in mind that it can take a while to upload the files, depending on your Internet speed.

The following section details these options and show you how to get CDs in your or your fan's hands.

CDs on demand

When you have a CD you want to copy, you can either make the copies yourself or hire someone to make the copies for you. If you do them yourself, you have to record CDs one at a time, just like the first one. This can cost less, but it takes a lot of time (as you undoubtedly found out when you recorded your first CD).

Doing it yourself

Well, you've done everything else yourself, so why not add the copying process to the list? If you have more time than money and you only need a few CDs, making them yourself may be a good option.

PROTECTING YOUR RIGHTS

Before you put your music out into the world, get it copyrighted. Getting a copyright on your music is easy and relatively inexpensive, so there's no reason not to do it.

The easiest and cheapest way to register your copyright is online through the Electronic Copyright Office (eCO). The online system is easy to use, allows you to upload your music files, and costs only $35. You can access the eCO at `https://eco.copyright.gov`.

If you still want to register by mail, you can. Just fill out an SR (sound recording) form and send it to the U.S. Copyright Office at the Library of Congress. You can find the SR form at `www.copyright.gov/forms`, or you can call the Copyright Office at 202-707-9100 and ask to have it mailed to you. Choose (or ask for) the Form SR with Instructions. The current cost for filing the form is $85, but double-check this fee before you send in your form, because the fee has been known to go up. You can fill out one form for each CD, so the cost per song isn't very high. Send your completed form, the fee, and a copy of your CD to the address listed on the form.

The form is pretty easy to fill out, but if you find that you have difficulty, you can call an information specialist to help you out. The number is 202-707-3000. Be prepared to wait on hold for a little while.

Several months after you complete your registration (whether by mail or online), you'll receive a certificate in the mail, but you can consider your music officially copyrighted as soon as you submit the form. If you use snail mail and you're especially protective of your music (paranoid?), you can wait until your check clears your bank. At this point, you can be almost certain that your form is being processed. If you can't sleep at night unless your music is copyrighted, it's best to wait until your certificate arrives in the mail before you start selling or distributing your CD. (This is a good reason to file for your copyright early.)

To make saleable CDs yourself, you need not only the CD recorder but also a graphics design software program and a printer to print the CD labels and cover material (the CD sleeve and tray card). Even with this equipment, your package won't look as professional as the package that a CD duplication or replication company can create, but what you create is probably good enough for you to sell a few copies to your friends and acquaintances.

Having someone else do it

If you don't have the gear to make your own CDs and don't plan on selling them directly to your fans, you can sign up for a service that will put your CDs online for your fans to buy without you having to pay any money upfront. The CDs are printed when your fan orders one, and you receive a portion of the sale (how much depends on the service you use). Do an Internet search for "CDs on demand" to find a list of current companies that offer this service.

Short-run CD duplication

Duplication involves making copies of your mastered files by burning CD-Rs. The only difference is that duplication companies use CD recorders that enable them to make more than one copy at a time. Duplication is great if you want to make a small number of copies — from 50 to 300. Bare-bones CD-duplication companies often provide one-color printing on the CD and either a vinyl sleeve or a jewel case to hold the CD. Most full-service companies can prepare retail-ready packages, which look like other commercial CDs and include CDs with printing on them, digipaks, and shrink-wrap. You can expect to pay $2.50 to $5 for each CD, depending on the quantity you order.

An advantage to having your CDs duplicated is that it can usually be done quickly. Many duplication companies can provide you with a finished product in as little as a few days (although seven days seems to be the average). The disadvantage is that you usually pay considerably more for each CD than if you do it yourself or go the replication route, which is explained in the section that follows.

To have your CDs duplicated, you need to provide 16-bit/44 kHz audio files (or a CD-R that was recorded as an audio CD). If you want the duplication company to create retail-ready packages, you also need to provide artwork that's laid out to the company's specifications.

If you're interested in going the duplication route, here are a few resources to get you started:

- CD\Works
- Disc Makers
- GrooveHouse
- NationWide Disc
- Oasis Disc Manufacturing

You can also do an Internet search for "CD duplication" for more places that offer this service.

Large-quantity CD replication

Replication is used for making commercial CDs and involves recording a glass master (the master disc from which all your CD copies will be made) from your mastered 16-bit/44 kHz audio files. The glass master is then used to transfer the data onto CD media. Replication is designed for larger runs of 300 or more copies.

CD replication usually comes with printing on the CD in one to four colors and a tray card and sleeve that are often printed in four colors. Most CD replication companies have retail-ready CD package deals that cover everything from the layout of your artwork (some do and some don't, so be sure to ask first) to printed CDs, digipaks, and shrink wrap. You can expect to pay $800 to $1,400 for 1,000 copies from most manufacturers.

If you want to go the replication route, you need to provide the replication company with mastered 16-bit/44 kHz audio files, artwork set to the company's specifications, and a completed order form. Oh, and you probably need to pay half the money upfront before the work can start (bummer).

After people at the manufacturing company receive your order form, the CD, and artwork, they make a reference CD and proofs of your finished printed material. Be sure to look over the art proofs carefully and listen to every second of the reference CD. Any mistakes you don't catch are your problem, so take your time and compare the reference CD very closely with the master recording. (You did make a copy of your master CD before you sent it out, right?) The master and the reference CD should be identical.

UPC BARCODES

If you make a CD that you intend to sell through major retailers, such as music stores or Internet retailers, you need a UPC barcode. A UPC barcode is a string of numbers that identifies your product. Every CD has its own unique barcode. You can get a barcode in one of two ways: Register with and pay $750 to the Universal Code Council (UCC) or pay $0 to $50 to a CD replicator or distributor.

Unless you intend to release more than 35 CDs, your best bet is to buy a barcode from a replicator or distributor, which can provide barcodes for a small (or no) fee with your CD order. Here are additional places where you can get a UPC barcode:

- CD Baby
- Disc Makers
- Oasis Disc Manufacturing

Having your CD replicated is a stressful thing. You're spending a ton of money and getting quite a few copies that you need to be proud enough of it to go out into the world and sell them. So, choosing a CD-replication company is an important task. Quite a few companies are out there, so choose the place that makes you feel the most comfortable and that makes a high-quality product. Following is a list of the larger CD-replication companies:

- Disc Makers
- DiscMasters
- GrooveHouse
- NationWide Disc
- Oasis Disc Manufacturing

For more possibilities, do an Internet search for "CD replication."

TIP

Many CD-replication companies can provide you with great resources, information, and even opportunities for promoting your work. Take advantage of these opportunities if you can, but don't choose a company based on its promotional promises. Choose a company because of its customer service, price, and the quality of its product.

REMEMBER

Be sure to ask for referrals — or at least a list of satisfied clients — before you choose a duplication or replication company. As always, your best bet when entrusting someone with your precious music is to ask friends for recommendations. Also, take timing estimates with a grain of salt — on a couple of occasions, a company promised to finish my CDs by a certain date and missed the deadline. So, leave plenty of time between when you print your CDs and when you need them.

Delivering Digital Files

Digital music files have often gotten a bad rap over the years for their poor sound quality. Early versions of digital download files were created to optimize file size over quality. However, high-speed Internet and the popularity of video online made the need for small audio files obsolete. Even the highest-quality audio file requires less bandwidth and space than a typical video file.

Digital sales are the main source of non-performance income for musicians. In most cases these sales are done online through streaming and download (I cover these later in this chapter), but there are also ways to make your digital music available at your shows. In this section, I introduce you to the two most common methods: download cards and USB sticks (flash drives).

Download card

For most musicians, a digital download card, also called a music download card, is an extension of a CD. Fans buy your CD and you give them a code so that they can download the files to their digital devices. This is essential for the gigging musician because you need to sell merchandise at your shows to make enough money to survive, but many fans no longer listen to CDs and few have the equipment to put the CD on their device. You can also skip the CD and just sell the card.

To offer a download card, you need to have a website to host your music files and a secure way to make them available to only those people who have a download card. For many musicians, this is a barrier that is too high for the benefits of printing a card.

Fortunately, several companies can take care of this for you. Here is a short list of popular download card makers (or do your own Internet search using "music download cards" as your search term):

- Digi-cards
- Dropcards
- ProCards

TIP

Most download card makers allow you to upload a variety of file types. They limit how much storage you can use for your files (typically 500MB), but for an album-worth of content, you can offer some pretty decent-sized files. Unless you also offer a player compatible with your type of file, I recommend sticking with MP3 or WAV formats.

USB sticks (flash drives)

Given that musicians need to be able to sell their music at shows, and digital files are preferred for many fans, the USB flash drive is a great option. USB flash drives are physical storage devices, often packaged as sticks (least expensive), but can be packaged in novel ways, such as mimicking a cassette tape complete with a printed J-card (more expensive).

This format has some advantages over other digital formats:

- **You can load high-resolution audio files.** Forget 16-bit/44 kHz CD quality. USB flash drives can handle 24-bit/96 kHz files, which sound so much better than CDs.
- **You can include videos.** A lot of artists add music videos or "making of" videos or backstage footage to give fans something extra.

» **You can offer multiple file formats.** USB flash drives can hold enough data that you can offer a variety of file types so your fans can choose the best format for their needs.

» **You can choose from some cool designs.** You don't have to go with a boring stick for your drive. Some manufacturers make cards with a tab or concert passes with a lanyard. You can even find USB flash drives that look like old-school cassette tapes, complete with a case and custom printed J-card insert.

You can find a multitude of manufacturers of USB flash drives, but I'd stick with the companies that focus on musicians. Any of the CD duplicator and replicators will also offer USB flash drive options.

Online music distribution

Several stores online let you sell your music as digital downloads. Some will allow you to upload the music directly, while others require a distributor (aggregator). Given that, managing these placements can be complicated and take time. I recommend going straight to a distributor for all your download sales outlets.

Here are a few of the more popular distributors (do an Internet search for independent musician distribution for more options):

» CD Baby

» DistroKid

» iMusician

» TuneCore

Streaming music sites

Streaming is now the top revenue source for the music industry. This may not yet be true for independent musicians, but it is an important distribution channel that you need to be aware of. Streaming services, such as Spotify or Apple Music, require an aggregator for you to get your music played. Fortunately, you can use the same aggregator for your streaming channel as you do for your download channel.

Creating MP3 Files

To create MP3 files, you need MP3 encoding software and a CD or audio file of your music (well, you need a computer, too). If you record using a computer-based system and you use one of the more full-featured, popular programs such as Pro Tools or Logic Pro X, you can probably create MP3 files without getting additional software. Most decent programs offer encoding capability built-in.

The actual encoding process is pretty simple. Just open your MP3 encoding software and choose the parameters you want for your file. However, there are some important points to keep in mind when you encode your music:

- **To ensure that you get the best sound quality possible, encode your downloadable digital files from a WAV or AIFF file instead of directly from your CD.** The process of ripping a song from a CD can create problems in sound quality. So, by converting your CD to WAV or AIFF files first, you get a chance to hear your ripped song and to correct problems that ripping may have caused before your music goes to MP3.
- **Import your WAV or AIFF file into a sound editor.** Sound editor programs, such as Sound Forge or Wave Burner, work fine. (You can find sound editors online.) When you have your file in the editor, use the Maximizer plug-in to raise the overall level of your song. You lose some dynamics, but they may not come through with the MP3 or AAC file anyway. If you recorded your music to your computer, you can use the recording software instead of a separate sound editor to do this procedure.
- **Choose the stereo or joint stereo modes for a better sound.** Most online music hosts require a stereo file. Choosing the force stereo option is fine if your encoder supports it.
- **If you want to put your music on the web, choose the 320 Kbps bit rate because it covers you for most situations.** If you're encoding for specific providers, check to find out what bit rate they prefer.
- **Experiment with different modes and encoding engines.** Some sound better than others on certain types of music.

Bit rate

The bit rate determines the quality of your encoded music. When you encode your music, you have to choose your file's bit rate, as shown in Figure 23-1. Bit rates range from 20 to 320 kilobits per second (Kbps). The higher the bit rate, the better the sound quality. The downside is that higher bit rates create larger files. When you convert your music to MP3 format, you're constantly balancing quality with file size.

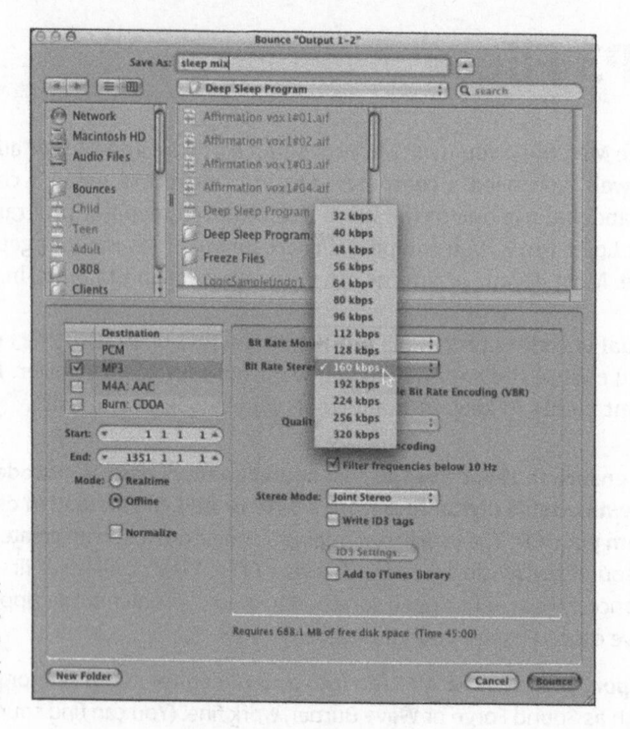

FIGURE 23-1: MP3 encoders allow you to choose the bit rate of your MP3.

The bit rate that you ultimately choose depends on how you plan to use your MP3 or AAC file. For example, if you want to put your music on a downloadable music host site (a website that makes people's MP3 or AAC music available for download), you most likely need to choose the 128 Kbps rate because this is what many host sites require for download. For Hi-Fi mode you may choose 192 Kbps or even 256 Kbps, depending on the provider. On the other hand, if you want to stream audio on the web, and you want anyone (regardless of connection speed) to hear it, you're better off choosing a lower rate, such as 96 Kbps or even lower, depending on your host's requirements.

Variable bit rate (VBR) is an option that many MP3 encoders offer. VBR allows the encoder to change the bit rate as it compresses the file. The advantage of this approach is that sections with fewer instruments or less data can be compressed further than sections with more critical information. The result is often a better-sounding MP3 file that takes up less space. The only drawback — and it's a big one — is that not all MP3 players can read a file created with VBR. So, you're probably better off not using this approach for your web-based files.

If you're making MP3s to listen to through your own player and it supports VBR playback, using VBR keeps your files smaller. If you do choose VBR, you're prompted to choose an average bit rate or a minimum and maximum bit rate. Try them both and choose the one that sounds best to you.

Mode

Modes essentially refer to whether your file is in stereo or mono; however, your choices include more than just plain stereo and mono. You have the option to choose mono, stereo, joint stereo, or sometimes force stereo (also known as dual mono), as shown in Figure 23-2. Again, choose the mode based on your music and how you prefer to balance quality with file size.

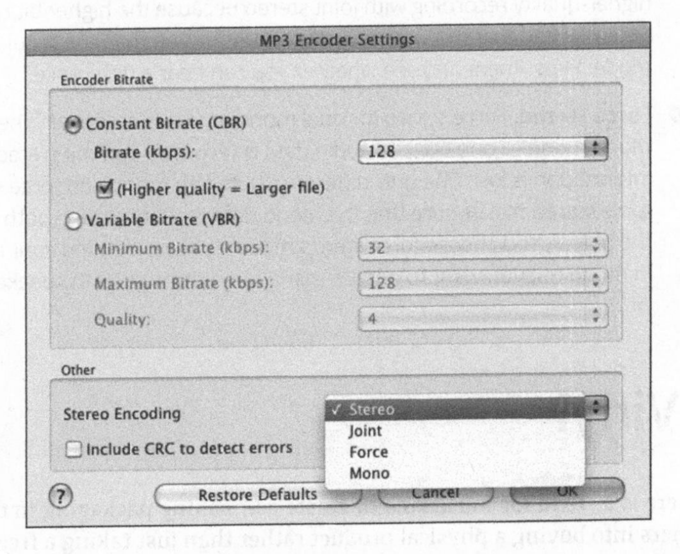

FIGURE 23-2: MP3 encoders have several modes from which you can choose.

Here's a look at the various modes and how they relate to quality and file size:

- **Mono:** Mono takes up little room because all the stereo data from your CD is contained on one track. The sound quality can be good, depending on the bit rate that you choose, but you lose all stereo-imaging data. Choose mono mode if the loss of the stereo image won't adversely affect your song or if the overall sound quality is more important to you than the stereo information.
- **Stereo:** Stereo mode consists of two mono tracks. With stereo mode, you retain all your stereo information. The drawback is that your two tracks are at half the bit rate of the mono track that uses the same bit-rate setting. For example, if you encode in stereo at 128 Kbps, each of your tracks is only encoded at 64 Kbps. So, if you want each track to be at 128 Kbps, you need to encode at 256 Kbps. This creates a file that's twice as large as the mono file at 128 Kbps but has the same sound quality.

  Stereo mode is a good choice if you have a song with complex stereo panning effects that you just can't live without and you don't mind a sound quality that's slightly lower.

- **Joint stereo:** Joint stereo mode is a cross between mono and stereo. This mode consists of creating one track of audio information and one track of information that tells the player to send certain sounds through one speaker or the other (called steering data). You get most of the stereo information with only a slightly larger file size than with mono mode.

  For most songs, the difference between regular stereo and joint stereo is indistinguishable as far as the stereo image goes, but you end up with a higher-quality recording with joint stereo because the higher bit rate is used. You may find that this option works better for you than the regular stereo mode. Experiment and see whether you can hear a difference.

- **Force stereo:** Force stereo (or dual mono) mode is essentially the same as mono mode — one track of audio data is recorded and the stereo panning information is lost. The only difference between mono and force stereo is that force stereo makes sure that the mono data is sent through both speakers of the player. You choose force stereo mode if you don't mind your music being in mono but you want to ensure that it plays through both speakers.

Pressing Vinyl

There is a trend for musicians to create compelling packaging to try to entice listeners into buying a physical product rather than just taking a free download. One of the ways artists are distinguishing themselves is to offer vinyl records.

This retro format is a viable option for breaking through the noise and getting your music heard. If you're interested in putting your music out on an old-fashioned record, here's what you need to know:

- **It takes a lot longer to make a vinyl record than a CD.** Expect to wait close to eight weeks for your finished record.
- **Not everyone has a record player.** In fact, as attractive as it may be to put your music out on vinyl, the vast majority of your fans will not have the proper equipment to play it. So, when you print, keep this limited market in mind. The average independent artist only prints a few hundred records at a time.
- **A vinyl record doesn't hold a lot of music.** You may need to cut songs from your CD to fit the constraints of the vinyl. A 12-inch 331/3 rpm record holds only about 18 minutes per side and a 7-inch 45 rpm record holds about 4½ minutes per side.

- **You may lose some fidelity.** If you're mixing your music with the modern style of having pretty heavy bass, you may need to dial that back to accommodate the limitations of the vinyl medium. You may also find that the high frequencies drop as you move to vinyl. You can deal with this and make an excellent-sounding record if you have the special know-how.
- **Most vinyl record pressing companies will include a download card** in your record's packaging so that your listeners can download your music to a portable device. This allows you to offer the best of both worlds.

If a vinyl record interests you, check out these resources for the many options and prices:

- GrooveHouse
- Rainbo Records
- Record Pressing
- United Record Pressing

Most CD duplicators and replicators also have recommendations for vinyl pressing companies that they work with regularly. So, if you have a CD manufacturer that you like and you want a vinyl record, ask the manufacturer for a referral.

6

The Part of Tens

IN THIS PART . . .

Discover ten tips you can use in your studio to improve the quality of your recordings.

Explore ten great promotion and distribution ideas as you begin to share your music with the world.

IN THIS CHAPTER

» Improving the sound of your recordings

» Making your room look and sound good

» Making edits easier

» Capturing and preserving an artistic performance

Chapter 24 Ten Invaluable Recording Tips

Throughout this book, I suggest things that you can do to make your recordings as good as possible. In this chapter, I present you with more simple and effective tricks that you can use to improve the quality of your recordings. You find ways to add more of that sought-after analog sound to your music, fatten up your tracks (add more depth), and increase the overall feel (artistic interpretation) of your performances. You also discover a couple of tips to help you improve the sound of your room, make the editing process easier and quicker, and double-check your mix before you call your song finished.

Using an Analog Tape Deck

If you have a digital recorder and yearn for that analog sound, you can run the tracks out of your recorder, into an analog tape deck, and back into the digital recorder. You can do this for drum tracks or even the final two-track mix. By blending the tape-saturated tracks back in with the original ones, you can add as much or as little of the distorted analog sound into your clean digital tracks as you want and reverse anything that you've done later.

This procedure is really simple. Just bus (route) the outputs of your recorder to the inputs of your analog tape deck, and run cords from the outputs of your tape deck back into two empty tracks in your digital recorder. Hit record in the tape deck and play in your digital audio workstation (DAW) to record your mix to the analog tape. Then hit record in your DAW and play on the tape deck to record the taped tracks back into your DAW You can then mix these two new tracks with your originals.

A slight time delay (a few milliseconds) may occur between the original tracks and the returned ones, depending on your computer and song settings (higher sample rates have less delay than lower sample rates). If you have a graphical editor, you can eliminate this time delay by following these steps:

1. **Choose a single snare drum or bass drum stroke on both sets of tracks.**
2. **Enter the waveform graphical mode and compare the two waveforms to see where they differ; you can use your cursor to determine the distance between the two beats.**

   See Chapter 14 to find out more about editing.
3. **Cut that distance from the front of the tape-returned tracks.**
4. **Double-check your work by listening to both sets of tracks.**

   If both beats play at exactly the same time, you're done. If not, just click the Undo button and try again.

If you don't have a waveform editor, you eliminate the time delay by listening. You can start by picking a time, 20 milliseconds (ms) for instance, and deleting it from the front of the tape deck–enhanced tracks. Listen and make any adjustments from there. With a little experimenting and a dose of patience, you can find the right amount to cut. Make a note of this amount because this number will be the same the next time you do this procedure.

TIP

If you don't have a tape deck, you can use this same approach to run your audio through any analog gear, such as compressors or preamps.

Layering Your Drum Beats

If you use a drum machine or an electronic drum set to play your drum rhythms, you can make these rhythms much fatter by layering one sound on top of another. Likewise, you can use this technique to add sampled drum sounds to your acoustic drum tracks to fatten them.

If you recorded your drums using MIDI, just duplicate the drum tracks that you want to add to, select the drum that you want to duplicate, and change its patch number to match a sound that you want to add. Depending on your drum machine's polyphony, you may need to record the original tracks to audio before you play the second set of drum sounds. (You can find out more about using MIDI in Chapter 11.)

If your original tracks are from an acoustic drum set, you have to trigger the sound from the drum machine by hand (press the trigger pads in time to the music) or, if your audio software has the capabilities (Logic Audio, for example), you can create a MIDI file from the audio track. Then just choose the instruments that you want to have triggered from the new MIDI track.

Decorating Your Room

When you set up your studio, think about the types of materials you use for furniture, floor, and wall treatments. You can improve the sound of your room simply by using materials and furniture to absorb or reflect sound. For example, you can use a couch to catch some of the room's reflections or a bookcase placed on the wall behind you to deflect some sound waves. Carpet on the floor or curtains over your windows absorb sound. In contrast, wood floors and bare walls add reflections and give your room a more live sound.

If you think about how the furniture and decorations in your studio affect sound, you can save time and money when you optimize your room for recording.

Setting a Tempo Map

Before you start to record, set a tempo map of the song within your system. You do this by entering the number of measures (on some systems), the time signature, and the tempo for each section of the song in the Tempo Map or Metronome dialog box of your system. Then, when you record, play to this metronome.

When it's time to do your editing, just choose the section(s) of your song that you want to edit by cueing the measure and beat that you want to work with. This enables you to choose edit points much faster and more accurately and makes quick work of producing loops or assembling a song from parts.

Listening to Your Mix in Mono

After all the effort that you put into getting each instrument to sit exactly where you want it in the stereo field, the last thing you probably want to do is listen to the song in mono. Doing so, however, enables you to see your mix differently and to hear whether any of your instruments are crowding out the others. Even if you like to have stuff moving in the mix, listening to your song in mono can help you to find problems in the arrangement.

REMEMBER

If it sounds good in mono, it generally sounds great in stereo.

Doubling and Tripling Your Tracks

If a track sounds thin to you in the mix, just make a copy of it onto an empty track (if you have one) and use both of them in the mix. Doubling or tripling a track is called *multing*, and it's especially useful for vocals, particularly backup vocals.

If you don't have the tracks to spare, make a copy of the track you want to mult onto a separate virtual track and then combine those two tracks by using a bounce procedure, which I explain in Chapter 10. You can do this as many times as you want with digital recorders because you don't lose sound quality in the process. If you want, you can mult dozens of times and end up with really thick tracks. Don't overdo it, though — lots of thick tracks added together can create a muddy mix.

Recording Dirty Room Ambience

When I started recording in the 1980s, I worked hard to eliminate the ambient bleed of the sound of the band playing together in a single room. We set up baffles and distanced the band members as much as possible to isolate each instrument. No matter how hard I tried, though, it was impossible to remove all the bleed from other instruments in each mic. This was a point of frustration because I was always looking for ways to remove noise and this ambient bleed was always there.

It wasn't until recording in the nearly noiseless digital world using separate tracks and performances for each part of the song, did I realize that how important this ambient bleed was to the feel of a mixed song.

Like with many aspects of digital recording trying to be more analog in sound, I now simulate this bleed by recording with an ambient room mic whenever I record. This is how to do it:

- » Each time you record using a mic, add an additional mic, placing it across the room to capture the room sound.
- » Choose this placement carefully. Try a variety of positions and angles until you find something you like. I tend to place it across the room facing away from the instrument or band to catch the reflection off the far wall. You're not looking for a natural sound. Instead you want the reflections in the room.
- » Add some effects, such as distortion, saturation, or reverb (Chapter 19 covers effects) to this track when you mix the song. This will add some more noise and distortion, making it dirtier sounding. Just add a little into the mix. Most times it doesn't take much to help the instruments blend together.

TIP

If you want to add an ambient quality to a group of instruments that weren't recorded together, such as the entire rhythm section, send a mix of these instruments to speakers and mic those speakers from across the room, facing the mic away from the speaker. Then add that into your mix.

Depending on your gear and settings, you may need to adjust the timing of the new track in your song session to remove any delay that may exist. I cover this process in "Using an Analog Tape Deck" earlier in this chapter.

Overdubbing Live Drums

If you're like most home recordists, you record most of your drum tracks with a drum machine or electronic drum set. You may find them thin-sounding or a bit stiff. A good remedy for both the thinness and the stiffness can be overdubbing some real drums or cymbals to add to the electronic ones. (*Overdubbing* is adding separate tracks.)

For example, you can add real hi-hats to a rock song. Eliminate the drum machine hi-hats, keep the electronic kick and snare, and play the hi-hat part to the other drums. In many cases, the variable nature of the hi-hats is what creates the feel of the drumming. I discuss overdubbing in detail in Chapter 10.

Pressing Record, Even during a Rehearsal

Get your instruments, mics, and levels set before you start to rehearse your part. Then when you start to practice, press the Record button. You may be surprised when you catch the perfect performance before you plan to record a serious take.

Leaving the Humanity in Your Tracks

Along the same lines of recording your rehearsals, don't be so hooked on getting every note just right that you miss the feel of a performance. Listen to some of the greatest records ever made, and you can hear little mistakes. In fact, it's those little mistakes that often make those records so great. So, before you go auto-tuning and editing the life out of your music, give it a good listen and see whether that note you want to fix is what gives the part its character.

IN THIS CHAPTER

» Marketing yourself

» Finding a music host site

» Utilizing social networking

» Promoting your music

Chapter 25
Ten (or So) Ways to Distribute and Promote Music

Congratulations! You have a final product to sell. The hard . . . oops, I'm sorry . . . the *easy* part is behind you. I'm sure you don't want to be stuck with boxes of expensive coasters, so now you have to work on getting people interested in buying your music. You've just gone from being a musician-composer-engineer-producer to being all those plus a record-company-owner-businessperson. (Exactly how hyphenated can a person get, anyway?)

Your friends and some acquaintances will probably buy a few copies, but after you've sold copies to all of them, you need to promote your music to the broader world. This can be tricky. After all, you're now competing with the big boys and — face it — you don't have nearly the resources they do. Traditional channels of distribution and marketing are pretty much out of the question for you. So, to succeed in selling your music, you need to try some alternative approaches.

In this chapter, I show you a variety of ways to get your music out to the masses. From basic promotional ideas to online distribution, this chapter covers a lot of ground. You explore how you can use the Internet to promote and sell your music.

You discover how to put up music files so that your potential customers can either download your music or listen to it online. You find out about some of the best ways to get your music hosted online, and you take a look at promotional ideas to get you started.

REMEMBER

Throughout this chapter, I list a lot of music promotion services that you can get involved in. Many of them are free, but others charge a fee. These fees can add up, so I recommend sticking with the free plans until you know whether the fee-based service can add to your bottom line. Also, keep in mind that if you have your music in a lot of places, it's easy to lose track of or be unable to keep up with updating your music.

Marketing Yourself

I'm no marketing guru, but I have managed to create a nice niche for myself and my music. So, trust me — you can do the same. All it takes is a little imagination and a lot of hard work. In the following list, I present a few ideas that have worked for me and other enterprising, independent artists:

- **Take yourself seriously.** What I mean by this is take the job of promoting and selling your music seriously — treat it as a business. Getting people to notice and buy your music is a lot of work, but it doesn't have to be a drag (if it is, you're better off getting someone else to do it for you).
- **Get organized.** Get your new business off on the right foot by developing a habit of keeping track of your sales and developing a contact list. One of the best investments that you can make is to get a contact management database (Act! is a good one for Windows, and Contacts is serviceable for Mac users) to keep track of promotion contacts (newspapers, radio stations, and clubs), CD and download sales, and fans. Also, do yourself a big favor and keep meticulous records of your income and expenses; you'll be grateful that you did when tax time comes.
- **Create a mailing list.** This is one of the most cost-effective and powerful ways that you can start to develop a following. Make a signup sheet for your mailing list available at every public appearance. (Ask people to include not only their postal mail addresses but also their email addresses.) Then enter those names into your database. You can then either send out snail mailings or email notices whenever you play or do anything worth mentioning. I talk more about email lists later in this chapter.
- **Get out and be seen.** This one is pretty straightforward. Get out in the world and let people know about your music. This can mean playing gigs or talking

about your music. I have a good friend who releases an album each year. He prints a thousand copies, which he sells at his gigs, and every year he sells out. (Hey, that's an extra ten grand a year after expenses — not bad.) He also uses his albums as his calling card to get more gigs.

» **Look beyond the music store.** It's nearly impossible to compete with the labels — indies and majors alike — in the music store. Unless you live in a small town or know of a music shop that has a section devoted to local bands and can sell your CDs, you need to think of other places to put your music. For example, another friend of mine has his CD at quite a few of the local businesses in his neighborhood around the holidays. Every place, from the local pack-and-ship to the video store, has a countertop display with his CD. He creates a small poster that fits on the counter describing him and his music. He sells quite a few CDs and gets a handful more gigs each year this way.

» **Capitalize on your style.** Another one of my friends composes folksy, New Age music, and he managed to get his CDs into a handful of New Age gift shops. He often puts them in the stores on consignment and checks each store once a week to refill the countertop display and collect money that the store took in (minus the store's cut, of course). Going into the stores every week helps him to develop a relationship with the store owners, many of whom have arranged for him to do performances in their stores, increasing exposure and sales.

» **Try something different.** Years ago, I teamed up with a local author and played at her book signings. (This is before I wrote books myself.) She read a passage from her book, and then I played for a few minutes. I always ended up selling a few dozen CDs at these events.

» **Don't be stingy.** Give away your CD. I usually count on giving away about 10 percent to 15 percent of the CDs I print. These can be for reviews, to try to get gigs, or for any purpose that may spread the word about your music. Giving out your CD as a promotional tool is an inexpensive way to let people know what you're doing.

REMEMBER

I'm sure you can come up with dozens more ways to promote and sell your music. Think outside the box and use your imagination. Don't be shy. Do whatever you can to get your music out into the world.

Setting Up Your Own Music Website

No matter what else you do, you need to have your own website. A website is your calling card — a place where you can showcase yourself and your music. With your own site, you can provide a lot more information for visitors to read. You can also offer more products that may make you more money than your CDs — T-shirts, for instance.

Having your own website is not without challenges. For example, you have to design and maintain the site, which can take a lot of time. You also have to pay for things like hosting (that is, a service that will host your site files on its servers so that people who visit your web address can see your site). If you intend to sell products on your site, you need to provide online ordering, which you can do with simple options like adding a Checkout button via PayPal or Google (which charge a small fee for each sale) or by setting up an account with a payment processing company, such as Stripe or Square. In all, having a website can be time-consuming and costs money, so be prepared to do a fair amount of work if you really plan on making money from your website.

Checking out musician-friendly hosting services

TIP

Some hosting services make it easy to create a website for you or your band and allow you to offer downloads or streams of your music, CDs, and other merchandise. All the following sites are geared toward musicians. The one you choose will likely depend on the fit for you or your band. Here are some options:

- Bandvista
- Bandzoogle
- Squarespace
- Wix

REMEMBER

Each of these sites offers slightly different features for the money. Take a close look at their plans and keep in mind that, while all offer free trials, you're unlikely to move from one host site to another, so choose the site that you feel best about and whose features most closely match your needs.

Designing your site

Your first step in getting a website up and running is designing it. When you design your website, keep the following points in mind:

- **Make your site easy to navigate.** Make sure that your visitors know where they are on your site at all times. It's often a good idea to have a menu bar on each page so that they can at least return to the home page without having to search for it.

» **Make sure your site is mobile responsive.** Smartphones and tablet computers are an important segment of online users, and having a site that utilizes responsive web design means that your site will look as good on a small screen as it does on a large one.

» **Include an email newsletter opt-in form.** Offer something of value, such as some music, for free to get your fans on your list. Then use your newsletter to develop a relationship with them. The more you engage with your fans, the more music and merch you will sell. You need an email service provider to do this. Check out the "Connecting with an Email Newsletter" section later in this chapter.

» **Make ordering your CD (or other stuff) easy.** Put a Buy My CD button or link on every page. Also, consider including upsells, such as T-shirts or behind-the-scenes videos, in your shopping cart sequence.

» **Double-check all your links.** Nothing is worse for a web surfer than clicking on links that don't work. If you have links on your site, double-check that each one works. And if you have links to other people's sites, check the links occasionally to make sure that the page you're linking to still exists.

» **Test your site.** Before you sign off on your site design, check it from a slow connection and multiple devices if you can (or have your web developer do this for you). You instantly get a sense of whether your site's download time is speedy. If it's slow to load or confusing to navigate, keep working on it until it works. You may also want to check your site using different Internet browsers and screen resolutions to make sure that your site still looks good.

» **Make your site your browser's home page.** Years ago, before I knew better, I had a site down for weeks because I didn't have it set as my default site in my browser. I didn't find out until I got a call from a friend who told me it was down.

For more tips and tricks on creating a great website, check out *Building Websites All-in-One For Dummies*, 3rd Edition by David Karlins and Doug Sahlin (Wiley).

TIP

When your site is live on the Internet, techniques such as search engine optimization (SEO), which makes your site appear higher in search results, and social media networking can help your site and your work get noticed. SEO techniques are constantly evolving and beyond the scope of this book, but you can check out *Search Engine Optimization For Dummies* by Peter Kent (also from Wiley) to find out details. You find a brief introduction to social media networking later in this chapter.

Putting Your Music on a Music Host Site

A *music host site* is a website that allows you to add your music to its list of available music downloads. Putting your MP3s on a host site can give you exposure that you wouldn't otherwise be able to get. You can direct people to the site to listen to your music and also benefit from traffic that the site itself, other musicians, and the site's fans generate. For some of the larger sites, that can be a lot of potential listeners. Although MP3 host sites are constantly changing, a few have managed to hang around for a while:

- **Bandcamp:** Bandcamp lets you offer downloadable music, physical CDs, and even merchandise like T-shirts. A basic plan is free (pro plan is $10 per month) to offer your music or merch, though it does take a cut of your sales. Bandcamp's cut is 15 percent for digital sales and 10 percent for CDs or merchandise.
- **CD Baby:** CD Baby, aside from letting you sell CDs and letting you sell your music digitally, also offers a place for you to put up your website.
- **Last.fm:** Last.fm is a streaming radio service with a dynamic community. You can put your music on the site plus offer links to your CDs and downloads. You can also sign up for a plan that pays you for the streaming, but it won't amount to much unless you have a ton of plays (check out the Terms and Conditions for details).
- **ReverbNation:** ReverbNation is kind of a one-stop-shop for releasing and promoting your music. It offers website hosting, digital distribution, email contact management, newsletter delivery, and more. It has a free plan that lets you upload and offer your music for download, but if you want to monetize it, you'll need to pay some money. The price varies depending on what services you want to use, but its basic full-service plan runs $20 per month.
- **Soundcloud:** Soundcloud lets you upload your music and make it available as a download or online stream. It's free and it's popular, so it's a worthwhile place to add your music. Soundcloud is very strict about ensuring no one is uploading material that he or she doesn't own the copyright to, which is a good thing for musicians.

WARNING

Be sure to read and understand the contracts (often called agreements) that each of these sites requires you to agree to. Make sure that you don't sign away your rights to your music. If you're not sure that you like a particular agreement, don't sign up for the service. You can find plenty of other places to put your music on the Internet.

Engaging in Social Media Networking

People are atwitter (sorry, I can't help myself) about social networking as a way to promote themselves. I'm personally still a bit cool on the actual sales that can be made using Twitter, Facebook, and the other social networking sites, but I won't deny that these sites generate a lot of activity, and activity is always a good thing. So, I'm not really going out on a limb to suggest that you join the social networking world, too. It can be a great way to connect with your fans (and possibly attract new ones).

Aside from the music hosting sites I list earlier in this chapter, musicians are also using general social networking sites as well. Here is a list of the most popular ones (as of mid-2020 anyway — chances are this list will be out of date before too long):

- **Facebook:** Facebook is the largest, most active community on the Internet. With its size and reach it's not going away anytime soon. So, if you're not already on Facebook, you really need to get to it. Because of its size, many of the other musician-centric sites, such as ReverbNation, have apps that allow you to connect your account to your Facebook page. This gives you the best of both worlds and makes it easier to manage your social networking.
- **Instagram:** Instagram started as a photo sharing app and has grown into a huge platform for musicians to develop a following. You can post videos as well as photos, and engagement is higher than with Facebook.
- **TikTok:** TikTok, a platform focused on short videos, has become an effective place for musicians to promote their music. Like Instagram, TikTok has a high engagement rate, and if you are comfortable making videos, is worth getting on.
- **Twitter:** Twitter lets you share news and videos in 280 characters. And for some reason, this type of blogging (called *micro-blogging*) has become popular. I'm willing to bet you're already using Twitter, regardless of how many tweets you actually create or if you just follow others. If you're not, you should at least try it out and see if you like it.
- **YouTube:** There are countless artists who have made a career from posting videos on YouTube. If you have any interest in doing videos to promote yourself, you should set up a YouTube channel and start posting your videos and music. Be consistent and before you know it, you'll have a following.

TIP

There have been a lot of complaints and concerns about privacy and content ownership with these social networks. If either of these are an issue to you, make sure you read and understand the user agreements that you are bound by when you sign up and use these sites. If you're unsure whether you have privacy or if you give up any rights to your music by posting it on these sites, you're better off erring on the side of caution and limiting what you share.

Offering Free Downloads

Offering a freebie can be a good way to get people interested in your music and a way to turn people into fans. Online promotion of your music almost requires you to make downloads available to your potential fans. You can talk about your music all you want, but what people want is to *hear* your music. The purpose of the free download is to get your listener excited enough about your music that he buys your music or comes to see your show.

Turning a freebie listener into a buyer isn't that difficult. My company offers a variety of free download demos, and we have found that over 10 percent of the people who take a free demo end up buying a CD, MP3 download, or program from us. This is an inexpensive way for us to get new customers and a very good return on investment. On top of that, by allowing our customers to try our recording first, we receive fewer requests for a refund (contrary to what most music creators do, we offer a money-back guarantee on all our music and programs). So, you won't be surprised to hear me suggest that you should offer free demos/downloads of your music. (I won't suggest a money-back guarantee unless you're doing something with a therapeutic purpose, as I am.)

Give people a taste of your music and sell an upgrade — other tracks, physical CDs, vinyl records, boxed sets, CD-and-T-shirt packages, tickets to a live concert stream — anything that turns a casual listener into a fan. There are some good models out there for monetizing your music if you look around.

TIP

I'm not a fan of making all your music free to download as a way of generating buzz. I see a freebie as a teaser. I believe that if you offer your fans something, they will buy it. Even if you're "not in it for the money," charging for your music says that you value what you do. And if you value it, your fans will too.

Selling Your Music Digitally

Digital delivery of your music will be the main source of revenue. Sure, you'll sell a few CDs at your shows and maybe a couple more through a local store or one of the online music sites, but fewer and fewer listeners own CD players and many more prefer listening on a phone or tablet and don't want to hassle with importing a CD into their device.

Aside from being the format of choice for listeners, digital music files is a better choice for musicians because you don't need to invest a ton of money in a garage full of CDs that you'll likely not sell.

There are two forms of digital distribution:

- **Downloads:** Downloads allow your listener to own and load the digital file onto a device so he can listen anytime, forever (or until he loses the file). You get paid once for this download, no matter how many times your buyer listens. You can sell a download directly to your listener, but most musicians will make more sales by putting their downloads on other sites, such as iTunes or Amazon.
- **Streaming:** Streaming delivers your music to your listener without downloading it on her device. You get paid every time your song is listened to. It's a much smaller fee than you get for a download, but you can end up with a lot more in the long run. Unless you can build an infrastructure and fan base to support serving the music yourself, you'll need to distribute through existing sites. This is not a problem because there are a ton of them.

Regardless of which digital distribution method you want (choose both), and channels you want to be on (Spotify, Apple Music, Amazon, Google, and others — the list is long), you'll need a distributor, also called an *aggregator*. Following is a list of popular music aggregators that can get your music on most, if not all, of the most common music sites:

- **AWAL:** AWAL doesn't charge an upfront fee for its distribution services, but it does take 15 percent of your sales. Depending on how much music you sell, that can add up to much more than you'll pay through some of the other services.
- **CD Baby:** As an aggregator, CD Baby charges a one-time fee for each album ($35) or single ($9.95) you want them to distribute your music beyond their site (you can get a free account and sell on their site for a 15 percent commission). They also take a 9 percent fee on all your digital sales.
- **Distrokid:** Distrokid also charges an annual fee for distributing your music and doesn't take a percentage of your sales. Distrokid also offer other services for distribution that can add to your cost.
- **Ditto:** Ditto charges $19 per year for one artist and no commission on sales. You can pay more for some other services, such as pre-releasing your music.
- **TuneCore:** TuneCore charges $50 per year for each album and $10 per year for each single you upload. Like Ditto and Distrokid, TuneCore doesn't take a commission on sales and passes on 100 percent of your revenue.

TIP

This is a very short list of music distributors. Look around for other places to sell your digitally formatted music. There are a ton of them — and more showing up every day.

Licensing Your Music

Licensing (also called "sync" licensing) gets you paid for your music and gives you exposure to audiences that may not otherwise find your music. You can license your music to film, TV, commercials, and a host of other outlets — I've licensed my music for dance videos and shows, conferences, and other unexpected places.

It used to be that you got lucky and someone called asking to license your music (this is how all my licensing happened), but nowadays there are services that offer listings of libraries or producers looking for music. Here are three worth checking out:

- **Audiosocket:** Audiosocket vets the music that it offers its buyers but doesn't charge its artists to list their music. So, if you're interested in offering your music through Audiosocket, complete an application and a few songs. If they accept your music and sell any, they take a 50 percent cut in the placement fee and 50 percent of the publishing royalties.
- **Broadjam:** Broadjam helps you submit your music to publishers. It's also a music hosting and download site. Membership starts at about $10 per month.
- **Taxi:** Taxi has been around a long time and has a very active member community, as well as a yearly "road rally" conference to help you get the most out of the service. Membership will cost you $300 plus a small fee for each submission, but for all they offer, this can be a bargain if you work to get the most out of the service. They don't take a cut of the money you make on placements for royalties.

Podcasting

Podcasting is another way to offer audio online. Typically, podcasts are media feeds that your visitors can subscribe to and get updates automatically as they're published. If you regularly update your music or if you want to have an audio blog (or video blog) that your fans can listen to (or watch), this can be a great way to keep them involved in your music.

The process of creating a podcast starts with recording the content and then putting it in an MP3 format (if you're doing audio). You have this book, so you can create audio content easily. Just follow the steps outlined throughout the book to record and convert your music. Next, you need to host it or have a podcasting site host it for you. This process can get pretty complicated, so I recommend checking out *Podcasting For Dummies* by Tee Morris and Chuck Tomasi (Wiley). You can also check out these sites to learn more about podcasting:

» **Apple podcast page:** This page on the Apple website contains tons of information on creating a podcast and publishing it. This is a good place to start.

» **Podcasting Tools:** This site has information, links, and tools for creating a podcast. This is a good place to find quality information.

If you're ready to get started podcasting, here are a few sites worth looking into:

» **Hipcast:** Hipcast is an easy-to-use site that lets you create and publish your audio or video blogs. This site offers a seven-day free trial period, with plans starting at $5 per month. You don't find a lot of information on this site about podcasting, but if you're ready to give it a try, this is a good inexpensive option.

» **Libsyn:** Libsyn offers plans starting at $5 per month and, for an added cost, offers Apple iOS and Android apps for mobile listeners.

» **PodHoster:** PodHoster, as the name states, hosts podcasts. With this service, you record your audio and PodHoster hosts it. This is a good option for musicians who record their own music and know the ins and outs of the audio-creation process (that would be you, after you've read this book). PodHoster offers a 30-day free trial, with monthly plans starting at $5.

Selling Your CDs

Regardless of whether you have your own site, you can always sell your CDs on the Internet through other outlets. An advantage to selling your music through other online stores is that you can capitalize on the traffic that the store generates. A number of online retailers are out there, but the following list gives you the low-down on some of the major players:

» **Amazon.com:** If you want to sell your physical CD on Amazon.com, all you need is a "retail-ready" package (professional manufacturer and with a UPC code on it).

» **Bandcamp:** Bandcamp is a way for you to sell, not only your CDs online, but also merchandise such as T-shirts, coffee mugs, and so on. Bandcamp doesn't charge a monthly fee but does take a cut — 15 percent or less, depending on how much you sell and the prices you set.

» **CD Baby:** CD Baby puts your CD on its site for a small setup fee ($35). For this, you get a web page (which the people at CD Baby design) with pictures, bios, MP3s, and streaming audio. The site sells your CD for any price you set, takes $4 from the sale, and gives you the rest. You even receive an email whenever someone buys one of your CDs.

Because the Internet is constantly changing and growing, you may find other sites that allow you to sell your music online. Use your favorite search engine to search for the phrase **sell your CD.** This gives you a ton of other places to consider when selling your CD online.

Promoting Your Music

The whole point of making CDs and putting MP3s of your music on the Internet is to promote and sell your music. To do this, you need exposure. As with any promotion technique, there are no hard-and-fast rules except to use your imagination. Experience will be your guide, but here are some ideas to get you started:

- **Start an email newsletter.** An email newsletter is an inexpensive way to keep your music on people's minds. Try to be somewhat consistent in sending it out, but don't just send out the same message on a regular basis. Give your subscribers something. Provide new information in your email, such as a press release about where you're playing next or a link to a new song that you've just uploaded. Check out the "Connecting with an Email Newsletter" section later in this chapter.
- **Put your website address on everything.** People can't come to you if they don't know that you exist. So, print your website address on all your promotional materials, including the CD itself. Also, include your website address on all emails and Internet correspondence that you do (as a signature on Internet forums if you belong to any, for example).
- **Network.** Check out as many independent-musician sites as you can. You not only learn a lot about marketing your music, but you'll also have an opportunity to spread the word about your music.
- **Stay up to date.** Keep track of where you put your music and check back often to make sure everything is working properly. Websites change and go out of business often. Unless you check the site occasionally, you might not know if your music suddenly disappears from there. Also, routinely search for new places to put your music.
- **Get linked.** Try to get folks to link from their sites to your own. Likewise, share the wealth and link to other sites that you like. Cross-promotion can be a good thing and allow you to pool your fan base with another band. This doesn't take away from your sales (after all, *you* listen to more than one band's CDs, right?). Visitors to your site will appreciate the link and will probably check back to see whether you added any new ones.

Connecting with an Email Newsletter

An email newsletter is an inexpensive way to keep your music on people's minds. Try to send newsletters to your subscribers somewhat consistently, but don't just send out the same message on a regular basis. Give your subscribers new information, such as a press release about where you're playing next or a link to a new song that you've just uploaded.

WARNING

Don't send your newsletter to anyone who hasn't asked to receive it. This is called *spamming*, and it's illegal.

To build a subscriber list, encourage people to sign up for your mailing list at your gigs and on your website. Or offer them a free download when they sign up on your website, and put a subscription form on every page. (Check out my day-job website to see this in action at `www.stronginstitute.com`.) Always provide an easy way for users to unsubscribe from your list.

If you're serious about sending out an email newsletter, an email service provider (ESP) can collect and manage addresses and send out your messages. The advantages of using an email service provider include ease of use, but the most important is that a good ESP will help your messages get to your subscriber. Sending emails directly from your email account can get your messages blocked — and if the email host (such as Gmail or Yahoo!) labels you as spam, they will ban your messages. The rules on this get pretty complicated, and trying to keep up with changes and be compliant is a full-time job.

Your best solution to make sure your messages go through is to use an experienced ESP. Here are a few I recommend:

- **AWeber:** AWeber has been around a long time (I've used them for the last five years) and has the best customer service I've come across in this industry. You can actually get someone on the phone. In fact, they encourage it. Their plans start at $19 per month (for up to 500 subscribers). You can try AWeber for a month for only a dollar, and they offer excellent email marketing advice (through a newsletter, videos, and blogs).
- **Constant Contact:** This is a popular ESP that is easy to use and offers a 60-day free trial. Their basic (500-subscriber) plan is $15 per month. Plans with more subscribers cost about the same as the other providers I list here. I haven't used Constant Contact, but I have friends who are very happy with this provider.

» **MailChimp:** I also use MailChimp, and what I like about this ESP is that it's super-easy to use and their data tracking (of clicks and whatnot) is very good. What I don't like is that they will not get on the phone with you if you have problems. You're stuck with instant chat or email (not the worst thing but kind of annoying if you have a complicated problem). They have a free account option that allows you to try them out and see if you like them. Once you get to a couple thousand subscribers, their cost is about the same as everyone else in this list.

You can find a lot more by doing an Internet search using "Email Service Provider" or "email marketing" as your search term.

TIP

If you choose a music-centric company to host your website (check out the "Setting Up Your Own Music Website" section earlier in this chapter), you may find that your blast email needs are taken care of and you don't need to hire a separate ESP. However, if you end up with a lot of fans, you may find the features offered by a dedicated ESP useful.

Index

A

B

N

O

P

Q

R

S

T

U

V

W

X

Y

Z

About the Author

Jeff Strong is the author of seven books, including *Pro Tools All-in-One Desk Reference For Dummies* (Wiley). Jeff is also the director of the Strong Institute (www.stronginstitute.com) — a music-medicine research organization and therapy provider — and the founder of Brain Shift Radio (https://brainshiftradio.com). Jeff graduated from the Percussion Institute of Technology at the Musician's Institute in Los Angeles in 1983 and has either worked in or owned a recording studio since 1985. Every week, he records dozens of custom client CDs using the equipment and techniques found in the pages of this book. He has also released over 35 commercially available CDs, including the *Brain Shift Collection: Ambient Rhythmic Entrainment* eight-CD set on the Sounds True label (www.soundstrue.com) and the best-selling *Calming Rhythms*, which is used in tens of thousands of homes, schools, and institutions worldwide. You can discover more about Jeff's music and recording studio at www.stronginstitute.com.

Author's Acknowledgments

I am grateful yet again to executive editor and fellow musician Steve Hayes for making this sixth edition possible. Also, my profound thanks to editor and sounding board Katharine Dvorak, who helped make an already great book even better. Thanks, as well, goes to my friend and technical editor, Michael Sheppard, for keeping me on track and up-to-date on the many technical aspects of this subject.

As always, I'm grateful to my family (Beth and Tovah) and my many friends (you know who you are), who indulge me in my obsession with recording and recording gear.

Publisher's Acknowledgments

Executive Editor: Steven Hayes

Senior Managing Editor: Kristie Pyles

Project Editor: Katharine Dvorak

Proofreader: Debbye Butler

Technical Editor: Michael Sheppard

Production Editor: Siddique Shaik

Cover Image: © AleksandarNakic/Getty

Take dummies with you everywhere you go!

Whether you are excited about e-books, want more from the web, must have your mobile apps, or are swept up in social media, dummies makes everything easier.

Find us online!

dummies.com

Leverage the power

Dummies is the global leader in the reference category and one of the most trusted and highly regarded brands in the world. No longer just focused on books, customers now have access to the dummies content they need in the format they want. Together we'll craft a solution that engages your customers, stands out from the competition, and helps you meet your goals.

Advertising & Sponsorships

Connect with an engaged audience on a powerful multimedia site, and position your message alongside expert how-to content. Dummies.com is a one-stop shop for free, online information and know-how curated by a team of experts.

- Targeted ads
- Video
- Email Marketing
- Microsites
- Sweepstakes sponsorship

20 MILLION PAGE VIEWS EVERY SINGLE MONTH

15 MILLION UNIQUE VISITORS PER MONTH

43% OF ALL VISITORS ACCESS THE SITE VIA THEIR MOBILE DEVICES

700,000 NEWSLETTER SUBSCRIPTIONS TO THE INBOXES OF *300,000* UNIQUE INDIVIDUALS EVERY WEEK

of dummies

Custom Publishing

Reach a global audience in any language by creating a solution that will differentiate you from competitors, amplify your message, and encourage customers to make a buying decision.

- Apps
- Books
- eBooks
- Video
- Audio
- Webinars

Brand Licensing & Content

Leverage the strength of the world's most popular reference brand to reach new audiences and channels of distribution.

For more information, visit dummies.com/biz

PERSONAL ENRICHMENT

9781119187790
USA $26.00
CAN $31.99
UK £19.99

9781119179030
USA $21.99
CAN $25.99
UK £16.99

9781119293354
USA $24.99
CAN $29.99
UK £17.99

9781119293347
USA $22.99
CAN $27.99
UK £16.99

9781119310068
USA $22.99
CAN $27.99
UK £16.99

9781119235606
USA $24.99
CAN $29.99
UK £17.99

9781119251163
USA $24.99
CAN $29.99
UK £17.99

9781119235491
USA $26.99
CAN $31.99
UK £19.99

9781119279952
USA $24.99
CAN $29.99
UK £17.99

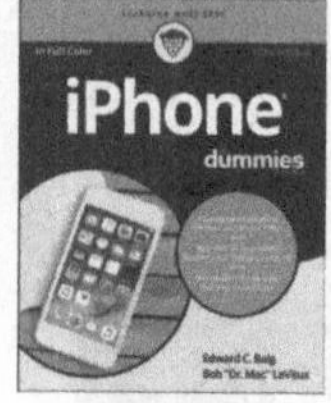

9781119283133
USA $24.99
CAN $29.99
UK £17.99

9781119287117
USA $24.99
CAN $29.99
UK £16.99

9781119130246
USA $22.99
CAN $27.99
UK £16.99

PROFESSIONAL DEVELOPMENT

9781119311041
USA $24.99
CAN $29.99
UK £17.99

9781119255796
USA $39.99
CAN $47.99
UK £27.99

9781119293439
USA $26.99
CAN $31.99
UK £19.99

9781119281467
USA $26.99
CAN $31.99
UK £19.99

9781119280651
USA $29.99
CAN $35.99
UK £21.99

9781119251132
USA $24.99
CAN $29.99
UK £17.99

9781119310563
USA $34.00
CAN $41.99
UK £24.99

9781119181705
USA $29.99
CAN $35.99
UK £21.99

9781119263593
USA $26.99
CAN $31.99
UK £19.99

9781119257769
USA $29.99
CAN $35.99
UK £21.99

9781119293477
USA $26.99
CAN $31.99
UK £19.99

9781119265313
USA $24.99
CAN $29.99
UK £17.99

9781119239314
USA $29.99
CAN $35.99
UK £21.99

9781119293323
USA $29.99
CAN $35.99
UK £21.99

dummies.com

dummies
A Wiley Brand

Learning Made Easy

ACADEMIC

9781119293576
USA $19.99
CAN $23.99
UK £15.99

9781119293637
USA $19.99
CAN $23.99
UK £15.99

9781119293491
USA $19.99
CAN $23.99
UK £15.99

9781119293460
USA $19.99
CAN $23.99
UK £15.99

9781119293590
USA $19.99
CAN $23.99
UK £15.99

9781119215844
USA $26.99
CAN $31.99
UK £19.99

9781119293378
USA $22.99
CAN $27.99
UK £16.99

9781119293521
USA $19.99
CAN $23.99
UK £15.99

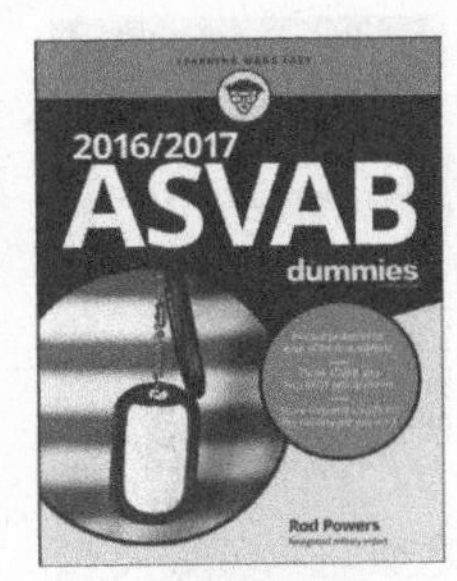

9781119239178
USA $18.99
CAN $22.99
UK £14.99

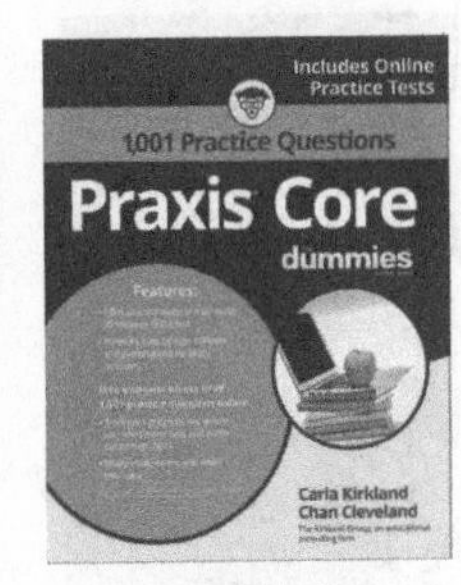

9781119263883
USA $26.99
CAN $31.99
UK £19.99

Available Everywhere Books Are Sold

dummies.com

NOV 2 0 2020

Small books for big imaginations

WITHDRAWN

9781119177173
USA $9.99
CAN $9.99
UK £8.99

9781119177272
USA $9.99
CAN $9.99
UK £8.99

9781119177241
USA $9.99
CAN $9.99
UK £8.99

9781119177210
USA $9.99
CAN $9.99
UK £8.99

9781119262657
USA $9.99
CAN $9.99
UK £6.99

9781119291336
USA $9.99
CAN $9.99
UK £6.99

9781119233527
USA $9.99
CAN $9.99
UK £6.99

9781119291220
USA $9.99
CAN $9.99
UK £6.99

9781119177302
USA $9.99
CAN $9.99
UK £8.99

Unleash Their Creativity

dummies.com

dummies®
A Wiley Brand